Appalachian Hiker II

Edward B. Garvey

D1563277

Published by
Appalachian Books
Oakton, Virginia 22124

Cover design and photograph by Rita Malone

Table of Contents

FOREWORD

This 1978 revision of Appalachian Hiker is written to update such things as the status of the Appalachian Trail since the passage of the National Trails System Act of October 1968; to include new items that are available in the backpacking equipment market; to record the deaths of colorful Appalachian Trail personalities such as Benton MacKaye, Grandma Gatewood, and others; to add chapters such as the ones on overnight accommodations, edible wild plants to be found along the Trail, and another on equipment; plus additional appendices and an update of the extremely popular Mileage Fact Sheet.

The last chapter of the original Appalachian Hiker was completed and put into the mailbox at 5 p.m. on May 31, 1971. One hour later I was on my way to Dulles International Airport with my wife Mary and my 12-year-old-son Kevin to begin a 4-month odyssey of most of the countries of Europe by automobile. If, in 1970 I had done "my thing" for over five months, my long suffering wife had decreed (with considerable justification!) that in 1971 we would do "her thing!" When we returned to the U.S.A. in October 1971, the book *Appalachian Hiker* was already at the printers. Much of the nitty-gritty work, customarily the responsibility of the author, had been done by others. For that I am indebted to Dan Couch of Appalachian Books; to my daughter Sharon who contributed ten pen and ink drawings; to my long-time hiking companion Maurice A. Crews; and to Father Richard J. O'Brien, Professor of Linguistics, Georgetown University, and an ardent backpacker, who contributed his expert editorial talents to the production of the book.

During the six years the first book was on the market I received several hundred letters from readers, many making suggestions, others asking questions which in themselves were clues to subjects I should have covered more thoroughly. I am especially indebted to forty-seven "2,000 Milers," class of 1976; each of whom completed a detailed questionnaire upon the completion of his hike.

Much of the preliminary work for this revision was done at historic Harpers Ferry, WV where I lived alone in two different houses during various periods in 1976, 1977, and 1978. Both places were but a few minutes walk from the new headquarters of the Appalachian Trail Conference (see September 1976, *Appalachian Trailway News*). Employees of the Conference graciously provided me with much background information. Others who made substantial contributions to this revision were my editor Estelle Mallinoff and Rita Malone of Appalachian Outfitters whose color pictures grace the front and back covers.

I have visited various parts of the Trail since 1970 but have hiked extensively only in the White Mountains of New Hampshire (1972 and 1976); in the southernmost 300 miles of the Trail in Tennessee, North Carolina, and Georgia (April 1976, April 1977, and May 1978); and the northernmost 114 miles from Katahdin to Monson, Maine in August 1977. An article describing my April 1976 hike of the Southern Appalachians appeared in the fall, 1977 issue of *Backpacking Journal*.

And lastly, even though this is an extensive revision, I have made only a few minor changes in the 190 pages of the book in the chapter entitled "My Hike: Day by Day Along The Trail." Those pages describe the Trail and Trail people just as they were in 1970 and both my publisher and I felt that it would be best to leave those pages essentially as they were written.

Edward B. Garvey
1978

Letters to the Author—Always Welcome. Send to Appalachian Books, Box 249, Oakton, Virginia 22124. If reply is desired, enclose stamped, self-addressed envelope.

Ed Garvey in his early Boy Scout days.

President Carter, after signing the Appalachian Trail Bill on March 21, 1978 (Public Law 95-248) authorizing $90 million for acquisition of Trail right-of-way. Pen used in the signing is given to Congressman Goodloe E. Byron of Maryland.

1
The Trail and I

This is a story of the Appalachian Trail, the famous hiking footpath that stretches for 2,000 miles along the crest of the Appalachian mountain chain from Maine to Georgia. More specifically, it is a story of my own hike along the beautiful Trail during the period April 4, 1970 to October 7, 1970. But let me go back a bit in time to explain how it was that I found myself, on a sunny spring day in April, sitting beside a bronze marker marking the southern terminus of the Appalachian Trail at Springer Mountain in northern Georgia.

As I sat there soaking up some of that warm Georgia sunshine, I contemplated the 2,000-mile hike ahead of me wondering if I would really make it to Mt. Katahdin way up north in Maine . . . and wondering what adventures would come my way during the months I would be on the Trail. My mind went back swiftly over events of the past 43 years . . . events that somehow or other culminated in my being there at Springer, about to embark on that 2,000-mile hike. In 1926 in the little town of Farmington in southern Minnesota two events were taking place that certainly had some bearing on my hiking activities. One was the announcement by the high school principal that a Boy Scout troop was about to be formed. This coincided with the fact that on November 13, 1926 I would be 12 years of age . . . then the minimum age for becoming a Scout. I became a charter member of that Boy Scout troop. One of those who assisted the high school principal in the formation of the troop was a 17-year-old high school junior named Kenneth E. Parr. Oddly enough, when on October 7, 1970 I completed my 2,000-mile-long hike at Mt. Katahdin and hiked back to the base camp at Katahdin Stream Campground, on hand to meet me was this same Kenneth E. Parr, now 60 years of age, who, with his wife Ingrid, had motored over from Vermont to congratulate me on my accomplishment. But let's get back to 1926.

As I moved through the Scouting ranks, Second Class, First Class,

1

and on toward Eagle, I found that many of the requirements placed heavy emphasis on hiking, camping, and outdoor cooking. The skills thus acquired in these years of Scouting were later to stand me in good stead. I drifted away from the Scouting and hiking bit for about a 15-year period and did not again become involved until 1952. My wife and I and three children had moved to Falls Church, Virginia, in 1949. In 1951 I had learned of the Appalachian Trail and of the Potomac Appalachian Trail Club, which not only maintained some 300 miles of hiking trails in the Pennsylvania, Maryland, Virginia area but also maintained some 19 trailside shelters, 13 locked cabins, and issued high quality maps of the hiking trails, primarily the Appalachian Trail, in those states. I promptly purchased a complete set of the 14 maps available at that time.

By this time my oldest son Dennis had joined a Boy Scout troop in Falls Church. In 1952 I was prevailed upon to accompany the troop for three or four days to the Herbert Hoover Boy Scout Camp in nearby Shanandoah National Park. In order to give the Scoutmaster a breather I volunteered to take 13 of the boys on an overnight hike to one of the nearby trailside shelters on the Appalachian Trail. We spent the night at the Lewis Falls Shelter, sharing it with its lone occupant, Francis A. Smith, M.D., of Buffalo, N.Y. Smith, although a lifelong resident of Buffalo, N.Y., had in 1950, joined the Washington, D.C. based Potomac Appalachian Trail Club. As we sat around the campfire that July night in 1952, we listened on Smith's radio to the proceedings of the Republican National Convention which was in the process of nominating Dwight D. Eisenhower as the Republican candidate for the presidency. I also listened to Smith as he urged me to join the Potomac Appalachian Trail Club (PATC).

I joined PATC in October 1952. One of the first publications I received from that organization was the January-March, 1953 issue of the *PATC Bulletin*. It contained an article describing the 2,000-mile hike of the entire Appalachian Trail by PATC member George Frederick Miller, age 72. This article captured my imagination. Quite possibly this is when I first entertained vague thoughts of someday hiking the entire Trail myself. Some 16 years later when plans for my own hike became rather definite I went to my stock of *PATC Bulletins*, and from near the bottom of the pile, pulled the one on Miller's hike. One of the features of his hike was a preprinted daily log form on which he recorded pertinent information on each day of the hike. This idea I borrowed lock, stock, and barrel. More on that later.

In 1953, two other events occurred which gave indication of my growing involvement with the Trail and its maintenance. I volunteered to become an overseer for a three-mile section of the Trail in Maryland . . . some 70 miles from my home. As an overseer, it was necessary for me to make from three to five trips a year to my section of the Trail, to remove any fallen logs or trees, to cut out summer growth, and to see that the Trail was properly identified by white paint blazes, by the four-inch diamond-shaped ATC metal marker, and by wooden directional signs. In addition to the overseer job, I did the planning for and participated in the first Appalachian Trail hike of any consequence conducted by Boy Scout Troop 681. This first hike was a modest affair in which two adult leaders, each with seven or eight boys, began hiking on the Appalachian Trail in the Shenandoah National Park. One group hiked north, the other south. After four days of hiking, staying each night at a trailside shelter, each group arrived at the Herbert Hoover Boy Scout Camp where they stayed for another week. I participated in these annual hikes for two more years and did the planning for another two before bowing out. The same Boy Scout Troop is still conducting these annual hikes along the Trail.

During the years 1952, 1953, 1954 I was beginning to become increasingly aware of the Appalachian Trail Conference and the role that it played in coordinating the activities of the many clubs that maintain the Appalachian Trail. In 1956, while on a three-week business trip to South Carolina, I attended the three-day Labor Day get-together at Roan Mountain, Tennessee, of the five hiking clubs that maintain the Trail in Georgia, North Carolina, Tennessee and southwestern Virginia. I was gradually extending my knowledge of the Trail and the hiking clubs that maintain it. My involvement in affairs of both the PATC and the Appalachian Trail Conference was to become increasingly heavy in the next few years. I became Supervisor of the Trails for PATC in 1959 and served in that capacity for six years . . . directing the efforts of some 60 volunteer overseers in trail maintenance work and in one season, 1962, directing the renovation of the Club's 19 trailside shelters. In 1960, I spent the night at the Indian Run Shelter in Shenandoah National Park and chanced to meet Lochlen Gregory and Owen Allen on their 99-day hike from Georgia to Maine. In the next few years I was to meet on the Trail a number of additional through-hikers: Ray Baker in 1964; Elmer Onstott and Everett and Nell Skinner in 1968, and Jeff Hancock and Eric Ryback in 1969. I met and talked to many others who had hiked the entire trail—to such an extent, that I had become acquainted with over half of the small fraternity of some 40 people who had hiked the entire Trail through 1969.

During these years I had also extended my own hiking on the Trail. Hiking frequently with Maurice A. (Gus) Crews of Bethesda, Maryland, I had hiked all of the 462 miles in Virginia, Maryland's 37 miles, plus sizeable chunks of the Trail in Pennsylvania and Maine. These, plus bits and pieces of hiking in Georgia, North Carolina, Tennessee, and New Hampshire, had given me a pretty good idea of what I could expect over the entire Trail. I had become active in the affairs of the Conference, serving as Secretary from 1964 to 1967 and remaining as a member of the Board of Managers from 1967 to 1972; and from 1977 to the present.

I had become an employee of the Federal Government on March 18, 1935. This meant that as each St. Patrick's Day rolled around I completed exactly one more year of service. I worked 23 years for the Soil Conservation Service in the Department of Agriculture; and then, in October 1958, I accepted the position as Finance Officer with the National Science Foundation, a position I held until I retired. For years I had planned to retire on March 17, 1975. That would have given me exactly 40 years of service; and for a person of Irish descent, March 17 seemed like an appropriate day to have a retirement party and call it quits. Unanticipated circumstances, however, can frequently cause a change in even the best laid plans. The National Science Foundation underwent a major reorganization in 1969; this included extensive personnel changes. In October of that year, I was suddenly faced with a situation in which retirement, then and there, seemed to be the expedient thing to do. Retire I did on October 31, 1969.

With retirement now a reality, my long-held dream to hike the entire Appalachian Trail moved from the realm of the possible to the feasible . . . even to the probable. True, I had a wife to consider; moreover, the two youngest of our five children were still of school age. There was the distinct possibility that my wife would take a very dim view of her husband being on the Appalachian Trail for over five months. Married men reading this book will certainly appreciate my predicament. I sent up a few tentative smoke signals. No outward reaction. I sent up more and stronger signals. Still no reaction. I interpreted this as calm acceptance of the inevitable, and I proceeded to make definite plans. There are two ways to plan a hike of this magnitude. One way is to tell no one of your plans. Then, if you decide you have had enough after a few days or a few weeks, no one is the wiser; and no embarrassing explanations are in order. The other way is to tell everyone of your plans. Then, you have no choice. Unless death or injury intervenes you *must* complete the entire hike. I chose the latter method. Notice of my hike appeared in the January 1970 issue of *Trailway News*. Shortly before my hike began I gave a midday talk to members of PATC on plans and preparations I had made. I was totally committed.

In late March, my wife, my 11-year-old son Kevin, and I took a short Easter week vacation trip to the Everglades in Florida. On our return we arrived at Amicalola Falls State Park in nothern Georgia on the afternoon of April 3. Bob Harrell, outdoor editor of the *Atlanta Constitution*, was there; and we talked at some length about my hike, my equipment, and the plans I had made for inspecting trailside shelters and Trail conditions. The Henry Morrises, the Ed Seiferles, and the Al Thompsons of the Georgia Appalachian Trail Club also arrived at the Park about the same time we did. We stayed overnight at a cabin with the Morrises and the Seiferles. After an early Saturday morning breakfast, we set out in a six-car motor caravan to Nimblewill Gap. There I met for the first time my hiking companion from Kansas City, Elmer Schwengel. Picture taking, a few words of prayer by Jim Engel of the Georgia Club, a farewell to my wife and son, and I was hiking with Schwengel toward Springer Mountain, the southern terminus of the Appalachian Trail. I reached the summit of Springer at 12 noon on a beautiful spring day, temperature 68. I signed the register and noted that one Branley C. Owen, of Brevard, North Carolina, had signed the register on April 3, one day ahead of me. He had indicated on the register sheet that he was hiking all the way to Maine. I thought it quite possible that I might catch up with Owen somewhere along the Trail, but this was not to be. Owen broke all existing records for speed, arriving at Mt. Katahdin in Maine on June 12, 1970, a mere 117 days ahead of me.

After signing the register at Springer, I walked a few yards south to the viewpoint directly beside the bronze plaque marking the southern terminus of the Trail. Here I met Major Garnett W. Martin of Denver, Colorado, who had hiked the entire Trail in 1964. Martin had come back to revisit some of the more interesting points along the Trail. The picture that appears on page 7 is the one taken by Martin as I sat beside the bronze plaque contemplating the long hike to Maine.

But now, before I take the first of those five million steps required to propel me to Mt. Katahdin, let me explain just what this Appalachian Trail is, who conceived it, who constructed it, who maintains it, and why so many people have the desire to hike it.

The Appalachian Trail is a 2,000-mile-long footpath extending from Maine to Georgia generally along the crest of the Appalachian Mountain chain. It is the longest continuous marked footpath in the world. Eventually the Pacific Crest Trail in the western United States will be 300 miles longer, but the latter Trail has not yet been completed. The idea for the Appalachian Trail was first conceived by a young man, Benton MacKaye, in the early 1900's. It was not until 1921, however, that MacKaye put his thoughts down on paper; his article "The Appalachian Trail, a Project in Regional Planning," appearing in the October, 1921 issue of the *Journal of the American Institute of Architects*. MacKaye's proposal for a long distance hiking trail caught the public fancy, meetings were held, and work was begun. The first sections of the Trail were constructed and marked in 1922 and 1923 in the Palisades Interstate Park in New York. The first meeting of the Appalachian Trail Conference was held in Washington, D.C., in 1925. Unfortunately, this early enthusiasm soon waned; and it remained for Arthur Perkins, a retired lawyer of Hartford, Connecticut, to rescue the project in 1926. Perkins promptly enlisted the aid of Myron H. Avery of Lubec, Maine, who was then residing in Hartford, Connecticut. Avery moved to Washington, D.C., the following year. For the next four years Perkins, as Chairman of the Conference, and Avery, as a loyal hardworking assistant, insured the eventual success of the Appalachian Trail project. Not only did they work assiduously on the project themselves, but they enlisted the support of scores of other capable people from Maine to Georgia. In 1930 Perkins died, and Avery was elected Chairman of the Conference in 1931. He was to occupy that post for 21 years; and during most of those same years he also served as President of the Washington, D.C., based Potomac Appalachian Trail Club. It was under Avery's stewardship that the Appalachian Trail was finally completed and the "Golden Spike" (to borrow the railroad term for

Ed Garvey at the beginning of his hike, April 4, 1970. The southern terminus plaque is on the rock next to him. (Photo: Garnett W. Martin)

completion of the first transcontinental railway) was driven on the final few miles of the Trail in Maine on August 15, 1937.

A complete history of the Appalachian Trail appears in *ATC Publication 5, The Appalachian Trail.* This history occupies 16 pages of small print. It was compiled largely by Dr. Jean Stephenson, herself a veteran of almost a half century in the Appalachian Trail Project. Although I have been involved in this project myself for almost 25 years, I still read this 16-page history with awe . . . marveling that people like the Perkins, the Averys, and others could have accomplished so much in so short a time. It strikes me that this was an amateur volunteer recreation effort with few, if any, parallels. It was, first of all, a tremendous promotional effort to inform and to stir the enthusiasm of people for the project, to stimulate the formation of hiking clubs, and to obtain commitments from people and organizations first to create the Trail and then to maintain it. During the 15-year trail-building period, there were various groups involved in studying feasible routes, in actually laying out the Trail, in clearing it, in marking it with paint blazes and directional signs, and in measuring it with a bicycle wheel calibrated to hundredths of a mile. Finally, there was the job of developing narrative descriptions of the Trail, north to south, and south to north, so that guide books could be printed to assist the hiker in his traverse of the Trail. That these things could have been accomplished by volunteers seems truly amazing. The Appalachian Trail Conference had no paid employees for the first 40 years of its existence. Those who worked on behalf of the project did so on their own time, and rarely were they even reimbursed for expenses incurred.

In these few words I have described how the Appalachian Trail came to be. Now to describe what it is. It is primarily a wilderness foot trail. It exists for those who wish to hike a few hours, a few days, a few weeks, or for several months. The Trail is marked with an extensive side trail system which permits the hiker to plan a variety of side hikes and circuit hikes while using the Appalachian Trail as his base of operations. The Trail is studded with simple, rustic, overnight trailside shelters which are available to hikers on a first-come first-served basis. Although the Trail generally follows the crests of the mountain ranges, it frequently cuts across valleys through rural areas and either skirts or goes directly through small villages and towns. It can be beastly hot in summer and alarmingly cold in midwinter. There will be days in midsummer when you will be dripping with perspiration, when gnats, mosquitos, deerflies, and no-see-ums will make life miserable and days when you walk through stinging nettles and poison ivy. There will be times when your feet will be wet for days either from rain, heavy dew, or wet spots on the Trail, days when firewood is wet and when campfire smoke with an unerring sensor system seeks you out, wherever you are, and makes your eyes water and your nose run. But more than compensating for these things are spring days, clear and sunny, cool at night, warm at midday, when you will walk through thousands of acres of wild flowers—bluets, spring beauties, and trilliums. There will be summer days, when you can hike lightly clad, with a cool breeze on your face, with a song in your heart and not a care in the world. There will be autumn days in Maine when you can look across a mirror calm lake—a lake framed by white birch and flaming red maples while spruce and fir trees provide a dark green background. There will be times when, hot and thirsty, you come across a delightful ice cold spring and when the simple act of drinking deeply of that cold clear water fills you with a feeling of gratitude and appreciation that you would never have thought possible. There will be cool nights when you put on additional clothes and sit quietly beside a campfire, watch it slowly die, and then crawl into your sleeping bag and revel in the delightful warmth that only a 98.6 degree body and a down sleeping bag can produce. Nights when you are overcome with that incredible sense of well-being that results from strenuous exertion, a good meal, and a mind free from worry. Nights when sleep will come so quickly that you barely have time to recall and fix in your mind some of the more outstanding sights and events of the day . . . nights when you will thank God for having the good health and great good fortune to be where you are enjoying some of Nature's best. This is the Appalachian Trail. Neither words nor pictures can adequately describe it. Only those who have partaken of its pleasures and endured its hardships can fully appreciate it. And, having made that statement, it seems appropriate to list the names of those who have hiked the entire Trail, either in one year or many years, either from north to south, south to north, or both ways from the middle.

The Office of the Appalachian Trail Conference in Harpers Ferry, West Virginia, does its best to keep track of those who are hiking the entire Trail, both during the hike itself, and after the hike is completed. Most through-hikers have been in touch with the Conference long before their hikes are scheduled to begin. For these people communication between hiker and the Conference is fairly simple during the course of the hike. Employees of the Conference take a personal interest in all through-hikers and alert hiking clubs and others to the through-hiker's itinerary. The editor of *Appalachian Trailway News (ATN)* also takes a personal interest in the through-hikers because occasionally a story is exacted from the hiker and published in *ATN* shortly after the hike is completed. On two occasions *ATN* has published an up-to-date list of all such hikers with a thumbnail sketch showing the dates that each hike was begun and completed plus any unusual incidents that occurred. The last such listing was published in the September 1969 issue of *ATN*. The following is the most current list available (thru 1970) and shows the names and years of each recorded Appalachian Trail Hiker, 59 in all. According to conference records, the 25th to hike the Trail was the oldest, at age 82, Dr. Frederick W. Luehring. The youngest was Mark Boyer, age 13.

Recorded Appalachian Trail Hikers thru 1970

1.	Myron H. Avery*	1936
2.	Dr. George Outerbridge*	1939
3.	Dr. Martin Kilpatrick	1939
4.	Mrs. Mary Kilpatrick (Dr.)	1939
5.	Mr. Orville Crowder*	1939
6.	Mr. Charles Hazelhurst	1946
7.	Mr. Earl V. Shaffer	1948 T
8.	Dr. Robert Sosman	1948
9.	Mr. Carl E. Jones	1951
10.	Mr. Eugene Espy	1951 T
11.	Mr. Chester Dziengielewski	1951 T
12.	Mr. Martin D. Papendick	1951 T
13.	Mr. George F. Miller*	1952 T
14.	Mr. Richard Lamb	1952 T
15.	Mrs. Mildred Lamb	1952 T
16.	Mrs. Emma Gatewood*	1955 T
17.	Miss Dorothy Laker	1957 T
18.	The Honorable William O. Douglas	1958
19.	Mr. Murray S. Chism*	1959 T
20.	Mr. Edward N. Little	1959 T

* Deceased   T Thru in one trip

21.	Mr. Owen F. Allen	1960 T
22.	Mr. Lochlen L. Gregory	1960 T
23.	Dr. Walter S. Boardman	1960
24.	Mr. Herbert S. Hiller	1960
25.	Dr. Max Bender	1962
26.	Dr. Frederick W. Luehring (Age 82)	1963
27.	Mr. James F. Fox, Jr.	1963
28.	Mr. Paul A. Gerhard*	1963
29.	Mr. Chuck Ebersole	1964 T
30.	Mr. John Ebersole*	1964
31.	Mr. Ray Baker	1964 T
32.	Mr. Garnett W. Martin	1964 T
33.	Mr. Richard Kuhl	1965 T
34.	Mr. Paul Macauley	1966 T
35.	Mr. Jim Shattuck	1966
36.	Mr. Michael Ebersole	1966
37.	Mr. Leon L. Barkman	1967
38.	Mr. Clarence Boyer	1968
39.	Mr. Marc Boyer (Age 13)	1968
40.	Mr. Howard E. Bassett	1968 T
41.	Mr. Elmer L. Onstott	1968 T
42.	Mrs. Nell Skinner	1968 T
43.	Mr. Everett Skinner	1968 T
44.	Mr. Albert Field	1969
45.	Mr. Wm. O'Brien	1969 T
46.	Mr. Jeffrey Hancock	1969 T
47.	Mr. Eric Ryback (81 days)	1969 T
48.	Mr. Andrew J. Giger	1969
49.	Mr. Carlton B. Colquitt	1969
50.	Mr. Branley Owen (70 days)	1970 T
51.	Mr. Richard A. Hudson	1970
52.	Mr. Joseph Simpson	1970
53.	Mr. Chas Konopa	1970
54.	Mr. Thomas C. Herring	1970 T
55.	Mr. Edward B. Garvey	1970 T
56.	Mrs. Margaret Smith	1970 T
57.	Mr. Clifford Smith	1970 T
58.	Mr. Bradley Greuling	1970 T
59.	Mr. Paul Longway	

---

* Deceased   T Thru in one trip

It is interesting to note that whereas only 43 people were reported as having hiked the entire Trail in the first 31 years of its existence as a complete Trail, 15 people were recorded in the two years of 1969 and 1970. Beginning in 1971 the Conference appointed a committee to receive and evaluate the evidence of those who claimed to have hiked the entire Trail. But that procedure had to be discontinued in 1973 because of the tremendous increase in the number of 2000-Milers. The records maintained by the Conference show the following number of people reported to have hiked the entire Trail:

1936-70	59
1971	23
1972	35
1973	92
1974	70
1975	63
1976	91
Total 1936-1976	433

Those who complete hiking the entire Trail are urged to notify the Conference of the year in which they complete it. A cloth "2000 Miler" patch is available at a cost of 60¢ (members 50¢) and a walnut plaque is available for $30 (member price $25). The plaque is illustrated on page 371. The patch is generally worn underneath the familiar round "A.T." patch either on shirt, jacket, or pack. If you have spent four to six months and from $1000 to $2000 hiking the entire Trail, by all means order the patch and plaque. Buy several of the patches and wear them. They are great conversation pieces and you may inspire others to try the long hike. You will also be surprised at the number of people who have long harbored a desire to hike the entire Trail. An 18-year-old high school senior Richard Vogt writing from New Jersey in 1975 commented that:

I first hiked on the A.T. in 1971 from Bear Mountain, NY, to the Delaware Water Gap. I met and talked to many people and it's kind of sad how many expressed a wish to hike the entire Trail at one point in life, and let it pass by. (Vogt didn't let the idea pass *him* by . . . he hiked the whole Trail in 1975.)

Probably 90% of the through-hikers start in Georgia rather than in Maine. There is a reason for this, especially if the hiker plans to begin his hike in the early spring. Spring comes early in Georgia but very late in Maine. There is frequently snow on the ground in Maine until June 1. Even after the snows melt, the ground is still soggy until well into the summer. In addition the mosquitoes, flies, midgums, no-see-ums, etc., make life miserable for the hiker until almost the first of August. Early spring in the Southern Appalachians is beautiful in the extreme. Spring flowers are already in evidence by April 1; and as the hiker walks north, it is like hiking in eternal spring. The hikers cannot hike north quite as fast as spring advances; but it is a fact that one who begins his hike in Georgia around April 1 will probably see and enjoy more of the spring season than ever before in his life. As I review my daily diary notes for those delightful April and May days with the entries describing the flowers— trillium, bluets, spring beauties, . . . the rhododendron, the beauty and fragrance of the wild azalea, the birds I heard and saw—I get the urge to revisit the beautiful area. For those planning to hike the entire Trail in the five or six months that should be allowed, I would strongly recommend the south to north route. In that way you can enjoy the best of both seasons, spring in the Southern Appalachians, autumn in Maine.

You may by now have made your decision as to whether you will hike from south to north or vice versa. An equally important decision is whether you will hike alone or with a companion. *ATC Publication No. 15* in its Chapter 13, Precautions, has three pages of *do's* and *don'ts* for the hiker. The final paragraph of that chapter consists of a single italicized sentence as follows: *"Above all and, as a final monition, do not travel alone."*

After reading this rather stringent monition you may wonder why it is that so many of the through-hikers have hiked alone. If safety were the only factor to be considered, there would be no solo hikes. Danger is always present in mountain hiking. There is the danger of bad falls when bones can be broken or severe cuts sustained from the thousands of knife-edge rocks that dot the Trail. A heart attack, a stroke, or a sudden severe illness could occur. There is danger of a poisonous snake bite or attack by a vicious or rabid animal. All of these things could occur, whether you are alone or in the company of others; but the possibility of getting help is greatly increased if you have one or more companions. Again, why so many solo hikes? The answer is that it is very difficult to find someone who is free to hike at the time you are free to hike, who wishes to or is able to hike at the same speed you wish to hike, and who has a personality compatible to yours. It is one thing to hike with a companion or several companions for a few days or even a week. It is an entirely different matter if you plan to hike with the same person or people for a five- or six-month trip.

Two of those who hiked the entire Trail together in 1960 (Owen F. Allen and Lochlen L. Gregory) in describing their hike (*ATN* January, 1961) had this to say: "It may be worth mentioning that the warning given us by Earl Shaffer against hiking together has solid foundations. On the Trail, 'mole-hills' can become 'mountains,' and on more than one occasion we found ourselves acting stupidly childish, although we had worked together for two years. It bears consideration by any who plan to hike together for very long."

Two other men who hiked together were Murray S. Chism and Edward N. Little who required (or permitted themselves the luxury) eight months in 1959 to complete the Trail from Georgia to Maine. Of all those who have hiked the entire Trail in a single year, I have always felt that these two men obtained the full measure of enjoyment. They hiked through three seasons (spring, summer, fall) and finished up amid winter conditions in snow and ice on Mt. Katahdin on November 8, 1959.

I had planned to do most of my hiking with Maurice A. (Gus) Crews of Bethesda, Maryland. We took two conditioning hikes in February and March, 1970; and on the second of these Gus developed an infection. His doctor advised against his taking the long hike, and Gus heeded the advice. Despite this, it seemed that I would have plenty of companionship because I had announced in the January 1970 issue of *ATN* that I planned to begin the hike at Springer Mountain during the first week of April and that I would welcome company for a few days or a few weeks. I received about 12-15 inquiries; but for various reasons I hiked with only one person of that group, and then only for part of one day. One of these, Tom Herring of Mobile, Alabama, did not receive his equipment in time to begin on April 4. He started later but finished ahead of me in Maine. Another hiker, Elmer Schwengel of Kansas City met me at the starting point in Georgia. He had not had previous hiking experience; and even though he had arrived at Amicalola Falls State Park three days early for some conditioning, it was not enough for the rigors of the Appalachian Trail. After one day he decided it was more than he had bargained for; and I learned he returned to

Kansas City. I, therefore, found myself traveling alone for about two-thirds of the entire hike. Sometimes I met friends by prior arrangement and hiked with them a few days to two weeks. Sometimes I met people on the Trail who were hiking north, and I joined them for short periods of time. I thoroughly enjoyed the company of all those I met, and it will be enjoyable in the years to come to reminisce with these people over areas hiked and experiences shared. And yet, even though I am naturally a gregarious individual, I did enjoy those days when I had the solitude of only my own company. No one, unless he be a total recluse, can live his life exactly as he pleases. Each day of a man's life is a series of compromises and accommodations, with members of his family, his co-workers, his boss, his neighbors, and others. It was pleasant, therefore, to have some days on which all the options were mine: the time of arising and the time of going to bed, the choice of food to be eaten at each meal, the speed at which to hike, and the side trails chosen to explore.

Someday a solo hiker on the Trail will die or be killed; and when that happens, the event will receive nationwide newspaper coverage. But in that same year some 45,000 people (the yearly average) will be killed in automobile accidents, which, unless it be a particularly horrible accident, will receive no more than minor local newspaper coverage. Strange that we have become so hardened and accustomed to the automobile death but would look upon a hiking death with horror.

There is a considerable segment of the population that harbors the view that the Appalachian Trail is a publicly owned recreation area and that the hiker has a *right* to be there. Unfortunately some hikers also labor under this delusion. As a result there have been some uncomfortable confrontations between hikers and landowners. The plain fact of the matter is that perhaps 600 miles, or 30% of the Trail, is still on private land; and the Trail is there by reason of verbal permission of the landowner. The hiker should treat each acre of land over which he hikes (1) as though it belonged to a close and respected friend or (2) as though it was publicly owned land and the hiker is there as a guest of the people at large.

Beginning in the 1950's those exercising stewardship of the Trail began to become increasingly alarmed at undesirable encroachments upon the Trail. The encroachments came in the form of ski developments on many of the major mountain tops, mountain top

summer home developments, roads, radio and television towers. It
soon became apparent that some type of legislation would be
needed if the Trail was to be preserved as a wilderness foot trail.
In May 1964 Senator Gaylord Nelson of Wisconsin introduced a bill
(Senate Bill 2862) in the United States Senate to protect the Appalachian Trail. The bill was introduced too late for any action to be
taken in that session of Congress. However, Senator Nelson and
other Congressmen introduced a number of Appalachian Trail bills
in the next two sessions. The Ninetieth Congress passed an Appalachian Trail Bill and President Johnson signed it into law on October
2, 1968. (Public Law 90-543, 82 STAT. 919). The complete text of the
law is contained in *ATC Publication No. 5.* The law which bears the
title *National Trails System Act,* provides for a national system of
foot trails of which the Appalachian Trail shall be one. It provides
that the Secretary of the Interior shall fix the route of the Trail and
publish same in the Federal Register together with appropriate maps
and descriptions. Once the publishing of the Trail route in the
Federal Register has taken place, the States and local governments
have two years in which to acquire the necessary Trail right-of-way.
After the two-year period has expired, the Secretary of Interior is
authorized to enter into the picture and to take such action as necessary to provide the Trail right-of-way where the States and local
governments have failed to do so. In providing the right-of-way the
Secretary is authorized to enter into cooperative agreements with
landowners and others, to obtain easements, to purchase or exchange land, or to accept donations of land. Where all other methods of providing the right-of-way have failed, the Secretary may
utilize condemnation proceedings without the consent of the owner;
but where resort to this procedure is required, no more than 25
acres to the mile may be acquired.

Although the National Trails System Act was enacted in October
1968, it was not until three years later, October 1971, that the Secretary of Interior published the official route of the Trail in the
Federal Register. The publishing consisted of 85 maps and seven
pages of narrative description. Under the terms of the law the states
and the local governments would have two years from the date of
publishing to acquire the Trail right-of-way. After the two-year
period had expired (October 1973), the states, local governments,
and the Secretary of Interior could each take the necessary action
to acquire the right-of-way. Although the Department of Interior

knew in October 1971 that it would be expected to begin land acquisition two years hence, it took no action to develop land ownership information nor did it develop a land acquisition plan. During the eight years of the Nixon-Ford administrations, it acquired *not one acre of land* nor did it obtain a single easement to protect the Appalachian Trail right-of-way. To Trail enthusiasts the attitude of the Department of Interior during those eight years seemed to be of almost contemptuous indifference to the plight of the Appalachian Trail.

Alarmed by the reported lack of progress, the Congress through its House Interior and Insular Affairs Committee held legislative oversight hearings on March 11 and 12, 1976. These hearings are the ones in which a government agency is asked to make an accounting of its progress in implementing a particular law and in which other interested parties are also permitted to have their day in court with respect to the same law. An excellent report on these hearings was written by Cliff Gaucher for the September 1976 issue of *Trailway News.* As pointed out in that article the *mere announcement* of the hearings brought these results:

> Interior Secretary Thomas Kleppe on March 6, in an announcement to commemorate the birth of the late Benton MacKaye, inspirer of the AT, made available $1 million for AT land acquisition from the Contingency Reserve of the Land and Water Conservation Fund to protect critical sections of the Trail.
>
> An allocation of $500,000 is included in the President's budget for 1977 to assist the states with preacquisition costs, largely as an incentive to get the states moving on needed AT survey, appraisals, and title evidence.
>
> The National Park Service on March 1 designated Dave Richie with full-time responsibilities for the AT.

Other than for these three "just before the hearings" accomplishments, Interior had precious little to report. Three representatives of the Appalachian Trail Conference were also permitted to testify: Stanley A. Murray, former Chairman; Paul Pritchard, Executive Director; and I. In my own testimony I traced the legislative history of the National Trails System Act in which there was every indication that Interior could, would, and should engage in direct acquisition of AT right-of-way and I quoted parts of a letter from the former Secretary of Interior in which he agreed completely with the concept of direct acquisition.

Not all was gloom at the hearings. The Forest Service of the U.S. Department of Agriculture has jurisdiction over 830 miles of the

AT that passes through eight national forests. The Forest Service reported that since the Act was passed in 1968 the Service had purchased, acquired through easements or through relocation 117 miles of the Trail. The 117 miles protected is 5.8 percent of the entire Trail! The published hearings, Serial No. 94-50, were released by the House Interior and Insular Affairs Committee in February 1977.

Since the Act was passed in 1968, 10 of the 14 states have passed their own Appalachian Trail Bills. As of December 1976 only Vermont, New York, Pennsylvania and West Virginia have failed to enact such legislation. Pennsylvania came so close to obtaining legislation in late 1976, with both houses of its legislature passing almost identical bills by huge majorities, only to have the bills snarled by committees in the closing days of the legislative session. In total the various states have acquired about 100 miles of the Trail since 1968. Maryland has perhaps the best track record to date and continues to systematically purchase land along the AT route. In general the state laws were written to supplement the federal law. Each of the state laws authorizes some agency of the state government to provide the necessary right-of-way for the Appalachian Trail. While both the federal law and the state laws authorize action to be taken in providing a Trail right-of-way, no substantial progress can be made until the United States Congress and the various state legislatures appropriate money for that purpose. It will be many years, therefore, before the hiker can hike the entire 2,000 miles of the Trail serene in the knowledge that he does have some legal right to be on the Trail. And even after that momentous milestone has been achieved, the hiker would be wise to go out of his way to be courteous and friendly to landowners along the Trail. Many of these landowners have permitted the Trail to go through their land for decades. Others will have even donated the legal right-of-way required by Public Law 90-543. Furthermore I found in my own hiking that the landowners and others living near the Trail were a most friendly and interesting group of people. I enjoyed visiting with them and my Trail experience was much the richer for having done so.

This then is the Appalachian Trail, how it came to be, what it is now, and what is being done to preserve it. In succeeding chapters I will discuss the preparations to make for an extended hike, maps and guidebooks, selection of a pack and the equipment to be carried.

On March 21, 1978 President Carter signed into law a bill, H.R. 8803, which provided very important amendments to the National Trails System Act of 1968. The new legislation, which is now known as Public Law 95-248, contains these following provisions:

1. It reestablishes the Advisory Council for the Appalachian Trail for a 10-year period beginning in March 1978.

2. It permits the Secretary of Interior to use the powers of eminent domain (condemnation) to acquire up to 125 acres per miles (a 1,000 foot strip) in lieu of the 25-acre, 200-foot maximum under the original law.

3. In increases the authorization for acquisition of land from the totally inadequate $5 million in the 1968 legislation to a new figure of $90 million and it directs the Secretary of Interior to complete the needed land acquisition within a three-year period beginning with the fiscal year 1979.

This is tremendously important legislation and it seems almost unbelievable that it moved so rapidly through the legislative channels. One of our own ATC members, Congressman Goodloe E. Byron of Maryland, introduced the bill on August 4, 1977 for himself and for Congressman Jonathan B. Bingham of New York, Phillip Burton of California, and John F. Seiberling of Ohio. The Chairman of the subcommittee for National Parks and Insular Affairs, Congressman Phillip Burton, held hearings on October 6. Those who testified on behalf of the bill were:

1. Congressman Goodloe E. Byron; Mr. Robert Herbst, Asst. Sec., Dept. of Interior; Charles McC. Mathias, U.S. Senator from Maryland; James Mallow, Dept. of Natural Resources, Maryland; Henry W. Lautz, Exec. Dir., App. Trail Conference; William Eischbaum, then with the Dept. of Environmental Resources, of the Commonwealth of Pennsylvania; Charles Foster, Dean, School of Forestry and Environmental Resources, Yale University and Chairman of the Appalachian National Scenic Trail Advisory Council.

2. Thomas Deans Appalachian Mountain Club, Boston; Edward B. Garvey, Appalachian Trail Conference; Destry Jarvis, National Parks and Conservation Association; Pam Rich, Friends of the Earth; Ray Page, Wilderness Society.

No one appeared to speak in opposition to the bill at the House hearings although later at the Senate hearings there was some landowner opposition from people in Maryland and Virginia. Suffice to say the bill moved swiftly through both House and Senate subcommittees and full committees. Senator Mathias of Maryland had introduced a companion bill in the Senate—S. 2066. The Conference sent a letter to each of its 10,000 members asking for support of the bills. A separate letter went to each of the 500 or so 2,000 Milers as it was felt that that group had received more benefits from the Appalachian Trail than any other one group. The Congressional climate was excellent. The vote in the House was 409 to 12 for passage. The vote in the Senate was by acclamation. The House accepted the Senate amendments to the bill and passed the amended bill, also by acclamation, early in March. The President signed it shortly thereafter. Those who desire a copy of the new law should write to either their congressman or senator and ask for P.L. 95-248 and ask also for Senate Report No. 95-636 which explains, in layman's language, the significance of the various sections in the law.

In the winter of 1978 the National Park Service issued invitations to bid on a title search project on 1,750 parcels of land along the center line of the Appalachian Trail from Georgia to Maine. Contracts for this vast title search job are expected to be awarded in the spring of 1978.

On April 19, 1978 the Potomac Appalachian Trail Club hosted a wine and cheese victory party at its downtown Washington headquarters. Those invited were Congressmen, Senators, professional staff members of the House and Senate committees, and many, many others who worked so diligently to secure passage of this sorely needed legislation. It would seem that 1978 will long be recognized as the turn-around year for the Appalachian Trail.

See picture of signing ceremony on page vii.

2
Along the Trail

If you have read Chapter 1, you now have a pretty good idea of *what* the Appalachian Trail is. You may now appreciate a word of information as to just *where* the Trail is and how you can find it. A quick study of the map will give you a rough idea of the route of the Trail through each of the 14 states through which the Trail passes. The next step, if you desire more precise information, is to obtain a road map. The road maps issued by most major oil companies show fairly accurately where the Trail intersects each primary highway. Furthermore, the highway departments of all the states involved erect highway crossing signs identifying intersections of the Trail and primary highways. These signs range in size from the modest 24 inch ovals in Connecticut to the huge 24 by 72 inch signs in New Hampshire. At secondary highways, the Trail is frequently identified by signs erected by trail clubs. If at this point your interest has been aroused to the extent that you desire to locate the Trail and see what it looks like, you have a good chance of doing so. By using the road map and your car and by keeping a sharp eye for road signs you should be able to spot a point where the Trail crosses a highway. Once having located a Trail crossing, you can park your car and hike on the Trail in either direction to find out what it is like. While hiking on the Trail you may find a wooden directional sign giving distances to points of interest in either direction, e.g., distances to an overnight shelter or to another highway intersection.

You may, however, be an individual who desires to have much more complete information before you hike the first step. Or you may not like the idea of exploring a strange trail all by yourself. There are a number of ways you can obtain additional information. You might telephone your local newspaper, ask for the sports department, and ask one of the editors for information on hiking clubs in your area. Or you might inquire from your local library if it has

Appalachian Trail. (Sketch by Sharon Garvey)

available one of the guidebooks issued by the Appalachian Trail Conference. Yet another possibility is to contact one of the eight National Forests or the two National Parks through which the Trail passes. But the surest way is to write to the organization that coordinates the activities of the clubs and individuals that maintain the 2,000 mile Trail. This organization is the Appalachian Trail Conference, P.O. Box 236, Harpers Ferry, WV 25425. Send 25 cents and ask to be furnished with the information packet. Ask also to be furnished with the names of hiking clubs in your area.

The Appalachian Trail Conference consists of 63 hiking clubs that share responsibility for maintaining the Trail. Most of these clubs schedule weekend or Sunday hiking trips on almost a year-round basis. If one of these clubs is located near you, you may (1) telephone the club office, (2) contact a club member, or (3) scan the leisure sports section of the newspaper to ascertain the date, locale, and other particulars for forthcoming hikes. In this way you can arrange to hike with a group of people; and the more experienced hikers will be glad to answer your questions regarding maps and equipment, overnight shelter accommodations, and so on.

If you live in a location where there are no hiking clubs, or if you prefer to hike alone, or with your family, or with a few close friends but have questions as to trail locations, locations of drinking water, shelters, and perhaps equipment, you should write to the Trail Conference. You will receive with their information packet a list of the publications that are available. One of these publications is *ATC Publication No. 15, Suggestions for Appalachian Trail Users.* Also on the publication list are some 10 guidebooks.

Each of the guides is a five by six inch book about one inch thick with durable plastic covers. Each book contains detailed trail data on some 200 to 300 miles of the Trail, describes interesting side trails, and frequently contains interesting and historical information concerning features found along the Trail or about the country through which the Trail passes.

Every book is divided into a number of chapters, with each chapter containing detailed information on a length of the Trail that extends anywhere from 5 to 20 miles. At the beginning of the chapter are listed the names of any maps that pertain to the section of Trail being described. Each section of the Trail is described twice in the book; once from north to south, and again from south to

Trail Description

Section 3: Nahmakanta Lake to Kokadjo-B Pond Road

21.6 Miles

Direction
N to S

Miles   Trail Data (see page 95 for opposite direction)

0.0m. At gravel lumber road next to Nahmakanta Lake, take road
SE and directly away from Pond. Trail north leaves road on
right. **Nahmakanta Lake Lean-to** is 50 yds. from shore of lake.
See section on **Lean-tos & Campsites** for description of lean-to
and its accommodations.
The Trail follows this road for the next 4 1/2 m. south.

1.0   Cross small brook.

1.5   At top of rise, turn **left** at junction of lumber roads. Descend
beyond.

2.8   Cross Tumbledown Dick Brook.

4.6   Turn **sharp right** off road and into trail. Road leads 0.2 m.
ahead to Mahar Landing on northwest tip of Pemadumcook
Lake. Trail is quite wet and muddy in next 1/2 mile through
boggy section.

5.4   Skirt to right, large beaver flowage.

6.6   Pass on left, west shore of Pemadumcook Lake, one of the
largest touched by the trail in New England. To left, side trail
leads to shore where views of Katahdin may be seen by walking
along shore.

6.7   Cross Twitchell Brook. Trail begins easy ascent of
Potaywadjo Ridge beyond.

7.2   Reach **Potawadjo Spring Lean-to** and spring. See section on
Lean-tos & Campsites for description of lean-to and its
accommodations. The Potawadjo Spring is one of the two major
springs on the trail in Maine; the other being the Rainbow Lake
Spring further north. This one is a 6 yds. wide bubbling spring.
with extremely cold water; truly a joy to the hiker.

8.0   Reach crest of ridge (elev. 837 ft.) and descend.

8.9   Near shore of Lower Jo-Mary Lake, trail swings NW along

THE APPALACHIAN TRAIL IN MAINE

lake shore. Here short side trail (blue blazed) leads to a **sand beach** on shore of lake (excellent swimming).

9.1   Blue-blazed **trail branches right to open ledges of Potaywadjo Ridge** (a pleasant hike of 1 mile).

9.3   Cross inlet brook to lake as trail swings around west end.

10.5   Reach old Antler's Camps, now in ruins, on lake shore. Trail **swings right** down lake shore (To left, a trail passes number of old camps out to a point with outstanding views the entire length of the lake).

11.2   Turn right onto old Cooper Brook Tote Road. Trail follows this for next nine miles up Cooper Brook Valley to Crawford Pond.

11.8   After skirting Mud Pond, to right, cross its outlet.

12.2   Pass through old lumber campground and beyond, swing right (upstream) along Cooper Brook. Cross gravel lumber road.

13.2   Pass 10 yds. to left, small spring.

13.4   On left, is blue blazed side trail 0.2 m. to shore of Cooper Pond. Main trail does not come in sight of it.

14.5   Cross G.N.P. gravel lumber road. (see **Road Approaches** for description of this road). Interesting falls and balancing rock just above road in brook. Continue on Tote Road.

18.3   To left, is side trail 25 yds. to **Cooper Brook Falls Lean-to.** See section on **Lean-tos & Campsites** for description of lean-to and its accommodations. Beautiful falls on brook just above lean-to.

20.6   Bear left and cross old lumberman's dam at outlet of Crawford Pond. Beyond dam, cross clearing and follow lumber road south.

21.6   Reach graveled Kokadjo-B Pond Road at end of section. Trail turns left onto this road. (see Sec. 4). To right road leads 2.8 miles to Yoke Pond Camps (privately owned) and on to Kokadjo. (See Road Approaches)

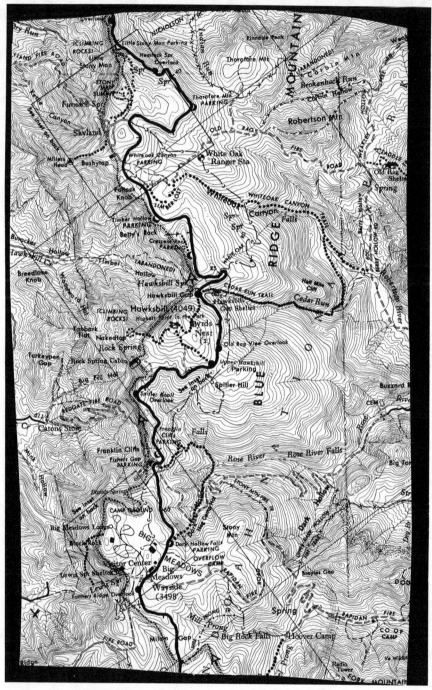

A section of Map No. 10 by the Potomac Appalachian Trail Club.

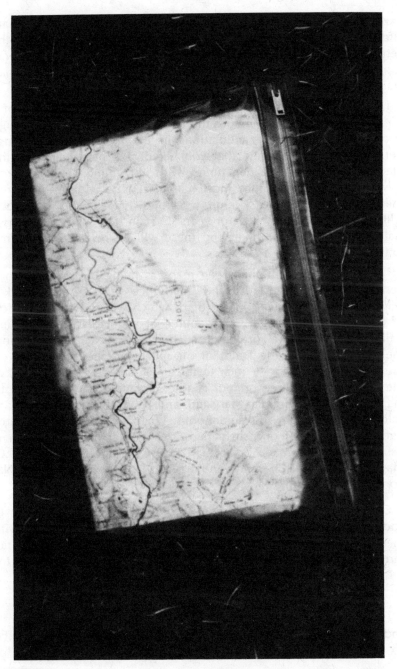
Trail map in a waterproof zippered plastic map case. (Photo: Appalachian Outfitters)

north. Moreover, each section of the book first prints the summary information for that particular section of Trail and then lists the detailed trail data. On the previous pages is a reproduction of a complete page of one such guidebook, the *Guide to the Appalachian Trail in Maine*, eighth edition.

I would advise any hiker to buy the guidebook. Half the fun of a trip is to study the book before the trip begins and then go through it afterwards and make annotations in the margins about things personal to you: the date that you hiked at a particular trail, the place where you saw a hen turkey with her young, the place you saw a fox or a bear. Since most hiking is done within a hundred mile radius of the hiker's home, it follows that a single guidebook will serve the average hiker for years. Certain trails will carry a special fascination for the hiker and these will be revisited from time to time.

I have already mentioned road maps as being of assistance to a person who desires to locate the Trail. Once *on* the Trail, the hiker will desire more detailed maps: maps which will show the location of each overnight shelter, each source of water, each intersecting trail, road, and stream. Fortunately such maps are available for almost the entire length of the Trail. For the most part these maps are on the scale of 1 inch or ½ inch to the mile; and the guidebooks, at the end of every three or four chapters, contain one such foldout map. In northern Virginia, Maryland, and Pennsylvania the maps are sold separately from the guidebooks. On page 26 there is reproduced a portion of one such map. This is Map No. 10, which is issued by the Potomac Appalachian Trail Club of Washington, D.C. Map 10 covers the 35-mile central section of the Shenandoah National Park in Virginia.

Over 800 miles of the Trail goes through eight national forests. In addition to the guide book maps, many hikers desire to carry with them the U.S. Forest Service maps that show the route of the Trail through each of the eight forests. If you desire these maps, write to:

U.S. Forest Service
1720 Peachtree Road
Atlanta, GA 30309

and ask to receive the maps showing the Appalachian Trail in the six national forests in the southern region. You may also write to:

U.S. Forest Service
633 West Wisconsin Ave.
Milwaukee, WI 53203

and ask to receive the Appalachian Trail maps for the White Mountains and Green Mountains National Forests.

Those who desire to have the ultimate in detailed map information may write to:

U.S. Geological Survey
1200 South Eads Street
Arlington, VA 22202.

Ask to receive the index of those topographic maps that pertain to the Appalachian Trail. The index will be mailed to you free of charge along with an order blank and a little booklet "Topographic Maps." This booklet has copious illustrations in color using the same colors and symbols that are used on the topographic maps (topos).

Many hikers planning trips of short duration on the Appalachian Trail either remove from their guidebook or otherwise reproduce only those pages that pertain to the area being hiked. These pages plus the pertinent map are then placed in a clear plastic map case. Such a practice cuts down on both weight and bulk in the pack. Furthermore, the map with its contents clearly visible through the case can be referred to even in wet weather without damaging the guidebook sheets.

Most of the information in this book relates to the Georgia to Maine hiker and there is no question but that one who is going all the way needs all the advance information he can get. But perhaps 98 percent of all AT hiking is done by those who are to be on the Trail but for a single day (day hiking) or on short backpacking trips of two days to two weeks. I have been urged to include a few suggestions for this category of hikers also. There seems to be a feeling in some circles that the person who hikes the entire Trail in one year is just a cut above the person who is tied to a job and who must squeeze in his hikes on weekends and on one and two week vacations in order to complete the entire Trail. I personally feel that it requires more perseverance, and requires much more money, to do it over a period of years. Which method results in the greater satisfaction is debatable. The through hiker has the thrill of walking through all or parts of three seasons . . . spring, summer, and autumn. He becomes lean and hard from the day-after-day hiking up and down and along mountains. He learns how to sustain himself and

to come up smiling through fair weather and foul. He becomes at-
tuned to the mountains and to the hiking routine and develops a
rhythm that the short distance hiker seldom experiences. And yet,
except for the Trail itself, the through hiker learns precious little
about the country through which he passes and the people who
inhabit that country. He leaves the Trail only to replenish his food
supply and to pick up and dispatch mail.

Instead of having one long five-month experience in a single year,
the short distance hiker has many, many experiences over a period
of many years. The planning, the picture taking, the reminiscing,
even the automobile trips themselves, each become a separate ex-
cursion to be enjoyed in full measure before getting ready for the
next trip to complete additional mileage on the Trail. One family in
Ohio completed the Trail over a period of years driving some 90,000
miles in the process. What a series of rich experiences about which
to reminisce at family get-togethers in the years to come.

Two hiking friends, Gus Crews and Norm Greist, mentioned elsewhere in this book are among the 2000-Milers who accomplished
the task (enjoyed the experience!) over a period of years. Gus hiking
his last mile in 1972 at the age of 70 and Norm in 1975 at the age
of 65. How long did it take them? For Gus it was a 15-year experience and for Norm a mere 45! Each of these men has a much better
knowledge of the Trail than I do because they have done so much
more planning for each trip and because they began hiking and
terminated short hikes from so many more approach points than
I have. And in doing so, they have become acquainted with the
small towns and villages along the Trail and with the local people.

Those using the short hike approach will make much more use
of road maps, Forest Service maps, and Park Service maps than will
the through hiker. The maps in the guidebooks generally show only
the Trail and perhaps two or three miles to either side (adequate
for the hiker on the Trail but not of much help to the man trying
to reach an approach point via an automobile). If you are a small
group and can get all members of that group and their gear into one
car, then by all means use but the one car. You may think that having
more than one vehicle will give you greater mobility. It doesn't.
It restricts your mobility because you have additional vehicles that
must be moved from place to place. I've been involved in some
hikes that involve much car shuttling and I find it extremely frustrating. You begin to wonder if the purpose of the trip was to enjoy

the mountains and to hike or to shuttle cars for long distances over poor roads each morning and afternoon.

If you have but one car and you wish to day hike for several days, it can be done by spotting part of the group each morning at one point on the Trail and the remainder at another point. The two groups hike in opposite directions and exchange the car keys at the point where the two groups meet for the midday lunch. If you have but one car and you wish to backpack rather than day hike, it is best to drive to the point where you will complete your hike and arrange for a local person to both drive your group to the starting point of the hike and then to drive the car back to the driver's home. In that way you are always hiking toward your car and regardless of what time you finish the hike the car is there waiting for you and it is in a protected place during the course of your hike. It is becoming increasingly risky to leave a vehicle unattended for several days or a week alongside a public road while hiking the Appalachian Trail.

So far in this chapter I have provided general information, information that would probably be of more value to one having no previous knowledge of the Trail than to one already having some experience of it. Now let's return to the central theme of this book, the long distance hike on the Trail—either mine or one by someone else.

Whereas the short-distance hiker needs but one guidebook, the hiker going all the way needs all 10 guidebooks. Or does he? Does a hiker *have* to have guidebooks to hike the Trail? The answer is that he does not. But without the guidebooks the hiker will miss so much. Many, many points of interest will not be seen because the hiker will not know that they are there to be seen . . . and even if he did, he would frequently not know where to look for them. Not all points of interest, trail-side shelters, or sources of water along the Trail are marked. They should be, but they are not. I think of the young man I met down in Georgia who had spent his first night on the Trail a mere half mile from the shelter where I stayed overnight. Why didn't he walk the additional half mile to the shelter? Because he did not know it was there. He was traveling without a guidebook. In the May 1970 issue of *Appalachian Trailway News*, Andrew J. Giger tells of his end to end hike on the Appalachian Trail. He tells of catching up with a couple who had been on the Trail for 55 days. He mentions that the couple was "carrying no guidebook, a severe disadvantage."

Let us assume that you purchased all 10 guidebooks and you wish to use them to the maximum advantage. If you plan to hike from

"I Still Say if Hansel and Gretel had followed the Appalachian Trail markers instead of those stupid bread crumbs they'd never have gotten lost!"

Cartoon by Sharon Garvey.

south to north you will find it advantageous to remove from each guidebook the north to south description. The next step is to combine into five guidebook covers the south to north descriptions that formerly appeared in the 10 books. The next thing is to go through each of your five consolidated books and underline in red those points of maximum importance, particularly sources of water and locations of overnight shelters. An additional precaution that will pay dividends is to obtain copies of *Appalachian Trailway News* for the past two or three years. Study each issue carefully and mark in the margin of your guidebooks any information that would be pertinent to your hike. Such information might be the location of new trailside shelters built since the last edition of the guidebook was published, the locations of old shelters that had been torn down, burned, or otherwise abandoned, and listings of areas where the Trail had been rerouted. Everett and Nell Skinner who made their leisurely traverse of the entire Trail in '68 documented the locations of eating places, grocery stores, and other valuable bits of information. Much of this information was published in the January, 1970 issue of *ATN*. Some of the parenthetical notes provided by the Skinners in their article are gems; for example, "we ate at every restaurant we passed in order to shop less and eat heartily without carrying surplus food." Again, in describing the Dodson South Mountain Inn in Maryland the Skinners said, ". . . restaurant, wonderful chicken Maryland! Waitress told us anybody would know we weren't bums. She meant it so sincerely we couldn't take offense. We still chuckle over it. Just off Appalachian Trail crossing U.S. alternate Rt. 40."

Just prior to my 1970 hike, my intended hiking companion for the trip, Gus Crews, studied all of the south to north sections of the 10 guidebooks. He then prepared a listing of all overnight shelters, highway crossings, and locations of conveniently situated grocery stores. He also listed the cumulative mileage after each item so that by reference to this fact sheet I could tell at a glance how far it was to the next shelter, the next grocery store, etc. The following is an excerpt from one such sheet for southwestern Virginia:

Item	Mileage
Cherry Tree LT	441.43
Iron Mt. (Rt. 16)	448.00
Racoon Br. LT	448.66
Brushy Mt. (Rt. 16)	457.7

The symbol LT means lean-to or shelter. The cumulative mileage shown is distance from Springer Mountain, Georgia. I carried these

Appalachian Trail white paint blazes. (Photo: Steve Wagner)

sheets with me at all times and referred to them constantly. In 1971 Mr. Crews and I reviewed and updated the sheets. They were included in the first issue of Appalachian Hiker as an appendix. Copies of the sheets were also furnished to the Appalachian Trail Conference. The issuance and revision of the Mileage Fact Sheets became a pet project of Les Holmes, the first Executive Director of the Conference (1968-75). In 1977 the Conference expanded the scope of the Mileage Fact Sheets and issued a new publication entitled *The Appalachian Trail Data Book* which is available at a cost of $3.00 (1977 price). By permission of the Conference, the contents of the new publication are reproduced as an appendix to this book revision. The publication will be updated from time to time to show new shelter locations and other changes that would be of interest to the hiker.

This chapter would not be complete without describing the manner in which the Trail is marked. In order of importance (to me at least) these markings are (1) the white paint blaze (2) the 4-inch metal marker (3) wooden directional signs (4) the blue paint blaze and (5) mileage markers. Each of these markings is illustrated by a picture in this book, and I will discuss them in detail in ensuing paragraphs. Readers desiring a thorough knowledge of trail markings and the methods of applying them may obtain *ATC Publication No. 1, Trail Manual for the Appalachian Trail*.

1. Without doubt the white paint blaze is the most important and infallible method of marking the Trail. The blaze is 2 inches wide and 6 inches high. The blaze is painted on trees, rocks, and other objects along the Trail. The blazes face the hiker like highway markers. When placed on trees, they should be at eye level. Blazes are supposed to be within sight of each other on narrow woods trails and at somewhat greater distances in more traveled sections. Generally, however, the hiker should always have a blaze in sight, either by looking forward or backward along the Trail. The paint blaze, if properly applied with precise 2-inch-by-6-inch dimensions and square corners, makes a most distinctive marking. Theoretically, the hiker should be able to find the Trail from Georgia to Maine by reference only to the white paint blazes. There are three reasons why it doesn't quite work out this way. For one thing, such occurrences as lumbering operations, road widenings, and fires can destroy all evidence of blazing over a considerable area. More recently, ski slope development and mountain home construction have done the same. A second reason is that those doing the paint blazing sometimes get a little careless. Since they themselves know the Trail so well, they assume that all others

Appalachian Trail wooden directional signs. (Photo: Abbie Rowe, National Park Service)

should likewise know it. They do not try to see the Trail through the eyes of the stranger. Therefore they omit blazes, particularly at trail and road intersections; so that the hiker must perforce stop and do some reconnoitering. To say that these interruptions to your hiking schedule are irritating and frustrating is to state it too mildly. Words like maddening and infuriating are much more suitable. If you as a hiker find areas like this on the Appalachian Trail, you will be doing your fellow hiker a great favor if you will promptly drop a postcard to the Appalachian Trail Conference describing the area that is inadequately blazed. The Conference, through its Trail Standards Committee, developed in 1971 an effective method for alerting maintaining organizations of any areas that were inadequately blazed.

The third reason the white blazes cannot be entirely relied upon is that one 70-mile section of the Trail is not blazed, or blazed so sparsely that most hikers do not realize that it is blazed at all. This is the 70 miles that lies within the boundaries of the Great Smoky Mountains National Park. For years I had thought that the omission of such blazing was because of the reluctance of the Park officials to permit it. I learned in October 1976 that the real reason is that the maintaining organization—the Smoky Mountain Hiking Club—had been unable to perform the blazing. When I hiked through the Smokies in 1977, I found that *some* excellent blazing had been done but it was so sparse that many of the through hikers were unaware of the blazing.

2. The 4-inch diamond-shaped metal marker with the familiar joined *A* and *T* is used sporadically along the length of the Trail. At the time of my hike it was used very frequently and effectively in Maine, to a lesser extent elsewhere. Unfortunately, the metal marker seems to have high value as a souvenir; and in a few areas of heavy Trail traffic the markers seem to disappear almost as fast as they are erected.

3. The wooden directional and informational signs are a great help. They tell the hiker the distance to the next shelter, the distance to a spring; they tell him when he has reached the summit of a mountain and inform him of the name of the mountain top and its elevation. I found some sections of the Trail to be very well marked with these signs. Maine was outstanding. Other sections of the Trail were almost devoid of such signs.

4. Blue paint blazes, the same size as the white ones (2 x 6 inches), are used to identify side trails leading off the Appalachian Trail. The

Appalachian Trail wooden directional sign in Maine. (Photo: Tex Griffin)

blue blaze trails lead to such things as overnight shelters, springs, and viewpoints. To be of maximum value the blue blaze trails should be further identified by signs informing the hiker where the blue blaze trail goes and how far it is to the shelter, spring, viewpoint, or whatever it is that lies at the end of that particular trail. Sometimes signs are not erected, sometimes they are destroyed or stolen. It is in such situations that the guidebooks prove of value. If the guidebook indicates that there is a shelter 200 yards to the right of the Trail at milepoint 13.52, for example, and if you should find a blue blaze trail leading off to the right at a point in the general area of where you think milepoint 13.52 should be, then it is a safe bet that ye olde blue blaze trail will lead you directly to the shelter.

5. The Trail route across open fields and over mountain tops where no trees exist is marked by piles of built-up stones, called cairns, or by blazes painted on rocks, or by both such devices. As the hiker proceeds from Georgia to Maine, he will find many spots where cairns could be used effectively; but he will find precious few cairns until he reaches New Hampshire. In that State and in Maine, the cairns are used frequently and effectively.

6. Mileage markers are another seldom used trail marking device. I found them used extensively only in Maine plus in one 7-mile stretch in eastern Pennsylvania. I found them to be extremely useful. The Board of Managers of the Appalachian Trail Conference in a November 1970 meeting made provision for extending the mileage marker concept throughout the entire length of the Trail. To understand the mileage marker concept you must realize that the entire Appalachian Trail is divided into a number of sections. These sections are generally delineated by road intersections. That is, if the Trail is intersected by two roads that are three miles apart, you then have a "section" that is only three miles. On the other hand, in some areas, such as the Great Smoky Mountain National Park, there is only one intersecting road in some 70 miles. In such areas you might have a "section" that would be 35 to 40 miles in length. Unfortunately, the hiker is seldom certain of his exact location within a given "section." The guidebook, for example, may state that at 13.82 m. trail to right leads 200 yards to Jones pond shelter. As nighttime approaches the hiker begins to wonder how much farther he must walk before reaching "13.82"; and, after he has walked a considerable distance, he will wonder if perchance he has missed the side trail at "13.82." The mileage markers, located at one-mile intervals,

Maine Trail blaze mileage marker. (Photo: Tex Griffin)

give the hiker some reassurance and permit him to orient himself with respect to the various points of interest described in the guidebook. The distances used on mileage markers are always reckoned from the *north* end of the section, and the mileages used are keyed to the guidebook mileages. The mileage marker is a painted arrow pointing to north end of section plus a figure, e.g., *3.0,* and the word *miles* or, more frequently, just the abbreviation *m*. The ones in Maine were usually painted on large rocks beside the Trail. See page 40 for picture of one such mileage marker that I observed in Maine.

The last marker that I shall describe in this chapter is the National Scenic Trail metal marker. The National Trails System Act directs the Secretary of Interior and Secretary of Agriculture to establish a uniform marker with a distinctive symbol for each National Scenic Trail. Such a marker has been established, and the one for the Appalachian Trail is pictured on this page. The Department of Interior is having these markers manufactured in only one size—9 inches. The markers will be used at points where the Trail intersects a road and where the intersection is not already marked with a highway crossing sign. These signs are very attractive and are located in particularly vulnerable areas—along roadsides. As a result, the markers disappear about as fast as they are erected.

National Scenic Trail marker. (Photo: Appalachian Trail Conference)

3
Food

Hikers, who have hiked long distances on the Appalachian Trail, have used three principal methods of supplying themselves with food. These are the following:

Method 1. Buy your entire supply of dehydrated food in advance of the trip, pack in watertight containers, and bury in food caches at various points along the Trail. This method was used successfully by Howie Bassett in 1968 and again in 1969 by Jeff Hancock.

Method 2. Buy your entire supply of dehydrated food in advance of the trip, repack in boxes suitable for mailing, and have these boxes mailed to you at prearranged mail stops along the Trail. This method is used by many through hikers.

Method 3. Buy all of your groceries from rural and small town grocery stores along the Trail. This is the method I used on my 1970 trip and most of the 1976 2000-milers also followed this procedure.

If the hiker's principal goal is to hike, hike, hike with the least amount of lost time, then he would do well to use Method 1. Its disadvantage is that it requires a substantial amount of automobile travel prior to the trip in order to bury the food containers. And, of course, there is always the possibility that one or more of the caches will be disturbed or stolen. This possibility is perhaps somewhat remote. Of the 100 caches buried by the Hancock family only one was found to have been disturbed, and about half of the contents of one gallon plastic jar had been damaged. But from the standpoint of speed, it is hard to argue against Method 1. The hiker checks his notes, locates the food cache, removes the food which has been previously repackaged into meal-size plastic sacks; and he is on his way. Just one disturbing thought occurs to me as I describe this method. What happens to all those one-gallon plastic jars after the food has been removed? Litter! Tsk! Tsk!

Method 2 is somewhat like Method 1 except that the food caches consist of boxes which, hopefully, are waiting for you at the post office stops you have previously selected. It is more time-consuming because the hiker must leave the Trail and either walk or hitch a ride into town. But most hikers desire an occasional break in town anyway. There they can get a square meal, have their clothes laundered, and receive mail. And since few places along the Trail have the variety of dehydrated foods the hiker requires, he would do well to consider Method 2 if he plans to eat dehydrated foods.

Method 3 is for those hikers who have sufficient time to hike the Trail in a more relaxed manner or for those who do not care for dehydrated foods as a steady diet. I fitted into both these categories. I also found that shelf items in the grocery store are generally much cheaper than their dehydrated counterparts. I frankly enjoyed the sashays into town to buy food, to visit with the townspeople, receive mail, write a few quick letters, launder my clothes, get a shower, and eat a couple of good meals which I did not have to cook myself. On the average, I found that I could buy groceries every four or five days without having to travel too far off the Trail.

But suppose you have decided to go the dehydrated food route. Where does one buy enough dehydrated food for a five- or six-month trip extending for 2,000 miles? Fortunately, there are a number of suppliers where such quantities can be obtained. Their names and addresses are listed in Appendix 2. A word of caution here. If there will be but one or two people in your party, be certain to choose a supplier who prepares dehydrated food in packages for one or two people. I remember the two young ladies I met on the Trail in April 1970. They had embarked on a three-month backpacking trip and had purchased $170 worth of dehydrated food only to find upon its receipt that all the packages were packed for parties of four people. This meant that before beginning their hike they had to open every package and repackage its contents.

A word of definition is in order as the term "dehydrated foods." Most of us tend to think of dehydrated foods (including freeze-dried foods) as those foods available only at backpacking, camping, or mountaineering supply houses. But Webster defines dehydration as "the artificial drying of food products to reduce weight and preserve them for future use." If this definition is strictly adhered to, all grocery stores carry a number of dehydrated items on their shelves; for example, rice, raisins, apricots, dried soups, etc., to name a few. For the purposes of this chapter, I shall consider dehydrated foods (including freeze-dried food) to be those foods put up in packets of 1, 2, or 4 servings and available at supply houses catering to campers, hikers, and mountaineers.

Your choice of food, then, will be determined first by your decision to go either the dehydrated food route or the grocery store route; and second by your decision as to whether you plan to cook one meal per day, two meals per day, three meals per day, or, perhaps, no meals per day. And lastly your decision will be governed largely by your personal preferences in food.

Many hikers I met during my five-month Appalachian Trail hike who were aware that I planned to write this book urged that I include in it the particular foods that I found most satisfactory and that I also include recipes for those dishes I used most often. This I will do. But first I must quote a passage from the book *Appalachian Trail* by Ann and Myron Sutton, published by J. B. Lippincott, Philadelphia, Pennsylvania. You will enjoy reading this if for no other reason than that it will make you happy that you are buying your trail food in the 1970's rather than in the early 1800's. The Suttons, after describing some of the tremendous walking feats accomplished by the English in the early 1800's, describe the diets followed by these hardy hikers of 160 years ago. Here is what they say.

> And what kind of diet were these feats performed on? If a man walked thirty-six miles to breakfast and thirty farther to dinner, what did he eat? The reply concerned more what walkers should not eat. 'Vegetables,' went the answer, 'such as turnips, carrots, or potatoes, are never given, as they are watery, and of difficult digestion. On the same principle, fish must be avoided, and besides, they are not sufficiently nutritious. Neither butter nor cheese is allowed; the one being very indigestible, and the other apt to turn rancid on the stomach. Eggs are also forbidden, excepting the yolk taken raw in the morning. And it must be remarked, that salt, spiceries, and all kinds of seasonings, with the exception of vinegar, are prohibited. . . .
>
> With respect to liquors, they must be always taken cold; and homebrewed beer, old, but not bottled, is the best. A little red wine, however, may be given to those who are not fond of malt liquor; but never more than half a pint after dinner. Too much liquor swells the abdomen, and of course injures the breath. The quantity of beer, therefore, should not exceed three pints during the whole day, and it must

be taken with breakfast, and dinner, no supper being allowed. Water is never given alone, and ardent spirits are strictly prohibited, however diluted.

It is an established rule to avoid liquids as much as possible, and no more liquor of any kind is allowed to be taken than what is merely requisite to quench the thirst. Milk is never allowed, as it curdles on the stomach. Soups are not used; nor is anything liquid taken warm, but gruel or broth, to promote the operation of the physic.

The you have it, fellow hikers! Right out of the Hikers' Manual of 1810 or thereabouts. I find the list of "don'ts" to be impressive and almost all-inclusive. I find the section giving advice on the eating of eggs to be especially repulsive. Imagine, if you can, on a cold raw morning, swallowing a raw egg yolk and then washing it down with a little vinegar! But let's get back to the 1970's and see what is now acceptable.

As a beginner I suggest you review ATC Publication 15, Chapter 18 on Food. I would also suggest a valuable but little known book called *Nutrition Scoreboard* published by Avon Publishing Co., 959 8th Ave., New York, NY 10019. Single copies of this book cost $1.75 in 1977 and can be ordered directly from Avon. Add 25¢ for postage and handling.

One of the more thoughtful reviews of my book appeared in the June 15, 1972 issue of *Appalachia*, the publication of the Appalachian Mountain Club of Boston. The reviewer was Edward N. Little who had hiked the entire Trail in 1959. While he gave me high scores on most points, he pointed out, quite correctly, that I had failed to adequately discuss the need for a balanced diet for a trip of five or six months duration. I still have not done so! I describe the foods that I ate and the method of cooking them but the development of a really balanced diet from the foods generally available to the long-distance backpacker is another project. I do think that the *Nutrition Scoreboard* book will give you some good ideas. The *Scoreboard* book is especially critical of the popular breakfast cereals pointing out that many are nothing but sugar-coated confections.

There may be a few long-distance hikers that stick to the three meals a day routine they have at home. I found it most advantageous to have three or four light meals and snacks during the day and then a full cooked meal at night. The great majority of the 1976 2000-Milers also ate but one hot meal per day, a few had 2 hot meals,

and a very, very few opted for three. I ate a light breakfast about
6:00 a.m., a snack about 9:30, a light lunch around noon, frequently
another snack about 3:00 p.m., and a hearty cooked meal around
6:00 p.m. About three-fourths of the time my breakfast consisted
of dry cereal only. For these meals, I would measure out a generous-
size portion of the cereal, then add dry milk and sugar. All such
meals would be prepared in advance; that is, at the time I bought
the boxed cereal during my hike, I would measure out meal-size
portions of the cereal, milk, and sugar and pack this into plastic
bags. Then each morning it was necessary only to pour the contents of one bag into a container, add water, stir, and eat. I varied
this by occasionally eating a slice of *Claxton Fruit Cake*, by drinking
a cup of one of the instant powdered breakfasts, or by eating one
of the many varieties of fruit tarts which have become popular in
recent years. Early in the hike, however, I discontinued the instant
powdered breakfasts, as I felt they cost too much for the food value
delivered. The same reasoning applied to the tarts. They made a
good combination with a cup of hot coffee, but I felt I was eating
mostly pastry dough with only a tiny amount of sweetened fruit
thrown in.

Near the end of my hike, in September and early October up in
Maine, I frequently heated water for breakfast and enjoyed the luxury of hot coffee (instant coffee). This practice proved so pleasant
that I seriously toyed with the idea of buying a small coffee pot at
Monson, Maine, and of making fresh-brewed coffee on each of the
last ten days of my hike. But reason prevailed over appetite, and
I contented myself with the instant coffee. Later I discovered (*Consumer Report* magazine, January 1971) that expert coffee tasters
believe the better instant coffees to be fully as tasty as the brewed
coffees. This explodes my long-held conviction on this subject and
bears out my wife's contention that my preference for the brewed
coffees "is all in the mind." So be it.

If cold cereals were my most frequently eaten breakfasts, what
particular cereals did I use? I found the combination of General
Mills' *Total* and Kellogg's *Concentrate* to be very good. I bought
these two cereals frequently and mixed them together before putting
them in the plastic bags. I also used Post's *Grape Nuts* frequently.
I bought corn flakes once, when I could not buy the others. Before
opening a package of *Total* or corn flakes I would put the package
on the floor and stamp on it to reduce the volume. As might be

imagined, this action required a hasty explanation to the grocery store proprietor and any other patrons. It was somewhat disconcerting at times to go through the stamping process on a large box of flaked cereal and then discover what a small amount of food was left. From the standpoint of weight versus volume, I would vote for *Grape Nuts*. Its large box contains 24 ounces of food. Some of the other cereals, in boxes half again or twice as big would contain only 8 to 12 ounces of food. Don't be deceived by the size of the box.

During the course of my 1970 hike, the breakfast cereal industry came into heavy criticism—being scored for valuable nutrients, which they lacked, and for undesirable elements, principally heavy concentrations of sugar, which they contained. The criticism continues to this day and the cereal companies continue to manufacture many junk cereals. Read *Nutrition Scoreboard* for details. The breakfast cereal I used most frequently, Post's *Grape Nuts*, emerged from this bombardment with a relatively high score—being mildly criticized for somewhat low protein count but scoring well on most other factors. Also since 1970, a number of the granola products have entered the market. Some of these are subject to the same criticism as other cereals, that is, much too much sugar. In recent years I have made much of my own granola from a recipe devised by Darwin and Eileen Lambert, two professional outdoor writers who live in a pre-Civil War house on the edge of Shenandoah National Park. Here is the recipe:

CRUNCHY GRANOLA

¼ lb. melted margarine	7 to 8 C. uncooked oatmeal
½ cup brown sugar	1 cup wheat germ
1 tsp. salt	1 cup coconut
1 tsp. vanilla	¼ c. sesame seeds—optional
½ cup water	½ cup chopped nuts—optional

In Dutch oven combine margarine, sugar, salt, vanilla, and water. Stir over low heat until dissolved. Add remaining ingredients and stir until moistened. Spread on ungreased cookie sheets (2). Bake 2 hours at 275° stirring occasionally with a fork. Or bake at higher temperature for less time—but be careful not to scorch.

Comments by the Lamberts, "We sometimes substitute honey or molasses for the brown sugar and use a little less water. And we sometimes use sunflower seeds instead of nuts—just for variety. We never seem to tire of this. We add raisins or bananas when we serve it but backpackers could add dry fruit.

Comments by Ed Garvey, "I mix this in a heavy aluminum pot of 8 to 10 qt. capacity instead of Dutch oven. In lieu of measuring out 8 cups of oatmeal, use the full 18-ounce package you buy at store— it equals 8 cups. I have made many batches of this—sometimes doubling the recipe. Excellent stuff!"

For snacks and lunches I ate such foods as peanuts, mixed nuts, raisins, apricots, dates, candy bars, cheese, bread, *Citadel Spread, Nonesuch Mincemeat, Claxton Fruit Cake.* When I could find them along the Trail, I also ate strawberries, raspberries, blueberries, blackberries, cherries, and apples. Of the above, the *Citadel Spread* and *Claxton Fruit Cake* require further explanation. When I mention bread, I do not mean loaves of bread that are available at grocery stores as these are too big and soft for backpacking. Something smaller and firmer is in order in the bread department. I found English muffins to be particularly good. Small packages of hamburger buns or hot dog buns are satisfactory, but they are somewhat softer than the muffins. One other bread I ate occasionally was French bread rolls flown over from Paris by Air France. I boasted that I was probably the only hiker on the Appalachian Trail who enjoyed the luxury of bread rolls baked in Paris and flown to this country. It just happened that my daughter Kathleen worked part time for Air France at nearby Dulles International Airport. On incoming flights from Paris there would frequently be sizable quantities of these delicious long keeping French rolls left over from the flight. These would be given to any Air France employees on duty at the time. Some of these found their way into our freezer and later into my Appalachian Trail food supply. I never ate one of these French rolls without marveling at the miracles of present day transportation. It seemed incredible that I could be sitting at a remote spot on the Trail eating a bread roll which had been baked in Paris, France.

Before leaving the muffin and bread subject, let me describe an excellent luncheon combination which I used extensively in 1976, that is, buttered muffins and hardboiled eggs. In 1974 fellow PATC-ers Bill Husic, Ed Hanlon, and I hiked for six weeks in the Alps of northwestern Yugoslavia and in the mountains of nearby Italy and southern Austria. Stopping each night at the doms, rifugios, and huts (the names given by the respective countries to their mountain top inns), we noticed the almost universal practice of using small rectangular tins which were used to transport such foods as luncheon meats, bread, crackers, jam, etc. Husic promptly bought one and has used it extensively on his long hikes on the AT. On our 1976 hike in the southern Appalachians, Hanlon came upon the ingenious idea of packing six well-buttered English muffins in a one-pound coffee tin with plastic top. In a separate plastic egg container, he carried six hardboiled eggs. That was lunch for six days. Margarine is better than butter for this purpose as it keeps much better before turning rancid. How long do the eggs keep? Well, in June 1976, hiking on the Laurel Ridge Trail in Pennsylvania, I too carried the six eggs and six muffins, and I ate the last of them eight days after the hike began—this was in hot humid weather. Even fresh eggs keep without refrigeration much longer than generally supposed. Ray Baker who hiked the entire Trail in 1964 would frequently purchase a dozen eggs at a time, and leave them in the original carton. He had no problems with spoilage. Eggs are high in protein and, when you think of it, the hen that lays them is really most considerate in providing the hiker with a bio-degradable container in which the egg can be carried. Eggs can be poached, soft-boiled, hard-boiled, or fried and the egg shells should be scattered in the woods, not left at the fireplace.

I can't leave the subject of eggs without passing on a method of keeping eggs fresh for incredible lengths of time without refrigeration. Here's how: immerse a fresh egg in boiling water for just five seconds . . . not five minutes but five *seconds*. It will then keep for weeks without refrigeration. When I first read of this little trick, it seemed hard to believe so I conducted my own test. On May 31, 1976, I put three fresh eggs in boiling water for five seconds. I then put them up in my attic which is 10-15 degrees warmer than the other rooms in the house. On June 14, two weeks later I fried one for breakfast. Just like a fresh egg. On June 28 I fried another one which tasted just like a fresh egg but the yolk was somewhat flatter when first put into the griddle. On July 21, some seven weeks after the 5 second boiling, I fried the last one. It too tasted just like a fresh egg but the yolk appeared almost flat when put into the griddle.

One other "bread" product that has come on the market bears the trade name "STOVE TOP" and it is labeled as a 15-minute stuffing mix. It comes in two flavors, Chicken and Cornbread. It could easily be called dehydrated chicken stuffing. One box sold for approximately 70¢ in 1977 and it makes six one-half cup servings. Inside each box are two packages. One contains a concentrated heavily seasoned soup-like mix. You pour this in water, bring to a boil, and simmer five minutes. From the other package you pour into your "soup" mix the required amount of dry bread crumbs, stir them thoroughly into the soup, wait five minutes, and that's it. The stuffing, still hot and giving forth a delicious aroma, is ready to eat. It satisfies your craving for bread in a most delightful way. I've made the mix several times, very simple. If you wish to add the gourmet touch, you can, after the stuffing is cooked, lift it slightly off the skillet bottom, pour in a little margarine, spread the dressing out so it forms a loose patty, and cook it a bit longer until the bottom is lightly browned and crisp. Serve with the crust side up.

A certain backpacker, who did his hiking about 100 years before most of us, stoutly maintained that for food he desired nothing more than bread, bread, bread, and more bread. I am speaking of John Muir who did his hiking and exploring in the Sierra Nevada mountains in the latter part of the nineteenth century. In the book *The Wilderness World* of John Muir (Houghton Mifflin Co., Boston), Muir in his journal of July 7, 1869 wrote,

> Bread without flesh is a good diet, as on many botanical excursions I have proved. Tea also may easily be ignored. Just bread and water and delightful toil is all I need . . . not unreasonable much, yet one ought to be trained and tempered to enjoy life in these brave wilds in full independence of any particular kind of nourishment. * * *

But in reading elsewhere in the book, I noted that where Muir described a particular meal he frequently mentioned other items in addition to bread. The bread only diet I would find about as uninteresting as the rice only diet described elsewhere in this book.

And now the explanation in regard to *Citadel Spread*, *Nonesuch Mincemeat*, and *Claxton Fruit Cake*. All three of these might be considered to be pemmican. American Indians, frontiersmen, and Arctic explorers were known to rely on pemmican on long overland trips. Webster defines pemmican as lean, dried meat pounded into paste with fat and dried fruit and then pressed into cakes. Two of the three foods I describe contain no meat, but they certainly qualify on the other counts. The third, *Nonesuch Mincemeat*, qualifies on all counts. Consider first *Citadel Spread,* a name rather jokingly given to a concoction devised by Bill and Beth Oscanyan, members of the Potomac Appalachian Trail Club, who live directly beside the Trail in northern Virginia near State Route 7. When my nephew, Shannon Garvey, and I arrived at the Oscanyan residence on June 16, 1970, I had covered 880 miles from Springer Mountain. Within minutes after reaching the Oscanyan residence, we were treated to hot coffee and a generous chunk of *Citadel Spread* fresh out of the refrigerator. The Spread was delicious, and I was very seldom without it during the remaining 1,100 miles of my hike. I hastened to obtain the recipe from Beth Oscanyan; here it is as it appears in my diary for June 16:

Citadel Spread

18 oz. jar Skippy Creamy Peanut Butter
2-4 oz. Bacon Grease (residue from 6-8 slices)
½ cup honey
2-4 cups granular powdered milk *(Carnation)*

Add milk and stir until mix gets crunchy. Put in pint plastic freezer containers. It will keep in refrigerator indefinitely; it keeps for at least three weeks unrefrigerated.

That's the recipe as given to me. I made the mix a number of times during the rest of the trip and made some alterations. I used any kind of peanut butter or powdered milk I could get. I love bacon grease, but sometimes I had to use vegetable oil. Also I added to the mix such things as mixed nuts, dates, raisins. I never did use it as a spread because I kept adding milk during the mixing process until I achieved a consistency as firm as soft fudge candy. I ate the *Citadel Spread* at various meals and between meals. If I had hot coffee for breakfast, I would finish off my cereal breakfast with a chunk of the Spread with more hot coffee. From northern Virginia to Mount Katahdin I gave little samples of this spread to many people. Almost invariably I was then asked to furnish the recipe; which I did. I recommend it highly.

Since the *Citadel Spread* recipe first appeared in my book in 1971, I have received comments on it from many sources. One was from Beth Oscanyan, who concocted it. She wrote that peanut butter, while high in proteins, is not a *complete* protein, since it lacks some of the essential elements found in animal proteins. However the addition of the powdered milk in the recipe overcomes the deficiency so that the final product is indeed a complete protein.

A most interesting series of comments came from John Shores in a sequence of letters to his parents in January, 1973. Writing from Columbia, South America where he was working in the national parks of that country, and living with and eating his meals with a Columbian family the younger Shores related:

> Jan. 5: Going to bus to the park tomorrow. Plan to make some Citadel Spread to carry with me. * * *I'm off to buy some peanut butter, honey, and dry milk, plus a container for it.

> Jan. 12: I ate another mixture of *Citadel Spread*, almost. I may mix up some more so that we can eat some in Cali this weekend. I really enjoy nibbling, which is probably indicative of my slightly undernourishing diet. But 8 table-spoons of peanut butter are supposed to supply protein necessary for one day (two servings of 4 tablespoons each, or two servings of 2 eggs.)

> Jan. 17: What scares me about making *Citadel Spread* is that I can eat all 8 oz. at a sitting, without looking up once. Something about mild forms of starvation that is disturbing. It's so slow I can't get fired up enough to do much about it except watch. I mean this can't really be happening to me! I have *Citadel Spread* on hand *not* to build my weight *up*, but to maintain it!"

And now the *Claxton Fruit Cake*, made by Claxton Bakeries of Claxton, Georgia. These cakes are individually wrapped, each cake being eight inches long and approximately two inches square. It is sold in three pound boxes (each box containing three one pound cakes) and mailed anywhere. In 1976 a three pound box cost $6.00. At Harpers Ferry, West Virginia, I mailed Claxton Bakeries a check and informed them where I wanted the first box sent. At later points I informed them where I wanted box number two sent, and later where I wanted box number three sent, etc. At each point the box was waiting for me. Well . . . almost. I arrived at Glencliffe, New Hampshire, at 8:20 a.m. on August 15 expecting to find a three pound package of Claxton Fruit Cake at the post office. No such luck. But my disappointment was short lived. Five minutes later, a mail truck arrived; and the postmistress promptly handed me my precious fruit cake. This fruit cake is easy to pack, keeps well, and is delicious to eat. What more could one ask? It contains flour, raisins, cherries, pecans, shortening, and pineapple, among other things.

The mincemeat that I recommend for backpacking is that which is sold in small dried cubes approximately 1½ x 2½ x 3½ inches in size. These cubes weigh 9 oz. and cost 99 cents in 1978. They are prepared and sold by Borden's, by A&P, and possibly by others. Each cube when cooked with water makes enough filling for an eight-inch pie. This gives you an idea of how much food is con-contrated in that little cube. I nibbled on the cubes occasionally for daytime snacks. At the evening meal, I would cook up part of one cube and use it as a sauce over cooked rice.

My evening meal was my most enjoyable meal, as you might expect. I tried to arrive at a trailside shelter about three hours before darkness was due to set in. This would give me about one hour to make my shelter inspection and to complete my paper work for the day. I would then have about two hours to gather firewood, prepare my evening meal, clean dishes, shave, and bathe.

Before going into the details of evening meals let me describe two variations of my usual routine upon reaching camp. If meal time is a good two hours away, your group may find it enjoyable to quickly heat up a pot of water and enjoy a cup of bouillon or some other light pick-me-up. A second variation enjoyed by some of my backpacking friends is to stop at the shelter say at about 4 p.m., promptly cook the evening meal, then begin hiking again during a cooler part of the day. This routine might be used to permit watching a sunset or sunrise from the top of the ridge, to sleep in a cooler spot, to seek more solitude away from an already crowded shelter, or simply to get an earlier start the next day to reach a particular destination.

What dinner dishes are available to the backpacker traversing the entire Appalachian Trail or large segments of it? If you are using the dehydrated foods, there is almost no limit to the variety of vegetable, meat, and dessert dishes available. But, since I followed the grocery store method, I am listing only those dishes made from ingredients generally available from such stores. Before I begin listing these foods and giving recipes, I must confess that I did eat some dehy-drated foods during my hike. Several times fellow hikers pressed upon me a package of their favorite dehydrated or freeze-dried foods with the request that I "give it a try." And during the first week of my hike at the Addis Gap shelter in northern Georgia I found a bonanza: six packages of freeze-dried food, each carrying a price tag of $1.55 and containing portions for two people. This meant 12 dinners, two of chili con carne, ten of chicken and rice. I should have been content to take one or two packages and to have left the rest. But you become very possessive about food when you are on a long hike of this nature and dependent upon the food you have in your pack. Accordingly, I took all six packages and alternated those freeze-dried dinners with my more conventional ones for the next several weeks. Many a time as I lugged those rather hefty packages of freeze-dried foods up and down the mountains of Georgia, North Carolina, Tennessee, and Virginia, I had reason to reflect on my greediness in taking all six packages. I ate the last half portion of the sixth package on May 16 at Niday shelter in the Jefferson National Forest in Virginia. That was five weeks and 500 miles after I had picked it up! The question arises, as to "How stupid can you get?" And the answer comes back, "Pretty stupid!"

My main dish at the evening meal generally consisted of one of the following; they are listed below in order of preference and frequency of use:

1. Creamed tuna or creamed chicken over either rice or instant potatoes,

2. Lipton's Green Pea Soup or Potato Soup, supplemented with various items from my larder,

3. One of the four Lipton's Dehydrated Dinners then available at most grocery stores (Chicken Supreme, Chicken Stroganoff, Beef Stroganoff, Ham Cheddarton),

4. Appalachian Trail Mix.

The creamed tuna and creamed chicken were my old reliable standbys. I never tired of either one. I had tried these dishes on previous hikes but not with too much success. But before I began the 2,000 miler in April, I took some extra tutoring from my wife; and the tutoring paid handsome dividends. These dishes are inexpensive, are nourishing, and are delicious. Where I could get them, I bought the small 3 oz. cans of tuna and chicken. At many stores only the larger 6 oz. cans were available, so I bought them. For rice, I preferred Uncle Ben's Five Minute Rice; but I used any of the quick-cook rices if Uncle Ben's was not available. Usually I used the two-pot method, cooking the rice in one pot and all other ingredients in the other. When time was short, I cooked everything in one pot.

Let's consider the two-pot method first. Light-up your stove or have a fire going with enough wood beside it for your entire evening meal. Nearby (hopefully on a table) put all the items you will need for the meal, . . . can of tuna, rice, cooking oil, seasonings, etc. In one sauce pan (use pans of three- or four-cup capacity) pour enough water to cook the amount of rice you plan to use. Add margarine or vegetable oil plus salt. Measure out the proper amount of rice and put it to one side. All the proportions are on the rice box cover. Put the sauce pan on the fire so that water begins to heat. Now let's proceed to the other sauce pan and the remaining ingredients. Using a can opener cut all around the top of the tuna can except for one inch. Then, using the top of the can as a squeezer and using both hands, you squeeze out all excess tuna oil into the second saucepan. Then add one tablespoon vegetable oil or margarine followed by 1/4 cup of water, one tbs. of flour and three tbs. of dried milk. Put all these ingredients into the second saucepan, put it over the fire, and stir vigorously. Bring the contents slowly to a light boil, stirring frequently. Keep a weather eye on saucepan number one so that rice doesn't stick or burn. Back to pan number two. Keep this pan over low heat and stir until you have a thick sauce. If it's too thin, add more flour. If it's too thick, add more water. You can't lose on this dish. When you have it the way you want it, spoon in the tuna chunks from the can and work them into the sauce. Then remove both pans from the fire and pour the cream sauce and tuna chunks over the rice. It will be too hot to eat immediately, so you will have a few precious minutes to immediately rinse out pan number two and fill it with water for your beverage or for dishwater. So far I've said nothing about the seasoning for the sauce. At the time you begin making it in pan number two, add salt, pepper, basil leaves, oregano, in any combination you please. After you have mixed in the tuna chunks, taste the concoction and add more of any spice you think is needed. I suggest you practice making this dish at home until you get the process letter-perfect.

Now the one pot method. You use the same ingredients, but you dirty only one cooking utensil. From a taste standpoint, the end result is not as good as the two pot method. Proceed to make the cream sauce first; and when it has cooked slowly for a minute or two, you simply add the tuna and rice and additional water for the amount of rice you have measured out. Bring to a boil and simmer slowly until the rice is tender. It's as simple as that.

For simplicity, I have furnished directions only for tuna and rice. Follow the same directions for canned chicken. Occasionally you will desire to use instant potato mix instead of rice. Use the two pot method and pour the cream sauce and tuna chunks (or chicken) over the potatoes.

In the immediate preceding paragraphs, I have explained how to make cream sauce starting from scratch. Here is a quicker way to make the sauce. Squeeze the oil out of the tuna can into a sauce pan. Add one packet of instant cream of mushroom soup. Add about one-fourth cup water—hot or cold. Stir and heat over fire. As mixture thickens keep adding water until you have a thick cream sauce. One packet of instant soup makes enough cream sauce for one 6½ oz. can of tuna.

Since I have already alluded to some of the spices such as salt, pepper, etc. this may be a good time to discuss the subject of condiments. In the earlier part of this chapter we read what the English hikers of the 1810 era thought about condiments, that is, no salt, spiceries, or seasonings of any kind except vinegar. Let's dismiss that philosophy as a bad dream. Writing about a hundred years later, George W. Sears under the pen name "Nessmuk" wrote his famout book *Woodcraft*. Nessmuk advises his readers to carry a single container of spice: this container is to include both fine white salt and white pepper, mixed at a ratio of ten parts salt to one part pepper. Not bad advice; not bad at all, even in this day and age. Nessmuk further advises, rather emphatically, not to carry any of the other numerous condiments such as oregano, thyme, etc.

Now let's consider what a more recent expert on condiments advises. In the January 1956 issue of *Trailway News* appears the excellent article "Gormandize on The Trail" by Ellen H. Connelly, an experienced nutritionist. Miss Connelly strongly recommends the addition of a few spices to your pack so that a little change and adventure can be achieved in your trail cooking. I quote a few sentences from that article: "Granting that some things can't be improved on—fresh springwater, the first cup of morning coffee, wild strawberries—nearly everything else you cook on the trail can be given new and different flavor with the addition of a bit of herb or spice. The wonderful thing about herbs and spices is that they pack so much flavor into so little bulky, weighable matter. A little of them goes a long way." And later in the article . . . "You don't need to take a wide selection; pick the three or four that will do the most for your cooking, and plan to alternate them."

I am a strong advocate of the Connelly philosophy. When I began my hike on April 4 in Georgia I was carrying salt, pepper, sugar, and cinnamon. Six weeks later on May 22 near the James River in Virginia I was joined by two hiking companions from the Washington, D.C., area: Gus Crews and Charlie Burroughs. If Ellen Connelly was enthusiastic about the use of spices, Charlie Burroughs was even more so. During each of the three days he hiked with me he gave me pep talks on the use of his favorite herbs and spices, concluding each talk with a "and it really doesn't weigh anything!" I was a receptive listener. On May 25 I left the Trail and returned home for a 12-day break. When I resumed hiking on June 6, I was carrying three additional items in my condiment bag: oregano, basil leaves, and instant minced onion. Shortly thereafter, at one of the post office stops along the Trail, I received a letter from Burroughs containing two things: typewritten instructions on the use of his favorite herbs and spices plus a small packet of one such herb, Krauterbutter. (Krauterbutter—a herb butter seasoning made by McCormick & Co.) It seems doubtful if any of the end to end hikers of the Appalachian Trail could boast such a variety of condiments. And did I regret carrying this wide assortment? Not at all. They made my meals ever so much more enjoyable; and before reaching Katahdin I had used up all of the condiments and had to resupply for a few of them.

I urge you to give some of these spices a try. Try them out at home or on short duration backpacking trips. You may decide that the simple salt and pepper condiments are all you need. Or you may be one of those (like me) for whom cooking and eating is one of the real pleasures to be enjoyed on a long traverse of the Trail. If so, you will probably wind up by carrying a few of these extra herbs and spices.

One other item I will mention at this time, although it is not a condiment; that is butter or margarine. Backpacking these items in their solid form is a messy proposition. I carried liquid shortening in a one pint plastic bottle throughout my entire hike. As an added precaution I put the plastic bottle inside a plastic sack and secured it with a wire twist top—this to prevent unsightly grease stains on my Kelty pack. And what specific liquid shortening do I recommend? If you can get it, buy Buttery Flavor Oil as made by Wesson. And

Ed Garvey's cooking gear. (Photo: Joan Knight)

why this one? Because it is flavored to taste like butter and because it has a yellow color to make it look like butter. This is important. Consider these facts. Real butter when it first comes from the churn has a very pale yellow look. Buttermakers add vegetable coloring to give it more eye appeal. Prior to about 1950 margarine was required by law to be sold in its white uncolored form. Millions of American families went through the weekly ritual of softening up two or three pounds of the white margarine and then working in the yellow coloring. It didn't make the product any better, but it made it look more like butter. The Wesson Buttery Flavor Oil is, as far as I know, the only oil now on the market that is made to look and taste like butter. And since you will be using it in all situations where you would ordinarily be using butter or yellow margarine, you may as well use a product that looks as much as possible like the article for which it is being substituted.

If you can't get the Buttery Flavor Oil, buy the clear uncolored variety. Then when you are sitting down to your evening meal with some instant mashed potatoes in front of you, you will add a tea-spoon or so of the clear oil to your potatoes and you will say to yourself in a convincing manner "These potatoes will be delicious with this rich yellow butter! These potatoes will be delicious . . . etc." You get the idea. Think positive!

Now that I have discussed the condiment and butter situation, let me return to the main evening dishes: Lipton's four Dehydrated Dinners, which were popular with backpackers in 1970, have been taken off the market—a sad day for backpackers. But other foods have appeared on grocery shelves which fill the void quite well. Two of these are Hamburger Helper and Tuna Helper. Of the two I prefer the Tuna Helper and have used it a number of times in the past two years. A single package provides generous servings for four people and the instructions suggest a 6½-ounce can of tuna. If your group is smaller than four people, it is a simple matter to use but part of the package and to save the remainder for another meal. For backpacking, throw away the outside box. In cooking these dishes, I add a tablespoon of cooking oil plus some of the herbs and spices I carry with me. These dinners are nourishing, filling, tasty, and inexpensive.

With respect to the Hamburger Helper one 1976 hiker reported that he had substituted soy protein for the meat and the substitution proved quite satisfactory.

Another product that I have carried in my pack for years is Lipton dried soups. I have on occasion used two other dried soups: Wyler's and Swiss-Knorr. Both are good, but I prefer the Lipton. At the time of my 1970 hike most of the available packaged soups required from six to eight minutes of cooking. The two varieties I used most were green pea and potato. But alas! Like its Dehydrated Dinners, Lipton has also removed the very tasty potato soup from the market. I am now using cream of mushroom. Both the pea soup and the cream soups are excellent when eaten just as soups with nothing added. But an added value of each is that they can be used as the principal ingredient for making rich nourishing stews or chowders. The cream soups generally contain some starch and flour and can be used for thickeners for cream sauces or gravies. The Lipton soups are sold in boxes and each box holds two aluminum foil packages which contain the soup. Each foil package provides three 8 oz. servings of soup. For backpacking, discard the paper boxes and carry only the foil packages.

Here are some of the combinations I used with these two soups. You will think of others. Make croutons by breaking bread into small pieces and frying it with a generous quantity of butter. Just before eating the soup add the croutons. With the green pea soup, I would occasionally pour in a handful of rice. Also with the green pea soup, I have added fresh sliced frankfurter (in cool weather) or canned sausages. At the Grafton Notch shelter in Maine, fellow hikers gave me small quantities of sardines and canned salmon. I added both to the potato soup I was making and finished up with an excellent main meal dish. Let me quote a few passages from my diary under date of August 24, 1970 to prove my point on these soups. This was a day on which Sam Steen, ATC member from Kingston, New York, and I had hiked 13 tough grueling miles from Pinkham Notch in New Hampshire over the Carter mountains all the way to the Imp Shelter. My diary for that day reads: . . . "Daylight beginning to fade when we reached Imp Shelter at 7:45 p.m. Both Sam and I beat. Made beds and cooked Green Pea Soup strengthened with can of sausages. Gad but it tasted good! Hot tea, instant pudding and fruit cake for dessert after which we collapsed into bed." A few minutes later while laying in our sleeping bags before drifting off to sleep Sam and I agreed on several things regarding the day's hike:—one of them being "how fantastically good that soup and sausage was at the end of a hard day."

During the 1970's Liptons came out with an instant soup called Cup-a-Soup; Nestle came out with an instant soup called Souptime; and I am sure there are others. These are individual packets which, combined with 6 oz. of boiling water reconstitutes in 10 to 20 seconds. These are great for a quick snack and I try to keep a few packages in my pack at all times.

I will describe one other main meal dish that I enjoyed a number of times during the last 500 miles of my hike. This dish I call "Appalachian Trail Mix." But before I describe it in detail, let me discourse a bit on one of its principal ingredients, short grain whole rice. During the first week of my hike down in Georgia, I met by chance a young college student, and I hiked with him almost a week. He had embraced an Eastern religious diet that dictated he exist on a diet composed chiefly of short grain whole rice, ½ cup each day. Occassionally, at lunch time, he would cook up a small batch of buckwheat groats. During the last two or three days of our hiking together he accepted some raisins from me to supplement that rather uninteresting rice diet, but he accepted nothing else. I admired him for his self discipline, and I listened carefully to his discourses on the value of the short grain whole rice diet. At the time the young man left me he had been on the rice diet for nine days. He appeared to be in excellent health but had lost considerable weight. He had not had a bowel movement in those entire nine days. Apparently his body was absorbing all of the little amount of food he was eating. One half cup of this rice weighs slightly over three oz. One pound of rice would therefore provide rations for five days. This young man was carrying a 15 pound sack of rice. At the rate of ½ cup each day, this would provide food for 75 days, or 2½ months. It seems doubtful if any one will every try such a feat, but it makes for interesting speculation.

Frankly I was impressed with the short grain whole rice idea, not as a steady diet but as the principal part of an occasional main meal. Even though I carried some of the rice with me for several hundred miles, I never did use it during the first four months of my hike primarily, because of the long cooking time required. Whole rice (as distinguished from the polished partially cooked rice) requires a solid hour of simmering over low heat in a tightly covered container. So much for the whole rice. Now let's return to Appalachian Trail Mix.

While hiking in Vermont I joined forces for about a week with four young men. One was George Wright, a traveling troubador type, now singing professionally under the name "Peregrine." Another was Craig Bumgarner, a University of Vermont student. The other two were two friends from Saddle Brook, New Jersey, Ken Lesenko and Jim Burdick. Shortly before beginning his hike, Bumgarner had eaten an evening meal with some friends and had been impressed by a tasty casserole type dish they served. He inquired as to its ingredients and concluded it would make an ideal dish for his forthcoming hike on the Trail. He brought about five pounds of the mix on his hike, cooked it almost every evening, and shared it with us on occasion. Here is the mix and the method of cooking it:

Appalachian Trail Mix

Mix two parts short grain whole rice to one part lentils and one part barley. Mix two cups water to one cup of the mix. Add seasoning. Cook one hour at low heat in a covered container.

All of these foods must be purchased at one of the health food stores. Fortunately one such well known store is located within a five minute walk from my home; namely Kennedy's Natural Foods of Falls Church, Virginia. Health food stores seem to be quite popular; look in the yellow section of the phone book under Foods-Health.

During my August 25-September 10 break from hiking I returned home for my daughter's wedding. During that period I visited the Kennedy store and purchased two pounds of rice, one pound of lentils, one pound of barley. I mixed the three of them together. I made one batch of the mix at home and added generous quantities of ham chunks. The result was excellent. I took some of the mix with me when I resumed hiking in New Hampshire and I mailed an additional quantity to myself at Monson, Maine. At one shelter I cooked the mix adding Spam as the meat ingredient. However it was at Potaywadjo Spring Shelter in northern Maine on October 2, five days before the completion of my hike, that I made my most successful batch of Appalachian Trail Mix. I arrived at the shelter at 2:45, found plenty of firewood, and placed the following ingredients into the only large cooking pot I had:

1½ cups A.T. Mix (all I had left)
1 pkg. Dehydrated diced potatoes
1 pkg. Dehydrated green beans

2 tablespoons Buttery Flavor Oil
6 oz. canned grated tuna
4 cups water

For seasoning I added salt and pepper plus all of the basil leaves and krauterbutter I had left. I cooked this for one hour at low heat over a "V" type fire which I will describe later in this chapter. I had no cover for my large cooking pot, but I fashioned a piece of aluminum foil over the pot. This served very creditably. When finished cooking, I had almost two quarts of tender well-seasoned mix. I ate more than half of it for my evening meal and finished the rest the following evening. The Appalachian Trail Mix costs about $1.10 per pound; each pound provides 2⅓ cups of the mix.

This is not intended to be an exhaustive treatise on evening meal dishes, but merely on the ones I used most frequently and which I know to be good. I have already mentioned two of the desserts I used frequently; namely Claxton Fruit Cake and Citadel Spread. My most frequent dessert for my evening meal, however, was instant pudding. My favorite brand was Royal, with A&P brand a close second. Each package of Royal pudding weighs 4½ oz. and makes four half-cup servings. For hikers of the Appalachian Trail it would be more accurate to say that each package makes two meal size servings. At each point where I purchased groceries it was my practice to retire to my motel room, to a booth in a nearby restaurant, or to the front porch of the grocery store and repackage my groceries. For the instant puddings this meant opening each package and pouring the contents into two plastic bags. Into each plastic bag I would add one third cup of powdered milk. I would then secure the top of each bag with a twist tie and put all the bags into a large plastic bag. Upon reaching my shelter each afternoon one of the first orders of business was to make the instant pudding. For this I used a one pint plastic shaker. Into the shaker I poured one cup of water and then poured in the contents of one of the plastic pudding sacks. I would shake this vigorously for perhaps 60 seconds and then put it aside. My dessert would be ready for me an hour or so later when I had finished my main dish.

Now that we have considered things to eat, let's consider how to cook them, cooking utensils, wood fires as opposed to gasoline stoves, portable fireplace grates. This seems to be an appropriate place to quote an article that appeared in the July-September 1970, issue of the *Bulletin* issued by the Potomac Appalachian Trail Club of Washington, D.C. The article seems to have been reprinted from a number of previously issued outdoor publications. It was originally written in 1966 by a Mr. John Echo. I quote it because it does contain some good ideas for simple cooking and even simpler ideas for pot cleaning the cooking utensils. If you think the techniques advanced by the author take you back too far towards the Stone Age, you may settle for some modifications I will suggest later in this chapter. Here is the article entitled "Courageous Cookery" or "Why Not Enjoy Backpacking?"

Courageous Cookery
Why Not Enjoy Backpacking?

John Echo

Once the convert backpacker has accepted the subtle gustatory nuances associated with sustained operations beyond the chrome, he should try the advantages of ultra-fringe living so that he will realize what he is paying for his nested pots and pretty pans carried so diligently and brought home so dirty after every "wilderness experience."

The following system works. It is dependable and functional. It works on the big rock. It even works when the weather has gone to hell, you are wet and cold, and the wind is blowing a Dirty Degan right down the back of your hairy neck. It is not for the timid. It consists of a 6-inch sauce pan, a Primus stove, a plastic cup, and a soup spoon. If you insist on a metal cup, you must never fail to mutter, "I'm having fun, I'm having fun," every time you burn your lips and spill the soup on your sleeping bag.

Breakfast: Instant wheat cereal—sugar and powdered milk added—ready 2 minutes after the water boils. Eat from the pot. Do not wash pot. Add water, boil, add powdered eggs and ham. You'll never taste the cereal anyway. In 3 minutes, eat eggs. Do not wash pot. Add water or snow and boil for tea. Do not wash pot. Most of the residue eggs will come off in the tea water. Make it strong and add sugar. Tastes like tea. Do not wash pot. With reasonable technique, it should be clean. Pack pot in rucksack and enjoy last cup of tea while others are dirtying entire series of nested cookware. Enjoy sunrise or take morning stroll while others are washing, in cold water, entire series of nested cookware.

Lunch: Boil pot of tea. Have snack of rye bread, cheese, and dried beef. Continue journey in 10 minutes if necessary.

Dinner: Boil pot of water. Add Wyler's dry vegetable soup and a beef bar. Eat from pot. Do not wash pot. Add water and make potatoes from dry potato powder. Add dry gravy mix to taste. Eat potatoes and gravy from pot. Do not wash pot. Add water and boil for tea. Fortuitous fish or meat can be cooked easily. You do not need oil or fat. Put half-inch water in pot. Add clean, salted fish. Do not let water boil away. Eat from pot when done. Process can be repeated rapidly. Fish can even be browned somewhat by a masterful hand. Do not change the menu. Variation only recedes from the optimum. Beginners may be allowed to wash pot once a day for three consecutive days only. It is obvious that burning or sticking food destroys the beauty of the technique.

If you insist on carrying a heavy pack, make up the weight you save with extra food. Stay three days longer.

[Reprinted from the Rambler (Wasatch Mountain Club, Salt Lake City, Utah), which reprinted from the I.A.C. News, Idaho Falls, Idaho, which reprinted from the 1966 Peaks and Trails.]

When I began my A.T. hike in Georgia I did not carry a frying pan. I love such fried dishes as bacon and eggs, pancakes, and hamburgers. There is a definite place for such foods in some types of camping, but they are not practical dishes for backpacking. I started with two small aluminum sauce pans which nested. These sauce pans are 5 inches in diameter and about 2½ inches deep. One cover served both pans. The total weight of both pans and the cover is 7 oz. A light weight pot holder weighed another ounce. Cleaning pads and a plastic bag to carry them in add another ounce. Already I have violated some of the "Courageous Cookery" concepts. I also violated another one: I cleaned the pots—not after each dish but after each meal. But, more importantly, I never, not even once during the whole trip, cleaned the outside of the pots, just the inside. I fully intend to wash the outside of those pots someday; but even as I re-write this chapter, some seven years after

Special alternate top for gas container designed and manufactured by Buck Canedy. (Photo: Buck Canedy)

the completion of my hike, I have not done so. I am still giving occasional talks on my 2,000 mile hike. In these talks I demonstrate the equipment I used. It is important that those pots have that blackened look that comes only from repeated use over countless cooking fires. In addition to the two cooking pots I started out with two stainless steel cups and two stainless steel soup spoons. Although I did use them, one each of the cups and spoons would have been sufficient. Contrary to the comments of the Courageous Cookery author, the metal cups gave no trouble in drinking hot liquids. The cups I had were made for the Sierra Club, and I could drink hot liquids from them just as safely as from plastic or china cups. At the 700 mile mark of my hike, I changed my cooking equipment. I kept the two sauce pans, got rid of one steel cup, and added a larger aluminum cooking pot which weighed 7 oz. and was 6½ inches in diameter and 3½ inches deep. It held 7 cups. I now had more weight; but I had more cooking capacity and I had a larger container in which to carry and heat water. I also exchanged my 1 oz. pot holder for a sturdier one weighing 3 oz. For the last 1,300 miles of my hike, my cooking equipment plus cup, spoon, and carrying sack weighed 20 oz. The equipment I was carrying would have been sufficient for a two or three man party; it was a bit elaborate for a single hiker.

Now the more difficult decision as to whether you wish to use wood cooking fires throughout your trip or whether you wish to carry a stove. Most of the long distance hikers whom I have encountered carry stoves. Some of them use the stove at almost every meal. Others only occasionally. Still others, like Everett and Nell Skinner who hiked the entire Trail in 1968, relied on wood fires entirely and spared themselves the 3½ to 4 pounds of weight occasioned by a stove and fuel supply. Bill O'Brien, who hiked the entire Trail in 1969 carried a stove and had this to say: "The stove was a Svea 123, with an extra pint of fuel; but I used it very sparingly and bought fuel only four times. Mostly I cooked by an open fire by preference or had cold meals."

Branley C. Owen, who hiked the entire Trail in 1970, started out carrying a lightweight tent and a primus stove. Later he abandoned both tent and stove in order to reduce weight and increase his speed. In my own case I carried no stove for the first 700 miles, but I did carry a Model 71L Primus the last 1,300 miles. I used it occasionally at first, and quite frequently up in Maine where I began regularly enjoying a hot breakfast and where I experienced a number of cold rainy days. So it becomes a matter of personal preference. If you have room for the stove and fuel in your pack, if you're not worried about that 3½ to 4 pounds of weight, if it is important to you to have hot meals day in and day out, rain or shine, then by all means carry a stove. On the other hand if you are concerned about that additional weight and bulk in your pack, if you don't mind eating cold meals occasionally, and if you greatly prefer the wood cooking fires and are skilled in making them even in wet weather, then forget the stove.

If you do plan to carry a stove, what kind should you carry? I have owned and used a variety of alcohol, kerosene, naptha, and gasoline stoves but have more or less settled on the Primus 71L model. Why that one? Because some years ago the Hiking, Camping and Mountaineering Equipment Committee of the Potomac Appalachian Trail Club made an exhaustive study of some 30 stoves and recommended the Primus 71L as tops. See the article "Stoves for Hiking Trips" by Arthur C. Lembeck in *Trailway News*, September 1961.

I have heard some heated arguments over the years as to the relative merits of the three Swedish gasoline stoves—Primus, Optimus, and Svea. Many of the parts or interchangeable and this is quite understandable when you learn that all three stoves are made in the same factory which is located at a small city some 30 miles south of Stockholm. After I had completed my assignment at the Outdoor Recreation Exhibit in Moscow in June 1973, my wife and I returned home with stops at various northern European cities, including Stockholm. While there, I received an invitation to visit the Optimus factory. Small backpacking stoves hold a special fascination for me and I have quite a collection—gasoline, kerosene, alcohol, and low pressure gas. I spent several very enjoyable hours at the Optimus factory examining stoves in all stages of construction. The most famous of all the Optimus stoves is the Primus, so much so that the word "primus" (small "p") has come to mean almost worldwide any small portable stove used on expeditions. Upon leaving Irkutsk in Eastern Siberia in October 1973 at the conclusion of my second assignment in the USSR, I was given a going-away present by an ardent backpacker with whom I had hiked on two occasions. The present, a small Russian-made gasoline stove was patterned carefully after the Optimus Model 8R. On the cardboard box containing the stove appeared two words, "TOURIST," the Slavic term for hiker or backpacker, and the word "PRIMUS!"

Unfortunately the Optimus made stoves have become terribly expensive. The Svea stove and its look alike cousin the Primus 71L sold for $9 in 1960 when I bought mine. They now (1977) sell for $29. Quite a jump! In recent years I have become very fond of an inexpensive little stove that is the soul of simplicity. It is an English made alcohol burning stove that sells in the $2.50-$3.00 range and it burns liquid alcohol, paint thinner, chafing fuel, or whatever you wish to call it. Trade names of two such alcohol products are Solox and Paco, available at paint and hardware stores. This stove's trade name—Picnic Special—is illustrated on page 58. I first began using this stove in 1972, and have carried it with me on backpacking trips in the USA and on trips all over Europe and the USSR. It never fails—burns for 20-30 minutes on a single filling of one-third cup of fuel. It has but one heat—HOT! And it will bring a quart of water to a boil in about eight minutes. The fact that the heat cannot be regulated is admittedly an inconvenience. But consider that perhaps 80 percent of all backpacker cooking is simply bringing water to a boil so that it can be used to reconstitute freeze dry foods, to make instant soup, or to make hot beverages such as coffee, tea, or hot chocolate. If you can put up with the inconvenience described, if that $2.50-$3.00 price appeals to you, and if you like a quiet stove that burns clean from the moment you apply the match, then I urge you to try this one. I keep one in my camper and another in my pack.

For a final stove suggestion let me take you from alcohol back to gasoline. This is a stove that I had been expecting to enter the market for years and my only surprise is that it took so long. For years Coleman has made a superb gasoline stove—one, two, and three burner variety that was great for car camping or even short hiking jaunts into a cabin or a somewhat permanent camp. But even their one burner Sportster weighed four pounds, too heavy for backpacking although a friend of mine from Guatemala, after surveying all the stoves available on the American market, picked the Sportster—feeling that its reliability, ease of operation, and tremendous heat output more than made up for that heavy weight.

But in 1977 as I was rewriting this chapter, Coleman (Coleman Co., Inc., Wichita, Kansas) came out with a line of backpacking equipment which will be sold only at outdoor stores. Included in

the new line was a two pound "Peak 1" gasoline stove. It has all
the good features of the time tested heavier camp stove plus a few
others and its two pound weight makes it only eight oz. heavier
than the Optimus 8R (which has no pump) and makes it 1½ pounds
lighter than the expedition type Optimus 111B which does have a
pump. The clean burning Coleman preheating system is much superior to the smoky dirty preheating operation of the traditional self-
generating gasoline burning backpacker stoves. However, having
become wary of glowing claims for new products, I promptly obtained one of the new stoves and took it with me on a 10-day
backpacking trip to the Smoky Mountain National Park in April
1977. Coleman overlooked one detail in designing the new stove—
a carrying case. I found that the new stove will just fit into a 2-lb.
coffee tin but the top of the stove with its sharp pot holding fins,
projects ⅜ inch above the coffee tin. By rounding out the bottom
of the coffee tin with thumb pressure the stove sinks down far
enough so that the plastic coffee can cover can be inserted on the
can. The slight extra weight of the coffee can is offset by the fact
that it can be used as a water carrying container in camp, as a pot
for heating water, or as an extra cooking pot. In all other respects
the stove performed admirably on our 10-day trip, bringing a quart
of cold spring water to a boil in about four minutes, burning for as
much as three hours at low speed on a single filling of gasoline (10
oz. fuel tank) and burning at full speed for well over an hour. Cost
of this new stove—$27.50.

I cannot leave the subject of stoves without commenting on the
two very handy accessories I observed during my hike. The stoves
with which I am familiar require preheating, and for this purpose
they have a small well at the top of the stove tank. This well holds
a teaspoon or so of fuel. The idea is to fill the well, light it, and by
the time the fuel has burned down, the stove will be hot enough
to generate its own pressure. But how to get that teaspoon of fuel
into the well? The instructions say that you should open the valve
wide open and then hold your hot little hands around the stove
long enough to cause the fuel and/or air inside the tank to expand
and force enough fuel into the well for your preheating operation.
Sometimes this process works well, sometimes it does not. At Three
Springs Shelter in Virginia, I met a high school student, Allen Levander of Charleston, South Carolina. For the preheating operation he
had purchased a small eye dropper (plastic, not glass). For preheat-

ing, he simply removed the filler cap from his stove tank, and with the eye dropper he quickly and cleanly extracted enough fuel for the preheating operation. Simple. Inexpensive. An eye dropper costs 10 cents.

The other accessory I observed was used for transferring fuel. Some backpacking stoves have small tanks, generally a half pint or less. This means that the tank must be refilled frequently from a larger container. These larger containers generally are made of aluminum. They have 1 pint or 1 quart capacity and are made expressly for carrying fuel. How to make the transfer? Some hikers carry funnels. Others (like myself) who fancy they have steady hands, pour directly from the larger container into the small aperture of the stove. One who does this resigns himself to a certain amount of spillage. At Kinsman Pond Shelter in New Hampshire I met young Buck Canedy, an apprentice optician from Fall River, Massachusetts. Buck has solved the transfer problem by fabricating an alternate top for his gasoline container. Into this alternate cover he has inserted a copper pouring tube about 1½ inches long and with an inside diameter of perhaps 3/16 of an inch. In another area of the cover he had drilled a very small air hole about 1/16 inch in diameter. (See illustration). With this alternate cover he could pour fuel into his stove without spilling a drop. By pressing his forefinger over the air hole he could prevent the flow of gasoline. When he removed his forefinger from the air hole, air could then enter the container, and the gasoline poured freely. I used one of these alternate tops during the last 3 weeks of my hike, and I can vouch for its efficiency. The cover weighs less than 1 oz. If you desire one of these covers, send $1.25 to Buck Canedy, P.O. Box 1685, Fall River, Massachusetts 02720. The covers come in two sizes, so be sure to furnish him the inside diameter size of your container top. Or you may mail your existing container cover to him, and he will return it with the one that he makes for you.

With regard to fuel, most stoves such as the Primus 71 or 71L, Optimus 80 or 8R, and Svea 123 are designed to be operated on naptha, Coleman fuel, or low octane white gasoline. Most can be operated with any kind of automobile gasoline but you will have to clean them more often with the leaded types. The higher octane fuels are more dangerous if malfunctions occur.

A few observations are in order for those who plan to use wood cooking fires. At some overnight trailside shelters you will find small efficient fireplaces with metal grates in which you can cook your meals with a minimum amount of wood. At others you will find deep, wide fireplaces as high as 14 inches off the ground. The individual backpacker or the two or three man party will wish to partially fill in these fireplaces with stones, dirt, or slow burning logs so that the firebox is about 8 inches high. At other shelters you will find piles of stones that have been piled into something that looks like a fireplace. But many of the shelters that provide no fireplaces as such do provide a variety of makeshift fireplace grates that are quite satisfactory for cooking purposes. Sometimes these consist of discarded shelves from old refrigerators or kitchen stoves, or they may be lengths of steel reinforcing rods, or 2 inch wide steel plates, perhaps 24 to 36 inches long. With any of these arrangements the hiker can fashion a very useable cooking surface. But, let's face it, you will find a number of shelters that provide no fireplaces or cooking aids of any sort. For these you must either carry your own light weight grate or rely on your ingenuity. You can buy these light weight grates, or you can make them. I have made several out of cake drying racks by simply putting a stiff wire leg at each corner. These legs swivel flat against the rack for carrying in your pack, and I carry the rack in a cloth sack with drawstring top. The one I carried on my hike was only 6 by 7 inches in size. I could level it on uneven ground, I could protect its three sides with rocks to conserve all possible heat, and I could cook a meal using only very small twigs, whereas larger fireplaces would require more and larger pieces of firewood.

There is available on the market a lightweight magnesium alloy Backpacker Grill. It is 15 inches long and four inches wide and does not require legs—you arrange two stones or two logs in such fashion that you will have a level resting place for the grill. After the fire is built you set the grill in place and cook the meal. Total weight of this grill and cloth carrying cover is but 3 oz. It sold for $4.25 in 1977.

It is not the purpose of this book to include comprehensive instructions on firemaking and wood fire cooking. I must assume you already possess these skills or that you will refer to other books or manuals for information on these subjects. I will, however, describe one particular type of cooking fire because is the most efficient cooking fire I know of for simmering foods at low heat for long periods of time. It is a backpacker's adaptation of the "Out-Door Cooking

Range" described by Nessmuk in his book *Woodcraft*. The Nessmuk affair requires an hour to build and is more suitable for a party of six or eight which plans to stay in one place for a number of days. The one you will make can be formed in perhaps 15 minutes. If it serves for but one evening meal, it will have done its job.

Start by locating two green logs, or two long-dead water-soaked almost unburnable logs, or two pieces of rock. The logs or rocks should be about 5 inches high and about 12 to 16 inches long. The idea is to build a firebox in the form of a V. The V should be open at its narrow end for approximately 2 inches; at its wider end about 5 inches. Be sure the logs are firmly bedded on the ground. Push in dirt or small stones so that the logs will not shift once you begin cooking. Once you have your firebox formed, start your fire by using plenty of dry kindling. Let it burn until it begins to burn down. Put your cooking pot on the wide end of the V so that it receives the maximum amount of heat. As soon as the contents of the pot begin to boil, move the pot to the narrow end of the V. Have on hand an adequate supply of small pieces of wood . . . preferably hardwoods. Stoke the fire just often enough to keep the pot simmering slowly. You will find that the small pieces of wood will, when placed on the glowing coals, burst into small flames for a few minutes. Then they too, will become part of the glowing coals. With only occasional fire tending and by using only a small supply of wood, you can simmer foods for hours.

WATER

In these paragraphs we will discuss that other life-maintaining substance—water—both how and where to find it and what to do with it after finding it. In the diary part of this book, I describe in several places the difficulties I experienced in locating sources of water that, according to the guidebooks, were supposed to be at or near certain points along the Trail. The situation in 1977 is much better, however, even now many of the water sources are unidentified and the government agencies that manage various parts of the Trail exercise what one Department of Interior attorney described as "a super abundance of caution!" This caution is attributable to a law entitled the Tort Claims Act—a provision of law which permits government agencies to settle up with private individuals for damage done to the person or the property of the individual because of negligence on the part of a government employee. Government attorneys exercising that "super abundance of caution" warn government managers not to identify sources of unprotected drinking water because hikers and others might drink that water, might become ill, and might sue the government under the provisions of the Tort Claim Act. As of February 1977 both the Shenandoah National Park and the Great Smoky Mountain National Park had begun eliminating signs indicating sources of water. What makes this extreme caution so illogical is that U.S. Government agencies also operate vehicles—tens of thousands of them (in calendar 1976 the Soil Conservation Service of the Department of Agriculture operated 10,500 vehicles and drove 95 million miles) and every time a government employee operates one of these vehicles he is subjecting the government to a possible claim under the same Tort Claims Act that would apply to someone getting sick from drinking impure water. And yet no one is seriously advocating that all government employeys cease driving vehicles! It seems so odd that we have come to accept the automotive vehicle and its consequences—45,000 deaths per year, many more thousands of personal injury cases, millions of dollars of property damage—and yet we seem to go into paroxysms of fear over what might happen if someone drank impure water. The Appalachian Trail Project Office of the Department of Interior is attempting to obtain a sensible government wide approach to this subject of identification of drinking water as it applies to government-owned recreation-type land. However, as of 1978, the matter was still in a state of uncertainty, and so the long distance hiker may or may not be able to locate the water sources that should be available to him.

But suppose you have located a spring or stream or cistern. Is it safe to drink the water? No one can guarantee that water from an unprotected source is safe. Anyone who drinks such water without treating it does so at his own risk. Many state health agencies flatly refuse to test water that comes from an unprotected source such as a stream or spring. The reason is that the purest of pure waters could become contaminated shortly after the sample was taken. Most of the long distance hikers on the Appalachian Trail drink the water from springs and small streams without treating it. But here again, each does so at his own risk. If you follow the same practice and become ill, you have no one to blame but yourself. If you plan to treat the water what treatment is recommended? Much hard research on this has been done by Dr. Bob Burrell of the West Vir-

ginia University Medical Center. Burrell, an immunologist, micro-
biologist, and long-time outdoorsman lists the following four methods:

1. Boil for at least one minute (full rolling boil).
2. Place 8 drops of iodine solution in a quart of water and let
   stand 10 minutes.
3. Place one Halazone tablet in a *pint* of water and let stand 30
   minutes after the tablet has completely dissolved, which may
   be quite sometime in cold spring water.
4. Add 16 drops fresh household bleach such as Clorox to a quart
   of water and let stand 10 minutes.

But in correspondence with Burrell, he qualified his conclusions
by stating that, while the latter three methods were equally effective
in killing disease producing *bacteria* in the water, it is uncertain as
to how effective they would be in killing some of the enteroviruses,
such as those that cause hepatitis. He, therefore, concluded that to
be fully safe one should boil the water. So there you have the pros
and cons and you are on your own as to how safe you wish to be.

(Note: Since Dr. Burrell did his research on this subject a new
product has come on the market which many outdoorsmen prefer
to the Halazone. The new product is Potable Aqua, an iodine type
purifier that works much faster than Halazone. The new product
was selling for $1.50 per 50 table bottle in 1977. My first use of the
Potable Aqua was rather startling. On a 1976 hike, I carried a canteen of water to which had been added one Potable Aqua tablet.
Prior to our evening meal I had eaten some chicken noodle soup
out of my trusty Sierra cup. I then poured water from the canteen
into the cup and the water immediately turned a bright blue. I
learned from a fellow hiker that when iodine treated water comes
in contact with any starchy product—noodles, potatoes, etc., it produces the blue coloring. It's not harmful, but neither is it appetizing!)

Adaptation of the "Outdoor cooking-range described by Nessmuk. (Sketch by Sharon
Garvey)

4
Equipment

In the next four chapters I will discuss equipment needed on a long hike—that which I used and that which is available on the market today. In this chapter I will make some general observations on backpacking equipment before getting into the detailed descriptions in the succeeding paragraphs.

In December 1971 at about the same time that *Appalachian Hiker* was published, I began working on a part-time basis at Appalachian Outfitters, a store specializing in equipment and supplies for backpackers, mountain climbers, cavers, canoeists, and cross-country skiers. I have continued that affiliation right up to the present time. The arrangement permits me to acquire first-hand knowledge of new equipment coming into the market and I receive feedback from knowledgeable customers and from fellow employees. During the years 1972–74, I participated in five outdoor recreation exhibits sponsored by the US Information Agency in Yugoslavia, the USSR, and in Hungary. In these exhibits I demonstrated various items of backpacking and camping equipment. I concentrated on the erection of a backpacking tent and the cooking of freeze dry foods primarily because these proved to be attention-getters and crowd-pleasers. In one city alone, Irkutsk in Eastern Siberia, during a 5½-week period, I put up the backpacking tent 441 times—always within the three-minute period I had allotted myself—and cooked 174 casseroles of chunk chicken! (Yes, I can still eat chunk chicken!)

I have continued to write articles on backpacking equipment. One such article appeared in the *Shoppers Guide,* the 1974 Yearbook of the US Department of Agriculture. The article has been reprinted and single copies can be obtained free of charge by writing to: Consumer Information Center, Pueblo, CO. 81009. Ask for Publication 225D, Backpacking Gear.

Beginning with my hike of the AT in 1970, I have now had over seven years of using, selling, testing, demonstrating, and writing about backpacking equipment. It has become a way of life for me and I have formed some very definite opinions on many aspects of shopping for such equipment. First and foremost is the fact that the longer I am involved in the equipment game the less opinionated I become. I have learned that there is very keen competition in the manufacture and distribution of such equipment, and there are a variety of hiking boots, packs, sleeping bags, tents, and stoves that will do the job for you. If I had any doubts on this score, they were removed in 1976 when I got in touch with 52 of the "2,000-Milers" class of 1976. I asked each of them to fill out a questionnaire for me on various aspects of their trip including the make and model of the equipment used. Near the end of the questionnaire appeared this question:

> Regardless of what equipment you actually used on your 1976 hike of the AT, if you were to completely re-outfit yourself for another complete hike of the AT, what equipment would you buy? (list make and model).

Most "2,000 Milers" take from 120 to 150 days to complete the hike and they have ample opportunity on the trail itself and at evenings spent at shelters to discuss and observe the performance of various makes of equipment. I had half suspected that, by consensus, one type of backpack might have emerged as the best pack, one particular type of tent might have emerged as the best tent, etc. Not so! Almost without exception these long distance hikers indicated that if they were to rehike the entire AT, they would purchase exactly the same make and model of hiking boot, tent, stove, or whatever. It made little difference as to what make or model was involved or how much or how little they had paid for it. The attitude seems to be that if a particular hiking boot or backpack had served them well for 2,000 miles that they would buy exactly that same boot or pack for another long hike. One develops a loyalty to a certain piece of equipment that performs well for you through good weather and bad for a 2,000-mile hike. And in my own case, I had to be careful that my loyalty to certain pieces of equipment did not bias my judgment against other makes and models of equipment that would have performed equally well.

The endorsement of products by the prominent and by the not-so-prominent is a type of sales pitch of which the would-be purchaser should be extremely wary. If you are a would-be purchaser of outdoor equipment, you would be wise to ignore the endorsements that appear in outdoor magazines. They tell you merely that

Tube tent utilizing walking stick and pack. (Chuck Young in tent) (Photo: by Sharon Garvey.)

the person making the endorsement has either (1) been paid hard cash to lend his prominent name to endorsing that particular product or (2) that he or he and his group were provided with free equipment and supplies for making an expedition with the proviso that there would be product endorsements lauding the particular equipment that was furnished free. I have before me a letter dated October 1976 from two people in Colorado. It is addressed to Appalachian Outfitters and it states that the two people are going to hike the entire Appalachian Trail in 1977 and that they are looking for sponsors to provide them with free lightweight hiking, backpacking, or camping equipment. In return, the two backpackers would carry an advertisement for Appalachian Outfitters in whatever form desired. The same letter was undoubtedly written to scores of other dealers and manufacturers.

Barry Bishop is a geographer with the National Geographic Society of Washington, D.C. and is one of the few Americans to have climbed to the summit of Mt. Everest. He and his wife Lila have designed a number of high quality tents (Bishop's Ultimate Tents). In his dual capacity as a tent designer and as a geographic expeditions expert, Bishop gets approached regularly for advice by those seeking free tents or sponsorship of an expedition. Recently he was approached by three different groups within a six-day period. Of this general practice, Bishop has this to say:

> Many groups think they can get free equipment but usually they are wasting valuable time in their attempts to do so. Their chances are about one in a thousand. Expeditions to far off places or long distance hikes are no longer extra-ordinary events but have become commonplace. Furthermore no one gets something for nothing. If equipment and supplies are accepted, then the enjoyment factor of the trip is lessened . . . there are pictures that must be taken, articles that must be written, or endorsements that must be made. But the person who goes on an expedition with responsibility to no one reaps the full measure of the enjoyment factor. He is beholden to no one.

So much for product endorsement. What about equipment evaluations? They are certainly better than product endorsements but the evaluations have their pitfalls too. How many times have you heard radio or TV commericals in which it is said that "a nationally recognized testing agency found the XYZ aspirin (or whatever) to be 44% faster acting than any other brand tested!" *What* testing agency? How many brands were tested? In what publication were the results of the tests published? On the other hand, if it is reported that the National Bureau of Standards has made laboratory tests to

Ed Garvey and Chuck Young showing a two-person tent.

determine the relative efficiency of goose and duck down as compared to certain synthetic fills, it becomes a different matter because the Bureau of Standards is a US Government financed testing agency whose testing would be thorough and impartial.

On balance I'm skeptical of evaluations made by magazines which accept advertising, especially if any of the products tested are made by corporations which regularly advertise in that particular magazine. There is always the suspicion that the magazine would be very reluctant to downgrade any product tested if such down grading would result in the loss of regular advertising.

One magazine whose evaluations have always seemed impartial is the magazine *Consumer Reports.* I like the way the tests are made—products are bought in the market place—no free samples to be submitted by the manufacturer. After the tests are made and the results analyzed, the products are resold. The magazine does not accept advertising. Another publication that achieved tremendous respect was the *Equipment Bulletin* published by the Potomac Appalachian Trail Club. The Equipment Committee was composed of a number of very knowledgeable outdoorsmen with a preponderance of rock climbers. They really did a thorough job of checking out equipment, evaluating the results, and publishing the information in an easy to understand *Bulletin.* The last such *Bulletin* was published in 1972. There was no advertising in any of the *Bulletins.* Club officials have expressed doubt that the *Bulletin* will be continued because of the tremendous increase in the amount of equipment to be tested and the time limitations of the volunteers who would do the testing. But it is that type (non-profit organization— no advertising) of evaluation that I would be much more inclined to accept and I would hope that PATC or some other like organization would produce another impartial comparison of backpacking equipment.

Would be purchasers can obtain valuable information simply by going out on weekend hikes with any of the various hiking groups in metropolitan areas. Experienced hikers are only too glad to discourse on their equipment and to disclose where they bought it. Another method is to look in the yellow pages of the telephone book under Camping Equipment listings. You will know you're in the right place if you see yellow page ads that feature backpacks with names like Kelty, Camp Trails, or Jansport; hiking boots with

Garvey's 16-year-old Kelty pack and his new Kelty pack. Note the damage caused by scraping when the car rack came off the car on the way to Springer Mountain.

(Photo: Appalachian Outfitters)

names like Vasque, Fabiano, or Danner; sleeping bags with names like Camp Seven, Sierra Design, or North Face. Visit one of the outdoor stores listed and talk to the salesmen. You will know in a short time if the salesman is merely a purveyor of merchandise or if he is an outdoorsman himself who has actually used the types of equipment you wish to buy. If you do not have access to an outdoor store you must resort to catalogs. Check outdoor type magazines at your local library or newsstand and send for catalogs. In an appendix to this book are shown a number of reliable outdoor dealers in the eastern United States and a number of organizations that sell outdoor merchandise through catalogs.

"When I die, bury me well
Six feet under the Appalachian Trail
Lay my packframe upon my chest
And tell Ed Garvey I did my best!"
A West Virginia Poet.
Received Nov. 1975

5
The Pack

It is an important decision as to what type of pack should be carried for a 2,000-mile hike. One has to choose not only the pack itself but the selection of articles to be carried in it. Today there are a variety of pack frames and packbags on the market that are suitable and durable enough for an extended hike (See Appendix 2). In 1954 I purchased my first Kelty pack and I have been an enthusiastic Kelty man since that time. These packs are made by Kelty Pack, Inc., P.O. Box 3453, Glendale, California 91201. Kelty also makes a number of backpacking accessories such as pack rain covers, polytents, stuff sacks. A postcard mailed to Kelty will bring you a brochure on their packs and accessories. Now these packs, frames, and accessories are being sold in stores specializing in backpacking and outdoor equipment in most major cities. (See Appendix 2). After you have decided upon the particular brand of packframe and packbag you wish to purchase, you must still decide whether you wish a compartmentalized bag or one with a large open space. You must also decide on the size frame and bag that is most suitable for you. Kelty frames and packs come in various styles; and four sizes in each style.

I started my hike with a 16-year-old Kelty, Model A4, large size. I had used the pack so much during these 16 years that I had worn out and replaced one set of shoulder straps and also the waist strap. As if age were not enough, I inflicted an almost mortal wound to that faithful pack during the automobile trip down to Georgia to begin the hike. While traveling on Interstate Route 95 near Richmond, Virginia, my luggage rack tore loose from my car. When it did so, my fully loaded Kelty pack also came loose and splattered over the pavement at 60 miles per hour. The fabric was torn here and there, but the metal frame was undamaged. As I neared the 1,000-mile mark in my hike, I noticed that the shoulder straps were wearing badly. I was also having trouble finding enough space in my A4

SHARON GARVEY
JAN. 1971

The various areas of Garvey's pack. (Sketch by Sharon Garvey)

model. I therefore ordered the big BB5 expedition size model pack and frame from Appalachian Outfitters, Box 249, Oakton, Virginia.

Less than three days after 1 placed my order, the new pack and frame were waiting for me at the post office in Delaware Water Gap, Pennsylvania. The new pack boasted almost 900 cubic inches of additional space (3,680 cubic inches total capacity) and weighed 25 ounces. It had no interior compartments which meant that it was necessary for me to buy additional carrying bags of various colors and sizes. The general appearance and arrangement of the pack is shown in the sketch. My original 1954 pack now hangs like a revered Civil War cannon on the walls of Appalachian Outfitters at Oakton, Va.

The following paragraphs indicate what articles I carried in each part of the packbag.

Area 1 is the area I refer to as "the hold" because it is such a big area in relation to the other six areas. In this area I carried 8 sacks, each sack containing items similar or related to other items in that particular sack. To the extent possible I used sacks of different colors so that I could readily identify and remove any needed item. The contents of each sack were as follows:

Sack   1. Extra clothes: underwear, socks, shirt, trousers, parka, my all-purpose deerskin mittens, pajamas, and (in cold weather) wool cap. Also included were my rain parka and rain chaps.

Sack   2. Condiments. Described in Chapter 3.

Sack   3. Food for dinners. Described in Chapter 3.

Sack   4. Food for breakfasts and lunches. Described in Chapter 3.

Sack   5. Cooking equipment, pot holder, cleaning pads. See Chapter 3.

Sack   6. Gasoline stove, eye dropper, alternate cover. See Chapter 3.

Sack   7. Toilet articles.

Sack   8. Miscellaneous: First-aid kit, newspapers, towel paper, plastic sacks, litter bags, nylon cord, string, clothespins.

Item   9. 1 quart aluminum gasoline container.

Item 10. 1 pint plastic shaker, which also doubled as an extra canteen.

Area 2 is the large-size back pocket. In this pocket I carried guide books, maps, trip diary book, sewing kit, extra clevis pins, beer can

Garvey carrying his pack. (Photo: F. Wm. Ader)

opener, whistle, and two plastic envelopes which contained stationery, pencils, stamps, address book, postcards.

Area 3 is one of two upper side pockets. In this packet I carried two plastic bottles plus an aerosol container of "Off" insect repellent. The two plastic bottles had a total capacity of about 5 cups. I used them for carrying water except for a few rare wonderful occasions when I used them to carry table wine! The larger of the two plastic bottles was green in color and its original white label was still very clear and prominent. The label read *Liquid Car Wash,* and whenever I took a copious drink from that container, eyebrows were raised and questions asked.

Area 4 is one of the two lower side pockets. In it I carried a rain cover for the pack, a tube of liquid soap, and a small flashlight.

Area 5 is the second of two upper side pockets. In it I carried a thermometer and a 14-ounce capacity plastic bottle which contained liquid vegetable oil. The therometer was a Taylor instrument with metal carrying case. The use of the liquid vegetable oil is described in Chapter 3.

Area 6 is the second of two lower pockets. In it I carried a waterproof match case, candles, fire starters, and a small camera.

Area 7 at the bottom of pack frame was used to carry a 3 pound sleeping bag, a ground cloth, a short foam pad mattress . . . all three carried in a large-size stuff bag.

Area 8 was myself and the things I carried on my person, my pocketknife, compass, watch, and metal cup, etc.

How much should your pack weigh? This is most difficult to answer. In fact, I have come to the conclusion that there is no one correct answer. From 1960 to 1970, I met, either by chance or by arrangement, some 16 through-hikers of the Trail. I have met and talked to perhaps another 8 or 10 who have made the long hike. I have read and reread in *Trailway News* and other publications the accounts of these hikers and the accounts written by most of the other through-hikers. In 1960, I met Allen and Gregory who hiked the entire Trail in 99 days (see *Appalachian Trail News,* January 1961). Their packs weighed 18 to 25 pounds. In 1963, Fox and Gerhard hiked the Trail in 94 days. They, too, traveled light, their packs ranging from 17 to 25 pounds. On the other hand two retired businessmen, Ed Little and Murray Chism, took a leisurely eight months (March 10 to November 8, 1959) to complete their hike. Their packs weighed from 37 to 50 pounds. You might conclude from these accounts that speed demons "travel extremely light" while the "take it slow and enjoy it" type carry much heavier packs. But, consider that 17-year-old Eric Ryback hiked the Trail in 81 days in 1969 and for the entire hike carried a pack weighing 70 pounds fully loaded but which averaged out at 55 pounds. The 47 "2,000 Milers" of 1976 carried packs generally in the 30 pound range (pack weight without food).

Experienced backpackers reading this chapter will chuckle at the weight of my own pack. Inexperienced hikers frequently start out with tremendously heavy packs and gradually rid themselves of unneeded items. Not Garvey! I started out light and kept adding weight. At the starting point on Springer Mountain, my pack weighed 34 pounds including 8 pounds of food. I kept the pack light during the first 725 miles and even managed to use up all my food on one occasion. I reached Roanoke, Virginia, with a pack weighing only 26 pounds. At that point, Roanoke, both my pack and I were at the lowest weight of the entire trip. My weight had dropped from 158 pounds with my hiking clothes on down to 143; and 158 is my normal weight. From then on things began to happen. Without going into whys and wherefores, I will simply say that when I left Reading, Pennsylvania, my pack weighed 43 pounds including one quart of table wine given to me by Bob and June Fisher of the Blue Mountain Eagle Climbing Club. When I left Glencliffe, New Hampshire, the pack was up to 46 pounds, including a 3-pound fruitcake mailed from Claxton, Georgia, and picked up at Glencliffe. Monson, Maine, was my last resupply point; and it is 118 miles from here to Mt. Katahdin. Furthermore, I deliberately planned a slow schedule for that last 118 miles as I wished to savor each day through that beautiful lake country of Maine. Consequently, I laid in a huge supply of food and staggered out of Monson with a pack which I estimated to weigh between 52 and 54 pounds. This seemingly violates all the rules of good backpacking. All I can say in defense is that I lived pretty well during those last 10 days out of Monson, Maine.

For those whose only goal is to hike, hike, hike each day as far as they possibly can, I would recommend a pack weight in the 18-25-pound range. Frankly, I have nothing but sympathy for the person who tries to race along the Trail with scarcely a moment to contemplate a beautiful view, to admire a rushing stream, to study a rarely seen bird, or to cook and enjoy an excellent meal. With all due respect to those who have accomplished it, I find myself invariably comparing the 70, 80, and 90-day hikers of the entire Trail with the American tourist just back from Europe. A cartoon shows the tourist exclaiming breathlessly, "Seventeen countries in eight days! We saw everything!"

Let us assume that you are one of those who plan a more leisurely pace, say 10 to 15 miles per day. I would advise a pack weight in the 25 to 35 lb. range. This will permit you to carry all the necessities and some of the luxuries. For each Ryback or Hancock who can seemingly carry a 50 to 60 lb. pack with ease, there are a hundred others (like myself!) for whom anything heavier than 35 lbs. becomes a real burden. And yet I shrink from recommending the more Spartan, necessities-only, 15 to 25 lb. load. Why? Because man's entire history has been one in which he tries to surround himself with a few tools, appliances, gadgets, and implements to make life on this earth a little more pleasant. Backpackers, for the most part, are no different in this regard from the rest of the population. You don't *have* to carry a mattress or pad. You *can* do without, but you sacrifice some comfort. You don't *have* to carry a gasoline stove and fuel. You can scrounge for wood and use wood cooking fires. You don't *have* to carry cooking pots. You can eat your food uncooked. You don't *have* to carry extra underwear and an alternate shirt and trouser outfit. You can wear the same dirty, sweaty, smelly outfit for the entire trip. Most hikers *will* wish to carry most of the articles I have mentioned because of the added comfort, convenience, or appearance. You, and you alone, must then decide which of the many desirable things available to you should actually be taken.

Elsewhere in this book I describe the various items you may carry in your pack and the uses to be made of them. Chapter 3 details food supplies, cooking equipment and stoves. Chapter 6 treats sleeping equipment, ground cloth, and mattress, etc. In the remainder of this chapter I shall say a few words about rain gear.

One of the most important of these is a rain cover for the pack itself. The pack that I am familiar with is not waterproof. The materials used for Kelty pack construction is a water-repellant nylon of the type that permits the passage of air (and also water!) for ventilation. Water does condense on the inside of a pack just as on the inside of a tent. There are a variety of rain garments available: some of them cover the pack only; some cover the hiker only; and some cover both the hiker and his pack. There are garments, known as ponchos, that fulfill a number of wet-weather purposes. A poncho

Garvey's current Kelty pack with its rain cover—note packet. (Photo: Appalachian Outfitters)

will protect the hiker and his pack, will serve as a ground cloth, and will serve as an emergency shelter. In my assortment of camping gear there are two ponchos, but I haven't used them for years. I feel that while they do a passable job of performing many functions, they are not ideally suited for any one function. On my own hike I carried separate rain gear for myself (See Chapter 7), a ground cloth (See Chapter 6), and a form-fitting rain cover for my pack. The Kelty pack rain cover weighs 4 oz. and comes in several sizes so as to fit the particular size pack you own. When not in use, it can be folded into a compact packet and inserted into one of the outside pockets of the pack. I used the rain cover extensively not only during rains but oftentimes when the woods were still wet from previous rains. The Kelty rain cover that was available in 1970 had one defect. The cover fit snugly around the pack and was further secured by two fabric straps with snap fasteners. In perhaps 90 percent of the wet weather situations this arrangement proved satisfactory. I found, however, that when I was exposed to strong winds, the rain cover had a tendency to creep up the pack thereby exposing it (and especially the sleeping gear at bottom of pack) to a wind-driven rain. In 1972 Kelty came out with an improved rain cover that was long enough to cover completely the sleeping bag at the bottom of the pack. Furthermore, the cover had a cord arrangement that fitted underneath the pack and the cord had a fastening device that permitted it to be snugged up tight. Both rain covers are available. Approximately two-thirds of the 1976 through-hikers, regardless of the pack used, did use the Kelty rain cover. Tom Lundberg, a '76 2000 Miler, stated that the Kelty rain cover was the "most valuable and most used item I carried."

I do not wish to convey the impression that Kelty is the only packframe available on the market. Far from it. The biggest chunk of the backpack market has been captured by Camp Trails which makes a variety of packs and frames within a wide price range under its own name and also makes the packs and frames sold under the label of the Boy Scouts of America. Most of the Camp Trails frames will accommodate a number of different packs and the literature provides information as to the combinations that are possible. Within recent years, the Jansport has made significant inroads into the market. Some of the Jansport packs have adjustable frames permitting a single frame to fit hikers from teenagers to adults. The heavy duty Jansports have aluminum harnesses which wrap around the thighs, providing better distribution of the pack load. In 1976 North Face introduced its new pack which it hoped would revolutionize the art of backpacking to the same extent the first Kelty packs did in the 1950's.

Except for hiking boots, there is no item of your equipment in which a good fit is as important as the pack. The better packs come in small, medium, large, and extra-large sizes. And there are devices provided by which each of these sizes can be adjusted a bit. In the fitting process, knowledgeable and helpful salespeople will insert weights in the pack so that the fitting can be done under more realistic conditions. Many items needed by the backpacker can be ordered by catalog, but hiking boots and the pack should, if at all possible, be fitted by an experienced salesperson.

LITTERBUGS NOT NEW

Litterbugs were active in the days of ancient Rome. Archaeologists excavating Herculaneum, a Roman city buried under lava from Mt. Vesuvius in the first century of the Christian era, found a sign at crossroads warning that litterers would be fined or subjected to corporal punishment. Visitors to William Shakespeare's birthplace in Stratford, England, may see a sign on the wall of one of the rooms reporting that "John Shakespeare, the poet's father, was fined for repositing rubbish in Henley Street in 1552."

One of the first recorded actions against litter in the United States was an editorial in a Boston newspaper in 1784 condemning the litter left behind after an Independence Day celebration. The city fathers urged to prevent a recurrence. The major difference between ancient and modern littering is that there is a lot more of it in present-day civilization. Litter today takes a half-billion-dollar-a-year tax bite out of the national pocketbook. That is the amount of the annual clean-up bill.

The species could be eliminated, however, if each person would assume responsibility for the proper disposal of his own litter and trash. It is the individual who creates litter, and only the individual can prevent it. This means you and me.

—*Texas Parks and Wildlife*

6
Sleeping

One third of the backpackers' hours are spent within the confines of his sleeping bag. And when I use the fraction "one-third" I am referring to the summer months. It follows, then, that such things as the sleeping bag, ground cloth, and mattress deserve attention. During the late September and early October days of my own hike, I was spending almost one-half of the twenty-four hours in the sack. For it was almost totally dark by 6:30 p.m. during those overcast rainy days, and it was 6:30 a.m. the next morning before it was light enough to distinguish objects.

You have already seen the sketch of my pack. Area 7 of the pack includes:

Stuff Bag	4 ounces
Ground cloth	13 ounces
Mattress (foam pad)	20 ounces
Sleeping bag (3 lbs. 3 oz.)	51 ounces
Total	88 ounces or 5½ pounds

The total weight of 5½ pounds does not tell the complete story. An additional item—quilted pajamas—weighed 1¾ pounds. I always wear pajamas and socks when using a sleeping bag. The pajamas and socks protect the bag from perspiration, provide additional warmth, can be used as undergarments in very cold weather, and permit me to carry a lighter weight sleeping bag than would otherwise be the case. Except for a one-week period (June 6–13), I used the combination of the 7¼ pounds of sleeping gear mentioned above. It kept me warm in the early spring and early fall when the temperature at night fell to the middle 30's. During the warm summer months I still wore pajamas and socks, but frequently slept on top of my sleeping bag and crawled only part way into the sack during the cooler hours of the night. If I were to do it over again, I would carry lighter weight sleeping equipment during the warmer

Garvey's sleeping gear; ground cloth, sleeping bag, stuff sack, nylon covered polyurethane foam pad (not visible). (Photo: Appalachian Outfitters)

months. More on that later. Now, let's discuss one item at a time. My stuff bag was the biggest one I could find, a Camp Trails bag that was 22 inches long and 10 inches in diameter. The following is the method I used to pack my sleeping gear into the stuff bag. There may be a better way, but this way is quick and practical. Step 1 is to roll up the mattress tightly, insert it in the stuff bag, and then fluff it out so it leaves an open space in the middle. Step 2 is to stuff your sleeping bag into the open space inside the mattress. Step 3 is to fold the ground cloth carefully (with the dirty side always folded on the inside) until you have a compact envelope size package about 18 inches by 4 inches. This can be slipped just inside the stuff bag between the stuff bag and the foam mattress. Simple.

The next item is the ground cloth. Mine is 7 feet long and 56 inches wide. It has a grommet at each of the four corners. I purchased it from Recreational Equipment Cooperative in Seattle in 1962, and it has served me well as a ground cloth only. The fact that it has grommets would indicate that it may have been intended for an emergency shelter, but it seems a little skimpy to be effective. If I were to hike the Appalachian Trail again, I think I would proceed a little differently. I would carry a 9 foot by 10 foot tarp with grommets (weight 1 pound, 8 ounces; cost $14.95 at Appalachian Outfitters). I would also carry a piece of 4 mil plastic 4 feet by 8 feet (cost 40 cents) as an emergency groundcloth. On nights when I used the shelters, I would use the tarp as my ground cloth, either opening it to its full size or folding it over once for a 5 foot by 9 foot size. On nights when I slept away from the trailside shelter I would use the tarp as an emergency shelter and use the 4 mil plastic as my ground cloth.

Now for the foam mattress. For years prior to 1970 I had used air mattresses. They were reasonably satisfactory, but the nuisance of inflating the mattress each night was exceeded only by the greater nuisance of attempting to deflate it the next morning. Foam mattresses have become increasingly popular within the past few years. They are bulkier than a deflated air mattress but also much lighter. I purchased one such mattress a month before my hike. Its size is 20 inches by 36 inches. I used the foam pad on two of my conditioning hikes and found it satisfactory. That 20 x 36 size may seem small but I found that it was adequate for my hips and shoulders. There are a few hardy souls who carry no mattress, but I am not in that category. Allen and Gregory began their hike in 1960 without mattresses, but early in their hike they made arrangements to have mattresses mailed to them. Unless you *know* that you can make out satisfactorily without a mattress I would suggest that you give the foam pad a try. The one that I have is made by Colorado Outdoor Sports Corporation and its cost in 1971 was $7.00. A similar pad made by Camp Trails cost $9.50 in 1977.

In the years since 1970 another product—closed cell insulation—has become very popular. Trade names of some of the closed cell products are Ensolite, Superlite, and Valera. Closed cell products do not absorb water and some are used as fillers for life jackets. The closed cell products are much less bulky than the foam pad, somewhat lighter, and much firmer. They are not as comfortable but they have terrific insulating qualities. I keep a piece of Ensolite on the seat of my camper vehicle the year round. No one enjoys the shock of sitting down on the icy cold plastic seat of a car when the vehicle has been sitting overnight in winter weather. And in summer I find the Ensolite more comfortable than the smooth plastic car seat.

In my backpacking I now alternate between Ensolite and the foam pad (*open* cell insulation) I bought in 1970. In summer time I use a piece of Ensolite that is one-fourth inch thick and 20 inches by 40 inches in size, 1977 cost $4. In cold weather I use a piece that is three-eighths inch thick and is 21 inches by 56 inches, 1977 cost $8. The Ensolite can also be purchased in one-half inch thicknesses for those who desire even more insulation.

The quilted pajamas that I carry are inexpensive, machine washable garments. They are not down filled. They were given to me in 1960 by my long time hiking companion, Francis A. Smith, M.D. of Buffalo, New York. Since that time, I have carried them on innumerable hiking trips, and they have gone through innumerable machine washings. I think kindly thoughts of Fran Smith every time I pull those warm pajamas over my shivering body on a cold night. On many occasions, especially in winter while sitting around a cold cabin, I have donned the pajamas early in the evening, wearing them underneath my outer clothes to ward off the inevitable chill that sets in on those long winter nights. The 1960 pajamas described above have, unfortunately, just about "had it" as of 1977. They are still intact but when I hold them up to the light, I can see right through them in areas where the synthetic fill has shifted or disintegrated. I am now experimenting with an item known as the Official Camp Warmer sold by the Boy Scout Supply Division. The outer shell is 100%

Ed Hanlon's sleeping system.

nylon, the inner lining is warm and soft and 100% cotton and the garments are filled with Dacron Polyester Fiber Fill. It is a two piece outfit and somewhat bulky but so very warm that I think in summer months I could be comfortable just using the pajamas plus a light sleeping bag shell or bivouac cover and omit the sleeping bag. The Official Camp Warmer sold for $14.50 in 1977. (BSA item 559) for adults; $13.00 for youth sizes 12–16 (item 558).

Many backpackers do not use pajamas per se but carry two piece thermal underwear. The winter of 1976-77 saw a great wave of underwear buying in the Eastern United States. Tops and bottoms were each selling for about $4 in department stores. While not as warm as the pajamas described above, they are much less bulky and serve very effectively both as undergarments and as a sleeping garment.

There are some who prefer to protect their sleeping bags from perspiration by using a thin-lightweight, cotton inner liner. This would be lighter weight than the pajamas which I use; but it would not give the additional warmth and could not be used in an undergarment as can the pajamas. However, if hiking is to be done in the warm summer months only, the cotton inner liner may be the more practical of the two items.

The last item to be discussed in this chapter is the sleeping bag. There are few areas in which I have done more studying. Over the years, I have spent hours reading about baffle construction, tube type construction, insulation, loft, compressibility, loss of heat from radiation, convection, etc., etc., etc. From my own experiences and observations, from the reading I have done, and from my conversations with people knowledgeable in this field, I think I can reduce the great bulk of information on this subject to the following four statements. (1) Down-filled bags are superior to bags filled with other materials. (2) Mummy type bags offer the most warmth for weight and bulk involved. (3) You need not buy the most expensive bags offered by the various manufacturers. (4) For hiking on the Appalachian Trail during the period April 1 to September 30 (when perhaps 90 percent of the backpacking is done), a down mummy bag weighing from 2¾ to 3½ pounds is adequate.

If you are in the market for a sleeping bag, what brand should you buy and what price should you pay? The sleeping bag, your pack frame and pack, and your shoes will probably be the most expensive items in your entire list of backpacking equipment. Buying any of these items is somewhat like buying jewelry, and the axiom "If you don't know your jewels, know your jeweler" certainly applies to these more expensive backpacking items. If there is a specialty back-packing store in your locality, visit it and become acquainted with the proprietor and/or the salesmen. Find one who seems to know his merchandise and whose opinion you think can be relied upon. Don't rush into the purchase of a sleeping bag. It costs too much for hasty action; and once it is bought, you will have it a long time. Don't get yourself in the position of buying a bag that is too expensive to discard and yet is a bag with which you are dissatisfied. If there is no outdoor store in your locality I suggest you send for catalogs from the suppliers whose names appear in Appendix 2. Good bags in the 2¾ to 3½ pound total weight range, were selling for $85 to $110 in 1977. If money is no object, you can spend another $25-$30 and get a better built bag weighing a few ounces less; but this is certainly not necessary for conditions to be encountered on the Appalachian Trail. Be sure the bag you buy will fit you. Most quality down sleeping bags are made in regular and extra lengths. Some are made in children's and extra-wide sizes.

The bag that I carried for all but one week of the trip is one made by Gerry of Boulder, Colorado (now the Colorado Outdoor Sports Corporation), purchased in 1956. It has no zippers or ties, but the hood can be drawn up snug around the heads by means of snaps. It is a down-filled mummy shape bag weighing 3 pounds, 3 ounces. It was entirely adequate in temperatures down to the mid-30's, and much more protection than necessary during the warm summer months at the lower elevations in the states from Maryland to New Hampshire.

I left the Trail and returned home on May 25 and did not resume hiking until June 6. During this second leg of my hike I had planned to leave the down sleeping bag at home and replace it with a home-made rectangular shaped bag made by my wife from a single cotton flannel blanket. I had used this previously on car camping trips. This bag weighs but 23 ounces, and I planned to supplement it with an 11 ounce space blanket. I am sure this would have worked, and plan to give it a test on another occasion. What I actually had in the way of sleeping gear beginning June 6 was another matter. In going through my assortment of camping gear while home, I came across a Gerry sleeping bag shell for use in winter weather. This shell is heavily padded and insulated at head, shoulder, hip, and foot areas.

Elsewhere the shell is just that; namely, a shell of thin nylon fabric. There is no insulation whatever on top. I took this shell with me for the second leg of my hike and I left my down sleeping bag and foam mattress pad at home. I figured that the heavy padding on the shell would suffice in lieu of the mattress. I also planned to carry the space blanket to throw over myself on cooler nights. Here are the weights of the two combinations:

Sleeping bag	51 ounces	Sleeping bag shell	36 ounces
Mattress	20 ounces	Space blanket	11 ounces
	71 ounces		47 ounces

The difference in weight between the two is 24 ounces or 1½ pounds, a significant weight reduction. However, in the excitement of getting back on the Trail on June 6, I forgot the space blanket. This saved another 11 ounces, but I found I was sleeping a wee bit cold on those early June nights at 4,000 feet altitudes. I should have realized that the warmer days of summer were near and that by June 15 I would be out of the 3,000-4,000 foot elevations in the Shenandoah National Park and would be hiking and sleeping in the 1,000-1,500 foot elevations of northern Virginia, Maryland, and Pennsylvania. Here again this is hindsight, and all of us seem to have 20-20 hindsight. When my 11 year old son Kevin joined me for three days of hiking in the Shenandoah National Park, he brought with him the down sleeping bag and foam pad. When he departed for home, I kept the sleeping bag and foam pad and sent home the sleeping bag shell. The net result of all these experiments and oversights is that I carried from 1½ to 2 pounds more weight than necessary for almost 1,000 miles. Not good planning . . . definitely not good planning!

The isssue of down as compared to synthetic fills—Dacron and Polorgard to name two—will probably never be settled to everybody's satisfaction. But there are a number of aspects to the controversy that most people do agree on. Ounce for ounce, down is the warmest fill and the most compressible, both important items for the backpacker. Down is totally useless when it becomes wet, and it takes days and days on the Trail to dry out a thoroughly wet down sleeping bag. The synthetic fills are heavier, bulkier, firmer, not as compressible; consequently they occupy more space in your pack. But they are much easier to wash, they retain some warmth even when wet, and dry out much faster than down. And they are much less expensive. Furthermore the firmness of the synthetic fills is an asset in that they require less insulation underneath than do the down-filled sleeping bags. Regardless of the merits of each type of fill, we may see a big switch to the synthetic fills beginning in 1977. The reason is simple, cost. Through 1976 goose down was being purchased by sleeping bag manufacturers for about $7 per pound. Most goose down comes from China and in 1977 the $7 per pound rate was increased to $21 per pound! That is an increase of $14 per pound so that a light weight sleeping bag using two pounds of down fill would cost $28 more to manufacture in 1977 than it did in 1976. Such price increases will put the cost of down sleeping bags beyond the reach of many people.

I have already described at some length the sleeping gear that I used on my 1970 hike and that which I am using today. I will now describe another sleeping bag arrangement which is the most compact and lightest that I have yet seen. It belongs to Ed Hanlon, a long time hiking friend, who hiked with me for a week on the 1970 hike (see Chap. 11). For some 20 years Hanlon had carried a very warm and very, very heavy sleeping bag issued to him when he served in the US Marines. In 1975 I prevailed upon him to purchase a much lighter weight bag. Hanlon went from a 9 lb. sleeping bag to a Camp 7 "Arete" model, extra long, warm to 20 degrees. When stuffed into a light weight stuff bag, it measured 7 inches in diameter and 15 inches in length. The total weight of sleeping bag and stuff sack was 2 lbs. The sleeping bag is then placed in a much larger Camp Trails sack along with other items of Hanlon's sleeping gear: one tube tent which doubles as a tent or a ground cloth, thermal underwear—two pieces which serves as pajamas—wool socks, wool cap, Ensolite pad, and an air pillow. Total weight of all sleeping gear including tube tent is 6¾ pounds. Size of stuff sack with all gear inside was 10 inches by 20 inches.

The Philosophy of John Muir

"Climb the mountains and get their good tidings. Nature's peace will flow into you as sunshine flows into trees. The winds will blow their own freshness into you, and the storms their energy, while cares will drop off like autumn leaves."

7
Shoes and Clothing

With the exception of rain garments, I did not purchase any clothing or shoes for my long hike. I used that which I already owned. Most of it consisted of items which were or could have been purchased at any nearby department store or shoe store. In saying this, I wish to discourage no one from visiting the specialty stores that cater primarily to outdoor equipment and supplies. I do wish to make the point, however, that the hiker planning a long distance hike on the AT may be able to use clothes already in his possession or he may be able to buy inexpensive articles of clothing at a department store or mail order house like Montgomery Ward or Sears and Roebuck. Let's start with shirt and trousers. I'll save the discussion of shoes until the very end of the chapter . . . it's a controversial subject.

My requirements for shirts and trousers were perhaps somewhat more demanding than most hikers. This is because as a member of the Board of Managers of the Appalachian Trail Conference I was most anxious to meet with representatives of the eight national forests, the two national parks, and one national monument through whose territory the Trail passes. I had written to each of these agencies prior to beginning my hike; and I wrote them again as I neared each forest, park, and monument. I also made arrangements to meet with the officers and members of many of the trail clubs that have responsibilities for trail maintenance. I desired, therefore, to look reasonably presentable for these meetings. In Chapter 9, I dwell at some length on the subject of personal appearance. At the risk of repetition let me say this: No one expects the Appalachian Trail hiker to wear shirt, tie, business suit, and shiny shoes. On the other hand, hikers on the AT need not and should not look like bums. We have an obligation to landowners and to our neighbors along the Trail to look reasonably presentable, and I maintain that this can be done without sacrificing one iota of comfort. If readers of this book remember nothing else about it, I would hope that they would remember that personal appearance and courtesy to others are never out of style . . . even on the Appalachian Trail. I may seem a little oversensitive on this issue; but I point out that in February, 1971, I had the privilege of testifying on two occasions at committee hearings at a special session of the General Assembly of Virginia. These were hearings on bills to protect the Appalachian Trail in Virginia. At both hearings, I listened to landowners from northern Virginia describe the disreputable characters using the Appalachian Trail. I suspect that the facts were embellished a bit because I did not run into a single undesirable character in my 2,000-mile hike . . . although some of them looked a little rough around the edges. I urge you, therefore, to select your Trail wardrobe with some consideration for personal appearance.

During the five month period I was on the Trail, I used four sets of trousers and four shirts. Two of these were medium to heavy weight garments with long sleeve shirts. The other two were light weight with short sleeve shirts. With one exception, all shirts and trousers were purchased at either Sears and Roebuck or Montgomery Ward. I wore the long sleeve, heavier garments in the cooler weather; the short sleeve, light weight outfits in the warmer weather. Here is a description of the garments:

Heavy weight: 2 lbs. (Shirt *and* trousers); Sears and Roebuck, green, Sears Perma-Prest, Koratron, Dacron, Polyester, cotton.

Medium weight: 1¾ lbs., blue; Montgomery Ward, Power House, cotton.

Light weight: Sears trousers (9 oz. green); Montgomery Ward shirt (8 oz. green).

Light weight: 1½ lbs., Farroh trousers (green); Sears Perma-Prest shirt, green.

I wore one set and carried one set at all times. I did not alternate from day to day but wore one outfit day after day, no matter how grubby it became. In that way, I always had that one shirt and trouser outfit that was spic and span clean. No matter how dirty and sweaty I became, I could, when I visited civilization, get a shower, shave, and don my clean clothes. I could then saunter forth looking (and even smelling) like a gentleman. People living in cities and towns along the Trail know deep down inside, that the Appalachian Trail hiker lives in a hot, sweaty world; but somehow you have the feeling that they would rather not have to come into too close contact

Ed Garvey on the Appalachian Trail. (Photo: George Huber)

with hot, sweaty individuals. I tried to please; and I felt that I suc-
ceeded reasonably well.

On the shoulder of each shirt I wore a trail patch. On two shirts I
wore the blue, white, and gold AT Maine to Georgia patch issued to
all members of the Appalachian Trail Conference. On the other two
shirts I wore the green, black, red, and gold patch issued to members of the Potomac Appalachian Trail Club of Washington, D.C.
With my 55 years, my gray hair, black hat, my matching shirt and
trousers outfit, with that prominent shoulder patch, I looked sort of
"official." People might not know to what organization I belonged;
but I at least gave the impression that I belonged to *some* organization. I know for a fact that this impression was responsible for my
getting a ride into town on a number of occasions when it was necessary for me to leave the Trail.

If you are a member of an outdoor organization that issues an
identifying patch by all means wear the patch, on your shirt, jacket,
and pack. If you are hiking as a member of an organization such as
the Boy Scouts, wear the uniform. I've always been puzzled at the
attitude of Boy Scouts toward their uniforms. There are few garments
made that are more suitable for the hard wear of outdoor living than
the Boy Scout uniform. Members of that organization will wear the
uniform religiously to indoor meetings throughout the year. Then,
when going on a 50-mile hike, for example, they wear everything
except the uniform. Strange?

No discussion of hiking clothes could be complete without entering into the issue of whether shorts should or should not be worn
when hiking the Appalachian Trail. *ATC Publication 15* contains a
rather positive statement that shorts are just not suitable for Trail
use. I then goes on to provide some pretty convincing reasons why
they are unsuitable. Nevertheless some hikers have worn shorts for
all or most of their hikes. While I enjoy hiking in shorts during the
proper conditions, I almost never wear them while hiking on the
Appalachian Trail. There are a number of places on the Trail where
you are forced to walk through stinging nettles. These sting even
through trousers; it would be much worse on bare legs. I am allergic to poison ivy. If properly clothed, I can walk through acres of the
stuff. With bare legs, it would be suicide. I know! It happened
once . . . in 1947 . . . requiring me to be absent from work for two
weeks, the only extended sick leave I took in almost 35 years of
Government service. There are many places along the Trail where

Waterproof rain parka. (Photo: Appalachian Outfitters)

Waterproof rain chaps. (Photo: Appalachian Outfitters)

poison ivy grows thick and lush. If you're allergic to the stuff, don't wear shorts. Despite the efforts of trail maintenance crews, briars and underbrush make inroads on the Trail. It is impossible to walk through these areas in shorts without getting badly scratched. In addition to these factors, I felt that the trousers gave me protection from insects, lessened the dangers from cuts and lacerations from rocks and trees, and also afforded some protection from snake bites. If, in spite of these things you prefer to wear shorts, more power to you. I would suggest though, that you carry along one pair of trousers for cool nights and other situations where the shorts are not suitable.

In selecting trousers or slacks for backpacking it should be remembered that a Kelty pack, or any pack with a waist strap, renders almost totally useless the four pockets on a conventional pair of trousers or slacks. Had I foreseen the difficulty this was to cause me I would have either: (1) purchased slacks with pockets in a lower position that would have been useable in spite of the waist strap or (2) purchased extra pockets and sewn them on my existing slacks.

Now, let's consider outer garments: windbreakers, parkas, and rain gear. Since I began my hike in Georgia during the first week in April, I knew that I might have a few nights when temperatures would drop below freezing. Chuck and Johnny Ebersole, who began their hike on March 30, 1964, reported a temperature of 16 degrees the first morning. I deliberated as to whether I should take my 4 oz. lighweight Montgomery Ward windbreaker with hood or my 25 oz. Holubar parka. I finally decided to take the 4 oz. windbreaker, and it turned out to be the correct decision. In no occasion did the temperature drop below freezing; but even if it had, I felt that I had enough other garments to keep me warm down to perhaps 20-25 degrees. During the last 13 weeks of my hike up in Maine, I wore the heavier 25 oz. parka and was glad that I did. There seemed to be more of a chill in those long autumn nights up in Maine than in the early spring nights of northern Georgia. Moreover, I had a healthy respect for the temperatures and winds I might encounter on top of Katahdin. On the basis of what I experienced, I would say that those beginning their hike in Georgia in early spring would be quite comfortable with a windbreaker with hood that weighed somewhere in the 6 oz. to 10 oz. range.

Two other outer garments are cap and mittens. I carried an orlon cap (Balaclava type) during the first three weeks of my hike and the last three weeks. The warmth of the cap was welcome not only during the daytime but also at night. During the remainder of the trip I wore a Stetson rainhat. A floppy brimmed inexpensive raincap that I could have stuffed in my pack would have been more practical. But vanity entered into the picture, and practicality lost out. On the other hand, my all purpose deerskin mittens were one of the most practical and frequently used items in my pack. I carried them with me the entire trip. They served not only for warmth but protected my hands when I was clambing in rough rock areas and also when I was gathering and breaking wood for fires. Moreover, I used them at many meals as hot pad holders.

The selection of raingear presents a problem. I consulted a number of people before I made my choice. Some advised me to buy the rain gear that breathes. Others informed me that the breathable type rain gear had distinct limitations and advised me to buy the kind that was airtight and waterproof . . . even though it might present a perspiration problem. On the basis of my own experience and after talking on this subject with many experienced hikers I have come to the conclusion that there is no really satisfactory rain garment. The breathable type is excellent for light showers of limited duration. In heavy rains of long duration, they become completely watersoaked, as does the person wearing them. Inasmuch as they do permit the passage of air, they are more comfortable to wear than the other type. I purchased the nonbreathable type, and bought a rain parka with hood known as an anorak that weighed 8 oz. and a pair of rain chaps that weighed 4 oz. for the pair. The parka, a pullover type, was made by Black of England. It is no longer available in the US and I am now using a Kelty anorak which is a jacket affair with zipper fastening. I use it both as a wind breaker and as a rain garment. The anorak that I wore on my hike was waterproof, no question about that. It kept all rain from coming in but it also kept all perspiration from escaping! It was not comfortable in temperatures above 45 degrees. Early in my hike I worked out a procedure which proved quite satisfactory. If the temperature was 45 degrees or above and if I was hiking, I wore no raingear. At those temperatures I knew I I would be wet, either from perspiration if I wore the raingear, or from the rain if I did not. I therefore chose the rain. I reasoned that it would have a more salubrious effect both upon me and my clothes than would the perspiration. At temperatures below 45 degrees, the chill factor entered in. Then I was glad to don the rain parka, and even the rain chaps.

I despised the rain chaps even though they did their job. Each chap weighed only two ounces. At the top of each there was a tie string which could be fastened to your belt loop. I never wore the chaps except in cool weather. This meant that my fingers and thumbs were also cold and clumsy, not the best situation for tying knots especially when those knots must be tied over on the right side and the left side of your body. Compounding the problem was the fact that the tie strings were thin sleazy affairs which were difficult to tie and which had a pronounced tendency to become untied after but a few minutes of wear. Even when I wore the chaps for brief periods of time, I could feel the moist heat building up in my crotch area; and I began to understand why so many babies (wearing rubber protective garments over their diapers) are afflicted with diaper rash. So much for rain chaps, a must for bone chilling rains in temperatures from 32 to 45 degrees, a nuisance at temperatures above 45.

I also offer two other types of rain gear for consideration—items I did not cover in my original book; one is ages old, the other has just come on the market. The first of these is the umbrella. That's right, the UMBRELLA. Before you scoff and write the umbrella off as a sissy approach to the rugged outdoor sport of backpacking consider these facts. George F. Miller, the super hiker who was hiking seriously before most of us were born, hiked the entire Trail in 1952 when he was 72 years old. He carried a huge umbrella, both for protection while hiking and for nighttime protection. I have read with great interest the journals of the Lewis and Clark expedition of 1804-1806. The journals throw little light on the day-to-day routines of cooking, making camp, etc. But occasionally a tidbit of information would appear such as the one where Lewis describes an experience where Clark and a small body of the men camped overnight in a cave near a river. Heavy rains caused the river to rise rapidly during the night and the cave began flooding. Lewis describes the hasty middle-of-the-night evacuation and remarks, "In the excitement Clark forgot his umbrella." Aha! So the expedition carried umbrellas, at least one! And lastly, I suggest you read the excellent and humorous article, VIVA LES UMBRELLA that appears in the Winter, 1975 issue of *Wilderness Camping*. In the article, the author, Jim Lockyer, describes his own experiences with the umbrella and the alternate expressions of ridicule and envy from other hikers.

Garvey's Ranger moccasin shoes. (Photo: Joan Knight)

Garvey's L. L. Bean Hunting shoes used the last 300 miles. (Photo: Joan Knight)

The other item—trade name—GOR-TEX is the most recent of a number of fabrics to appear on the market in the last 15 years which are claimed to be both breathable and waterproof. GOR-TEX rain garments are already being sold and other items (tents, sleeping bag covers) either have or soon will be available. I have heard and read the comments of both scoffers and enthusiastic endorsers of the new product. I have not yet used it myself and I offer no comment other than to provide the information that it is available.

Another useful article which I consider as an item of clothing is a jumbo-size bandanna handkerchief. L. L. Bean sells the 22-inch by 23-inch size. However, any size, 18-inch square or larger, will suffice. These can be tied around the forehead to serve as a sweatband; they can be worn around the neck as a kerchief, or they can be tied triangular fashion so as to protect ears and neck from insects. I found the kerchief to be particularly effective against gnats. Those little insects are especially fond of the hikers' ears; and the kerchief was more effective than insect repellant in giving me protection.

Now let's proceed to underwear; both the light weight variety and long johns for colder weather. As to underwear pants, that's entirely a matter of preference and I do not discuss the topic. As to underwear tops, it seems to be primarily a choice between the fishnet T-shirt which sells for about $3 a shirt (1971) and the more common cotton T-shirt which sells for about $1. I've never worn the fishnet type, although many of my hiking friends wear them regularly. I did find the ordinary cotton T-shirt very satisfactory. I recommend buying dark colors for hiking purposes. They do not show soil and they look more presentable when worn without an outer shirt. I carried one green and another yellow one. The latter was a mistake. Not only did it show soil quickly but in time the combination of pressure from the shoulder straps of my pack and body perspiration resulted in a wide band of green or of blue being imparted from my outer shirt onto the T-shirt. In recent years, I have found that gray is an extremely satisfactory color. The T-shirts with their short sleeves and low neck cut leave much exposed skin surface which is a hazard in mosquito country. During the course of my hike I tried unsuccessfully to buy a light weight knit shirt with long sleeves and roll collar which would have given me more protection without being too warm.

If you plan to begin your hike in Georgia before April 1, or if you plan to finish at Katahdin after September 30, it is advisable either to carry long handled underwear (full length drawers, long sleeve upper garment) or to carry warm pajamas that can double as undergarments in the event of sudden cold weather with high winds. The weather at Mt. Katahdin can become vicious anytime after September 30. As I write these words, I have before me the January 1964, issue of *Appalachian Trailway News*. In that issue there is related the tragedy of late October 1963 in which a 52-year-old woman who had hiked to Baxter Peak lost her life. And a park ranger attempting to rescue her also lost his life. Their bodies were not recovered until May of 1964. What started out as a pleasant hike on a fair, warm October day turned into a nightmare when winds of Arctic gale proportions arose accompanied by rain, then sleet, then 16 inches of snow. It was probably knowledge of this tragedy that convinced Elmer Onstott that he should (after hiking all the way from Georgia) turn back after getting within a few thousand feet of Baxter Peak on October 25, 1968. A severe storm was raging on the crest of the mountain at the time. It is well, therefore, to carry warm clothes when climbing Katahdin in October, even if the weather is mild when you start out. For cold weather hiking, I have found that light weight Duofold underwear is very satisfactory. The Duofold products have a light layer of cotton next to the skin and a light outer layer of wool. The size 40 shirt and the 32-inch drawers weigh a total of 14 ounces.

Now for shoes and socks. In 1969 I had the audacity to write an article entitled, "How High the Boot, How Heavy the Shoe?" This article appeared in the July-September, 1969 issue of the *Potomac Appalachian Trail Club Bulletin*. I am still receiving comments on this article, some good, a few bad. Many people, quite probably knowing more about the subject than I, have graciously contributed to my store of information on the subject. In my article I poked a little fun at the trend towards the very heavy hiking boots. I even mentioned that pro football players had switched from the high top shoe to the low cuts, and I suggested that sturdy low cut shoes might be suitable for hiking on the AT. My article produced so much reaction that Jim Shores, the editor of the *Bulletin*, felt compelled to print another article on hiking shoes in the next issue. That article, written by a William A. Turnage, makes some very effective arguments for the heavier weight hiking shoe. Another *Bulletin* reader, Mr. William A. Kamper wrote a most interesting article "How Vibram Came to the U.S." His article appeared in the July-September, 1970, issue. It seems that sometime around 1942 an Italian bootmaker named Bramani developed a new type boot with molded rubber lugs on the soles and heels. After the war, the bootmaker VItale BRAMani began marketing the boot under the name VIBRAM.

Vibram has become the most prominent of the composition soles and heels used by hikers and backpackers in the post-World War II decades. The success of the Vibram product resulted in widespread

---

SHOES

5 Million Steps! That's what it takes from Georgia to Maine on the Appalachian Trail. And for each one of those 5 million steps the pressure on your feet is intensified by a pack that may weigh from 25 to 50 pounds.

Be kind to your feet. Buy a good pair of socks and a pair of shoes big enough to allow for the swelling that comes from constant hiking day after day and from the added weight of your pack.

Never start a hike with new shoes. To do so is to invite misery. Break in new shoes *thoroughly* on short jaunts. Hike in them for at least 50 miles. Half of that distance should be with a pack on your back.

I have seen so many hikers suffer so much needless misery from sore and blistered feet that I long ago vowed that this book would contain this warning for all.

Edward B. Garvey, 1971

---

promotion of other composition type soles and heels, usually dark colored, fairly hard and long wearing in which the lugs are in the form of crosses about an inch long. Two of the other post World War II composition soles and heels with which I am familiar are Galibier and Patons. Vibram itself comes in various qualities, thicknesses, degrees of hardness, and price. There have been other composition soles and heels on the market, long before Vibram. The earlier ones were softer and more comfortable but they did not have the long wearing or gripping qualities of Vibram.

Having given that little bit of background, I shall now describe the four types of shoes that I wore on my 2,000-mile jaunt. I will also describe the shoes worn by some of the other through-hikers of the AT. Then I shall offer a few suggestions for those who are in the market for their first pair of hiking shoes.

I began my hike with a pair of Red Wing Irish Setter shoes, 6 inches high, weight 3 pounds 9 oz. These have a light colored composition sole with a rather shallow tread. These were very comfortable and I wore them for over 700 miles, or until May 25, when I returned home for the first of my two 2-week breaks from hiking. I had purchased the Red Wing shoes in 1967 at a cost of $32. I had used them for perhaps 150 miles of trail walking, and they were thoroughly broken in. After that first 700 miles, the tread was nearly gone; but the composition soles were still 3/8 of an inch thick at their thinnest point; and I felt that the shoes still had several hundred miles of comfortable wear without resoling. Had I planned to use these shoes for the entire trip, I would have had them resoled during the May 25-June 6 break; and I am certain they would have made it all the way to Katahdin without further repairs.

In 1968 I had purchased a pair of Bean's Ranger Moccasins, low cut (less than 4 inches) and weighing only 2 pounds 2 ounces. In my *Bulletin* article on hiking shoes I had mentioned the Ranger Moccasins. I had speculated that they might be suitable for Trail hiking, and I had stated that I planned to give them a thorough testing. Little did I realize, when I made that statement, what a wonderful testing opportunity I was soon to have. When I returned to the Trail on June 6, 1970, I was wearing the Ranger Moccasins. I wore them through part of the George Washington National Forest, all of the Shenandoah National Park, northern Virginia, through Maryland, and through all of Pennsylvania. And Pennsylvania is about as tough a 200-mile stretch of walking as there is to be found, not because of its strenuousness or altitude (the mountains range from 1,000 to 2,000 feet) but because of the ever present rocks on the Trail that hour after hour punish feet, legs, and shoes. Midway through Pennsylvania I realized that my Moccasins had had it, and I wrote my wife asking that she mail me the Red Wing shoes. My wife is not quite as familiar with my hiking shoes as I am (I wear them; she doesn't!), but when I checked in at the post office in Delaware Water Gap, Pennsylvania, a box of shoes was waiting for me. But when I opened the box, I found that instead of the Red Wing shoes, my wife had mailed me a pair of six-year-old Pathfinder shoes, sold by L. L. Bean.

At this point, let me discourse a bit on the Moccasin shoe. Neither sole nor heel had any tread whatsoever. They were slippery on wet inclined surfaces. They lost their shape badly, so that near the end of their use I seemed to be walking almost as much on the inside

New Red Wing Boot. Similar to those worn by Garvey for the first 700 miles of his hike. (Photo: Banbury)

part of the leather uppers as I was on the sole of the shoe. Yet I did enjoy the lightness of these shoes and the fact that I could get in or out of them in seconds. Also in defense of this shoe, I must again point out that they served me for over 400 miles of tough Trail hiking with a 35 to 40-pound pack. Would I wear them again for this type of hiking? No, I would not. For casual weekend hiking with no pack or a light weight pack they would be quite adequate. But for just a few more ounces of weight and a few more dollars one can purchase a 6-inch sturdier shoe with ankle support and with a thicker sole that provides better traction and gives much more protection against the bone-bruising capabilities of the ever present rocks. So much for the light weight, low cut shoe. It was a noble experiment; and while one *could* hike the entire Trail in such shoes, I am now convinced that there are better ways of getting the job done.

Now to return to the L. L. Bean Pathfinder shoes which I received at Delaware Water Gap, Pennsylvania. I had purchased these shoes in 1964. They are a 6-inch-high shoe that weighed 3 pounds 8 ounces new. I had had them resoled once by a local cobbler who repaired them with materials on hand; namely a composition sole and heel which had no tread whatever. I used them as work shoes around my home; but now, for seven weeks, they were to be my hiking shoes through New Jersey, New York, Connecticut, Massachusetts, the Green Mountains of Vermont, and the White Mountains of New Hampshire. I wore them all the way to Gorham, New Hampshire where I took my second two-week hiking break to return home for my daughter's wedding. Except for the fact that they provided very little traction, these shoes performed admirably; figuratively giving up their lives for the cause. By the time I reached Gorham, the soles had worn through to the leather inner sole; the leather uppers had burst; and one heel was almost off. They are not worth repairing and I use them and the Ranger Moccasins as Exhibits A and B in some of my talks to hiking groups in order to show what the Trail can do to a pair of shoes.

After my daughter's wedding I returned to the Trail on September 11 for the last 300-mile lap to Katahdin. Almost until the moment I left home, I was undecided as to whether to resume wearing my Red Wing shoes or to hike in my 9-inch-high Bean Hunting Shoes with their rubber bottoms and leather tops. The Hunting Shoes are a light weight shoe . . . even the 9-inch-high ones weigh but 3 pounds per pair. The soles are rather thin; there is very little arch support; and all rubber bottom shoes can be uncomfortably warm on even mildly warm days and can be uncomfortably cold on cold days. I had hiked in Maine on two previous occasions, and I knew that the footing can be pretty wet. I did not relish the idea of having wet feet for long periods of time during some of those cold damp days of late September and early October. I therefore chose the Bean Hunting Shoes. I reasoned that the comfort of dry feet would more than compensate for the other recognized shortcomings of the Hunting Shoes. Even though my reasoning may have been logical, my choice was a mistake. The thin, soft, rubber soles with their rather shallow chain tread provided me almost no traction; and I suffered more falls in Maine than in the previous 13 states. The thin soles also afforded little protection against sharp rocks; and for several months after I completed my hike, my left foot was still sensitive because of bruises received from stones. But the most revolting feature of the Hunting Shoes was that my feet became wet and stayed that way for days. Near the end of my hike it rained for eight days out of nine. On the one day that it did not rain, the woods and underbrush were saturated from a three-day rain. The leather upper part of the shoes became watersoaked and the water ran down inside the shoe into the rubber bottoms. Once that happened I was doomed. It was next to impossible to dry out socks during the short late summer and early autumn days. At one point I washed two pair of socks and hung them from my pack with clothes pins for two days. At the end of that time, they were still wet.

When I reached Rangeley, Maine, some 200 miles short of Katahdin, I purchased a pair of lightweight fleece-lined shoes called "after ski" boots. They added two pounds more to my pack and were very bulky, but they were more than worth these minor inconveniences. Each day thereafter, promptly upon reaching my shelter, I would take off the wet soggy boots, don dry socks, and put on those warm fleece-lined "after ski" boots. What pure unadulterated pleasure. The only fly in the ointment was the knowledge that sometime the following morning I would have to reverse the procedure. How I dreaded those moments. I would perform all other camp chores first. Then just before leaving camp, I would take off the warm dry boots and socks and put on two pairs of cold, wet, clammy socks and an equally cold, wet, clammy pair of rubber-bottomed boots. If I was not fully awake before that, I can assure you pulling those cold, wet socks and boots over my warm, dry pinkies thoroughly completed my awakening process. In defense of the Bean Hunting Shoes, I should state that I probably could have avoided some of my miseries if I had done a thorough job of waterproofing the uppers. Even so, I doubt if any leather shoes, no matter how well waterproofed, could have withstood the day in and day out soaking to which these shoes were subjected. I dreaded the thought of slipping and sliding up and down Katahdin in those shoes, so I sent an S.O.S. home for my Red Wing Shoes. The Red Wings were waiting for me at the ranger's office at Katahdin Stream Campground, and I wore them on the final day of my hike to the summit of Baxter Peak. Having thus described the shoes that I wore, let's consider in the ensuing paragraphs the types of shoes worn by some of the other hikers who have hiked the entire Trail.

In the previous paragraphs I told of my difficulties with the Bean Hunting Shoe. Two hikers, Murray Chism and Edward N. Little, in their 1959 eight-month traverse of the Trail, wore Bean Hunting shoes the entire distance. They wore the ten-inch height in the cooler weather; six-inch in the hot weather. In commenting on the Bean Hunting Shoe, Chism and Little wrote, (*A.T. News*, May, 1960): "The soles are flexible and not very thick, so many persons use a separate insole in them. Without such insoles (we used none) the feet must be conditioned to stand travel over rough and stony trail."

Erick Ryback, who began his 81-day hike in Maine in June 1969, wrote these words about his boots (*A.T. News*, January 1970):

> My boots are Italian, 10 inches high, with the trade name Voyageur; they served me well. They were insulated and worn with two pairs of heavy Norwegian ski socks. I had blisters from the start because I hiked in about a foot of snow and got the boots soaked for the first few days; once my blisters healed I never had a foot problem. The soles of my boots were Vibram and lasted until Harper's Ferry. With one-day shoe service in Brunswick I had neoprene resoles added. The next time I would purchase extra soles of vibram and have them mailed ahead with my food drop. The neoprene had to be replaced twice.

One of those who seemed to have the least trouble with shoes was 69-year-old Elmer Onstott who hiked the Trail in 1968. In his January, 1969 article in *Trailway News* Elmer wrote as follows:

> The shoes I wore were the best grade of 9-inch boots sold by Sears. The Goodyear soles went all the way and have several miles of hiking left in them. I wore from two to four pairs of socks, one nylon pair next to the skin and three pairs of medium-weight wool socks to fill my shoes after I lost 32 pounds in weight. I had no blisters.

Bill O'Brien (*A.T. News*, January, 1970) writes:

> My boots were Fabiano, and I got in 1,400 miles to Massachusetts on one set of mountain soles and had them replaced in Boston during my visit home. Unfortunately the new sole on the right shoe began peeling off fairly soon, and when the trip was over the sole was fastened to the toe by less than an inch. The boots were very durable, but I should have bought them unlined so that they could dry out better. Wet feet were a continuous problem the last month because of the heavy rains and the type of terrain.

One could go on and on as to the types of shoes worn by the different through-hikers. Let me describe just three more which justify inclusion, principally because they are so different. Allen and Gregory in their 1960 hike wore the lightweight (approximately 2½ pounds) Maine Guide Shoe which is 6 inches high. Mrs. Emma Gatewood (Grandma Gatewood) hiked the entire trail in 1955, again in 1957, and again over a five-year stretch from 1960 to 1964. And what kind of shoes did she wear? Sneakers; that's right, Sneakers! I don't know whether they were the low cuts or the 6-inch-high variety, but I have it on the word of many people living on or near the Trail that Grandma Gatewood wore sneakers. George F. Miller at age 72 hiked the entire Trail in 1952. Miller may have been one of the most experienced hikers to have ever hiked the entire Trail. He had hiked regularly since his youth. In 1913 he walked the highways from Farmington, Missouri, to New York City, an estimated 1,000 miles in 26 days and three hours. He had performed other noteworthy hiking feats. For his 1952 hike he fashioned his own pack, part of it resting on his chest, part of it on his back . . . perfectly balanced. What kind of shoes did he wear? The article describing his hike (*PATC Bulletin*, January-March, 1953) says this:

> Two pairs of Bean's high-topped shoes headed Mr. Miller's list. Walks over Washington's streets, aggregating 100 miles or more, were sufficient for the 'breaking in.' When pair No. 1 became muddy, cold, and damp, he switched to No. 2, and he was prepared to visit a cobbler when soles or heels became worn.

Miller was the twelfth hiker to have completed the entire Trail. The article on his hike was the first I had ever read about one of the through-hikes. I often pondered over the wisdom of carrying that extra pair of shoes. It seemed as though Miller was adding a needless three pounds to his pack load. Had Miller been an inexperienced hiker, I would probably have dismissed the idea as a novice's over-cautious approach to the subject. But Miller was anything but inexperienced. He had made painstaking preparation for every aspect of his hike, even to a printed daily log form. He kept his pack weight under 30 pounds. He carried no camera or field glasses. Considering all the facts, one must ascribe considerable significance to his decision to carry that extra pair of shoes. I make no recommendations on this point. I merely recite the facts for what they are worth. Even though it has been 24 years since I first read the Miller article I am still "pondering" the issue of that second pair of shoes.

We have seen in the preceding paragraphs that through-hikers of the Trail have worn everything from sneakers to 10-inch-high boots. Now let's examine what is available on the market in 1977 and then to move into the delicate area of recommending a type and price of shoe for the person who has had little previous experience with hiking. We will discuss such things as the height of the boot, the weight, the type of sole, and the cost. And before getting into details let me explain that in the years 1974 to 1977 in my affiliation with Appalachian Outfitters I have concentrated on boots—the fitting, the waterproofing and general care, the breaking-in process, and the type of socks to be worn with the boot. I feel that the hiking boot is the most important part of the backpacker's equipment. It is particularly enjoyable to work with people who are just getting into the hiking game because I know the questions that are going through their minds and the doubts they are assailed with as they view and sometimes heft the many weights, sizes, and styles of hiking boots on the display shelf.

The first recommendation comes easy: the height of the boot. A 6-inch-high boot is high enough for the walking you will do along the Appalachian Trail, and for most other trails for that matter. Experienced hikers will already have established decided preferences for the weight of the boot, the brand name, the model, and the price. For the person venturing into the hiking game, I would suggest a light weight boot. And what is a light weight boot? I've had to revise my thinking on this but as of 1977 a light weight boot for a size 10 would weigh from 3 to 3½ lbs.; medium weight 3½ to 4½; and anything over 4½ is getting into the heavy weight category. The weights given are for a *pair* of boots, not a single boot. The light weight boot is especially suitable for those who do not weigh over 160 of 170 lbs. and who plan to use the boots primarily for day hiking with only occasional backpacking. Lightweight boots were selling for from $38 to $43 in 1977. I am a 160-pounder, I have used a pair of these light weight boots for the past four years, both for day hiking and extensive backpacking and I find them quite satisfactory.

The medium weight boot is better suited for heavier people or those who expect to do extensive backpacking particularly in rocky areas. They generally are stiffer in the ankle area and thus provide more protection. Generally they also have one or two extra midsoles which build up the overall thickness of the sole and this in turn provides more protection from stone bruises in rocky trail areas. The medium weight boot was selling for $50 to $65 in 1977. Since 1975, I have either bought or experimented with four different pairs of medium weight boots. They *do* provide more ankle support, they *do* provide more protection from stones and, after four or five hours of continuous hiking you do become painfully aware of the fact that you have an extra pound or so of weight on your feet! When I give lectures and slide shows on backpacking equipment on the Appalachian Trail, I generally wear the heavier boots because they look and sound quite impressive but at heart I'm still a light weight boot man.

I rarely recommend or sell heavy weight boots to backpackers. The heavy weights—those in the 5-lb. and 6-lb. class—are ideal for those on expedition-type mountain activities especially where snow and ice are involved. They are also very suitable for people like the Appalachian Mountain Club hut boys who carry tremendously heavy supply loads up and down the mountain day in and day out. But for the backpacker, these extra heavy weights are overkill and are really not necessary.

There are times though when logic or functional use is excluded from the transaction in favor of looks, prestige, elitism or whatever you wish to call it. Like the man for whom a 4-cylinder subcompact is the logical car to buy but who prefers to mortgage his soul to buy an 8-cylinder, heavy, gas-eating monster. Or like the 16-year-old girl who came into Appalachian Outfitters in December 1974. She was slight of build, not more than 100 lbs. and was accompanied by her parents. They inquired as to hiking boots and I explained the merits of the lightweight Fabiano boot. The parents liked what they heard—lightweight boots, extremely durable, could be resoled, easy to break in—and the cost only $35. Daughter expressed neither enthusiasm nor disinterest and allowed herself to be fitted. After the fitting process she was silent for a long moment and then said somewhat apologetically, "Sir, these are a good fit but could I just try on those Vasque Hiker II boots?", referring to a pair of boots that were 1½ lbs. heavier and $15 more expensive. Papa became angry questioning daughter as to the need for the heavier boots. I fitted her with the Vasque boots at which point she became even more apologetic and asked if I could fit her with the still heavier Vasque Whitney model. If papa was angry before, he was now furious and he stated flatly that $35 was his top price, and demanded to know of his daughter why she needed such heavy boots. She countered by stating that she had some of her own money and would pay any price in excess of $35, and as to her need, she stated that she might be going to Montana in the spring. I then fitted her with the heavier $60 Whitneys and for the first time she began to show enthusiasm. When she looked at herself in the full-length mirror, she was ecstatic. Expressions like, "these are cool . . . these really look cool. These are exactly what I want," poured forth. As she took the boots and headed for the check-out counter, I explained to her parents what they already knew, that I hadn't really *sold* her the heavy boots . . . she had *bought* them. They weren't happy but they understood.

Of equal importance with the brand of shoe, its weight, and its price, is the fit of the shoe and the breaking-in period required before embarking on a hiking trip of extended duration. If you plan to wear two heavy pair of socks for your hiking, then you should be wearing two heavy pair of socks when you are being fitted for your hiking shoes. If you plan to hike (as I do) with a thin pair of inner socks and a heavier pair of outer socks, then you should be wearing such socks when you are being fitted for shoes. Take plenty of time with the shoe fitting until you are certain you have the fit you want. Put your full weight on the shoes. Be sure there is a half inch of wiggle space between the end of your toes and the shoes. Be sure they are loose across the instep. Remember that the addition of a 30-pound pack will cause your feet to spread slightly. Remember, also, that the hour after hour pounding of carrying that same pack will cause them to swell a bit. So be certain that you have a roomy fit.

It has been six years since I wrote the preceding paragraph and experiences of others and my own have come to make me almost a fanatic on insisting on a roomy fit on hiking boots. In 1976 Roger Leavitt of New Vernon, New Jersey, hiked the entire AT. He began with a well-broken-in pair of Raichles which he stated "fit fine at the start of the trip but after 3 or 4 weeks of continuous hiking they were tight with only one pair of socks and my toes were getting sore." He left the Trail in southwestern Virginia, thumbed a ride to the Appalachian Outfitters store in Salem and purchased a bigger pair of boots, boots that were long enough and wide enough to be comfortable even when wearing two pair of socks.

Again in 1976 three of us hiked the 140 miles from Wesser, North Carolina to Springer Mountain and on into Amicalola Falls, in nine days. After about the third day, my feet had swelled so much that by mid-afternoon of each day the little toe on each foot became very painful. The swelling and pain would disappear overnight, only to reappear by mid-afternoon of the following day.

Now a word about lined shoes as opposed to unlined shoes. In November 1970, I gave a talk in Baltimore, Maryland, before some 75 members of the Mountain Club of Maryland. I had on display all of the hiking shoes I had used on my long hike. After the talk was over, one of the veteran members of MCM examined my shoes, noticed that my Red Wing shoes were unlined, and proceeded to berate me for my stupidity in using unlined shoes. He made it sound as though I had committed a felony, at least a misdemeanor. I really had no defense, as I had never given the matter any serious thought. Later, in reviewing *ATC Publication No. 15* I found the following two sentences. "An unlined shoe is preferable. If there is no lining, a wet shoe can be wiped out; and by putting on dry socks, there is all the comfort of a dry shoe." Still later in reviewing Bill O'Brien's story of his hike I noted (*A.T. News,* January, 1970) his comments regarding his boots. He said, ". . . I should have bought them unlined so that they could dry out better. Wet feet were a continuous problem the last month because of the heavy rains and the type of terrain." The lined shoe provides additional warmth, and the smooth surface of the lining is less apt to irritate the feet. These are the pros and cons; but the matter may be becoming academic because in my last survey of available hiking shoes, I noted that the great preponderance of the shoes available were lined. But since you have now read these comments on lined versus unlined shoes, you can at least act knowledgeably if your judgment on the matter is challenged.

I cannot overemphasize the importance of thoroughly breaking in a new pair of hiking shoes before embarking on a long hike. Even a two-day weekend hike can be torture if you are wearing new shoes that have not been well broken in. I took my first overnight Boy Scout hike in the spring of 1927. To this day I can remember the name of the boy, the appearance of his new black shoes, and the misery he endured for two days on that first overnighter. Don't let it happen to you. On my 1970 hike I hiked with companions, and I met others on the Trail who were suffering the tortures of the damned because of ill-fitting or inadequately broken-in shoes.

How much breaking in is required? I would say a minimum of 50 miles. And, if you are planning on a long-distance hike on the Appalachian Trail, then half of that 50 miles should be with a pack on your back, a pack of the weight that you plan to carry on your hike.

Before embarking on a long-distance hike you will wish to make your leather shoes water repellent. The Hiking, Camping, and Mountaineering Equipment Committee of the Potomac Appalachian Trail Club has been testing boots, shoes, and waterproofing products for years. The Committee has this to say on the subject:

> For waterproofing leather—and leather should never be fully waterproofed— a good treatment is to apply 3 coats of silicones in a volatile solvent, spacing the treatments 24 hours apart, followed by routine rubbing in of a wax-type boot grease. The leather should be re-siliconed about once a season.

Don't be confused by that term "volatile solvent." If you ask at a shoe store for a silicone waterproofing compound such as "Shoe Saver" or "Gard," to name two, the product you receive will already have been diluted in a volatile solvent.

From shoes we proceed to the socks that you will wear inside of them. There have been so many opinions expressed on this subject that I have come to the conclusion that there is no one "right" method or combination of socks that is superior to all others. Over the years I have found it very satisfactory to wear a thin pair of socks next to the foot plus a heavier pair of outer socks. There are those who stoutly maintain that the outer sock should be wool. I have worn wool, cotton, and nylon; and all have been satisfactory. My only objection to the heavy cotton socks is that it takes forever to dry them if you try to wash them on the trail during your hike.

Allen and Gregory in their 1960 hike each carried three pairs of Ward's cushion sole 100 percent nylon outer sock. I promptly purchased two pairs of such socks. That was 17 years ago. I have used those socks extensively over the years and wore them well over one thousand miles on my 1970 hike. They are still in good shape and seem to be almost indestructible. In more recent years I have been wearing Norwegian Rag Wool socks as the outer sock—and on some occasions the WickDry heavy duty sock which is 50% cotton—50% synthetic.

For inner socks I have generally worn cotton, but on my 1970 hike I purchased 2 pairs of WickDry Inner socks as manufactured by Rockford Textile Mills. These proved very satisfactory and very durable. The instructions provide that they are to be worn under wool or cotton which would seem to exclude nylon. I wore them under wool, cotton and nylon and they proved satisfactory for all three fabrics. The cost in 1977 was $1.20 per pair—machine washable—machine driable, and almost indestructible.

VIBRAM

In the six years since my book was first published, the number of backpackers, backpacking magazines, retailers, and manufacturers of backpacking equipment has increased at a phenomenal rate. Competition is keen and, with one exception, no one product dominates the field. The one product that does is VIBRAM, the heel and sole product that adorns perhaps 95% of all backpacking boots now sold in the United States. Domestically, Vibram soles are manufactured by Quabaug Rubber Co. of North Brookfield, Mass. 01535.

The backpacking fraternity is generally familiar with only one of the Vibram soles, this being the conventional lug sole with its eight one-half inch crosses in the sole and one in the heel. However, even the conventional lug sole comes in six models . . . Montagna, Montagnabloc, Roccia, Rocciabloc, Lacima, and Kletter lift. With the huge increase in the number of people using the existing hiking trails and the erosion that is taking place on some of those trails, it was inevitable that someone would attempt to determine if some or most of the trail damage might not be attributable to the hard Vibram lug sole. Actually it was two someones, Dr. E. H. Ketchledge and Dr. Ray E. Leonard of the State University College of Forestry, Syracuse University. Their research was conducted over a four-year period in the Adirondack High Country of New York. The results of their research were published in the October-November, 1970 issue of the *New York State Conservationist* and I will quote just a few sentences of the article to illustrate the point I wish to make:

> * * * But after studying three trails for days on end, in all kinds of weather, and at all times of year, we believe the greatest share of the disturbance is due to the pounding from the hikers' boots, particularly those with the cleated Vibram-type soles. The constant cutting-in of boots roughens the surface, thereby creating an easily eroded topography. With each step of

Vibram soles.

the hiker, soil is depressed further into the bottom of the cut, where the stream flowing downhill in the trail during and after a rainstorm carries it off the slopes.

While the Ketchledge-Leonard research shows that lug type soles are responsible for *some* of the trail damage, my own observations lead me to believe that the greatest trail damage is caused by (1) improper trail design (i.e., trails installed at too steep a grade), (2) inadequate maintenance (i.e., failure to install water bars or other devices to divert the flow of water off the trail bed), and (3) the utterly indefensible practice of some hikers in taking short cuts on graded trails.

If we accept the premise that sharp lug soles do more damage than a smoother sole, what can we do about it? Vibram (i.e., Quabaug Rubber Co.) is not insensitive to the problem. When I wrote them on this issue, I promptly received a letter from Herbert M. Varnum, the President. He furnished me with one pair each of two other Vibram soles, the Security sole and the Sestogrado sole. Each is pictured in this chapter. Each type would, I believe, be quite acceptable for backpacking purposes and would do less damage than the conventional lug sole. The problem now is to convince boot manufacturers that the hiking public will settle for or actually prefer a hiking sole that might be somewhat softer and have less prominent cleats and lugs than the present hard lug sole being furnished. Furthermore some of the professional forest and park manager types have begun switching back to the composition soles that were in use prior to the advent of Vibram soles. Even one of the 1976 through hikers of the Appalachian Trail, Jim Gardner of Union City, PA, wrote that he had a pair of heavy duty hiking boots with lug soles gathering dust in his closet and that he found it more expedient to use industrial type boots with smoother tread soles on his 2000-mile hike.

It is regretable that the Vibram sole which is such a superior product for technical rock climbing and other high mountain activities, is coming under fire because it is being used for situations for which it was not primarily designed. John Kettlewell writing in the Washington, D.C. Speleograph (Feb. 1977) states that:

After many years of caving, thousands of hours underground, and introducing considerable numbers of amateurs to caving, I have seen massive evidence that a standard hiking or climbing boot with Vibram soles is *extremely hazardous* for caving, * * * for two reasons: (1) the hard rubber becomes extremely slick when wet, and (2) the 'waffle' pattern collects mud, reducing the traction of the boot to nothing.

This is the situation as it exists in 1977. I will terminate this chapter with a final quote from a letter written by Dr. Ray Leonard to Herbert M. Varnum of Quabaug Rubber in January 1977. Leonard writes:

> There is certainly a place for Vibram soles among the climbing public. It is unfortunate in terms of trail degradation that the lug type sole became such a fad. Its use by the casual hiker on lower slopes is probably not necessary and injures trails in these locations.

The year 1977 produced three excellent magazine articles on hiking boots—covered just about everything from construction details to getting the proper fit. The articles are listed in date order of publishing:

1. "Boots," *Wilderness Camping*, June/July 1977, Vol. 1, No. 1
2. "What Do You Want in a Hiking Shoe?" Len Wheat, *Potomac Appalachian Magazine*, No. 5, Potomac Appalachian Trail Club, Wash, DC
3. "Stop Walking Away the Wilderness" by William M. Harlow, *Backpacker Magazine*, Vol. 22, August, 1977

In June 1978, Quabaug Rubber Co. issued a delightful little 48-page booklet *Stepping into Wilderness*. The book provides practical suggestions on how to use (and at the same time protect) our fragile wilderness areas. Among other subjects it addresses the "Lug versus non-Lug" issue. Available from Quabaug for a $1.00.

The silence of the forest, the peace of the early morning wind moving through the branches of the trees, the solitude and isolation of the house of God: These are good because it is in silence, and not in commotion, in solitude, and not in crowds, that God best likes to reveal himself intimately to men.

Thomas Merton

8
Not Necessary but Nice

This chapter is about those things which are not necessary but are nice to have along with one, such items as a camera, binoculars, books, a thermometer, an altimeter, a radio, a diary, and that most wondrous camping article—the Swiss Army Knife. Before buying, borrowing or carrying any of these articles on a long hike you should reread Chapter 4 and consider carefully the weight maximum that you intend to set for yourself. You must consider how often you will use some of these articles, how much enjoyment you will derive from them, and you must weigh these benefits against the energy and sweat of carrying them for days on end, in hot weather and cold, in hot sun, and in a slogging rain. No two backpackers think alike in their preparations for a long hike or in the particular type of enjoyment they expect to obtain. There are those who desire nothing more than to hike, hike, hike—and who consider as wasted time any interruption to study and identify a flower, to listen to the song of a bird, or even to stop for minutes to enjoy a beautiful view. There are others who have a hobby in a particular field, such as photography or bird study. Such persons will stop occasionally to indulge in these hobbies, and will carry equipment and supplies for these purposes.

There are some through-hikers of the AT who have carried no camera whatever, feeling that a camera was excess baggage. At the other extreme was Elmer Onstott (1968) a 69-year-old man who carried a tremendous amount of camera equipment. Elmer believes he is the only through-hiker to have carried a tripod the entire distance. I don't know exactly how much his camera equipment and supplies weighed, but it was probably in the 10-15 pound range. But photography was a big thing for Onstott, and he obtained some of the most complete and expert photographic coverage of the Trail of all those have hiked it from end to end. And, since Onstott ate uncooked foods on his trip, he did not have the weight of cooking equipment or of stove or fuel.

I carried a small camera; but if I could have foreseen the mishaps I was to have with it and how I would not obtain any acceptable pictures, I would not have carried it at all. My camera was a compact little 6 ounce 16 mm. Minolta with a built-in light meter and a built-in close-up lense. I knew it had limitations for distance shots, but I was not too much concerned about that. I was however, anxious to document by color slides such things as the word content of signs and obtain pictures of flowers, people, and grouse chicks (if I could catch them). I had two things operating against me: my general incompetence as a photographer and the fact that I dropped the camera in the water twice during the first week! But even later in the trip, after I had had the camera checked over at a camera shop, I was unable to get any clear, sharp pictures.

Somewhere in between the Garveys and the Onstotts are those who have carried other cameras, not too heavy in weight, and who have obtained some very good color slides. Garnett Martin in 1964 and the Skinners in 1968 obtained some very acceptable slides. Reproductions of Martin's slides appear in Ray Baker's delightful book, *Campfires Along the Appalachian Trail.* Another 1964 hiker, Chuck Ebersole, obtained color slides of high enough quality to be accepted by the National Geographic Society for some of their publications. Since an end-to-end trip on the AT is usually a once in a lifetime experience, I would advise hikers to carry a camera. You may not get professional quality pictures; but if you have just a little more skill than I have, you will be able to obtain pictures good enough for home consumption and for illustrating a lecture.

I have an excellent pair of compact, light weight binoculars. They weigh but 11 ounces including their leather carrying case. I did not carry them on this trip although I have carried them on a number of trips of shorter duration. There were times on my hike when I would have liked to have had them; but all things considered, I think I made the right decision. If you are one of those who derive much pleasure from bird watching, then by all means carry binoculars and forego something else.

I carried only one book, the ATC guide book for whatever section of the Trail I was hiking. I carried a mountain of other paper in the form of daily log sheets, green calling cards, ATC literature, and writing materials. Some hikers carry a small version of the Bible. Others carry instructional type books for the identification of birds,

flowers, trees. If you are not in too much of a hurry, I would recommend carrying one or two such books; but again, be careful. Books
with slick paper run into weight. The two young ladies, Pat and Ann
(See Chapter 11) whom I met in April were carrying such instructional books. They were nice, but heavy. When I met them later, the
books were missing; they had been mailed home!

Another item which can provoke much discussion is a radio. Some
hikers carry one and maintain that it does much to relieve the
loneliness and that it is useful for getting weather reports. Other
hikers spurn the radio; they feel that the noise of radio and television is something they prefer to do without. I did not carry a radio.
As to the weather reports, the radio would have been of little
value as I generally walked each day, rain or shine. As to loneliness,
if you read Chapter 10, I think you will conclude that my days were
so full that I rarely had time to be lonely. Yet I concede that if one
is hiking alone for days at a time, loneliness can be a problem. Here
again—weight versus enjoyment.

I did carry a Taylor thermometer in a metal carrying case. After
all I was documenting conditions of the entire Trail—and weather
is certainly one condition of interest to a would-be hiker of the Trail.
I have carried this instrument for years, but it is definitely not necessary. I have never carried either an altimeter or a windmeter. I feel
that these two instruments are like the thermometer, really not
necessary.

I did carry a diary and wrote in it religiously. In Chapter 11, I have
quoted frequently from it. Much of the pleasure of an AT hike, in
addition to the actual hike, is in its planning and later in the reliving
of the experience. For this a diary is invaluable. While not necessary
to your survival, I definitely recommend a diary or daily journal.

And now we come to the last item in my "Not Necessary But
Nice" category, the Swiss Army Knife. Actually there is not one but
several models of the Swiss Army Knife. All models contain a knife
blade. The model you may wish to purchase will be governed by
how much money you wish to spend and how many tools and
gadgets you either feel are necessary or you are willing to carry.
Albert Field hiked the entire AT over a 12-year period and wrote
about his 12-year hike in the September 1969 issue of *Trailway
News*. Field mentioned that in his pack he carried a Swiss Army
Knife, that he often admired it, and seldom used it. Among my
assortment of hiking acquaintances are those who dismiss the Swiss

Army Knife as an unnecessary gadget and others who consider it a very essential part of their hiking equipment. I make no recommendation on this item except to comment that in my own backpacking I have found it adequate to carry only a simple two-bladed pocket knife.

I'd Pick More Daisies

By a Friar at the Graymoor Monastery in Garrison, NY

If I had my life to live over, I'd try to make more mistakes next time. I would relax. I would limber up. I would be sillier than I have been on this trip. I know of a very few things I would take seriously. I would be crazier. I would be less hygienic. I would take more chances. I would take more trips. I would climb more mountains, swim more rivers and watch more sunsets. I would burn more gasoline. I would eat more ice cream and less beans. I would have actual troubles and fewer imaginary ones. You see, I am one of those people who lives prophylactically and sensibly and sanely, hour after hour, day after day. Oh, I have had my moments and, if I had it to do over again, I'd have more of them. In fact, I'd try to have nothing else. Just moments, one after another, instead of living so many years ahead of each day. I have been one of those people who never go anywhere without a thermometer, a hot water bottle, a gargle, a raincoat and a parachute. If I had it to do over again, I would go places and do things and travel lighter than I have. If I had my life to live over, I would start barefooted earlier in the spring and stay that way later in the fall. I would play hooky more. I wouldn't make such good grades except by accident. I would ride on more merry-go-rounds. I'd pick more daisies.

9
Trail Etiquette

Let me begin this chapter on Trail Etiquette by relating an incident that occurred during the latter part of my hike. The date was Sunday, August 2, 1970; and the place was southern Vermont just north of Route 11. I was hiking northward with George Wright, a traveling troubador, who now sings professionally under the name "Peregrine." Approaching us from the north was a well dressed middle aged couple who, as it developed, had spent the day enjoying a pleasant summer outing in the mountains. As the couple drew near the lady said, "I hope you men are not planning on spending the night at Bromley Shelter." When we confessed that Bromley was exactly the point where we planned to spend the night, we were informed that the shelter (1) was inhabited by a bunch of hippies, (2) that it looked like a pigpen inside, and (3) that it looked as if a commune of some sort had been established there and had been in operation for weeks. The information was given us in a spirit of helpfulness, and George and I discussed it soberly as we trudged north to Bromley Shelter which is a scant mile north of Vermont Route 11.

Minutes later, when George and I arrived at the shelter, we had an opportunity to assess the facts more objectively. The three "hippies" were three young men, average age 20. The inside of the shelter had the usual array of camping gear, plus a broom, and a few implements of the shelter. It did *not* look like a pigpen. Since the three young men had arrived there that very day, any suggestion that they had been part of a week-long commune was a gross exaggeration. Now as to the appearance of the "hippies." One had not shaved for several days, a not unusual practice for those living in the out-of-doors. One had long hair and a drooping mustache. All were dressed in respectable looking hiking gear. Later that evening, when we became better acquainted, I related to the three the impression they had created upon the middle aged couple who had

136

stopped briefly at the shelter earlier in the day. It stung them a bit to think that others would form such impressions on the basis of such brief observation. I did notice that shaving became more frequent thereafter. I hiked with these three men, Craig Bumgarner, a University of Vermont student and Ken Lesenko and Jim Burdick of Saddle Brook, New Jersey, the rest of the week. These three plus George Wright formed one of the most pleasant groups with whom I have ever hiked. It was with real regret that I said goodbye to them the following Saturday night at the Long Trail Lodge in Sherburne Pass.

I have related this story a number of times because there are two important lessons that can be derived from it. First, the middle-aged couple should not have made the statements they did. They were based on hasty observation and an almost complete ignorance of the facts. I wonder how many times the story was repeated, first hand, second hand, third hand; and I wonder how much the story was embellished in the retelling. The second lesson to be learned is that appearances do count. First impressions frequently become lasting impressions.

In Chapter 7 on Clothing, I have already alluded to the desirability of wearing presentable looking clothing. The hiker can look presentable without sacrificing one iota of comfort. There is a segment of the hiking community whose clothes look as though they had been rescued from rag bags. Many of these people are impeccably attired in their day to day business activities. Yet they feel the need, when preparing for a camping or hiking trip, to seek out the most disreputable clothes they own as being most appropriate for an outing. I hiked an entire week with a well-to-do corporate executive whose clothes were so ragged that I felt they should be burned. Apparently I made my point because, on the last night of our trip, with a good fire burning, the clothes, after a sad farewell, were consigned to the fire.

If the Appalachian Trail were truly a wilderness trail where you could hike for 2,000 miles without coming into contact with civilization, then it would make little difference what kind of clothes you wore or how careless or uncouth you became in your personal appearance. Although Trail enthusiasts fondly allude to the Appalachian Trail as a wilderness trail, the plain facts are that there are scores and scores of places where the Trail hiker will come into contact with evidences of civilization; for example, ski resorts, rural and urban roads, homes, small towns, Boy and Girl Scout camps, etc.

Many of these people judge the Trail by the appearance of the people who use it. Furthermore, many people having homes on or near the Trail feel just plain uncomfortable when they see legions of rough-looking characters using the Trail and the trailside shelters. So much for personal appearance. Pay heed to it because it is important.

There are certain other aspects of our relations with those living along the Trail that deserve consideration. In 1965 the Bureau of Outdoor Recreation of the Department of Interior made a comprehensive survey of the Trail. They found that some 866 miles or 42 percent of the Trail was on private land. Much of this 866 miles is on wooded land; but a substantial amount of it is on pastures, private lanes, and through the yards of landowners. Be considerate of the fences you cross. Trail clubs maintaining the Trail over private land are urged to construct stiles both for the comfort and safety of the hiker and for protection of the fence. If the Trail takes you through a gate, be certain to close and fasten the gate if you found it that way upon your arrival. If the Trail takes you directly through or close by the yard of a private home, stop in to see the landowner. In most cases the Trail goes close to the private home because the landowner wants it there; he likes to know and visit with the hikers going over his land. Norm Greist, of North Haven, Connecticut, a long-time hiker of the Trail, relates the following incident. When he and his party were more or less tiptoeing through the yard of a New England landowner, the landowner spotted them, came out of his house, hailed them, and engaged them in conversation. The landowner was, as Norm described it "exacting his toll for the Trail going through his land . . . not demanding money but expecting some good old-fashioned visiting from the hikers." Where the landowner extends you courtesies in the form of food or drink, you can repay the courtesy by obtaining his name and address and by writing to him further along your hike . . . and by being certain to write him when you have completed your hike. Landowners, post offices, and small grocery stores treasure these communications from hikers. At any number of places where I stopped along the route, letters and picture cards would be proudly produced from hikers who had hiked through there in previous years. Through-hikers who had been especially considerate in this regard were the Ebersoles, Elmer Onstott, Howie Bassett, and Everett and Nell Skinner.

Many of these landowners have an affection for hikers that is heartwarming, indeed. I think of Mrs. Latta Shelton near Devils Fork Gap in North Carolina with whom I visited on April 28, 1970, a rainy day. Mrs. Shelton produced a scrap book in which she had posted letters, cards, and newspaper articles of her own observations on many of the through-hikers who had stopped in to see her. One such clipping was a picture of Grandma Gatewood cutting her 83rd birthday cake in the spring of 1970. I think of the Pink Winters family near Roan Mountain, Tennessee (watch out for their two big black dogs!) who invited me into their house for a home-cooked meal. And of the J. L. Hodges family near Catawba, Virginia, who treated me to a Sunday dinner. And of Mrs. Fred Hutchinson at Washington Town Hall, Massachusetts, whose very old and very interesting home was once a way station for those traveling by stage coach on the old Boston-Albany Post Road. Mrs. Hutchinson and her deceased husband have befriended Trail hikers for 40 years. I could go on and on, naming people and incidents. Whether he knows it or not, the hiker has ever so many friends along the 2,000-mile-long Trail.

On the Trail itself, away from homes, roads, and stores, there is a certain code of ethics which the hiker is expected to observe. One aspect of the code relates to litter. The hiker will see signs reading: "Pack it in . . . Pack it out" or "Take nothing but pictures . . . leave nothing but footprints." Carry a supply of litter bags. Even though you may see piles of trash at a shelter or even a covered garbage dump do not use them. Carry out everything you bring in. Don't bury anything! Be able to say at the end of your 2,000-mile hike that you did not leave a single item of trash at any point along the entire 2,000-mile Trail. And, if you have the strength and determination to do it, you are urged to pick up *any* litter you find on the Trail and dispose of it at any suitable trash receptacle point such as a highway litter barrel, picnic area or Forest Service Recreation Area.

A second aspect of the code relates to fires and firewood. Keep cooking fires small. Also keep after-dinner, companionship-type fires small. This conserves wood and reduces the chance of a fire getting out of control. In private property areas landowners become uneasy when hikers build unnecessarily large fires. When the woods are tinder-dry, do not build any fires. Use gasoline stoves, or eat food that requires no cooking. At shelters always try to leave a supply of firewood for the next party. Be certain that in the supply you leave there is an ample amount of small twigs and tinder to get a fire started. You should follow this rule even though you are using nothing but a gasoline stove for your own cooking.

A third aspect of the code relates to the need for leaving instructions at trailside shelters and at other points for fellow hikers. If you have located a difficult-to-find water source near a shelter, leave a note in the shelter as to the exact location of the water source. If there is a gap in the shelter chain, and if you have been fortunate to find satisfactory lodging elsewhere, leave a note at the next shelter to inform fellow hikers of the point where you obtained lodging. If you have passed a home with a particularly vicious dog, leave a note so fellow hikers will be forewarned. A number of the shelters are located at some distance from the Trail, and a few of these are marked with neither a sign nor blue blazes to indicate their presence. If you encounter situations like this, leave a note on a tree beside the Trail so that ensuing hikers will be alerted to the existence of and directions to the unsigned shelter. A quantity of 3 x 5-inch white cards and few thumb tacks will serve admirably for this purpose. If your notes are to be left in spots exposed to the weather, do your writing with a soft lead pencil rather than with a pen.

On my own hike I did leave a number of such notes. In reflecting back on my entire trip, however, I realize that there are many more points at which I should have left an informative note of some sort. Nevertheless, one of the few notes I did leave certainly bore fruit as the following letter received just before Christmas 1970 witnessed.

December 15, 1970

Mr. Edward B. Garvey
c/o Appalachian Trail Conference
1718 N Street, N.W.
Washington, D.C. 20036

Mr. Garvey,

I've put off writing this letter of thanks long enough.

Last summer I and one of my friends started out hiking across Iron Mountain, beginning at Watauga Dam (near Elizabethton, Tenn.). We found the water scarce, or polluted, or almost dry. We had no maps of the trail. We simply put on our packs and took off, rather blindly, with one canteen of water each. The temperature was 93 F. We had walked about 6 miles, having a rough walk because the trail was overgrown (around June 15). We aren't exactly used to hiking so far). We were getting desperate for water as we had used up our

1-quart canteens in a hurry because of the heat. At one of the shelters about halfway between Watauga Dam and Shady Valley, Tenn., we discovered one of your cards with directions to water about 700 yards below the shelter. Your card saved us a great hardship. It was nearly 10 miles out of there and that water hole carried us through.

The enclosed card came from one of the other shelters. I left your card and directions on the shelter for someone else. Once again I thank you and wish you a Merry Christmas.

> Wallace G. Wright
> Route 10 Kodak Heights
> Kingsport, Tenn. 37664

The above letter expresses, more eloquently than anything I have said or written, the need for clear identification of all sources of water along the Trail. Secondly, I was pleased that the simple directional information I had written on one of my 3 x 5 green cards had proven so helpful to a fellow hiker. The shelter to which Mr. Wright refers is Vandeventer Shelter. The water is far distant from the shelter; there are no directional signs and the blue blazes are inadequate.

The first pages of this chapter on Trail Etiquette are repeated exactly as they were written in the first writing of this book. The following comments are written to reflect the state of affairs as they exist in 1977.

It sounds somewhat paradoxical, but, the most gratifying and yet the most disappointing aspect of my 2,000-mile hike was my effort to improve the litter situation. I started out my hike with a goal of picking up all litter on the Trail for the entire 2,000 miles. With very few exceptions I stuck to my litter pickup for every day of the hike. In a few situations I would find my litter bag completely full with no place to deposit the litter but these were the exceptions. On page 144 is a picture taken of me with a full litter bag. I was unaware of the existence of this picture until April 1976 when viewing a slide show in Charleston, West Virginia. The photographer, Bob Tabor, graciously furnished me with his color slide. The picture is one of the very few that illustrates one of the most strenuous aspects of my hike. The newspaper writers and photographers I met seemed particularly anxious *not* to have the litter bag in evidence. There seems to be feeling among both hiking clubs and the general population that there is something pure, noble, and adventuresome about long-distance hiking but that the act of picking up litter, especially some-body else's litter, is a degrading activity that is reserved for a less privileged class of society than the noble hiker. And this attitude must have been observed by the person who contributed a one-sentence paragraph in a monthly letter to constituents sent out by former Congressman Gilbert Gude of Maryland in 1973 (circa). Here is the sentence:

> It is easier for most people to organize a conference on clean up of the environment than it is to stoop over and pick up one gum wrapper!

Why did I persist in that back-breaking litter-pickup project? To set an example. I reasoned that if a not-so-young man with a 35-45-lb. pack on his back could pick up litter for 2,000 miles, then surely the hiking clubs would make it a practice to regularly provide and use litter bags on all of their weekend hikes. To the best of my knowledge it has not worked out that way. I am very cynical of those clubs that devote time and money to develop slogans, prepare placards, and have thousands of copies of literature printed, all relat-ing to the need for a clean environment, and who fail to provide and use litter bags on their weekend hikes.

If my litter campaign failed to impress the hiking club organiza-tions, it did impress individuals. Like a letter from Kim Hastings, a Dartmouth College student who told me of her litter-pickup activities on her frequent hikes. Or the letter from Sam Waddle of Chuckey, Tennessee, who, having read my description of the filthy condition of Jerry's Cabin leanto, has made regular trips there to clean it up, and who sent me a picture to prove the point. And a letter from Jim Shanahorn of Columbus, Ohio, who writes of his deep concern about the litter problem and then relates what he is doing as an individual to alleviate the problem.

We are making progress. Hiking with Ed Hanlon and Bill Husic for 9 days on the AT in North Carolina and Georgia in April 1976, we kept a tally on pieces of litter picked up and number of hikers encountered. There were six times as many hikers on the Trail in 1976 than there were in 1970 and *only half as much litter.* I am con-vinced that a much higher percentage of backpackers is carrying out litter in 1977 than was the case in 1970. Our job now is to convince some of these individuals that they should carry out not just their own litter, but at least some of that left on the Trail or at shelters by their less-thoughtful fellow hikers.

I do not wish to leave the litter subject without recognizing the activities of some of the clubs who do acknowledge the problem. The New York-New Jersey Trail Conference annually conducts a well-publicized well-organized campaign to remove all litter from all shelters under their jurisdiction. Dump trucks are arranged for and the participation of many individuals and organizations is obtained. Litter—almost by the cubic acre—is removed each year. The Green Mountain Club of Vermont has an ongoing program with trash collection receptacles provided at reasonable intervals and signs erected at shelters indicating where these receptacles can be found. The US Forest Service in the Chattahoochie National Forest in Georgia has placed animal-proof trash receptacles at strategic points along the Trail, and has erected signs informing hikers of the precise mileage in either direction at which the trash receptacles are located. I am sure other clubs are likewise engaged in similar activities. I have described only those whose programs have come to my attention.

Litterbugs do not enjoy an enviable reputation in any country. In 1972 two Russian correspondents traveled the length and breadth of the US visiting our parks and forests in particular and writing a series of articles which were printed in Russian (and later in US) newspapers. They were very interested in the Appalachian Trail and the State Department arranged for them to walk on part of it in the Shenandoah National Park and later to meet with me at the downtown Washington, D.C. headquarters of the Potomac Appalachian Trail Club. One of the two, Vasily Peskov, a noted writer of outdoor books, is an avid outdoorsman and dedicated conservationist. I showed slides of my AT hike, answered many questions about the role of the hiking clubs in the Appalachian Trail program, and then served them the standard Garvey PATC lunch . . . grilled cheese sandwiches washed down with wine, followed by ice cream and coffee. One year later it was Peskov's turn to be the host during my six-week tour in Moscow participating in the Outdoor Recreation Exhibit. On a beautiful June day he took Roy Feuchter of the US Forest Service and me on a hike through the huge green belt that surrounds Moscow, an area so vast that all of the city's seven million people could visit it at one time without getting in each other's hair. We walked through miles of spotlessly clean wooded areas, clean that is except at one point where a large sign requested people not to litter. Beside the sign were the remains of a discarded broken bicycle and about two bushels of other household trash. I

Ed Garvey on Bear Mountain carrying well-filled litter bag.

can still see Peskov standing there, hands on hips, viewing that mess. Finally he barked out something in Russian and walked away disgustedly. The interpreter looked at me, grinned, and explained "Mr. Peskov just said two things in Russian which in English translate out to 'Bastard' and 'Son-of-a-bitch'!"

Now, having described the litter problem and our mutual disgust with litterbugs, we will discuss a few other problems of Trail manners—subjects which both managers and hikers have suggested I include.

As described in Chapter 7, the lug soles and cleats of the heavy hiking boots damage both the trail and the vegetative cover. Upon reaching your destination for the day, whether it be shelter or camp site, you are urged to remove hiking boots and wear some type of soft-soled footwear around camp. This will give your feet a much-needed rest, and will lessen damage to the camp area.

The old-time practice of cutting balsam boughs for a bed is now verboten—just as is the former practice of digging trenches to divert water from your tent. One reader took me to task for cutting balsam boughs—a practice in which I do not engage or condone.

The long-distance backpacker hiking from Georgia to Maine has a heavy responsibility for exemplary conduct. The example he sets in his meetings with others along the Trail—especially young hikers—is tremendous. Some of the long-distance hikers, upon reaching the AMC huts in New Hampshire, seem to expect certain privileges which they have no right to expect. Granted that hiking from Georgia to Maine for 2,000 miles is a significant feat, the fact remains that the hut boys and hut managers in the huts have seen scores of 2,000-Milers and they are not inclined to get down on their knees and pay homage to each would-be 2,000-Miler who enters the doors of the hut. So act accordingly and do not expect to receive privileges not accorded to the other guests. Most long-distance backpackers reach the White Mountains during August which is the busiest time of the year for the huts. Be sure to make reservations through AMC's Pinkham Notch hut (by mail: Gorham, NH 03581; by phone: Reservations (603) 466-2727; other business (603) 466-2721).

Purple rhododendron at Roan Mountain, North Carolina. (Photo: U.S. Forest Service)

10
The Sixteen Sections of the Trail

The 2,000 miles of the Appalachian Trail may be conveniently divided into sixteen easily identifiable sections. As I hiked during the first days of April, I began sorting out these sections in my mind. Some of the dividing lines are state boundary lines, some are physical features such as a major river (Nantahala, James, Potomac, Delaware, Connecticut), and some are national parks such as the Great Smoky Mountain and the Shenandoah. I had originally considered only fifteen such sections; but, for reasons which I shall explain later, I found it necessary to divide the 79-mile stretch from the Georgia-North Carolina line to the Smokies into two sections. As I finished hiking each of these sections, mentally I ticked it off; each was one more hurdle completed. In the following paragraphs I describe the boundaries of each of the sixteen sections, provide information on the overnight shelter for each section, and describe briefly the type of terrain over which the hiker will hike.

1. *Northern Georgia, Chattahoochee National Forest (78 miles).* This section begins at Springer Mountain and ends at Bly Gap on the Georgia-North Carolina line. There are 10 of the typical trail-side shelters in this 78 mile stretch plus a stone structure atop Blood Mountain, a covered picnic pavillion at Lake Winfield Scott (off the Trail), and several good campsites. The Trail in Georgia is entirely within the Chattahoochee National Forest. State highways are crossed five times. From these points a hiker can hike or hitch a ride to a grocery store, post office, or town. Other than for highway crossings, the hiker walks through a wilderness area of high mountains and hardwood forests. Elevations range generally from 3,000 to 4,400 feet. Wild flowers and flowering woody plants (azalea, mountain laurel, rhododendron) abound.

2. *North Carolina, Nantahala National Forest (79 miles).* This section begins at Bly Gap on the Georgia-North Carolina line and extends to the Nantahala River at Wesser, North Carolina. There are

seven trailside shelters in the 54 miles. This 54 mile stretch is especially beautiful; it includes Standing Indian Mountain (5,498 feet), well-graded trails, magnificent stands of rhododendron, excellent water, and spectacular views. Well-graded trails take the hiker over the top of the most prominent mountains and balds; they skirt the less prominent ones. A side trail near Wallace Gap leads one-half mile to the largest known specimen of Yellow Poplar in the United States (discovered by Forest Service Ranger Duke Barr at Franklin, North Carolina). At chest height, this tree is 98 inches in diameter. The entire length of this 54 miles of the Trail is within the Nantahala National Forest, a particularly fascinating area of the Trail to which I would like to return.

3. *North Carolina, Stekoah Region (27 miles).* This section begins at the Nantahala River at Wesser, North Carolina, and extends to the Little Tennessee River (Fontana Dam, North Bank). There are two trailside shelters in the 27 miles. It, too, is within the Nantahala National Forest; but in its trail design and other aspects seems so different from the previous 54 miles that it merits designation as a separate Trail section. It begins at an elevation of 1,700 feet at Wesser, North Carolina, and in 2.7 miles attains an elevation of 3,050 feet. In another 4.3 miles it attains an elevation of over 5,000 feet going straight up and straight down several knobs and balds in between. Whereas the 54 miles of the Trail south of the Nantahala River are pleasantly graded, the Trail in this 27-mile stretch is brutally steep. There are some spectacular views from the rim of the Nantahala Gorge and from the summit of Cheoah Bald. For those who have hiked the entire Trail, it is a tossup as to which area of the Trail is the most strenuous to traverse: the Stekoah region or the Mahoosucs in Maine. My vote goes unhesitatingly to the Stekoahs.

4. *Great Smoky Mountain National Park (70 miles).* This section begins at the Little Tennessee River (Fontana Dam, North Bank) and extends to the Big Pigeon River. There are 15 trailside shelters in the 70-mile stretch. It is impossible even to begin to describe the beauty and grandeur of the Smokies. The guide book provides an extensive, but admittedly incomplete, bibliography of the books, articles, and publications relating to this region. One recent book on the Smokies that I have found especially fascinating is Michael Frome's *Strangers in High Places, The Story of the Great Smoky Mountains* (Doubleday & Co., Inc.), 1966. I have two principal regrets with respect to my hike through the Smokies: (1) that I hiked

through them so fast (four and one-half days) and (2) that I hiked through them so early in the spring. At the 4,000 to 6,600 foot elevations which the Trail traverses, I was too early to enjoy the full spring beauty. A fascinating one day side trip in the Smokies is the 5 mile hike to LeConte Lodge atop 6,350 foot Mt. LeConte. Permits are required for overnight stays in Park.

5. *Tennessee-North Carolina (196 miles).* This section begins at the Big Pigeon River and extends to the Tennessee-Virginia boundary line near Damascus, Virginia. There are 18 trailside shelters in this 192 miles. The hiker literally straddles the Tennessee-North Carolina state line for most of the 192 miles. He finds himself in the Pisgah National Forest while in North Carolina and in the Cherokee National Forest in Tennessee. The shelters in the Cherokee are distinctive in that they are constructed of cinder block and painted inside and out either a light green or a light tan. The roof extends five feet beyond the front of the shelter and underneath this overhang there is a very clever metal firebox set in concrete that makes for an excellent cooking arrangement. In this section, as in the Smokies, the hiker will sleep on wire bunks. If I were to use one expression to describe this section of the Trail, I would call it "big bald country." There are a succession of towering mountain tops ranging in elevation from 4,500 to 6,000 feet referred to inconsistently as "knobs," "balds," or the more common "mountain" but devoid of trees. Vegetative cover is grass, or grass and woody plants, such as laurel and rhododendron. The hiker can see the Trail clearly winding its way up to the top of each knob or bald, and has the feeling of being on top of the world as he reaches the summit of each and can look out upon other mountain tops for miles in every direction. For me it was a big, big day (May 6, 1970) when I reached the end of this section at the Tennessee-Virginia boundary. At this point I had over one-fourth of the Trail behind me. I was now in my home state of Virginia; and for the next 700 miles I would be hiking on sections of the Trail that, with a few minor exceptions, I had hiked one or more times on previous occasions.

6. *Southwestern Virginia, Jefferson National Forest (240 miles).* This section begins at the Tennessee-Virginia boundary line near Damascus, Virginia and extends to the James River. Approximately 150 miles of the Trail is on Forest Service property, the remaining 90 miles being either on private land, on rural roads, or on lands administered by the Blue Ridge Parkway. There are 25 trailside shel-

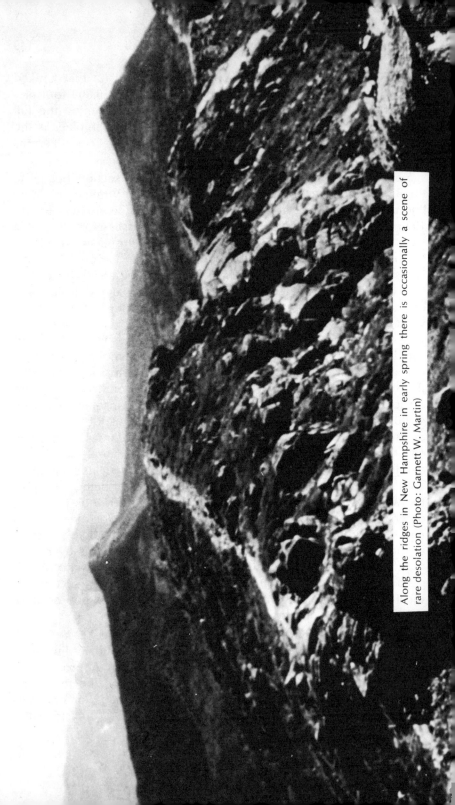

Along the ridges in New Hampshire in early spring there is occasionally a scene of rare desolation (Photo: Garnett W. Martin)

ters. This is a delightful 240 mile section of the Trail, and the 1971 Mt. Rogers relocation made it even more attractive. The shelters in this area are uniformly equipped with tables, toilets, and fireplaces. The shelters and environs are particularly well maintained by employees of the Jefferson National Forest. North of Roanoke, the Trail comes into close proximity with the Blue Ridge Parkway and crosses the Parkway in a few places. Except for White Top Mountain (5,344 feet) and Mt. Rogers (5,729 feet), the Trail is generally in the 2,500 foot to 4,500 foot elevation. At Apple Orchard Mountain the Trail attains an elevation of 4,244 feet, an elevation which is not again attained until the hiker reaches Mt. Killington in Vermont. There are tremendous rhododendron displays in this section in late May and early June.

7. *Southwestern Virginia, George Washington National Forest (69 miles)*. This section begins at the James River and extends to Rockfish Gap (US Route 250). There are seven trailside shelters. It is 27 miles from the last shelter in this section (Maupin Field) to the first shelter (Sawmill Run) in the Shenandoah National Park. This is a rugged and beautiful 78 mile stretch. It is marked by a series of mountains in the 3,500-4,100 foot elevation range, divided by river gorges. The hiker begins at the James River (elevation 750 feet) and climbs within a few miles to 3,550 feet. Further north the hiker descends into the Tye River Gap (elevation 900 feet) and begins a strenuous 3,000 foot climb to the summit of Three Ridges.

8. *Shenandoah National Park (104 miles)*. This section begins at Rockfish Gap (US Route 250) and extends to Chester Gap (US Route 522). Only about 94 miles of the Trail lie within the boundary of the park. The famed Skyline Drive extends along the crest of the Blue Ridge Mountains, and the Drive and the Trail intersect at 25 points in this 104 mile stretch. The 94 miles of the Trail within the Park are, in my opinion, the best designed, the best constructed, and the best maintained of any comparable area in the entire Trail distance. The Trail grades are so regular and the footway is so free of rocks and other protuberances that Park Service employees are able to mow the Trail regularly to a four foot width with gasoline powered mowers. There are 16 trailside shelters plus a number of developed camp grounds, campsites, and locked cabins. Permits are required for overnight stays. Hikers may *not* stay in shelters overnight. If the hiker's schedule permits he would do well to allow a few extra days to examine some of the many side trails within the Park

LOG FOR EDWARD B. GARVEY

1. Date _Tues., Sept. 29, 1970_   2. Log No. _154_
3. Travel From _____Chairback Gap Shelter_____
   To _____White Brook Shelter_____

   Beginning _9:00_ a.m.   Finishing _2:45_ p.m.

4. Number of Miles Hiked
   (a) By Trail _10.4_   (b) Other _.4_
   (c) Cum. Miles by Trail _1941.1_   (d) Other _149.5_
5. Weather _40°-6am; 50!-4pm & Cloudy   Alt. Clear   Brief rain at 4pm_
6. Food _bread, Cit.Spread, Fruit Cake.   B: hot oatmeal, Citadel Spread, bread, coffee. L: Cheese, S: hot soup, Appal. Trail Mix, Spam, hot choc. inst. pudding, coffee, popcorn._
7. Condition of Trail _Footway generally very good; 8 to 10 blowdowns; Blazing generally very good; identification_
   Section No _of blue blaze trails is excellent; sign work_
   Section No. _is excellent; frequent use of metal markers._

8. Shelter and Bed _Wood sapling floor at White Brook Shelter_
9. People _none_
10. Plants _Impressed with tremendous acreage of wild raspberries_
11. Money Spent _none_
12. Lean-Tos Inspected (see reverse)
    Section No. _____ Lean-To Name _White Brook_
    Section No. _____ Lean-To Name _____
    Section No. _____ Lean-To Name _____
13. Incidents _Impressed with grove of virgin white pine .15 miles off Trail at Hermitage.   Now owned by Nature Conservancy_
14. Trash Pick Up _3 pieces litter.   Am discontinuing litter pickup in Maine.   Too clean!_
    Noted two broken wood signs on ground .03 miles north of Chairback Gap Shelter.

Garvey's Daily Logs.

1. Name of Lean-To _White Brook_   *15' x 15' log structure; 6"-8" logs; aluminum roof*

2. Capacity_____ 3. Sleeping Facilities _sapling floor_ ~~wood~~

4. Guide Book Description _o.k._

5. Location of Water Supply _From stream 60 yds. South of A.T._

6. Fireplace _no_ _Yes, 30" x 60", pretty old._ 7. Toilet _no_

8. Table _____ _dump, 20 yards in rear of shelter_   _5 bushel open trash_

9. General Condition _Very Good. Area very clean. Limitless supply of firewood_

10. Date Inspected _9-27-70_ 11. By _/s./ E. B. Garvey_

---

1. Name of Lean-To _____

2. Capacity_____ 3. Sleeping Facilities _____

4. Guide Book Description _____

5. Location of Water Supply_____

6. Fireplace_____ 7. Toilet _____

8. Table _____

9. General Condition _____

_____

10. Date Inspected _____ 11. By_____

---

1. Name of Lean-To _____

2. Capacity_____ 3. Sleeping Facilities _____

4. Guide Book Description _____

5. Location of Water Supply _____

6. Fireplace _____ 7. Toilet _____

8. Table _____

9. General Condition _____

_____

10. Date Inspected _____ 11. By _____

(See *Circuit Hikes in the Shenandoah National Park*, published by the Potomac Appalachian Trail Club). During the warmer months of the year, the hiker will find camp stores, hot showers, snack bars, and dining rooms available. Some hikers will find the frequent automobile crossings (one crossing every four miles on the average) to be rather annoying. Except for this, most hikers agree that the Shenandoah National Park furnishes one of the most delightful sections of the Trail.

9. *Northern Virginia (48 miles)*. This section begins at Chester Gap (US Route 522) and extends to the Potomac River (Virginia-Maryland State line). There are four trailside shelters in this 51 mile stretch. Landowners in this area, fearful of the effects of the National Trails System Act, Public Law 90-543, have been serving legal notices for removal of the Trail from the private property involved. Each such notice forces the Trail out onto the road and in some cases makes a trailside shelter off limits to the hiker. In February 1971, the Commonwealth of Virginia enacted its own version of an Appalachian Trail law and is taking steps to acquire rights of way for the Trail in Northern Virginia. Until that goal is achieved the hiker must resign himself to road walking for much of the distance in this 48-mile section. The end of this section (Potomac River Gorge) provides some of the most spectacular views of the entire Trail. These are the views from several points on Loudoun Heights of the confluence of the Shenandoah and Potomac Rivers and of the historic town of Harpers Ferry. Harpers Ferry, now restored as a National Park Monument, is well worth the side trip of approximately one mile.

10. *Maryland (37 miles)*. This section begins at the Potomac River (Virgina-Maryland State line) and extends to Pen-Mar on the Pennsylvania-Maryland State line. There are six trailside shelters in this section. A sixth shelter (Wolfe Shelter) was closed by landowner action in 1970. This section begins at the Potomac River, and it is a steep climb from there to Weverton Cliffs. Once the elevation at Weverton Cliffs has been obtained, it is pleasant hiking all the way to the end of the section.

11. *Pennsylvania (223 miles)*. This section begins at Pen-Mar on the Maryland-Pennsylvania State line and extends to the Delaware Water Gap. There are 21 trailside shelters in Pennsylvania, plus a number of campgrounds and campsites. The Trail seldom attains an

elevation higher than 1,500 feet, but the Trail is so rocky through most of the State that it is rough on shoes and feet. The shelter situation east of the Susquehanna River is not too good, and springs have a tendency to go dry early in July. There are some lengthy gaps (25-30 miles) between shelters, thus requiring a tent or use of nearby motels. The 15-mile St. Anthony's Wilderness in the middle of the State is one of the most interesting 15-mile stretches on the entire Trail. The mountain ridge east of the Susquehanna is narrow, and the hiker frequently obtains excellent views to either side of the ridge. As the hiker in Virgina enjoys the spectacular Potomac River Gorge at the end of the Trail in that State, so does the hiker in Pennsylvania enjoy an equally spectacular view as he nears the end of the Trail in that State. The view of the Delaware Water Gap which separates Pennsylvania and New Jersey is truly outstanding, and the hiker is urged to tarry a bit and enjoy the view.

12. *New Jersey-New York (159 miles).* This section begins at the Delaware Water Gap and extends to the New York-Connecticut State line. There are 10 trailside shelters in this section. Beginning in New Jersey and extending all the way to Maine, the hiker will now find the Trail route dotted with lakes and ponds. From the Delaware Water Gap to the Hudson River, the Trail receives extremely heavy use during the summer months. Beyond the Hudson much of the Trail is on rural roads, through the rock-walled fields of former farms, and through or near small villages and Boy and Girl Scout Camps. The Trail in these two States seldom attains an elevation exceeding 1,500 feet. During the summer months mosquitoes and tiny black flies are a menace. In the Harriman State Park area the hiker will walk over the first six miles of the Appalachian Trail which was established and marked in 1923 by the now familiar AT metal markers. In the Harriman and Bear Mountain State Parks the hiker will, moreover, encounter a system of trails that were established even before the Appalachian Trail. Some of these run concurrently with the AT and the hiker will become accustomed to various color combinations used to identify this extensive network of trails: blue dots, red dots, white dots, etc. It does make for variety!

13. *Connecticut-Massachusetts (139 miles).* This section begins at the New York-Connecticut State line and extends to the Massachusetts-Vermont State line. There are 13 trailside shelters and one campground. Five of the shelters are located on the 56 miles of the Trail in Connecticut; four shelters in the 84 miles of the Trail in

View of the Shenandoah River near Harpers Ferry. (Photo: Steve Wagner)

Massachusetts. Trail elevations begin to rise in these two States; they reach 2,316 feet at Bear Mountain in Connecticut and 3,491 feet at Mt. Greylock, Massachusetts, the highest point in that State. Although the Trail does not attain high elevations in Connecticut, the hiker will experience some strenuous ups and downs. The Trail in Connecticut sticks largely to the wooded mountainous areas in the western part of the State. Surprisingly beautiful views of the rural countryside abound along the Trail. In Massachusetts, much of the Trail is on roads; but Trail officials in that State are making determined efforts to move much of the Trail off the roads and to develop a more continuous chain of trailside shelters.

14. *Vermont (134 miles).* This section begins at the Massachusetts-Vermont State line and extends to the Connecticut River. There are 32 trailside shelters in this 134 mile section, 28 of them occurring the first 95 miles. This is the most dense concentration of shelters anywhere on the entire Trail. The Trail goes through the Green Mountain National Forest for the first 73 miles. For the first 95 miles, the Appalachian Trail and Vermont's famous Long Trail coincide; the two trails diverge one-half mile north of Sherburne Pass (US Route 4). From this point the Trail changes its course from almost due north to almost due east as it crosses the Connecticut River Valley on its way to Hanover, New Hampshire. At Killington Peak (4,241 feet) the Trail attains its highest elevation since crossing Apple Orchard Mountain in Virginia. The Green Mountain Club, which maintains both the Long Trail (extending to the Canadian Border) and the Appalachian Trail, is a prolific building organization and the hiker will encounter a variety of different type trailside shelters. Not only will he find the conventional three-sided shelters but also a number of four-sided closed shelters equipped with inside tables. In its first 95 miles the Trail is routed near and around several delightful ponds and lakes. The Trail is heavily used from the Massachusetts-Vermont line to Sherburne Pass, less heavily used from there to the Connecticut River. The last 40 miles of the Trail require much exertion as they go through a number of extensive forested areas and a succession of high ridges, cleared slopes, and abandoned farms.

15. *New Hampshire (148 miles).* This section begins at the Connecticut River and extends to the New Hampshire-Maine State line. It has 13 trailside shelters plus 8 of the Appalachian Mountain Club "huts" which provide food and lodging during the summer months.

Garvey alongside Nesowadnehunk Stream on the day before he completed his hike on Katahdin. (Photo: Tex Griffin)

Approximately 100 miles of this section lie within the boundary of the White Mountain National Forest. Here, as in the Great Smokies further south, the hiker will be hiking at very high elevations, generally above 4,000 feet, frequently above 5,000 feet, and to an elevation of 6,288 feet in crossing the summit of Mt. Washington. The area within the White Mountains bears another distinction. Much of it is above tree line, and it is subject to sudden and violent changes in weather. The occasional white wooden crosses the hiker encounters bear mute testimony to the points where other hikers have perished, some of them during the summer months. This has a most sobering effect on the hiker. The hiker is urged not to hike in these higher elevations during bad weather, and he should so plan his hiking that he is certain of reaching a shelter well before darkness sets in.

Aside from the danger involved, this is a spectacularly beautiful section of the Trail. On clear days, when above tree line, the hiker can see for miles in every direction. The views offered are some of the most magnificent in all New England. All of the Trail in New Hampshire, but especially that within the White Mountains, is very heavily used by hikers during the summer months. The few trailside shelters are frequently fully occupied, and hikers are urged to carry tents or tarps for emergency shelter. Hikers who plan to use the accommodations at the eight AMC huts should make prior arrangements with the Appalachian Mountain Club, Pinkham Notch Camp, Gorham, New Hampshire 03851.

16. *Maine (278 miles)*. This section extends from the New Hampshire-Maine State line to the northern terminal of the Appalachian Trail atop Baxter Peak on Katahdin. There are 32 trailside shelters in this section plus campgrounds, campsites, and Maine sporting camps. At the latter, meals and lodging can be obtained by prior arrangement. Maine has a little bit of everything. It has rugged mountains, the formidable Mahoosuc Mountain range and the almost incredible Mahoosuc Notch, a deep narrow gorge, 0.9 miles long, filled with huge boulders and surrounded by high cliffs. The Trail in Maine takes the hiker past an unending succession of beautiful lakes, ponds, and springs with ice cold water. Maine is wilderness, and the hiker can go for days without seeing a soul. It is the domain of the moose, and the hiker will see frequent signs of this animal on the Trail. The Trail is extremely well marked in Maine; and the shelters, since they do not receive the heavy use they do in

other sections, are particularly attractive. Maine is the only State on the Trail where the hiker comes to the edge of a large river (the Kennebec) with no bridge available on which to cross. Fifty miles from the end of this section, the hiker obtains his first view of mighty Katahdin and suddenly realizes with both gladness and sadness that his 2,000 mile hike is almost over. Five miles from the end of the Trail, the hiker will reach Katahdin Stream Campground. The hiker who appreciates a magnificent mountain and spectacular views will tarry at Katahdin Stream Campground until he is assured of a clear day for the final climb. The hiker who reaches the summit of Baxter Peak on a clear day and who surveys the lesser mountain peaks and the lakes dotting the landscape for miles in every direction will enthusiastically agree that Katahdin is indeed a fitting point to mark the northern terminal of the Appalachian Trail.

OFFICIAL ROUTE OF THE TRAIL KEEPS CHANGING!

The National Trails System Act (Public Law 90-543) was enacted on October 2, 1968. Among other things, it directed the Secretary of Interior to establish the official route of the Appalachian Trail and to publish the route in the *Federal Register*. Three years later, on October 9, 1971, in some 86 pages of maps and narrative description, the official route was established and published. As of May 1977, there had been 254 official changes in the Trail route. Authority for this information is Col. Lester L. Holmes, the retired Executive Director of the Conference. Col. Holmes, as a volunteer, has completed the time-consuming task of writing up new trail descriptions and developing maps so that the records of the National Park Service, the *Federal Register*, and the records of the Appalachian Trail Conference reflect the trail route changes.

Sign at southern terminus of Appalachian Trail. (Photo: Garnett W. Martin)

11
My Hike: Day by Day Along the Trail

During the course of my hike, I walked 2,028 miles on the Appalachian Trail and another 157 miles to shelters, springs, small towns, and other points off the Trail. Under such circumstances one is almost certain to have a number of interesting experiences, and I felt that I had my share. Each day was a new experience . . . different scenery, different vegetation, different people (when I chanced to meet people!), and each night a different place in which to sleep. In recounting my experiences, I am now most thankful that I do have complete and copious notes on each day's activities. I had committed myself on this hike to an ambitious schedule of trail and shelter inspection and documentation of the same. The voluminous note-keeping became a chore at times; but I stuck to it religiously, writing up to my notes wherever and whenever I had a few minutes to spare. Much of my documentation was done on 5½ inch by 8½ inch printed forms. The front of the form provided space for showing condition of the Trail, weather, miles hiked etc. The reverse of the form provided space for detailed information on each of the 238 trailside shelters I inspected. I completed these forms with ballpoint pen. The sample log reproduced is typewritten for easier reading. In addition to the printed daily log form I kept a daily diary in a 4-inch by 6-inch bound book. I used two such books during the entire hike and devoted one or two pages for writing up each day's activities. Frequently, the material in my diary—written as events took place—is more accurate, more spontaneous, and more colorful than any words I can call to mind as I write this book. Therefore, throughout this chapter, I have quoted verbatim sentences, paragraphs, and at times almost whole pages from my diary. Whenever you find quoted material you may assume it is from my diary.

In Chapter 10, I provided a brief description of 16 different sections of the Trail. For consistency I have described my day-to-day experiences using this same 16-section Trail frame.

1. GEORGIA, APRIL 3 TO APRIL 11, 1970

On April 3, 1970. My wife Mary, my 11 year old son Kevin, and I arrived in Gainesville, Georgia at the tail end of an Easter-week vacation to the Florida Everglades. I spent an hour and a half after lunch visiting with employees of the US Forest Service Office. Gainesville is the headquarters for the Chattahoochee National Forest. Among other things, I made arrangements to meet with a small group later in the week. The Forest Service had already made plans to develop a five or six mile section of a model foot trail and to build one shelter which would incorporate the best ideas of present day thinking on trailside shelters. They planned to build this model trail on that part of the Appalachian Trail between Tray Mountain shelter and the Addis Gap shelter. They wished to hike that particular section of Trail with me so that we could exchange ideas. This was the first of many meetings or encounters with personnel of the US Forest Service—beginning in Georgia and extending as far north as the White Mountain National Forest in New Hampshire. The Trail goes through eight national forests in all; and during the course of my hike, I was to meet Forest Service personnel in many places. There were people from the regional office in Atlanta, from supervisor offices in four of the eight forests visited, district ranger personnel, and many construction, maintenance, and custodial personnel whom I chanced to meet on or near the Trail. Almost without exception, these employees proved to be competent, courteous, and dedicated to their jobs. At the conclusion of my hike I had formed the firm conviction that our national forests, yours and mine, are in good hands.

From Gainesville, my family and I drove to nearby Amicalola Falls State Park where Bob Harrell, a reporter from the Atlanta Constitution, was waiting for me. I talked to him about an hour; I discussed the plans for my hike, the things I was carrying, the inspection duties I intended to perform. Strangely enough, the article he wrote in the *Constitution* resulted in my later receiving an invitation to be a guest of the Crawford House Hotel in New Hampshire some four months later. But I am getting ahead of my story. At the Park I also met Major Garnett Martin, Denver, Colorado, who had hiked the entire Trail in 1964 and who had returned to revisit various points of the Trail that had made a vivid impression on him. Later in the evening I was privileged to view some of his many excellent 35 mm slides which document his 1964 hike.

Some 40 members of the Georgia Appalachian Trail Club had planned a big weekend of Trail maintenance work and paint blazing. Some of the members congregated at Amicalola Falls that Friday night. We met the Henry Morrises, the Ed Seiferles, the Al Thompsons. The Morrises and Seiferles had rented one of the Park cabins and invited us to spend the night with them. We had been sleeping in our Ford Travel Wagon for almost 10 nights. The temperature was expected to drop to the low 30's, so we gratefully accepted the invitation. I inspected my pack for the umpteenth time and made preparations for an early start the next day.

April 4. Up at 6. A quick hot shower (my last for some time); a ham and pancake breakfast; and shortly thereafter, we were part of a six-car caravan heading over some rough mountain roads for Nimblewill Gap. At the Gap, I met for the first time my hiking companion, Elmer Schwengel of Kansas City, who planned to hike with me for the first several hundred miles. Picture taking, a few words of prayer by Jim Engel of the Georgia AT Club, goodbyes to my wife and son and others, and at 10:40 a.m. Schwengel and I were hiking up toward Springer Mountain.

It was a beautiful spring day, warm and sunny with the temperature reaching 67 at noon. Here I experienced my first disappointment. It became painfully obvious within minutes that Schwengel, a retired railroad switchman, age 67, was not in proper physical condition to hike at anywhere near the pace I knew we would have to set if I were to reach Maine before snowfall. Schwengel had arrived at Amicalola Falls three days earlier for some conditioning, but it was not nearly enough. After about 30 minutes I reluctantly pushed on ahead, hoping he would catch up with me either at the summit of Springer Mountain (2.3 miles) or at the first lean-to which is a mere 1.6 miles north of Springer.

I reached Springer at noon, signed the register, and noted that one Branley C. Owen had signed the register the previous day and had indicated he was hiking all the way to Maine. I took some pictures, visited with Garnett Martin and Jim Engel, and then pushed on to the first of the 238 shelters I was to see during the next six months. I reached the Big Stamp shelter at 1 p.m., ate lunch there with the Morrises, the Engels, and other members of the Georgia ATC, made the first of my 238 shelter inspections, and had the misfortune to drop my little 16 mm Minolta camera in the spring. By 1:45 p.m. Schwengel had not shown up. I left a note for him at the shelter urging that he not give up his hike but that he continue it at a pace he could manage. I never did see him again nor have I ever heard from him. I learned later that he did not reach the first shelter until about four in the afternoon. At that point he discontinued his hike and returned to Kansas City. I felt badly about going ahead without him, but I had warned all would-be fellow hikers in early March that I would be hiking at a rate of about 14 miles a day.

After leaving Big Stamp, I pushed on steadily toward Hawk Mountain shelter, 8.0 miles further north, reaching it shortly after six. I barely had time to make camp and cook my evening meal before darkness set in. The afternoon's hike had taken me along beautiful streams bordered by rhododendron, laurel, and hemlock. I was fascinated by the mica particles imbedded in the soil. They looked like thousands of jewels sparkling in the bright afternoon sun. On the other hand, I was disturbed by the serious erosion along the foot trails and fire roads this first day in Georgia. It was the most serious I was to see until I reached the Smokies. And on this first night on the Trail I was to be entertained in a most unusual way. A scant 50 yards from the shelter, the US Army was conducting helicopter maneuvers. The choppers would zoom across the mountain, land quickly near the shelter, soldiers would rush out, and within seconds the chopper would take off and zoom away. These maneuvers continued until darkness intervened. I had hiked 12.2 miles this day despite the late start at 10:40 a.m. Sleep came quickly that first night, and it would continue to do so for most of the 158 nights I spent on the Trail.

April 5. Breakfast eaten and ready to hike by 7:10, except that I then had to spend one full hour catching up on my paper work. Joined by 20-year-old Jim Meredith of Charlottesville, Virginia, who would hike with me for a week. Leisurely hike of 9.1 miles to Gooch Gap shelter. Reached there 2:00 p.m. Met seven members of Georgia Club working on Trail. Hiked a mile beyond shelter to residence of Mr. and Mrs. Homer Gooch and had 45 minute visit. Was given four eggs. The Gooches had befriended Everett and Nell Skinner when the Skinners temporarily lost one of their dogs on their 1968 hike. Back at shelter I tried out my one pint plastic shaker, mixing powdered milk, water, and instant pudding. Worked fine. Instant puddings in various flavors became one of my most frequent desserts.

April 6. Cooked the four eggs at breakfast time, ate two of them poached, the other two hardboiled for lunch. One of few times I had fresh eggs on trip. Should have cooked them more often. Have been hiking during these past two days on "Foot Travel Only" trails, these trails being (hopefully, at least) protected by Forest Service signs designed to exclude two-wheeled and four-wheeled vehicles. During hunting season, it seems that the signs are taken down and hidden; and vehicles enter. Violators profess innocence . . . claiming they saw no signs excluding vehicles. To combat this, the Forest Service erects heavy wooden posts. The posts are cut down with chain saws, and vehicles obtain entrance. The Forest Service retaliates with more wooden posts, and this time drives one-inch thick steel rods diagonally through the posts and into the ground. And so the battle goes on . . . each side thinking of new ways to outwit the other.

I left Trail twice today. First, at Woody Gap where I hitched a ride to and from the village of Suches where I talked to Postmaster Lloyd Gooch and visited the grocery store. Mr. Gooch has been lending a helping hand to AT hikers for many years . . . frequently helping them pack and mail unneeded items back home. Back on Trail I hiked north to Jarrard Gap, and again left the Trail and walked the 1½ miles west to Lake Winfield Scott Recreation Area where I slept on the stone floor of a picnic pavilion. Cooked my evening meal in an inside pavilion fireplace that appears not to have been cleaned out for many months.

April 7. Up at 6 and by 6:40 I am hiking on road toward the Appalachian Trail. Should have reached it in 30 minutes; but kept hiking, hiking, hiking. Finally realized I have taken the wrong blue-blaze trail out of Lake Winfield Scott. I intersected the AT at Slaughter Gap instead of at Jarrard Gap where I left it the day before. Made good time to shelter at Tesnatee Gap, which I reached at noon. Found a note there from Meredith. He had left the shelter an hour or so before I arrived. No water at shelter; but a passerby gave me a ride to a stream two miles away . . .then drove me back to shelter. On my way again, not desiring to stay at Tesnatee which is cold, windy, and directly beside the highway. Realize I can't make it to next shelter, so stop at a Forest Service campsite 5.3 miles north of Tesnatee Gap and make camp out in the open. I have no shelter and am "camping in open night, gambling it won't rain. Heated water . . . had sponge bath . . . washed T-shirt . . . shaved . . . feel like new man. Hiked 16.5 miles today . . . my best yet. Paper work

1¼ hours. Trail very pretty . . . almost all 'Foot Travel Only.' Am enjoying the day-by-day advance of spring. Am finishing this 7:20 p.m. . . . almost out of light." (end of diary quote).

April 8. "Was awakened 5 a.m. by owl hooting nearby. Stars crystal clear. Big dipper had swung around from N.E. to due west. Very still except for owl who departed after 10-12 hoots. Watched stars slowly grow dimmer and sky brighter. Bright enough to see at 5:45 and I arose. Had a quick cold cereal breakfast. Temperature 38 at 6:00 . . . very still. On my way at 6:30. Many springs during first four miles. Reached Cold Spring Gap at 8:00 and scared up full grown black bear 30 feet down Trail just south of Gap. Saw two deer at Chattohootchie Gap. Beautiful views of Brasstown Bald with the imposing tower."

I reached Rocky Knob shelter at 11:00 and found Meredith and a second man, a Julius Broghman(sp?) from Elmira, New York, who hoped to hike the entire Trail. He had hiked the almost 50 miles from Springer to Rocky Knob without realizing that the white paint blazes signified the Appalachian Trail. He (as well as Meredith) was hiking without benefit of guide books.

Meredith and I went on ahead of Broghman and the two of us arrived Tray Mountain shelter at 4:45. Saw three deer north of Unicoi Gap. Never did see Broghman again or learn how far he progressed on the Trail.

April 9. This morning I reverse directions. Meredith continues hiking north. I backtrack south on AT to Tray Mountain Gap for my meeting with Forest Service personnel. At 10:00 I was met by Paul Sweetland, assistant regional engineer from Atlanta, by James Milner, engineer from the Gainesville office, and by Neil Hunt, a reporter from the *Gainesville Daily Times.* We hiked north to Tray Mountain shelter where I packed my gear, then the four of us walked in leisurely fashion north to Addis Gap shelter. The Forest Service had money budgeted for a prototype trail and for one shelter. We stopped many times during the hike to discuss trail design and construction, location and design of shelters, etc. I made a resolution to return to Georgia after the prototype trail was completed so I could hike that particular section again. We reached Addis Gap shelter at 3:30, and shortly thereafter the three men left, and Meredith and I are alone. This shelter has been extensively modernized as compared to other Georgia shelters. Instead of dirt-floor sleeping quarters, it has wire bunks. The other shelters have neither table nor fireplace. This one has a monstrous table made with 4-inch by 10-inch planks and 6-inch by 6-inch support members. It has a curved stone wall in front of shelter to reflect fireplace heat. At the top of this wall there is a built-in cooking fireplace with grate. What a delight to cook from a stand-up position. Slept on wire bunks covered with leaves. Went to sleep with the pleasant sound of the stream gurgling beside the shelter.

April 10 and 11. Two pleasant days in which Meredith and I hiked about 10 miles each day. Stayed at Plum Orchard Gap shelter April 10 and at the new Standing Indian shelter in North Carolina on the 11th. Crossed over into North Carolina at Bly Gap at 8:30 a.m. on April 11 . . . my first big hurdle behind me. Dropped my camera in spring for second time . . . which finished it as far as getting any decent pictures.

A few comments about the Trail in Georgia. The footway was in excellent condition and the paint blazing was excellent. There was, regrettably, an almost complete lack of signs. Litter on the Georgia Trail quite high . . . 25-30 cans per day and perhaps 40-50 pieces of other litter. Shelters well built but not the best design . . . too open on the open side and shelters have no conveniences (Addis Gap a notable exception). There are no tables, shelves, fireplaces, toilets, or direction signs at shelters. Trail throughout Georgia extremely beautiful. This was tremendous chestnut area before the blight. Even now one could walk for hundreds of yards stepping from one fallen chestnut to another. In early April the spring flowers were already in bloom. I enjoyed Georgia immensely, my principal regret being that I was too early for the displays of wild azalea, mountain laurel, and rhododendron.

2. NORTH CAROLINA, NANTAHALA NATIONAL FOREST, APRIL 11 TO 15.

Meredith and I entered North Carolina at Bly Gap early on April 11. At noon on that day we reached Deep Gap and spent 45 fruitless minutes looking for a nonexistent shelter described in the guide book as being located near the Forest Service recreation area at that location. Finally concluded that the shelter had burned or been torn down and we began hiking north. In 30 minutes we came upon a new shelter which turned out to be the Standing Indian shelter. Extremely nice . . . wood floor, nice location, swift flowing stream 20 feet in front of shelter. We washed clothes, bathed, aired our sleeping bags, cooked a leisurely evening meal, and generally enjoyed life on a beautiful warm spring day.

April 12. Meredith and I parted company at Mooney Gap. He planned to walk to the nearest primary road and hitch a ride back to Charlottesville, Virginia. During the week he hiked with me he subsisted almost entirely on short grain, whole rice . . . one-half cup each day. The last several days of our hike he had accepted some raisins from me. He was losing weight and had not had a bowel movement in nine days. I was sorry to see him go. He was a good outdoorsman and pitched in willingly on my litter pickup campaign. Began raining in early afternoon. Stopped at a fire tower and visited with the guard which was a mistake. The fellow was rabid on subject of politics and religions and would talk about nothing else. I was glad to get away. Reached Big Spring Gap shelter at 3:00 after 14.0 miles of hiking.

April 13. Left shelter early . . . raining slightly . . . quite foggy. Had difficulty following Trail. Lost it twice, and after one hour and 40 minutes I found myself back at the shelter from which I had started! Not too hard a trick to do in foggy weather. Started out again and made it to Wallace Gap (US Route 64) at 10:30 and immediately caught ride on a logging truck carrying 25 tons of hardwood timber. We roared . . . and I do mean roared . . . the full 17 miles into Franklin, North Carolina. The trucker informed me that his outfit was logging near the Appalachian Trail but that they were cutting no timber within 300 feet of the Trail itself. He offered to give me a ride back to the Trail on his return trip, but as it turned out I didn't need it. Frankly, I was surprised that he would stop that big rig on a curve on a narrow highway; but he recognized the AT patch on my shirt sleeve. At Franklin I visited the US Forest Service Office and met District Ranger Duke Barr. Tried unsuccessfully to contact Rev. Rufus Morgan, an Episcopal priest and the grand old man of the Nantahalas and the Appalachian Trail. In his 80's and almost blind, Rev. Morgan still hikes extensively; and this month, April, 1970, he was to climb to the top and stay overnight at 6,593 ft. Mt. Leconte Lodge for the 100th time. Had a hearty lunch with Barr, then a quick trip to local newspaper office for a picture after which Barr drove me back to the Appalachian Trail. "Began hiking 2:30 and made the 6.9 miles to Siler Bald shelter in three hours for 2.3 mph. Picked up trash for first four miles until my bag got full. Had given first bag to Barr. Another 6.9 miles of beautiful country.

Studied Winding Stair Gap where State Highway Dept. desires to cut huge 250 foot wide notch for new US Route 64; Forest Service recommends tunnel. Cold and windy at Siler shelter. Cooked some potato soup . . . huge bowl and hot coffee. Had eaten my main meal at noon with Barr. Wrote on my notes 'til darkness. Crawled in bed 7:45 . . . rained hard around 9 or 10. Slept well. Very glad I went into Franklin. Resolve I will visit every ranger office I can."

April 14. This was one of those ideal hiking days. Got an early start (up at 5:30 . . . on Trail at 6:10). Temperature cool . . . 38° at 6:00 . . . high of 55 at noon. Was hiking in the 4000-5000 ft. range most of day. Trail took me over the top of two impressive "balds." These were Wayah Bald (elev. 5336) and Wesser Bald (elev. 4627). There were towers on top of each that afforded magnificent views. Ate lunch at the delightful Cold Springs shelter . . . a 30 year old shelter built by the Civilian Conservation Corps of 10 and 12 inch chestnut logs. This shelter is fenced in, located in a rhododendron glade with clear cold water coming from a walled spring with pipe. Reached the Wesser Creek Shelter at 4:10. Had made 18.2 miles . . . my best so far. Saw no one during the day except the fire tower guard at Wesser Bald, Carl Smith, with whom I visited half an hour and prevailed upon him to carry out my two full trash bags. Went to sleep to the subdued roar of Wesser Creek some 40 feet in front of shelter.

April 15. Quickly hiked the three miles, almost all down grade, reaching first US Highway 19, then the Nantahala River, and finally the little village of Wesser, elevation 1723 feet. Enroute I hiked past a number of small mountain homes; four or five of them had tiny little boxwood nurseries in their yards. Had eaten but the scantiest of breakfasts and looked forward to a substantial meal at the restaurant in Wesser . . . only to find that it would not open until May 15 . . . a revolting discovery! Grocery store was open even at this early hour of 7:15; and I bought a few supplies and sat around the pot-bellied stove visiting with Larce Mashburn, the store manager, while I slowly ate a quart of ice cream.

Wesser provides a very distinct dividing point between the 55 miles of the Nantahalas nearest Georgia and the 25 miles nearest the Smokies. The 55 miles I had already hiked were indeed beautiful . . . high elevations, spectacular views, well maintained Trail with frequent clearly painted wooden signs. Litter on this 55 miles of Trail was heavy; and I was distressed to find each day some eight to 12 aerial survey panels still on the ground, almost two years after the aerial photography of the Trail had been completed. These panels are made of white plastic, about 24 inches wide and perhaps 15 to 20 feet long. At various points along the Trail two panels would be placed on the Trail in the form of a huge "X" as an aid to those who were flying and photographing the Trail. Although the many trail clubs had worked like beavers to put the panels in place, some of them had been rather derelict in removing them. Paint blazing, while generally good, left something to be desired. There was no use of blue blaze trails leading to water sources or other points off the Appalachian Trail. There was infrequent use of the double blaze to alert the hiker to an impending change in the Trail route or its direction. All things considered, however, this was a most beautiful and interesting section of the Trail . . . a section to which I certainly desire to return. (Rehiked this area April 1976—see article in *Backpacking Journal*, fall issue, 1977.)

3. NORTH CAROLINA, STEKOAH REGION, APRIL 15 TO 17

This 25-mile section of the Trail proved for me to be more strenuous than any 25 mile area in the entire Trail. From Wesser at 1723 feet, I climbed, in 4.8 miles, to top of Swim Bald with an elevation of approximately 4,800 feet, made descent to Sassafras Gap and then to top of Cheoah Bald at 5062. The entire day was a succession of climbing straight up the sides of many knobs, mountains and balds, and straight down the other side. There were no switchbacks or attempts to provide a graded trail as had been the case during my previous four days of hiking. Although the steepness of the Trail literally begged for serious erosion, there was almost none. Neither was there much litter. The absence of both erosion and litter was due, I think, to the brutally steep grades which discourage all but the very hardy few from hiking in that area. There are some Appalachian Trail enthusiasts who argue that there *should* be some areas like the Stekoahs that are so physically demanding that all but the few will be excluded. I personally do not share that view. I believe that the Appalachian Trail, even at more moderate grades, is strenuous enough and that blue blaze side trails should be provided for those who want the maximum in solitude and the extreme physical exertion that would be afforded by trails with excessively steep grades.

Blue blaze trails are not used in the Stekoahs, and I was unable to locate most of the sources of water described in the guide book. The trail to Sassafras Gap shelter was identified by neither sign nor blue blaze trail. I was lucky to find it. Had intended staying there overnight but changed by mind after seeing it. It was located in an uninviting spot directly beside a dirt road that provided automobile access and the inevitable accumulation of litter that such easy access provides.

I made one pleasant discovery this day. Discovered the high insulating qualities of a fully loaded pack. At Wesser I had planned to buy a pint of ice cream; but finding none of that size, I bought a larger size which I thought was the one quart size. Upon opening the package I discovered I had purchased a half gallon package. Even with my tremendous capacity for ice cream, I thought this to be too much . . . especially with those steep climbs to Swim and Cheoah Balds directly ahead on the Trail. Therefore, I ate but one quart, put the remainder in a plastic bag, and prevailed upon Larce Mashburn to put the plastic bag in his freezer until it was frozen hard. I then transferred the plastic sack with the now frozen ice cream, into the middle of my pack, where it was protected by a cloth sack containing my extra clothes. Even though the temperature reached 80, the ice cream stayed firm. I nibbled at it on three different occasions; finished the last of it at Sassafras Gap, a full four hours after I had left the store.

Realizing I could not reach Cable Gap shelter, I stopped hiking at 6:00 and made camp out in the open near a spring 2.57 miles north of Stekoah Gap. And . . . quoting again from my diary . . . "By 7:40 p.m. I had made all sleeping preparations, cooked evening meal, boiled four eggs for use on Thursday, and cleaned utensils. Climbed into bed at eight, staring up at half moon directly overhead. Experienced incredible feeling of well being . . . pleasantly exhausted, well fed, warm in my sleeping bag. A beautiful moonlit night . . . air pleasantly cool. Lay on my back and recounted experiences of the day and of the trip so far. Good night's sleep . . . never got very cold."

April 16. I reached North Carolina Highway 28 at 1:30, and within a few minutes I caught a ride into the Goverment owned and operated village of Fontana Dam. Picked up some very welcome mail at the General Delivery window, enjoyed a second lunch at the delightful cafeteria, and weighed myself on an accurate scale. Was shocked to learn I had lost 11 pounds in the first 12 days of my hike. Had my clothes laundered, bought groceries, obtained room in the Lodge. Had a late Swiss steak dinner at cafeteria, but had to eat cautiously as my stomach was not used to rich food. I was approached during meal by Mr. and Mrs. Monroe Wetmore, members of Appalachian Mountain Club, Connecticut Chapter. Back at my room, I brought all my records up to date, wrote some letters, and collapsed into bed between white sheets at midnight.

April 17. Up at 6:15 next morning, breakfast with the Wetmores, back to my room where I repacked all the groceries I had purchased.

4. GREAT SMOKY MOUNTAIN NATIONAL PARK, APRIL 17 TO 22

The Wetmores picked me up at 11:30 and drove me out to the Trail intersection on Highway 28. Raining steadily. I donned my rain parka and also rain chaps . . . the first time for the chaps. Took them off shortly as they were insufferably hot . . . was not to wear them again until I reached Maine. I reached Birch Spring shelter 4:30. Dark, damp, and dripping. Shelter has no vegetation around it, is located in a low spot, was muddy with much litter. A most depressing place to spend the night. During the night mice jumped on my head several times, and I chased two of them out of my pack at 4 a.m. I long ago developed the practice of carrying a stout nylon cord attached to the top cross bar on my pack frame. The cord has loop in its free end. Just before going to bed in the shelters I fasten the loop of that cord over any convenient nail and let the pack swing free. This is most effective in keeping the mice out . . . except at Birch Spring where they were smarter. I surmised that these mice climbed along the rafters overhead and then dropped down in to the pack. To provide protection from bears, all the shelters in the Great Smoky Mountain National Park are equipped with a sturdy steel fence extending all the way across the open side of the shelter. I fastened the steel door securely, although I learned later that my precautions were probably needless, as mid April was too early for the bears to be active at the higher elevations of the Park.

Saturday, April 18. A clear, pleasant day. Shelters are frequent in the Smokies. This slowed my hiking progress as it was necessary for me to visit and inspect five shelters. I trudged into Derrick Knob shelter at 6:00; found eight people already there and cooking fires burning. A Dr. Kintner and daughter gave me some fresh fruit which

I thoroughly appreciated. Finished my notes for the day long after darkness by using the light from the Kintner Coleman lantern. Had observed serious erosion during the day . . . especially on north side of Thunderhead Mountain where the Trail is already a small gully some three feet wide and two feet deep. The side trail to Old Spence shelter is horrible . . . gullied to a depth of five feet.

Sunday, April 19. A most pleasant day. Up early. On the Trail at 6:05 with the Kintners. We parted company after ½ hour . . . they returning to their home in Tennessee . . . I continuing on AT. Just east of crest of Siler's Bald I met Gus Crews of Bethesda, Maryland. We had arranged to meet the next day at Newfound Gap, but he surprised me. We hiked together as far as Mt. Buckley after which Gus returned to his car and to his tent at Indian Creek Campground near Cosby, Tennessee. I proceeded to Clingman's Dome, 6,643 feet elevation, highest point on AT. There were scores of people at the observation tower, and they looked at me and my pack as though I were a man from Mars. Proceeded on AT, walked over snow and ice on the north side of Clingman. Trail badly eroded from Clingman all the way to Mt. Collins shelter . . . gullies two feet to three feet deep. "Reached the Mt. Collins shelter at 3:30 and met Lionel Edney and LeRoy Fox, long time members of the Smoky Mountain Hiking Club. They had all the makings for a steak supper. We had a delightful meal and visited around a blazing balsam fire. They left at 8:00. Shortly after, a torrential rain set in, rain and wind. The rain on the metal roof was a continuous roar. Fire burned brightly for an hour. Lay in bed, head propped up, watching fire, and musing over the events of another full and very pleasant day."

Monday, April 20. On Trail at 6:20. After the 1.95 inch rain the Trail was a mess; the name Appalachian Creek would have been more suitable than Appalachian Trail. Reached Newfound Gap (US 441) at 8:30 and met Gus. I repacked my gear, put in some supplies from home that Gus had brought up in his car. We ate lunch at Ice Water Springs shelter. Shortly after, we left the AT and began hiking the Boulevard Trail toward Mt. LeConte (elev. 6,593). Reached there at 3:30. I had been waiting to visit this place for 14 years. Visited with the two employees, Al Bohannon and Mark Worsham and later talked on phone to the proprietor, Herrick Brown, who was in town. Had huge supper at lodge with six other guests. Other guests slept in cabins; Gus and I slept in the Trailside shelter about 400 yards from the Lodge. At midnight we were surprised and

These hikers joined Garvey near the beginning of the hike in the Smokies. (Photo: John Burton)

touched to be awakened by Mark Worsham who asked if we wished to exchange the rigors of our open shelter for the warmth of his closed cabin. We assured him we were comfortable but we were both most appreciative of his very thoughtful act.

Tuesday, April 21. Up at 6:15, and down to the Lodge for a delicious sausage and egg breakfast. Began hiking under cloudy skies, but at eight the skies cleared, making for beautiful views. Gus and I parted company at junction of Boulevard Trail and the AT. He returned to his car at Newfound Gap and I proceeded northward. Met eight people on trail, walked with group of four into the Tri-Corner Knob shelter. Reached shelter 5:30 p.m. Had hiked 19 miles and I was bushed. It was turning very cold and prospects of finding wood for a cooking fire did not look too promising. At this point John Burton and his three 16 year olds from Boston came to my rescue. They had hiked in the last mile or so with me, and Burton offered me the use of his propane stove so that I could cook my meal before they began. How I appreciated that courtesy. Not only that, but Burton and his boys began stripping balsam boughs from a large balsam tree that had blown down in a recent storm. They tossed in a large supply of balsam boughs on one of the wire bunks that I was to use. Worked on my notes until darkness; then put on all the clothes I had and climbed into my lightweight sleeping bag. Even though the temperature was near freezing, I was warm and enjoyed my best sleep of the trip.

Wednesday, April 22. A pleasant day, my last one in the Smokies. Made 18 miles. The pleasantly warm temperatures at 5,000-6,000 feet became unpleasantly hot at 4,000 and then 3,000 feet. Temperature in the 80's at Davenport Gap. Gus Crews met me in his car; and we drove to Cosby, Tennessee, for a fried chicken dinner at restaurant. Then we went over to the very nice AAA approved Indian Creek Campground. Showered and shaved. Gus slept in tent and battled a hard rain. I spread my ground cloth and foam mattress on the clean concrete floor of the laundry room and slept well.

It was with regret that I said goodbye to the Smokies and to the fascinating 70 miles of the Trail that lies within its border. I still regret that I hiked through them so fast; but I was glad that I took one day for that side trip to Mt. LeConte. I was surprised and distressed at the amount of erosion on the graded trails in the Smokies. The trails are laid out on moderate grades but because of heavy human travel and horse travel even these grades cannot sustain the traffic. There are miles of the Trail where erosion has already bitten down 24 to 30 inches, and there are a number of places where it is much deeper than that. I saw no evidence of water bars or other engineering devices that would check or reduce the erosion. Except for the erosion factor, the maintenance of the Trail was excellent.

The shelters in the Smokies are different from those I found on the Trail elsewhere. The typical Smoky shelter is 24 by 18 feet, stone, metal roof, with a bear-proof cage across the open side. There is one small 36 inch wide inside fireplace. The shelter has six double deck wire bunks (capacity 12) with floor space providing additional sleeping area. There is a toilet at each shelter, but no table. There are no garbage facilities. Hikers are urged by signs to pick up and carry out all trash. The shelters have no shelf spaces. All walls are stone, straight up and down with not even a fireplace shelf on which to put articles. When four to six different parties occupy one shelter it can become a 4 to 5 hour job for all to get their turn at the fireplace to cook an evening meal.

5. TENNESSEE-NORTH CAROLINA, APRIL 23 TO MAY 6

With the Smokies behind me I now turned my sights to the Virginia state line and to Damascus, Virginia, some 192 miles to the north. I looked forward to this section with eagerness. First, it was to be over trails not previously hiked. I would be hiking through the big bald country of eastern Tennessee and western North Carolina. Second, at the end of the section I would be in my home State of Virginia with over one-fifth of the 2,000 mile Trail behind me. Spring was coming on rapidly now. Each day the trees were leafed out a little more. Views through the trees were slowly becoming obscured. Spring flowers were out in profusion, violets, irises, trillium, dogwood, bluets, and May apple, to name the most common. Birds were becoming more frequent, and I could hear, see, and smell the many unmistakable signs of spring.

Thursday, April 23. Up at 5:30. Gus drove me to the starting point. Warm day . . . hiked in T-shirt. Reached Groundhog Creek shelter at 10:00 and found a table there, only the fourth table in 240 miles of hiking. Reached the Max Patch road and hiked on it for 3.8 miles. Joined Gus and his car at Lemon Gap where I repacked my Kelty for the hike into Walnut Mountain shelter. We reached there at 4:30 to find it already occupied by two young ladies, Patricia Wenner of Williamsport, Pa., and Ann Longanbach of Columbus, Ohio. They were seniors at Wittenburg University in Ohio, had completed all the requirements for their degrees, and had three months to kill before commencement exercises in June. What was more logical and adventurous than that they talk their folks into driving them to Fontana Dam, Tenn. and that they then begin hiking the AT north? They had hiked through the Smokies; and here they were at Walnut Mountain shelter. They planned to leave the Trail at Hot Springs, N.C. and hitchhike to Cosby, Tenn. to attend the annual ramp festival. And what is a "ramp"? It is a luxuriant leafy plant, a member of the lily family that grows well in the mountains of the southern Appalachians. It has an undergound bulb like an onion. In taste it is said to combine the potency of onion and of garlic; and they say that if you eat much of the stuff the odor seeps out through the sweat pores of your body. It is highly prized for seasoning. So much for ramps. We had an enjoyable visit with Pat and Ann and were most interested to hear of their experiences on this, their first attempt to hike the AT.

Friday, April 24. "Up at 5:30. I built the fire; and the girls cooked dehydrated eggs, bacon bars, and oatmeal. On my way at 6:40. Very pretty country . . . some small farms tucked away here and there. Began raining around 9:00, rained hard, much wind; but I kept hiking in my T-shirt, choosing not to use rain parka. Made the 3.44 miles from Garenflo Gap to Deer Park Mountain shelter in one hour 10 minutes reaching shelter at 11:00." Ate lunch at shelter and made my shelter inspection. Rain stopped at noon and I proceeded on to Hot Springs, N.C. meeting Gus Crews who had hiked in to meet me. We reached the town of Hot Springs at 1 p.m., and I now began to experience the first of many days of extreme discomfort due to diarrhea or dysentery. I suspected that I had drunk impure water . . . not too surprising when you consider that I was drinking water from perhaps seven to 10 unprotected water sources each day. I fought the dysentery business for almost 10 days. At one point I was almost ready to return home temporarily until I could shake the ailment. "Dr." Crews gave me his supply of lomotil pills which his doctor had prescribed for situations like this. I took the pills faithfully every time I had a bowel movement, but they proved ineffectual.

At Hot Springs we visited Ranger Jim Lunsford of the US Forest Service. He gave me my Gerber Pixie knife and sheath which I had lost in Ranger Duke Barr's truck at Franklin, N.C., two weeks previously. We spent three nights in Hot Springs staying at the Forest Service Rocky Bluff Recreation Area three miles south of town. Slept in Gus' tent each night. This particular Recreation Area is one of the best designed areas of its type I have yet to see. Situated on rolling terrain, each campsite is protected by a stone retaining wall. These walls serve both to prevent erosion and also to give each individual campsite its own little island of privacy. The combination of this delightful recreation area and the Henderson Grill in nearby Hot Springs made for a pleasant three day stay. Would have enjoyed it much more if I had not been battling the dysentery.

Saturday, April 25. By prearrangement we met Stanley A. Murray, Chairman of the Appalachian Trail Conference, and hiked with him from Hot Springs to Allan Gap, 10.4 miles. Gus had recently been appointed Chairman of the Conference's Trails Standards Committee, and I was about to assume the chairmanship of the Shelters Committee. Therefore, we had many things to discuss with Murray. On one of my "frequent visits to the woods" I mislaid my parka. Efforts to find it late that evening were futile, but next day I backtracked two miles and found it. Near the end of our hike with Stan Murray he confided to me that he had been somewhat apprehensive about hiking with me. He had done very little hiking recently, and he was aware that I had now had three weeks of hard conditioning. He said he was afraid I might embarrass him by walking his legs off. In view of my condition his fears were groundless. I was walking slowly and gingerly, with frequent unscheduled stops; and I would have had difficulty outwalking a 10-year old Cub Scout.

Sunday, April 26. Gus drove me over to the Catholic church, and I attended Mass for the first time since the beginning of my hike. A whopping ten people participated in the services. Talked to the pastor, Father Graves, after Mass and learned that the Church had a small guest house on the premises which they make available to hikers. Ate a big breakfast at Henderson Grill. Afterward Gus drove me to Allan Gap. Hiked a mere 10 miles for the day . . . all of it in a steady rain. First, I backtracked the two miles south to find my parka, then hiked the six miles to Camp Creek Bald. Gus met me en route. We climbed to the top of fire tower on top of the 4,844-foot Bald and drank in the magnificent views. Drove back to Hot Springs and our last night at the campground. Gus treated me to a delicious trout dinner at Henderson Grill . . . really living it up today.

(See January 1978 issue of *Appalachian Trailway News* for story of Hot Springs Campers Hostel.)

Monday, April 27. Packed Gus' tent and said goodbye to the Rocky Bluff Recreation Area. Into town for a final meal at Henderson Grill. Picked up mail at Post Office, telephoned my wife at Falls Church, Va. (our 32nd wedding anniversary . . . and I did remember!). Gus then drove me out to Camp Creek Bald Firetower, and I began hiking the 12.6 miles to Devils Fork Gap. Pleasant day for hiking, but witnessed one very depressing sight . . . the new Jerry's Cabin shelter, an attractive stone and concrete affair, whose builders had unwisely built directly beside a road which was traversible by—and obviously used by—both vehicles and horses. The amount of litter inside and immediately outside this new shelter was unbelievable. I estimated 20 bushels of litter including three rotting bed mattresses and discarded food of many sorts. The flies were so thick I was forced to walk down the Trail some 50 yards or so to complete my notes on my shelter inspection. In my 2,000 miles of hiking this was to be the most litter strewn shelter I was to encounter. Lesson: Do not build trailside shelters near roads!

Gus picked me up at 5:00. We drove into Erwin, Tennessee and put up at Morgan Motel. Ate our meals at the excellent Elms restaurant. Visited with Forest Service Ranger Fred Foster and staff.

Tuesday, April 28. A short hiking day. Bothered with diarrhea all day. Rained hard throughout the morning. Hiked only 7.8 miles to Sam's Gap where Gus met me and we decided that was enough for the day. Trillium, May Apple, and dogwood blooming in profusion. Filled my litter bag in the first five miles: 20 cans and 25 pieces of other litter. Then according to my diary: "Back to motel and I hit the sack for three hours. Gus took all dirty clothes to laundry. I ate light supper of beef stew, crackers, and tea. Raining off and on all day and evening. Erwin is a very pretty town; we walked around it after supper. If I can't see any improvement in my condition by Thursday night, I may have to return home for a few days. Depressing thought."

Reflective thought: Hikers are a democratic and helpful group. Here is Crews, a successful retired patent lawyer, a former Commissioner of the US Patent Office, chauffering me around the mountains, cooking some of my meals, and washing my dirty clothes. Such thoughtful acts are always appreciated . . . doubly so in my case with that persistent diarrhea robbing me of much of my usual zest.

Wednesday, April 29. Hiked 15.8 miles from Sam's Gap to the No Business shelter. "Reached summit of 5,516 foot Big Bald after first meeting two men who were digging ramps. I had an opportunity to see the ramps and recognized a plant I had been seeing for over a week. It looks like an oversized lily." Later Gus and I dug up some of the plants and nibbled on the bulbs . . . potent! Reached shelter at 7:00. Gus cooked a Lipton chicken stroganoff supper while I worked on my notes. So good to sleep in a lean-to again. This one is a concrete-block job: Clever design. Still bothered with diarrhea, but feel I am on the mend.

Thursday, April 30. Hiked from No Business shelter to Cherry Gap shelter today, 22.4 miles but only 7.4 miles with full pack. Am definitely recovering from the diarrhea. Hiked without shirt during much of day, quite warm, nice breeze. "Reached Cherry Gap shelter 6:30. Had delightful supper cooked over wood fire. Most pleasant day. Writing this at 8:10 . . . birds singing . . . daylight fading . . . water on fire steaming for my evening shave. Feel in excellent shape after 22.4 mile hike. Now for 6,207 foot Roan Mountain tomorrow!"

In building the food fire I found the charred remains of an envelope with enough writing still legible to convince me that the two young ladies, Ann Longanbach and Pat Wenner were some-where ahead of us. We reasoned that, after attending the ramp festival at Cosby, Tennessee, they had leapfrogged a big chunk of the Trail—how far ahead of us, we had no way of knowing.

Friday, May 1. Apple orchards in bloom at 4,000 feet elev. on Iron Mountain. A 17.1 mile day over the top of Roan and my last day of hiking with Gus Crews. Reached Hughes Gap, elevation 4,040 feet, at 1:15; it was marked by huge roadside garbage dump. Was sorely tempted to leave my full sack of trash there but resisted the temptation and carried it all the way up to top of Roan where I deposited it in a Forest Service trash can. Reached top of Roan (6,200 feet plus) and Gus' car at 3 p.m. Spent 45 minutes sorting all the stuff to be sent home and repacking all my food. Then I began the short hike down to Carver's Gap. Reached there at 5:00. Saw a patch of snow coming down Roan, my first since the Smokies and, hopefully, the last I will see on this trip. Gus was waiting for me at the Gap; we shook hands and said goodbye. He was leaving for his home in Bethesda, Maryland. I will now be hiking alone for most of the next three weeks. I shouldered my now heavy pack and began climbing up the Bald. I headed for Grassy Ridge shelter and arrived there at 6:00. "Very poor wood supply (alder) and not plentiful. Was almost 8:00 before I finished eating a very good meal. Worked on notes until dark. In bed at 9:00. Can hear an occasional car down in valley and see the valley lights. The shelter is sliding down the hill as soil around foundation erodes on this very steep slope. Elevation here is close to 6,000 feet. Grassy Ridge is my last 6,000 footer until Mt. Washington in New Hampshire.

Saturday, May 2. Hiked through big bald country; climbed over summits of five balds with elevations exceeding 5,400 feet. Reached home of Pink Winters (mentioned in guide book) about 1 p.m. Was promptly invited in for dinner: meat loaf, hot biscuits, homemade apple butter, the works! Left there at 2:30 and hiked to US Route 19E where I caught a ride into Elk Park, N.C. Checked in at Trivett House . . . $4.00 for lodging and breakfast. Bought half a gallon of ice cream, ate half, put the remainder in the Trivett freezer, and finished it off before going to bed.

Sunday, May 3. Ate 7 a.m. breakfast with the Trivetts. Hiked the 1.5 mile back to the AT as I was unable to catch a ride. Began hiking north from US 19E and lost the Trail twice in first 1½ miles. I was forced to obtain directions from landowners on both occasions. Paint blazing very poor from US 19E to Moreland Gap shelter, excellent thereafter. Had rained all night and rained occasionally during the day . . . my feet and legs thoroughly soaked. Even in the rain I could appreciate the breathtaking beauty of Laurel Fork Gorge. Reached the Laurel Fork shelter at 7:30 after a 19 mile hike and was lucky to find the shelter. It is marked by neither a sign nor a blue blazed trail. Without a guide book I would never have known where to even begin looking for it. I wonder how many hikers have missed that shelter.

Saw my first rhododendron in bloom at the lower elevations in the Gorge. Regretfully left a full sack of litter at Moreland Gap shelter . . . had no place else to dispose of it. Picked up no more litter the rest of the day. Disposing of litter is a real problem.

Monday, May 4. Resumed my hike down the Laurel Fork Gorge. Trail extremely beautiful. Enjoyed the rustic foot bridges, the high sheer cliffs, the roar of the water. Reached Tennessee Highway 67 at

8:15 and the Post Office in Hampton, Tennessee at 8:45. Received letter from home. Repaired to restaurant next door, had second breakfast, and brought all my notes up to date. Hiked back to Trail and resumed hiking on it at 11:45. Reached South Pierce shelter at 1:30.

Around 3 p.m. I caught and photographed a flying squirrel. He was lying in the middle of the Trail and hopped awkwardly toward a nearby tree. Upon reaching the tree, he shot upwards like a rocket. When I shook the tree slightly, he spread his "wings" and soared into space, landing some distance from the tree. Remarkable creatures. Hiked along one-half mile of freshly burned ridge area in Wautauga Dam area . . . such a fresh burn that the strong odor of charred wood and vegetation was unmistakable.

Reached Vanderventer shelter at 7:30. Spent one-half hour locating water a half mile down the mountain on an unsigned, faintly blazed trail. Barely had time to cook supper before darkness set in. Even cooked some grits I had found at a shelter in the Smokies. Vanderventer is another of the concrete block shelters and commands a spectacular view of the Wautauga Valley. I only wish the water supply were closer. On one of my green cards I wrote down explicit directions for finding water and fastened the card to the shelter wall. I learned later that my directions proved invaluable to other hikers.

This seems as good a place as any to describe a going-to-sleep memory routine I began practicing early in my hike and which I continued throughout the rest of my trip to Maine. Sleep generally came quickly after a hard day's hike; but in the few minutes before it did come, I would call to mind the name of the shelter or other spot where I had spent each night of my hike and I would associate the shelter name with the date and day of the week that I had stayed there. In all, I was to spend 158 days on the Trail; and even as I write this chapter some eight months after completion of the hike, I can still recall all the essential facts for each of those 158 days.

Tuesday, May 5. Overslept. Had hot breakfast for a change, much coffee. Even shaved! Noticed inscription on inside of shelter reading: "1964 Chuck and Johnny Ebersole—136 days Georgia to Maine; 1965 Chuck and Mike Ebersole, etc."

"The view this morning from Vanderventer shelter really something . . . looking down steep east slope . . . all the mountain tops dancing in bright sunlight . . . valley area obscured with white snow-like clouds."

A perfect day for hiking. Temperature 45 at 7 a.m., a more comfortable 68 at noon. Walked through two large areas dominated by two plants, violets and May apple. In another area observed large concentration of shagbark hickory trees. Saw a few clumps of those delightful bluets. Saw a chipmunk today . . . very few of them on the entire trip. Seems strange since they are so numerous in Shenandoah National Park. Reached Tennessee Highway 91 and talked to landowner briefly who mentioned two men hiking one day ahead of me. Reached Double Spring shelter at 4:20 and in fireplace I found a piece of plastic with one word, "Humanities," inscribed on it. I knew then that the two men hiking one day ahead of me were none other than the two young ladies, Pat and Ann. The "Humanities" tape was the clue because they had re-packaged all their dehydrated food with this particular tape.

This had been a most enjoyable day. Scared up numerous grouse hens nesting near Trail. Found the nest of one with a clutch of 15 eggs. "This was the most time I have had at a lean-to in some time, so I did some extra cooking. Had creamed tuna and rice which was perfect. Got the sauce just right. I also used some of the rice and cooked it with mincemeat. Made excellent dessert. Found three one-gallon tins here with handles, so heated lots of water, washed dishes, and shaved . . . twice today! Writing this at almost 8:40 p.m. . . . big owl hooting nearby . . . birds singing gently . . . fire dying down . . . a real good day. I'm 18 miles from Damascus, but only about 12 from Virginia line!"

Wednesday, May 6. Up as early as I could see, on the Trail by 6:30. Reached Abingdon Gap shelter, 8.1 miles, at 10:25. Another beautiful day . . . temperature 60 at noon with a nice breeze. Reached Damascus at 3:00, 18.7 miles, good time for me. Checked into city hall and signed the Appalachian Trail register. I saw two heavy backpacks there without owners, and I queried the state trooper who was there for the day as to the pack owners. He informed me that the packs belonged to two girls who had arrived about 30 minutes ahead of me. He asked if I knew the girls; and when I replied that I did, he asked me what type of girls they were. I was disturbed at his question: partly at the question itself, but more so at the manner in which it was asked. It was as though the trooper had already formed his own opinion and it was not good. I answered his specific question by saying that the young ladies were two of the nicest I had ever met and that they were the kind that a man would be proud to intro-

Fireplace at a camping spot along the Appalachian Trail. (Photo: Steve Wagner)

duce as wife or daughter but I don't think he was convinced. Perhaps his opinion would have been different had he seen them three months later: one was in Japan on a church-sponsored two-year teaching assignment; and the other was doing professional social work in Pennsylvania . . . but that is speculation. Most of us are loath to change our opinions of people even though the opinions are formed too hurriedly and without knowledge of the facts.

Damascus is a small town. The Trail goes through the main part of the town, and people generally are especially friendly to hikers. I made arrangements to stay overnight at the home of Mrs. Keebler who has been providing lodging for AT hikers for years. Cost of overnight lodging: $3.00. I met the two girls, Pat and Ann, shortly after leaving the city hall. They arranged to sleep in the back yard of a Mrs. Hall, a member of the Mt. Rogers Appalachian Trail Club. I laundered my clothes in Damascus, had a good supper, and was visited in the evening by Mr. and Mrs. Dave Thomas, also members of the Mt. Rogers Club, who live in nearby Abingdon.

6. SOUTHWESTERN VIRGINIA, JEFFERSON NATIONAL FOREST, MAY 7 TO 23

Thursday, May 7. Breakfast at Carney's restaurant where I was joined by my long-time friend, Keith Argow, Administrator of the new Forest Service Mt. Rogers National Recreation Area. Argow was new in the area, having been assigned to the office at Marion, Virginia, but two months previously. He made arrangements to hike with me that day as he was anxious to see for himself the condition of the Trail and the shelters in the area. Pat and Ann also hiked with us. Two things were disturbing: (1) the Appalachian Trail was obviously being used for sanctioned motorcycle races, and (2) there was a great amount of litter left by road survey crews who were surveying for the new scenic highway to be built through the Mt. Rogers National Recreation Area. The litter we picked up, almost 100 pieces on a 12-mile stretch of Trail; but Agrow was still wrestling with the motorcycle problem when I left there. Having crossed into Virginia I would now be hiking for days in the Jefferson National Forest. The two shelters we visited were most inviting, well-signed, attractive, immaculately clean, equipped with tables, fireplaces, and toilets. I was to find all shelters in the 240-mile stretch of Trail in the Jefferson to be among the best of my entire hike.

Ann and Pat elected to stay overnight at the Straight Branch shelter whereas I drove into Marion, Virginia, and stayed overnight with the Argows. Met Keith's wife for the first time, had a delightful dinner with much good visiting afterwards. Keith outlined some of the development plans for the Recreation Area. When finished, it promises to be one of the most delightful recreation areas in the country. Mt. Rogers itself, elevation 5,720 feet, is the highest point in Virginia and together with nearby White Top, which is almost as high, dominates the area. I make a firm resolution (one of many similar ones on my trip!) to return to this area another time.

Friday, May 8. Breakfast at Argows and then over to the US Forest Service Office where I was furnished with a desk and typewriter. Began typing critique of the Trail hiked in North Carolina and Tennessee but was shortly invited to a meeting in Argow's office involving Ralph Moyle, Supervisor of the Jefferson National Forest in Roanoke, one of his staff men, Charlie Blankenship, plus Argow and his assistant, Joe Baker. We discussed many aspects of the Appalachian Trail but dwelt most heavily on the problem of identifying water. Moyle informed me that the Atlanta, Georgia Office of General Counsel of the US Department of Agriculture had issued a ruling with respect to identification of water sources. The ruling, in effect, would prohibit the Forest Service from erecting signs reading "Water" or even "Spring." It was feared that such signs would mislead hikers into believing that the water so identified could thereby be considered to be safe, drinkable water whereas no State Board of Health could give a "Safe" rating to any unprotected spring or stream. In the same legal decision it was ruled that a sign containing the word "Stream" could be safely erected as this could not be interpreted to be a guarantee of the water supply. A fine point of law, perhaps, but in response to it the Forest Service had removed most of the "Spring" and "Water" signs. Since the new "Stream" signs had not yet been erected, the hiker was in somewhat of a dilemma as to location of water supplies. In the Shenandoah National Park, the Park Service solves the problem nicely by erecting a sign at each spring reading essentially as follows: "Unprotected water supply. Recommend Boiling or Use of Purification Tablets." It has always seemed strange to me that these two agencies of the Government, each providing outdoor-type recreation opportunities to the public, could not get together on this single vital issue of drinking water. If a legal opinion is needed, it would seem that a single opinion from the Attorney General would be applicable for all Government agencies without each one attacking the problem piecemeal. So much for the drinking water problem.

Argow had a speaking engagement in Abingdon; so shortly before noon, we dashed back to his home, where I obtained my pack and a large sack of groceries I had purchased the day before. He dropped me off at the intersection of the AT and the Skulls Gap road. (That name, Skulls Gap, has always fascinated me. I wonder about its origin.) I repacked all my groceries at the side of the road, burned all the excess wrappings, and began hiking at 12:30. Reached the very pleasant Cherry Tree shelter at 3:30; found Ann and Pat already there. Saw one of the rather rare pileated woodpeckers at the shelter. Am still seeing the May apples coming out of the ground; they look like little unopened umbrellas as they first emerge. With each day of growth the "umbrella" opens up a bit more, and in a week or so the "umbrella" is fully open. Fascinating little plant. It has a single flower, and later in the season it puts forth a single, small egg-shaped apple. The "apple" is edible but I never got a chance to eat one as the animals beat me to it.

Saturday, May 9. Up at 5:30 and built a fire. Had hot breakfast with the girls; then said goodbye to them. They planned to hike only the seven miles to Raccoon Branch shelter, whereas I planned to hike the 20 miles to Killinger Creek shelter. Much of the Trail between Cherry Tree and Raccoon Branch shelters had recently been relocated, and the new Trail was a big improvement. It substituted some delightful woods walking for several miles of the uninspiring road walking that I had hiked in 1968. Reached the first shelter before noon and ate lunch there; then pushed on towards Killinger. Thought I never would make that last four miles into the second shelter. Had visited during the afternoon with two families in the little village of Teas, Virginia, and learned that two young men with packs had been seen hiking from Sugar Grove, Virginia, towards Killinger Creek shelter. I therefore half expected to have company for the night, but I was certainly not prepared for what was in store for me. As I neared the shelter I was dismayed to see six or seven cars parked in the parking lot near the shelter (this is another of the trailside shelters too close to the road). When I reached the shelter, tired and hungry, I found that a big Saturday night picnic supper was in progress. A group of truckers and their families were having a farewell party for one of their members who was leaving them. Two girls, noticing my arrival, disengaged themselves from the group and advanced toward me with a huge plate of hot baked beans, salad, potato chips, and a hamburger. And who were these two maidens feeding a hungry stranger? None other than Ann and Pat! Their story comes later. The truckers and their families were a delightful group. They had two cooking fires going, and there was plenty of food and drink for all. I thoroughly enjoyed visiting with them. Shortly after darkness the truckers, their wives, and children, cleaned up the shelter site spic and span and departed. A wonderful group.

Ann and Pat then proceeded to tell me how they had arrived at Killinger ahead of me. Minutes after I had left Cherry Tree shelter that morning, they hurriedly packed their gear and also began hiking the Trail. However, when they reached the highway, they hitched a ride into Sugar Grove, bought a few groceries, and then both hiked and hitched a ride to a point near Killinger. They were "the two young men" who had been hiking near Sugar Grove. They told me gleefully of their second ride in the truckbed of a pickup truck. At the end of the ride they were asked to settle a wager for the two men in the truck cab. The wager concerned their sex: were they young men or young women? That matter settled, they proceeded to the shelter, found the truckers already there, and informed the group there about this character who was hiking all the way from Georgia to Maine and who would arrive with an empty stomach and unquenchable thirst. To cap off the day's events, the girls proudly produced a package of popcorn they had purchased in Sugar Grove. We cranked up their gasoline stove and popped a large panful of the delicious stuff for a late evening snack. Another full day . . . and a very pleasant one.

Sunday, May 10. A big breakfast of food given us by the picnickers: chili sauce, hard-boiled eggs, bread, and much coffee. I again said goodbye to the girls and left the shelter at 7:30. Saw two deer close to the shelter. Reached US Highway 11 at 9:20 and promptly caught a ride directly to the church in Marion. I was an hour early so I went next door to visit Ben Price and his wife who had been in the group at Killinger the previous evening. They were not in. So I sat on the church steps and spent the time bringing all my notes up to date, a never ending job. After church and a lunch at a nearby diner, I caught a ride with Father Fahey, the priest who had just offered Mass. He let me off two miles west of Groseclose, Virginia, on US Highway 11, the same point at which I had discontinued hiking some three hours earlier. The newly relocated Trail seemed to evaporate at this point, so I pounded the pavement the two miles into Groseclose, where I knew the Trail had previously gone. When I arrived at the little store in Groseclose, I found Ann and Pat holding up a hitchhiking sign reading "Wytheville." Pat's pack was broken; and although I had lashed it firmly at the shelter, the crossbar was rubbing her back raw. We enjoyed some ice cream at the store; and I telephoned my wife on this, the second Sunday of May, Mother's Day. I was informed by the store owner that the hiking club, The Piedmont Appalachian Trail Hikers (PATH), was relocating the Trail to cross US 11 west of Groseclose. Since the relocation seemed to be still in a state of flux, I elected to follow the old route. I said goodbye to the girls for the umpteenth time and began hiking at 2:30. I was following both the familiar white paint blazes and many now green blazes (white blazes obliterated with green paint). I visited briefly with Rev. Atwell, who for years has furnished shelter and food to AT hikers. I reflected that I would be one of the last AT hikers to visit him now that the Trail was being relocated. Just before leaving the now very narrow dirt road and climbing back up into the mountains, the Trail led past a small mountain home with a huge vicious German shepherd dog chained to the door frame of an old outbuilding. No one seemed to be at home. The dog made repeated lunges at me, but was brought up short at the end of each lunge by the big chain around his chest. I studied both the dog chain and the wooden door frame and hoped that neither would fail before I was able to get out of that area. Another good reason for getting the Trail relocated out of this area.

This was not my first encounter with dogs, nor would it be my last. They plagued me from North Carolina to Maine. How many hikers of the AT have actually been bitten, I do not know. Through-hiker Bill O'Brien was bitten in 1969, and Charlie Konopa, who finished the entire AT in 1970 was bitten in Massachusetts, a day or so before I met him. During my hike, people would invariably question me about the danger from bears and snakes. Danger from these two sources is slight; danger from domestic dogs is much more serious. Whenever I was approaching domestic dog territory, I picked up a stout cudgel. If the dogs approached, I would also pick up several stones, or just go through the motion of picking up a stone. Dogs associate pain with the sudden movement of a man picking up a stone, and this would frequently discourage many of them. Nevertheless, I felt many times that there should be some other weapon (short of a double-barrelled shotgun!) that would discourage those domestic dogs who seem to be enraged at the sight of a hiker with a pack on his back. Since the completion of my hike, I have had several conversations with officials of the Post Office Department. That Department loses one million dollars a year because of lost-time accidents which involve mail carriers being bitten by dogs. Each carrier now wears, clipped to his mail pouch, a small pressure can bearing the trade name "HALT!" One squirt of this spray is alleged to immediately discourage a dog. The spray has a range of up to 10 feet. I have written to the manufacturers, Animal Repellants, Inc. of Griffin, Georgia 30223. They inform me that their product is available at many retail stores. If the hiker cannot buy the article locally, he may send $2.98 (plus shipping charges . . . 25 cents in 1977) to the manufacturer and a can will be mailed. There are two sizes of cans, one weighing 1½ ounces (good for 8-10 shots) and the other weighing 2½ ounces (good for 15-20 shots). Both sell for the same price. I have not used the article myself, but I have received comments from many readers who inform me that HALT! is extremely effective.

Monday, May 11. Hiked all day along top of Walker Mountain. Apparently water sources are not too plentiful along the top of this mountain because the Forest Service has seen fit to install concrete cisterns at the four shelters in this area. These are very clever affairs. Water from the shelter roof drains off into the underground cistern; the water is then available from a pressure-type spigot. Forest Service officials are somewhat apologetic about these cisterns because untreated water in cisterns will not receive approval from State Boards of Health. From a practical standpoint the cisterns are a very ingenious arrangement. They permit shelters to be erected at convenient spacings along the Trail without being dependent upon either a nonexistent spring or an intermittent spring. Hikers using cistern water will ordinarily wish to boil it or purify it.

At 10:45 I reached US Highway 21 and stopped for a snack at restaurant there. From the restaurant I made several phone calls. One was to the Maritime Administration in Washington, D.C. My wife had informed me that two officials of the Administration were most anxious that I call them regarding the qualifications of a job applicant of whom I had knowledge. The officials I talked to were both surprised and grateful that someone would interrupt a 2,000-mile hike to telephone them from a rural restaurant. Another phone call was to the Forest Service office in Wytheville, Virginia.

I began hiking at 12:00. It was almost all road walking for the next 10 miles to the Turkey Gap shelter. On the way I scared up a wild turkey. I also stopped to admire the tremendous road construction job almost directly below me where a $30-million tunnel was being built underneath the mountain and underneath the Appalachian Trail as part of Interstate Highway 77. At 3:30, Forest Service Ranger Gerald Barnett and his assistant, Dan Sullivan, overtook me by car; and we visited for an hour. I arrived at Turkey Gap shelter at 4:30, 17.8 miles for the day. This is another cistern shelter, so I boiled the water. At the Walker Mountain shelter the previous night I had not boiled the water, since at the time I had not realized that it was cistern water that I was drinking. There were no ill effects!

On the food side, I find that I am eating large quantities of Mounds candy bars of late. I seem to have a tremendous craving for sweets.

I saw May apples in bloom today for the first time. I am still finding aerial survey panels littering the landscape, four to six per day.

Tuesday, May 12. On Trail at 6:10, one of my earliest starts. Reached High Rock shelter at 9:30. Climbed the fire tower and drank in the views. Pleased to see so many examples of Soil Conservation Service (my former employer) work in the valley farms below: contour strip cropping and farm ponds, to name two. Reached the little settlement of Crandon at 11:30 and spent an hour at the excellent grocery store there eating two pints of ice cream and visiting with Mrs. Bernard. Encountered extensive lumbering operations before reaching Crandon. Blazes obliterated and Trail blocked in some places. After Crandon, it was road walking all the way to Wapiti shelter—too much road. The Trail should be relocated. At 3 p.m. I was overtaken by Wayne Kelly, District Ranger for the Blacksburg, Virginia district. By prearrangement, he brought me two big sandwiches and a bottle of Taylor Lake Country White Wine. Talked with Kelly until 5:15. I ate both sandwiches and later cooked a chicken and rice supper which I washed down with that excellent white wine. Coffee and instant pudding for dessert. Never had it so good.

Quite a day. Walked through six miles of trillium north of Turkey Gap. The new Dismal Creek Road built by Forest Service is superb, a nice grade and an excellent job of vegetating the road banks. And from my diary: "Stoked up fire around 9:00, put on my pajamas, and watched fire die down. Whippoorwill perched near shelter and serenaded me. He then got real curious and fluttered down within 3-4 feet of the fire. I guess the heat and smoke frightened him, as he flew away and serenaded me from a safer point. They have entertained me at many shelters all the way from Georgia."

Wednesday, May 13. I was awakened at 5:30 by sharp blast from Mr. Whippoorwill. Scared up a deer at 7:00. If yesterday could be called "Trillium Day," then today could be called "Wild Azalea Day." They are in full bloom, and air is heavy with their delicate aromatic scent. Made the 15.5 miles into the town of Pearisburg by 1 p.m. Had reached Angels Rest, the prominent peak overlooking Pearisburg at 12, and enjoyed both the views and the rhododendrons that crown Angels Rest. Upon reaching the highway (US 460) in the outskirts of Pearisburg, I was stopped by a young man who drove up beside me in his car. He inquired politely as to what I was doing and how far I was going. When I told him he said something like this: "Sir I admire you. I would love, dearly love, to do something like you're doing. But I'll never do it. I'm trapped. I'm a manufacturer's salesman. I've got a wife and three children. I'm making mortgage payments on a $32,000 home. By the time I get out from under all of my obligations I'll be too old to do something like you're doing." I felt sorry for the young man and in so doing I became increasingly aware of my own great good fortune in being able to enjoy a six-month-long adventure on the Appalachian Trail.

I proceeded to the Post Office in Pearisburg. As soon as I opened the door and walked in the building, a mail clerk looked up from his work and said, "you're late! We've been expecting you for three or four days!" I learned early in my hike that Post Office employees in towns along the Trail have developed a strong empathy for the long distance hiker. If a letter is addressed to General Delivery and if it contains those magic words, "Hiking Appalachian Trail," the Post Office employees will make every effort to see that the hiker receives his mail. They will hold letters long after the 10 days or so prescribed in the postal regulations. They know the next towns north or south where AT hikers might be apt to pick up mail, and they will forward letters even without instructions if they learn that a hiker has passed by their particular post office without getting his mail. In my case, they had several letters for me, including one from the Skinners up in Vermont (hikers of the entire Trail in 1968) and another from my 15-year-old nephew, Shannon Garvey of San Diego, California, asking if he could hike with me after school was out. I wrote back immediately to Shannon extending a warm invitation to join me in early June.

I barely had time for a good lunch before Ranger Kelly picked me up and drove me out to a recreation area near Pembroke. The area, known as the Cascade Trail, was one that Kelly was very proud of, and well he might be. It comprised a circuit hike of some four miles winding in and over a clear rushing stream which culminated in an 80 foot cascade. The bridges, the trail, and stone work along it has been constructed by unskilled and semiskilled labor with money made available from the US Department of Labor for employment and training of people who were chronically unemployed. Supplies, supervision, and construction plans had been supplied by the Forest Service. Before beginning the four mile circuit, we were joined by Rangers Ed Johnston and George Todd of the New Castle district. The Cascade Trail was most impressive . . . another one of the many spots to which I shall someday return. The outhouse near the high point in the Trail is a classic. Built by a former owner of the property, it is a sturdy structure built among and fastened to three large hemlock trees. When you look down through the toilet seat holes, you are looking down 30 or 40 feet at the side of the mountain below you. This is one outhouse that would never fill up! Kelly informed me that an appropriate sign would be erected directing people to the outhouse (for viewing . . . not for use!). I suspect that that particular outhouse will bring forth many a chuckle over the years.

Back to Pearisburg and dinner at Hapiday Restaurant. Then over to the home of Miss Mary Finley, 204 E Woodrum St. for a night's lodging at the modest price of $2.50. Laundered all my clothes at nearby laundromat.

Thursday, May 14. The comments for this day are copied from my diary. "A wild, wild day! Up at 5:00, wrote more postcards. Breakfast with Mary Finley at 6:30. On my way at 7:30. Hiked a good mile . . . had forgotten the guide book. Dashed back to Finley place . . . 40 minutes lost. Blazing in Pearisburg streets very dim. Motorist stopped and gave me directions. Crossed two bridges, saw Highway Appalachian Trail crossing sign. Turned off US 460 and blundered ahead on the old Trail where paint blazes were not obliterated. Back to US 460. A State Trooper helped me out. This time found the new Trail. Rough going especially climbing the second mountain at a very steep grade on the road in the hot sun.

First day I have been bothered by insects to any degree. Had to wear kerchief around by head and ears. Chugged into Interior at 6:30; reached Bailey Gap shelter at 7:45. Quickly made bed . . . put water on dehydrated food, and dashed to spring with upper part of my body clad in a paper-thin T-shirt. Trail to spring horrible. No sign. No blue blazes. No trail . . . period. Finally found the water; and promptly got lost.

"Took an East-West compass bearing trying to pick up the AT. No luck. What a predicament. My open pack beside the table at the shelter . . . all my gear there including matches and flashlight. Nothing I could do except bed down . . . bare arms and all, pull leaves over me for warmth, and grit through eight hours of misery. Slept but little . . . watched the moon slowly sink. Luckily it stayed clear, no rain."

Friday, May 15. Again from my diary. "Up at 6:00, collected my water bottles, shook leaves and dirt out of my clothes. Took a South reading on compass and climbed to the top of the mountain and found the dirt road. Followed it north for 10 minutes and hit the AT. Turned left, hit the shelter from the north side in 5-10 minutes. All my stuff O.K. Promptly cooked supper (now breakfast!) Ate a huge meal, then brought all my notes up to date. Leaving shelter at 9:00; not an early start.

"Rest of day uneventful. Ate lunch at the beautiful War Branch shelter with its rushing stream. Would have loved to have tarried there the rest of the day. Cooked a hot meal for lunch. Pushed on to the not so beautiful Big Pond shelter. Water supply here is a stagnant looking pond which at this time of year is covered with pollen. Most uninviting. Luckily on my way to the shelter I met Forest Service employee, Bane Burton, who gave me a quart of good water. Cooked a light supper. This day most unusual in that I had three hot meals. In bed at 8:45 and to sleep immediately. First sleep in two days!"

Saturday, May 16. A cool, rainy, foggy day. Reached State Highway 42 at 7:40. Grocery store closed. Began hiking Sinking Creek Mountain at 8:40. Reached the beautiful Niday shelter with its big apple tree at 3 p.m., 16.2 miles for the day. Visibility about 30 yards most of day. Big event of the evening meal was that I finally finished the last portion of the dehydrated chicken and rice packages that I had found at the Addis Gap shelter in Georgia. Carried that last package over 500 miles. Stupid! I love to arrive at these shelters early. Cooked huge meal. An hour later I was hungry again and cooked a snack of grits. Resolve that when I reach US Highway 11, near Roanoke, I will stop at the pancake house and fill up. It is amazing how much food I eat, and how often my thoughts dwell on food.

Sunday, May 17. On Trail at 6:25 and made the six miles to Trout Creek shelter in one hour, 55 minutes. Mostly road walking. Cool and overcast. Enjoyed the new trail relocation south of Dragons Tooth. Reached Dragons Tooth at 11 and began the 1½ mile hike through deep pink rhododendron. First I had seen in several days and the biggest display to date. Reached home of J. L. Hodges around noon and was invited in for huge Sunday dinner. Hodges, a retired railroad man, collects hives of wild bees and sells wild bee honey. He is also an expert woodworker and showed me the huge grandfather clock case that he had built. Pushed on toward US 311 meeting Tony Whitwell and Nancy Rogers of Roanoke on Trail. They hiked with me to the highway and gave me a ride to grocery store where I bought some ice cream. My fact sheet lists two shelters north of US 311, but no one in the area seems to know anything about them, including four hikers I met at the highway who had just returned from a hike in that area. Fifteen minutes later, I noticed clear blue blazes leading to the right. I followed these for 250 yards and found a huge 32 foot long shelter, apparently little used. I was the only occupant. (1978 comment—Jack Hodges died in 1974 (circa). The Trail has since been rerouted away from the Hodges house.)

Monday, May 18. "On Trail 6:20. Cool, 48 degrees at 10. Delightful day for hiking. October blue sky. New Trail location a big improvement. Reached power line at 1:15 and took a 30 minute sun bath. Walked through acres of poison ivy and jewel weed. Delightful views all day. Trail is routed right on cliff edges. At mile point 18 I met Robert J. Donahoe of Roanoke who is building two Adirondack-type shelters one-fourth mile off the AT which will be available to AT hikers." (Note: As of 1978 these shelters had not been built.)

Reached US 11 at 4:20 and proceeded to the Travelton Pancake House for a big sausage and buckwheat pancake feast. Called Tom Campbell in Roanoke. Campbell is a long time member of the Roanoke Appalachian Trail Club and has been vice chairman of the

Appalachian Trail Conference for many years. Tom picked me up at the pancake house, drove me to the grocery store where I laid in huge supply of groceries. We then went to his home. Had delightful visit with Tom and his wife Charlene. Weighed myself and found that I was down to 138 pounds stripped, 143 dressed, some 15 lbs. below my normal weight. I had used up all my food so that my pack weighed 26 pounds, the lightest it was to weigh the entire trip. The next day it weighed 35.

Tuesday, May 19. The Campbells were slightly horrified but mostly amused to find that the bed they had provided for me had not been slept in. When staying at private homes throughout my trip, particularly for one night stands, I rarely used a bed. Since I was sleeping on the wood floors of shelters alomst every night, it was no inconvenience or hardship to me to spread my sleeping gear on the floor of a private home.

After breakfast Tom and I visited the headquarters of the Blue Ridge Parkway. We talked to Granville Liles, the superintendent of the 468 mile parkway. North of Roanoke the Appalachian Trail roughly parallels the Parkway and crosses it at several points. After lunch we visited the headquarters of the Jefferson National Forest and talked to Charlie Blankenship, the recreation specialist, and to Steve Law, the forest engineer. Arrangements were made for me to meet with both Forest Service and Park Service people later in the week.

At 3 p.m. Tom deposited me on US Highway 11 at the point where I had stopped my hike the day before. Hiked the 4.7 miles to Fullhardt Knob shelter. Reached there 5 p.m. Having forseen that I would have a short hike into the shelter, I had purchased a 19 ounce can of Bounty Beef Stew plus a can of crushed pineapple. Consuming these two items for supper reduced my pack weight by 30 ounces. This is the last of the cistern shelters. The water comes out of the spigot clear and cold, but I boiled it to be on the safe side.

During the past three or four days I had noticed that the tree foliage had completely closed in on me. Gone for another season were the winter views. And now an amusing incident from diary: "At 6:10 p.m. I was startled by loud flapping of wings. Two big buzzards where headed straight for all the food on the table when they suddenly detected life in the silent figure writing notes. They frantically changed course at a point 25 feet above my head. Amusing!"

Wednesday, May 20. Awakened at 5:20 by my wrist watch alarm. On trail 6:05. I loved these early starts and felt very smug when I could perform my early morning chores and be on my way by 6:00 or shortly thereafter. The small alarm on my watch was not too loud, especially if I left the watch on my wrist and if that wrist happened to be inside the sleeping bag when the alarm went off. Therefore I hit upon the idea of putting my watch in my metal cup and putting the cup inside the metal cooking pot. The noise resulting from that combination rivalled a conventional alarm clock.

From Fullhardt Knob north, I walked through miles of deep pink rhododendron. Absolutely gorgeous. Warm Day. Reached Wilson Gap shelter at 8:30 and reached Bobblets Gap shelter at 12:50. Left a note there for Ranger Bob Wilson and then I quickly caught a ride to the Peaks of Otter Recreation area on the Blue Ridge Parkway. Visited the nature building and talked to Naturalist Ken Ball. I finally learned the name of the flower I had seen all the way from Georgia to Roan Mountain in Tennessee. The flower is Spring Beauty, Claytonia Virginia, an early spring delicate five-petal flower with muted violet lines running through the white petals.

Caught a ride back to Bobblets Gap shelter. Arrived there 15 minutes ahead of Bob Wilson and Steve Law. I chided Wilson as I did some of the other rangers on the condition of the shelters; they were so clean that I accused them of having sent their wives out to scrub the wooden floors. It was also very obvious that the work crews had visited each shelter shortly before my arrival. In all fairness, though, I must state that on other occasions when I hiked unannounced through parts of the Jefferson, the shelters were always in excellent condition.

Wilson and Law had brought with them the makings of a steak dinner, and Steve proceeded to do the honors. He stated that he knew only one campfire recipe, one that his father had taught him, in which steak, small potatoes, and onions were cooked in a large frying pan. Either the father was a good teacher or the son an apt pupil, for the resulting dish was excellent. A loaf of French bread and a bottle of wine added the gourmet touch. A very delightful evening.

Thursday, May 21. Quoting from diary: "Woke up at 2:00 . . . didn't sleep much thereafter. Put more wood on fire at 3:00. Up at 5:20. Had hot coffee. On Trail 6:25; late for me. Was still disorganized from last night. Saw wild turkey on drive. Picked my first wild strawberries. Arrived Cove Creek shelter 10:25, exactly four hours after I started. Started fire. Had hot coffee and more substantial lunch than usual. Another delightful day; brought all my notes up to date, even shaved. Leaving 12:15. Have eight hard miles to Cornelius Creek. Pushed hard from 12:15 to 4:30: up, up, up. Reached shelter to find Bob Wilson and Malcomb Edwards. Edwards is from the Forest Service office in Roanoke. He took a picture of me as I came off the Trail, bare from waist up, red handkerchief over my head to ward off gnats, black hat, guide book in one hand, trash sack in the other. It should be a dilly! After I got cleaned up, Edwards took a number of additional shots of Wilson and me . . . wants to run an article in a Roanoke paper. During these proceedings, Ann Longanbach and Pat Wenner popped in. After Edwards and Wilson left, Pat and Ann recounted their exploits since I left them at Groseclose. It had been a fabulous 10 days during which time Pat bought a used '67 Dodge Camper in Roanoke and drove all the way to Harrisburg, Pennsylvania for a job interview. They were now headed back to Roanoke.

As they were leaving about 7:00, Newton Sikes arrived. He is the Park Service Ranger for nothern Virginia district of Blue Ridge Parkway. We visited until 8:15. During that time I cooked and ate my favorite creamed tuna and rice dinner. We made plans for Sikes and his wife to meet me the next night at Marble Springs shelter. He promised to bring in the makings for a hamburger and onion dinner and as a special concession to me, a big coffee pot with which we would brew real coffee.

A very full day. Have had trouble with gnats last 2-3 days. Expect I will be wearing my red kerchief over my head for next 2-3 months."

Not all of my days were as full as May 21 but I had many like that. From what you have read so far in this chapter, you might suspect that Ann and Pat were to meet me at various points during the rest of my hike; but it was not to be. I walked out from the shelter that night to admire the Dodge Camper and waved goodbye to them as they headed for Roanoke on the Blue Ridge Parkway. I was not to see them again. As I write these words a year later, Ann is completing the first year of a two-year teaching assignment in Japan and Pat is doing social service work in Pennsylvania. I shall be forever grateful to them for the companionship and for the good-natured bantering and gaiety they provided. (1977 comment—Ann and Pat now working and living in Washington, D.C.; I had an excellent visit with them at ATC bi-annual meeting in Shepherdstown, W.V. in May 1977.)

Friday, May 22. Another busy day. Hiked only 12 miles today. Climbed over Apple Orchard Mountain (4,244 feet) and reached Thunder Hill shelter at 9:00. Scared up two wild turkeys and located a towhee nest while hiking. Tremendous wild azalea display extending for a mile north of the Thunder Hill shelter. Reached Marble Springs shelter at 1:20. Last two miles before shelter marked by heavy nettle and poison ivy growth. I was joined at 5 p.m. by Charlie Burroughs and Gus Crews, who had driven down from Maryland. They too had brought the makings for a delicious steak dinner, complete with a bottle of Rosé wine. I had expected Newt Sikes and wife and was concerned when they failed to show. Learned next day that Sikes had had a death in the family and was on emergency leave. He had not forgotten his commitment and sent a note that the hamburger onions, and coffee would be provided on another occasion.

It was a mild pleasant evening with a light breeze. We kept a few coals in the fire all night. Were entertained . . . then annoyed by whippoorwill who kept up the music off and on all during the night.

Saturday, May 23. Up early; added wood to the fire and had hot coffee, bacon and eggs on the table before 6:00. Hiked with Charlie while Gus ferried the car north. Reached Matts Creek shelter at 9:00 after pleasant walk through flowering rhododendron. Reached US Highway 501 and the historic James River at 10:00. The James River marks the dividing line between the Jefferson National Forest and the George Washington National Forest.

7. SOUTHWESTERN VIRGINIA, GEORGE WASHINGTON NATIONAL FOREST, MAY 23 TO 29 AND JUNE 6 TO 8

At this point I took some of the heaviest gear out of my pack and transferred it to the car. Gus and Charlie left me at this point, and I began the 10 grueling miles to the shelter. Elevation at the James River is 600 feet and I climbed to 3,350 at Bluff Mountain. At 3:30 I was startled by an ominous buzzing sound. I heard it in midstrike and my reaction was immediate . . . I jumped away from the sound! A timber rattler, eight rattles, 1½ inches in diameter, and about four feet long. I went back and studied him, and he rattled again. Close call.

Reached Punch Bowl shelter at 5:30, 18 miles for the day. After a big supper we were visited for 1½ hours by W. G. Pettus and his son Bill of nearby Monroe, Virginia. This shelter has a dam and a small pond in front of it. The bull frogs, tree toads, and insects make a continuous din in and near the shelter.

Poisonous Snakes. The encounter with the rattlesnake was the first of only two such encounters during the entire trip. To the uninitiated, the fear of poisonous snakes seems to be the principal reason for reluctance to hike or to sleep out in areas like the Appalachian Trail where poisonous snakes are known to exist. I think it appropriate to make a few observations at this point to put the danger of snake bite in its proper perspective. First, in 18 years of hiking on the AT, I had never seen a poisonous snake until my 1970 hike. Of the two I encountered in 1970, only one was coiled and ready for business. The other, in Pennsylvania, was lolling on the Trail and showed no belligerency whatever. Each year some 6,680 people in the US are treated for venomous snakebites. Of this number, about 14 or 15 die, less than one-fourth of one percent. My authority for these statistics is *Emergency Medicine* magazine, July 1969. Compare this to the 45,000 who die annually in automobile accidents.

I did not carry a snake bite kit and have not carried one for years. This is admittedly a calculated risk. For those of you who prefer not to take this risk, I refer you to an article on Snake Bite Treatment that appeared in *Patient Care* magazine, June 1968, pages 55-67. The *Patient Care* article contains excellent concise instructions for the person who is bitten. The instructions are as follows:

If you are bitten
by a poisonous snake
Start immediately for medical aid. By getting there within two hours, you'll greatly increase your chances of a good recovery. If you are with friends when the bite occurs, have them carry you out by litter. But if you are alone, walk slowly. *Avoid running.*

- Immobilize the bitten arm or leg with a support or sling, but don't let it interfere with getting to medical aid quickly.
- Apply a tourniquet (a shoe string, tie or even a belt can be

Rattlesnake. (Sketch by Sharon Garvey)

used) around the bitten extremity about 2-5 inches above the wound. Make it just tight enough to cut off some of the lymphatic and venous channels. (Warning: The tourniquet shouldn't be so tight that it constricts the blood flow in the arteries; you should be able to wedge your finger under it.) If the wound is in the finger or toes, use the tourniquet on the wrist or ankle.

- Loosen the tourniquet slightly as swelling appears, but do not release it.
- Wash or wipe off the area around the bite. Some venom may have been deposited on the surrounding skin.
- Sterilize a knife and the area of the bite. An antiseptic and small knife are provided in a snake bite kit. Otherwise, use a match flame on a pocket knife and wash the bite area with alcohol, even whiskey. (DO NOT DRINK ANY WHISKEY.)
- Make longitudinal incisions across the fang marks (not cross-shaped), about one-eighth to one-quarter inch long. Make the incisions only as deep as the fang penetration—probably only through the first layer of skin (like cutting through a thin orange peel).
- Squeeze and apply the suction cups from your snake bite kit over the incisions to remove the venom (wetting the rim of the suction cup will make it stay in place). Otherwise, press hard with your fingers, gradually working toward the fang marks, or use oral suction.

NOTE: Wear heavy clothing in snake-infested areas and always carry a snake bite kit in your pocket. Check the contents of the kit regularly: Rubber suction cups will lose their elasticity over a period of years. Parts of the kit, such as the lancet, may be removed from the kit for other reasons and never be replaced.

Sunday, May 24. Although we hiked 17.7 miles from Punch Bowl shelter to Wiggins Spring shelter, the day was more notable for eating than hiking. Charlie Burroughs had brought with him several freeze dried goodies, and what better place to try them out than on a 2,000 mile AT hike. We started off at breakfast with ham a la king over toast, plus cereal and coffee. At Wiggins Spring we began with an appetizer of cream tuna over rice and finished up with a pork chop dinner complete with green beans, apple sauce, and hash brown potatoes. Fruitcake and coffee for dessert. Let no one offer me sympathy for roughing it on the Appalachian Trail!

Monday, May 25. My last day of hiking for almost two weeks. Hiked the 12 miles from Wiggins Spring shelter to the Crabtree Farm Road. Hiked with Burroughs. Gus Crews waited for us with his car at the very rough road. We changed clothes at the car and proceeded to Charlottesville, Virginia, via the little settlements of Tyro and Massies Mill . . . or what was left of those two areas. Both little settlements and the surrounding country were almost wiped off the map by Hurricane Camille in August 1969. Much home, road, and bridge construction is in progress. Our efforts to buy strawberries in this area were to no avail because all the strawberry beds had also been washed out by Camille.

Arrived home 8:30 p.m. and promptly ate another supper to top off the big meal I had eaten at Charlottesville. I weighed 140 pounds, 13 pounds under my normal weight, but two pounds heavier than at Roanoke. And so, the first leg of my long hike is finished. My daily log No. 52 shows that I have hiked 713 miles on the AT and 60 miles of other hiking. The 12 days I was off the Trail were much more strenuous in many ways than the 52 days I had already spent on the Trail.

I ate like mad all the time I was home. I gained one pound each day so that when I resumed hiking my weight was back to normal. During this period at home, I was bothered by severe leg cramps at night; and at the end of each day I had badly swollen ankles. It seemed that after 52 days of strenuous hiking, my body rebelled at the sudden inactivity. I spent one day in downtown Washington, D.C. at the office of the Appalachian Trail Conference and visiting the Red Cross Blood Bank. Over a 28 year period I had made 54 successful trips to the blood bank with never a rejection. My last visit had been one month before commencing my hike. But this time I was rejected. The reason: a slight lack of iron! Was my trail diet deficient? Or was this the aftermath of the almost two months of strenuous hiking? Some months after finishing my hike, I again visited the blood bank and donated pint number 55 with no problem whatever. Strange.

On Thursday night, May 28 my wife and I were most happy to have a party at our home at which we announced the engagement of our daughter, Kathleen, to a young man from Guatemala City, Guatemala, Hector Alfonson Menendez Castejon. The sizeable Menendez family and their attractive, diminutive, full-blooded Mayan maid Pauline were present in force as well as a number of intimate family friends. Kathleen looked beautiful in her full length Guatemalan dress. A most enjoyable evening.

Friday, May 29. Up at 5:30 after 3½ hours sleep and drove the 100 miles to Shippensburg, Pennsylvania to attend 9 a.m. meeting of the Executive Committee of the Appalachian National Scenic Trail Advisory Council. A good meeting, in which the National Park Service people present reported on progress made to date in implementing the provisions of Public Law 90-543, the National Trails System Act. I came to the meeting armed with a typewritten resolution which was introduced and passed without dissent. The resolution reads as follows:

> That it is the sense of the Executive Committee that the Forest Service of the US Dept. of Agriculture, the National Park Service of the US Dept. of Interior, the Appalachian Trail Conference and its member clubs make a concerted attempt to identify all sources of water described in the ten guide books pertaining to the Appalachian Trail. Identification would consist of (1) A sign indicating direction and distance to the source of water, (2) Blue paint blazes leading to the water source, and (3) A maintained trail leading to the water source.

Two days later the Board of Managers of the Appalachian Trail Conference adopted a similar resolution.

Page after page of the ten guide books I carried on my hike are studded with annotations in my handwriting pertaining to the sources of water described in those books. Generally I have circled the water source described in the book and added the following comment: "No sign. No blue blazes. Did not find." It is my fervent hope that in the immediate years ahead a hiker can proceed with guidebook in hand anywhere on the Appalachian Trail and be confident of finding every water source described in the book. He could not do so in 1970.

On the afternoon of May 29 I attended the opening session of the triennial ATC meeting at Shippensburg. I left at 4, drove back to Falls Church and attended the annual banquet of the Falls Church

Bowling League. Both my wife and I are avid duck pin bowlers, and in the 1969-70 season we bowled in two leagues.

Early on May 30, my wife and I drove to Shippensburg to attend the final two days of the ATC meetings. This was an exhausting two days for me. I chaired two group discussions on trailside shelters and worked until midnight summarizing the material for presentation to the full membership the next day. From the recommendations produced, an ATC policy on shelters eventually was adopted. The interim policy was published in the May, 1971 issue of *Appalachian Trailway News*.

On *Sunday, May 31*, in addition to presenting the trailside shelter recommendations, I gave a 20-minute talk on that part of my 2,000-mile hike which I had accomplished through May 25. I later presented and read a prepared paper on a constitutional amendment proposal which would have limited the tenure of members of the ATC Board of Managers. This later provoked the most heated discussion of the entire meeting, and the matter was finally tabled for lack of time. I came away feeling I had lost the battle but would eventually win the war. (NOTE: The amendment was re-introduced at the 1972 ATC meeting in Plymouth, N.H. It passed unanimously!)

I attended the Sunday afternoon meeting of the Board of Managers and stayed until 5 p.m. at which time I begged off from further participation. Mary and I left Shippensburg at 6:00, arriving home at 8:00. I made a resolution that at the June 1972 meeting in Plymouth, New Hampshire, I would arrive early, stay for several days for hiking trips after the meeting, and that I would not get so heavily involved in the conduct of the meeting. Time will tell.

From *June 1 to 5*, I relaxed a bit, spent one day in Washington, and make plans for the resumption of my hike. My nephew Shannon Garvey arrived by plane from San Diego, California, on June 5. That same night Mary and I attended the second bowling banquet, this one pertained to the National Science Foundation Bowling League.

Saturday, June 6. Left home at 1 p.m. in my 1961 Volkswagen camper with Shannon and my long time friend, Ed Hanlon of nearby Oakton, Virginia. We arrived at the Visitor Center on the Blue Ridge Parkway at 4 p.m. (much later than I had hoped) and left our VW camper there. Park Service employee Nick Eason drove us to our starting point on Crabtree Farm Road, and we began hiking at 5:30 p.m. We stopped very briefly at the Priest shelter, just long enough for me to make my inspection, then pushed rapidly north; we hoped to reach Harpers Creek shelter, 7.8 miles from our starting point. The evening was overcast, and I was doubtful if we could make that last mile. Therefore, when landowner W. D. Fitzgerald hailed us (after first calling off his dog), I explained our predicament; and he offered to let us use the wood floor of his apple packing shed. We readily accepted. He invited us into his home, and we cooked an evening snack on his stove and visited with him and his family.

Sunday, June 7. Up at 5:30 and invited into the Fitzgerald home at 6:00 for hot coffee. Ate some of McGuire's Musli for breakfast. Began hiking at 6:30. Reached Harpers Creek shelter at 7:15. And now I must explain the term "McGuire's Musli." Many readers will be familiar with a nourishing breakfast cereal called "Familia." Another name for it is Musli. Among other things it contains oatmeal, slivered nuts, currants, sliced dried apples, and brown sugar. Dr. Donald C. McGuire, a fellow worker at National Science Foundation, a fellow member of Potomac Appalachian Trail Club, and a member of my car pool, had, with his family, prepared and given to me a batch of this precious Musli to take with me to Georgia. When I wrote them saying how much I enjoyed it, they promply prepared a huge batch of the stuff. The McGuires also bowl; and so it was that at the National Science Foundation bowling banquet, four members of the McGuire family arrived and ceremoniously proceeded to our table and plunked down a four-pound sack of the precious Musli. Neither Hanlon nor my nephew was particularly fond of the stuff, but I loved it. I ate every morsel of it over the next 10-day period.

Left the shelter at 8:00 and hiked the six miles to Maupin Field shelter. Both Shannon and Ed Hanlon were quite tired at this point, and understandably so. They had hiked 14 miles since 5 p.m. the previous day, and they were not conditioned for such strenuous exercise. I therefore proceeded on alone while they walked out to the Parkway and hitched a ride north to where the VW was parked. I reached Humpback Rocks Picnic Area at 5:50 and was met by quite a delegation. Ed Hanlon and Shannon were there, as well as Charlie Huppuch and Joe Hudick of the George Washington National Forest and Pat Velenovsky, Managing Editor of the Waynesboro, Virginia, *News-Virginian.* They had been there several hours waiting for me to appear, and I felt badly that we had not made more precise arrangements. After the interview with Velenovsky, the three in our group

plus Huppuch and Hudick drove to the Forest Service Sherando Lake
recreation area and put up for the night at a bunkhouse for Forest
Service employees. This had been a hard day's hiking, and I did not
object at all when Huppuch and Hudick proceeded to do the honors
with a steak supper over a charcoal fire. The Sherando Lake area was
not new to me, as the Boy Scout Troop (Troop 681 of Falls Church),
with which both Ed Hanlon and I had been associated, had used the
Sherando area on several occasions for week-long camping trips. I
would have enjoyed a swim; but we arrived too late and left too early
the next morning.

Monday, June 8. Cooked breakfast in style over an electric stove.
Left Sherando in the VW at 8:30. Shannon and I began hiking at
Humpback Rocks at 9:00. Paint blazes on the AT are, by standard,
two inches wide and six inches high. I have seen them larger and
smaller than standard but never any as big as those in the six miles
north of Humpback Rocks. Many were three inches by 10 inches, a
few 3 x 14. I judged that some hard-working trail worker had been
given a paint can and brush but had not been told what size the blaze
should be painted.

Scared up a hen grouse with chicks which were already big enough
to fly. We met Hanlon near Rockfish Gap and hiked together for an
hour and then ate lunch. Shannon and I then pushed on north, meeting Hanlon at Sawmill Run Parking Overlook. Had planned to stay
overnight at Sawmill Run shelter, but Ed had already checked it out
and reported that the water supply was inadequate. We drove north
to Dundo Hollow campground. "Closed." Drove still farther north to
Doyle River cabin, one of the PATC locked cabins. I had a key and a
reservation for the following night, but we gambled that no one
would be using it this date. Did our cooking over my two-burner
Coleman stove. We were bothered during our evening meal and until
bedtime by a persistent raccoon who we judged had received untold
numbers of handouts from previous cabin users. He was not easily
discouraged.

8. SHENANDOAH NATIONAL PARK, JUNE 9 TO 15

Tuesday, June 9. Began hiking from Sawmill Run at 7:00. Reached
shelter within minutes. Shannon cleaned out the spring while I made
shelter inspection. Made excellent time hiking the 10 miles to Black
Rock shelter in four hours. We saw three deer and another hen grouse
with chicks barely able to fly. Ate lunch at Black Rock shelter and then

pushed north, reaching Doyle River cabin parking area at 3:00. Had hiked 16 miles before 3 p.m. I packed camping gear the .3 mile into cabin while Ed Hanlon and Shannon drove to Waynesboro for supplies. Sat at table on spacious stone porch at Doyle River, brought my notes up to date and enjoyed beautiful view to the south. And from my diary: "Legs and ankles O.K. since I resumed hiking . . . no more cramps and my ankles have stopped swelling. My right foot is a mess, am losing toenail on second toe, may lose big toenail, have a numb feeling in right big toe and a huge callous on the second toe of each foot, bigger on right. Biggest problem right now is sore rear end, chafing. Can't figure why I should suffer so much from that area now when it gave me so little trouble in first seven weeks. Ed and Shannon returned at 6:00. Delicious supper of hamburgers, onions, and lettuce salad, coffee, Gallo Rhinegarten wine. Visited by raccoon, deer, and kangaroo mouse. Another mild pleasant evening. Half moon trying to shine through the trees in the clearing in front of the cabin."

The reference to chafing immediately above is the first reference I find in my notes on this problem. It was to bother me during much of the hot weather season. In talking to many hikers I was to find that chafing is a common source of discomfort in long distance hiking, probably second only to ill-fitting shoes. Chafing can occur on any part of the body where skin rubs against skin or even where clothes or equipment rub against skin. I had always naively assumed that mentholatum was a cure-all for chapped skin, dry skin, or chafed skin. I found that it was not the answer for constant chafed skin, especially in the crotch area. Later I was to learn that medicated powder (I used Ammens) or corn starch provides very effective relief.

Wednesday, June 10. Left Doyle River cabin at 7:00. Enjoyed our stay there. Reached Ivy Creek shelter at 9:20 and Pinefield shelter at 10:45. Saw two deer, eight rabbits, and grouse with chicks. Picked strawberries for third day, excellent patch at Powell Gap. Visited with Park Service Ranger Dallas Koehn at Simmons Gap ranger station. Met Ed Hanlon at Smith-Roach Gap, repacked our gear, and the three of us began the hike to High Top shelter. Reached there 3:30 p.m. after a day's hike of 17 miles.

Thursday, June 11. Reached Swift Run Gap (US Highway 33) at 7:30 and reached South River shelter at 9:15. Hiked through much mountain laurel in bloom. Saw three deer and grouse with chicks, now an almost everyday occurrence. Reached the locked Pocosin cabin at 11:00 with its big concrete box never-go-dry spring. This is the first

Kangaroo mouse. (Sketch by Sharon Garvey)

PATC cabin I ever used (1951) and one of my favorites. After a quick lunch we drove to nearby Big Meadows, showered, laundered our clothes, and were interviewed and photographed by Hugh and Aggie Crandall, seasonal employees of the Park Service. I phoned home and learned that my 16-year-old daughter Sharon, her friend Liz Sorgen, and my 11-year-old son Kevin had already left home and were headed for Pocosin Cabin. They arrived at 5:30. My nephew Shannon was most happy to see them as he was a little homesick anyway and welcomed companionship from those his own age. We had a glorious evening. First a big supper. As darkness set in, we lit up the Coleman lantern, and the four young people played cards and visited on the outside table. Ed and I sat down in the clearing a short distance from the cabin and drank in the view. The entire mountainside was bathed in bright moonlight, and the valley in the Piedmont area to the east was dotted with blinking lights. The entire cabin area and the spacious clearing surrounding it seemed to come alive and respond to the glow of the Coleman and to the hearty peals of laughter coming from the four young people. One of those perfect evenings that we have relived many times since. Regretfully, we finally went to bed well after 11:00.

Friday, June 12. Shannon and I began hiking at 8:45. Reached Milam Gap at 11:30. Met Ed Hanlon and Kevin where Sharon had dropped them off. Sharon and Liz Sorgen had driven back to Falls Church. The four of us hiked into Lewis Falls shelter for lunch. Met a Class D (individual) member of the Appalachian Trail Conference there, a Mr. Sam Steen of Kingston, New York who was to hike with me later in Massachusetts and New Hampshire. Reached Hawksbill shelter at 5:30. Three people already there, but there was room for us. Has been fair and warm throughout the day, but began raining steadily at 7:30.

Saturday, June 13. Up at 5:30. The four of us ate quietly while the other three occupants of the shelter slept. Met Sam Steen at Hawksbill Gap where he had slept in his van. Shortly after he left for his home in New York; and I promised to contact him when I reached that area so that he could join me on the Trail for a few days. Then Shannon, Ed Hanlon, Kevin and I began hiking north. Reached Shaver Hollow shelter at 11:00, and shortly thereafter, the huge stone shelter known as Byrd Nest No. 3 (named after former Senator Harry F. Byrd). About 3 p.m. we arrived at Panorama (US Highway 211). Had a snack at the coffee shop and learned from a stranger there that a fellow looking remarkably like me had been seen hiking toward Pass Mountain shelter looking for his brother and his son. This would have to be my brother Jerry from San Diego (Shanon's father). Shannon and I then pushed on rapidly and found my brother near the Pass Mountain shelter. They returned to Jerry's car on Skyline Drive while I inspected the Pass Mountain shelter and then hiked north to Beahms Gap where Jerry picked me up in his car. Then we all drove to the Elk Wallow Picnic Grounds for supper. After a late supper Ed Hanlon packed his gear in my VW camper and headed for home. I hated to see him go. It had been a pleasant week hiking with him and having the VW handy for extra mobility.

Friday, June 12 was the last day of school for many schools throughout the country, and it seemed that all boys of Boy Scout age had immediately headed for the Shenandoah National Park. Whereas on previous days we had seen but a handful of people on the Trail during the day, today we saw scores. Furthermore, there were 40 or more Scouts camped in little green tents in the area surrounding the Elk Wallow shelter. The shelter itself had only one occupant, John Baldwin of Culpeper, Virginia, who had been in residence there for several days trying to recuperate from a case of nerves as he described it. Hanlon (Col. Edward Hanlon, that is, USMC pilot with an unmistakable air of authority) had made an advance visit to the shelter and sought to make certain that sleeping spaces would be available for us. Baldwin had been properly impressed and was prepared to defend the shelter against all comers. A big sack of potatoes established a claim for one bunk and various other pieces of gear established claims for others. When I identified myself as the man hiking from Georgia to Maine, the magic welcome carpet came out immediately, the sack of potatoes was moved, and the four of us brought in our sleeping bags and enjoyed the huge fire which John tended continually.

Sunday, June 14. Up at 6:00 and immediately had hot coffee as John Baldwin had tended fire all night. Drove into Luray to attend Mass. Had huge breakfast at Brown's restaurant. Then back to the Park, and Shannon and I began hiking north from Beahms Gap. Jerry and my son Kevin returned to Falls Church; Jerry, a design engineer for Gulf General Atomic, continued on to York, Pennsylvania, where he was assisting on a nuclear installation.

We reached Elk Wallow shelter again, this time by foot, and found that John Baldwin had hot baked potatoes waiting for us. The thoughtfulness of people like Baldwin, expressed in dozens of ways throughout my trip, really touched me. There is so much good in this world, but unfortunately it does not receive the headlines. Also at the shelter were Fran and Jean Marburg, fellow members of PATC from Falls Church, who spent over two hours with us taking movie pictures. We pushed on north on a cool, cloudy, windy day. Stopped briefly at Range View Cabin, then on to Gravelly Spring shelter. Saw more deer and grouse and caught, photographed, and released one grouse chick.

Reached Gravelly Springs at 5:30 to find that the shelter (bunks for six) already had eight Boy Scouts and their leaders from Dayton, Ohio. Another 20 to 30 people were camping in the shelter area. Shenandoah Park is popular in the summer time! The Dayton group permitted us to use their cooking fire. Shannon cooked supper while I worked on my notes. We slept on the ground underneath the roof overhang at the shelter. It rained during the night, and we kept inching further into the shelter. Togetherness! It's wonderful!

Monday, June 15. Cool, cloudy day with intermittent rain in after-noon. Reached Indian Run shelter at 10:15 and pushed on to Mosby shelter arriving there at 2:00. Had planned to stay overnight there, but elected to push on. Enjoyed wild strawberries, wild cherries, and mulberries. Reached little town of Linden at 4:00 and visited with Postmistress Lee White and enjoyed a pint of ice cream. Reached Manassas Gap shelter at 6:30 having hiked 22 miles for the day. The Manassas Gap shelter has always been one of my favorites (only 55 miles from my home), and it was in excellent condition. It has an excellent spring, three tables, three fireplaces, and is equipped with broom, saw, grass whip, food storage box, and register board. It is maintained by the Potomac Appalachian Trail Club of Washington, D.C. It is located on private land; and in April 1971, the landowner felt constrained to give notice that his land and the shelter would be barred to the public as of May 1, 1971. A severe loss to the Club and to hikers generally. (In 1977, this shelter again became available to hikers after a 6-year period of unavailability; the State of Virginia had purchased the property.)

9. NORTHERN VIRGINIA, JUNE 16 TO 18

Tuesday, June 16. Reached Yellow Rose shelter at 9:15. At 11:15 reached Ashby Gap (US Highway 50) and had snack at George Frye's

Weathered Trail marker near Harpers Ferry. (Photo: Steve Wagner)

store. While there, a car drove up and a wounded, bleeding man was assisted from the car. He remained at the store until an ambulance arrived. We saw his car on Route 601 shortly afterward. Totally wrecked. The Yellow Rose shelter was also closed to the public early in 1971. More and more of the Trail is being forced out of the woods onto Route 601 in this area, and we walked for miles on the hard top 601. Reached Three Springs shelter at 3:30. All hikers, hiking north from Three Springs shelter, marvel at the huge ant hills beside the Trail. Most of them are round, being about four to five feet in diameter and 30 inches high. The biggest was rectangular, 14 feet long, six feet wide, and 36 inches to 42 inches high. It takes a lot of ants to produce an ant hill that big!

At 5:30, having hiked 20 miles, we reached the home of Bill and Beth Oscanyan whose home is directly beside the Trail on Highway 601. The Oscanyans, fellow members of the Potomac Appalachian Trail Club, had extended a written invitation to me months earlier to stay overnight there when I reached that part of the Trail. Shortly after arriving, I was introduced to the very delicious trail food called "Citadel Spread" which is described in detail elsewhere in this book. Enjoyed the luxury of a shower, laundered our clothes, and enjoyed a delicious dinner and an evening visit. Beth is a wonderful cook, an expert on simple foods with high nutritional value. The Oscanyans are planning a trip to Vermont in August, and we made tentative plans to get together if my schedule permits.

Wednesday, June 17. Left Oscanyan residence 8:45. My pack weighed 40 pounds, the heaviest of the trip, as I repacked it with much food that Ed Hanlon had left at the Oscanyan residence Saturday night. Ed had left us at Shenandoah Park rather late and arrived unannounced at midnight at the country home of the Oscanyans! A good way to get acquainted and to make a lasting impression! We were shortly joined by Allan Levander, a 17-year-old of Charleston, South Carolina, and then to our surprise, by 16-year-old Maurice Gordon of Falls Church. I was surprised to see Gordon as he had made plans for months to hike the entire Trail from Maine to Georgia, and I thought he had already started it. He told us that he had started hiking at Mt. Katahdin in Maine on Sunday, June 14. He started in Maine with a 70 pound pack and had twisted his knee badly at the top of the mountain. This forced him to discontinue his hike and fly home. He was now carrying a much lighter pack and

View of Harpers Ferry. (Photo: Steve Wagner)

Shenandoah River near Harpers Ferry. (Photo: Steve Wagner)

testing his knee to determine if he could still do some extensive hiking during the summer.

We ate lunch at Wilson Gap shelter and then pushed on toward Keys Gap. We stopped en route to inspect the remains of a recent light airplane crash on the Trail. I later learned that the airplane crash was not recent; it just looked recent.

Reached Keys Gap shelter 4:30. Big supper and plenty of time to work on my notes. Enjoyed having company of three young men.

Thursday, June 18. Awakened at 3:30 by heavy wind and rain. Shelter roof leaked, and we hurriedly moved our sleeping bags to the dryest part of the small shelter. Shannon and I left the shelter at 6:15. Skies cleared; and as we approached the Potomac River, we were able to obtain beautiful views from several points on Loudoun Heights. The views here command the two rivers, the Shenandoah and the Potomac, and their confluence, with the town of Harpers Ferry nestled in between the two rivers. This is one of the most spectacular views provided on the entire Trail. In addition to the rivers, three arteries of transportation are also visible: the Baltimore and Ohio railroad, the old Chesapeake and Ohio Canal, and U.S. Higwhay 340. Upon reaching the highway, we left the Trail and walked into Harpers Ferry. The town and surrounding area is now part of the Harpers Ferry National Historical Park and many of the old buildings have been restored. Hikers should definitely schedule enough time to leave the Trail and visit this fascinating place.

I visited the Park Service office and talked to Ben Davis, the Super-intendent. He very graciously made available to me a desk and type-writer. Maurice Gordon arrived at noon and informed me that his knee was still acting up. My nephew Shannon had also decided that Harpers Ferry was as far as he wished to hike, and it was agreed that both of them would go back to Falls Church the next morning.

I found it best to stay off the streets in Harpers Ferry. It was a nice day, and there were hundreds of visitors strolling along the streets. I was wearing my "Forest Service Green" shirt and slack outfit with the very official looking PATC four-color patch on my sleeve. Appar-ently I looked more "official" than the Park Service employees, even though I did not have a broad brimmed hat. Whatever the reason, I found myself continually being stopped and asked to supply infor-mation or directions.

Spent most of the afternoon in "my office." Col. Lester L. Holmes, Executive Director of the Appalachian Trail Conference, joined me at one o'clock, and we transacted ATC business until four. Les brought me some mail which had been addressed to me at the Appalachian Trail Office in Washington. One letter was of particular interest. It was from a Mrs. Margaret Hill, director of a dance studio in Dublin, Georgia. Mrs. Hill spends her summer months as social hostess for the well-known Crawford House hotel, situated near the Appalachian Trail in the White Mountains of New Hampshire. She had read about my hike in the *Atlanta (Ga.) Constitution* and extended me an invitation to be a guest of Crawford House and to speak to the other hotel guests when I reached New Hampshire. I wrote to her promptly that I would be happy to accept.

I worked in the office until 6:30, then locked the place up, and dashed over to High Acre, a PATC owned house in Harpers Ferry. Cooked my evening meal over my Primus gasoline stove. Ray Fadner, Supervisor of Trails for PATC, arrvied at 8:30 and stayed for an hour. The three of us, Maurice, Shannon, and I spread our sleeping gear on the porch floor of High Acre and slept well.

It had been a full day. I had written 12 to 14 letters in the Park Service Office notifying a number of the hiking clubs further north of my tentative itinerary. It had been very convenient having an office and typewriter with coffee privileges thrown in for good measure.

10. MARYLAND, JUNE 19 TO JUNE 20

Friday, June 19. Up at 5:15, said goodbye to Maurice and Shannon and was on my way at 5:50. I would now be hiking alone, for the most part, all the way to the New Jersey-New York State line. I was sorry that Shannon discontinued his hike so soon, but he was having foot troubles, and I had been setting a pretty stiff pace. Shannon was a growing boy, 15 years old and 110 pounds The shoes he started hiking with were, I think, a wee bit tight. His father had given Shannon a new pair at Elk Wallow the previous Saturday. Although the new pair were larger, they were new; and this was an unfortunate time to break them in. He began getting blisters on top of blisters. Even so, he hiked over 180 miles in 12 days, rain or shine, which is mighty good for one coming directly out of school without a chance for proper conditioning.

At 7:00 I crossed the Potomac River, left Virginia, and entered Maryland. At 7:30 I reached Weverton campsite on the C&O Canal and had a second breakfast cooked by a group of Boy Scouts from Steubenville, Ohio. Met a number of hikers on the Trail including Joe Simpson of Miamisburg, Ohio, who is hiking all the way to

Springer Mountan, Georgia. Met Joe Mahlie, Scoutmaster of BSA
Troop 15 of Wintersville, Ohio. I concluded that the Trail was saturated with people from Ohio, for I had spent Sunday night in Shenandoah National Park with a group from Dayton, Ohio.

Visited for 45 minutes with Howard DeGrange, Superintendent of
the Gathland State Park in Maryland. He is very interested in the
Appalachian Trail and expressed a strong desire to receive issues of
Appalachian Trailway News. Later as I talked to the state game warden and other State Park, State Forest, and other State officials, I
concluded that the Conference has been derelict in not getting the
Trailway News to these State employees who continued to express
such a strong interest in the Appalachian Trail.

DeGrange had told me of the four local yokels who made frequent
nightly trips to the nearby Crampton Gap shelter to harrass the occupants. Since it was not on State property, DeGrange was powerless
to take the type of action he would have loved to have taken. I
visited Crampton Gap shelter and warned 14-year-old Mike Harris of
Garrett Park, Maryland and his two companions of the nightly visitors.
They were somewhat apprehensive and expressed a desire that I
stay overnight. I would have liked to have stayed, but this was one of
many instances when I had committed myself to be at a certain
shelter, so I reluctantly pushed on. Reached Rocky Run shelter at
4:00 having hiked 17 miles for the day. Laid in a large supply of firewood in anticipation of a visit from Les Holmes and some friends
from Frederick, Maryland. Les arrived at 6:00 without the friends. He
said his plans had changed, his wife was in their car, a half mile away,
and would I join them for a chicken dinner at the Dan-Dee Restaurant near Frederick. I would indeed! Delicious dinner with enough
food left to fill a doggy bag with pieces of chicken, fritters, and small
loaves of bread. Can't understand why my pack gets heavier each
day. Les drove me back to shelter; and I got to bed after 10:00, the
only occupant that night. (*1978 note:* the State of Maryland now
owns the land on which Crampton Gap shelter is situated.)

Saturday, June 20. At 9:00 I reached the trailer home of Walter and
Vera Onheiser directly beside the Trail. I had met them in March
when Gus Crews and I took a conditioning hike in this area. Had a
delicious second breakfast there and was given a jar of homemade
jam which Vera had been saving for me since March. Left there at
11:00, and within 10 minutes met George Huber, outdoor editor for
the *Washington (D.C.) Star.* George took several pictures; and then

we hiked to Pine Knob shelter where we visited and George took some notes for a newspaper article on my hike. It appeared in the July 5 issue of the *Star*. George makes it a point to get at least one story each year of those hiking the entire Trail. In 1968 he and I journeyed to the Pinefield shelter in the Shenandoah National Park and met Everett and Nell Skinner. In 1969, at the same shelter, we met Jeff Hancock. George is a veteran backpacker himself, a long time member of both the PATC and the Conference. He has the knack for extracting from each hiker the type of information that will make a good story.

I left Pine Knob at noon. Observed a young six-inch woodchuck shortly thereafter. Reached Wolfe shelter at 4:20. Had seen 18 people on Trail today, 31 yesterday. At Wolfe shelter I met Tom and Cheryl Cox and Art Robson and his 10-year-old son Brad, all of Maryland. The Coxes were ATC members; and while I was at the shelter, Art Robson filled out an application in the name of his son and gave me a check for $7. I was a walking salesman for ATC memberships all during my hike and know that I inspired many to join. The Robson situation, however, was the only time that I actually received a completed application form and had the money in hand.

Shortly after I arrived at the shelter another group of 11 people from New Jersey and New York arrived. After darkness, they built a huge fire at a point about 30 yards from the shelter. This disturbed me . . . not only from the standpoint of conserving the small firewood supply but also because this was on private land and landowners become justifiably alarmed when hiking groups build large fires. I felt constrained to walk over to the group and ask them to cut down the size of the fire. They immediately did so. This is another shelter that has recently been closed to the hiking public by the landowner.

11. PENNSYLVANIA, JUNE 21 TO JULY 6

Sunday, June 21. A horrible day weatherwise, hard steady rain most of the day. It was still raining when I went to bed that night. Visited four shelters, Devils Racecourse, Mackie Run, Antietam, and Tumbling Run. Found groups of people in each, 25 in all. At Mackie Run I met Bob Bernhardy, another ATC Class D Member, and 10 Boy Scouts from Levittstown, Pennsylvania. Had a nice visit with Mr. Kaufman, the Forest Foreman at Camp Michaux. Had tentatively planned to stay at Tumbling Run; but it was partially occupied, not in the best of shape, and the locked PATC Hermitage Cabin was but 6 miles beyond it. I gambled that the Hermitage would not be occupied on a Sunday night and it proved not to be. The Hermitage, which has a dark interior on even a bright day, was particularly dark and gloomy on this rainy dark night. (1978 note: the Hermitage was burned by arsonists in 1975; the arsonists were apprehended and convicted; and a new Hermitage was built by PATC.)

Monday, June 2. Reached Raccoon Run shelter at noon. Reached US Highway 30 at 2:00 and walked off Trail .4 mile to the office of Richard Thorpe, the District Forester for the State of Pennsylvania. Thorpe was not in, but I was permitted to use his desk for 2½ hours. Wrote letters and critiques on two of the major trail sections I had recently completed. Back to Caledonia State Park, where I visited with Hilary Vida, the Park Superintendent. The following is from my diary: "Reached Quarry Gap shelter 6:30 p.m., cooked an excellent supper: soup, Lipton's chicken dinner with six ounces canned chicken added, instant pudding. All done and eaten by 7:45. Washed dishes, cut kindling for breakfast, and put on fire to dry. Then to work on notes. Getting cool, 60 degrees at 9:00. This Quarry Gap is a delightful place to camp, bubbling stream, three tables, rhododendron in bloom surrounds the shelter. As I wrote these notes (9:05 p.m.) a whippoorwill fluttered down five feet from where I sat, sang his piercing call for a full three to four minutes, then fluttered off and resumed close by. Must stop now, getting too dark to see. 9:10 p.m."

The Quarry Gap shelter is maintained by the Alpha Phi Omega fraternity of Gettysburg College, and they do an excellent job.

Tuesday, June 23. Clear, pleasant day. Reached Milesburn Cabin at 8:30 and Birch Run shelters at 10:00. Found 18 young people there headed by John S. Bishop of Gettysburg who is Director of Camping for the Central Pennsylvania Synod, Lutheran Church of America. At noon I reached the pride and joy of the PATC locked cabin system, the beautiful Michener Cabin, built carefully and expertly by the loving hands of many PATC members. I had checked on occupancy and received a note from Ray Fadner that a Ken Lehman of Harrisburg, Pennsylvania, had the cabin reserved for part of the week. Which part? I heated up huge quantities of hot water, washed clothes, bathed and shaved. Found a 12½ ounce can of tuna, in the cupboard and had a monstrous dinner of creamed tuna and instant potatoes. At 6:00, who should show up but Ken Lehman with his bride of three days! They had been married in Goshen, Indiana, on June 20 and were on their honeymoon. I hastily packed my gear and departed; no time for a third party to hang around. Michener Cabin is becoming steeped with matrimonial tradition. Bill and Beth Oscanyan had been married here.

I hastened on to Tom's Run shelters. Arrived there just at dark, 9 p.m. Five young men were already occupying the two small shelters. Room for one more . . . me!

Picked my first blueberries of the season today.

Wednesday, June 24. Fair weather until 6 p.m., then overcast and windy. Reached Pine Grove Cabin at 7:00 and Pine Grove Furnace State Park at 8:45. This marks the end of the PATC territory through which I have been hiking since June 8, 225 miles. For the next 1,000 miles I will be hiking over trails with which I am only partially familiar.

I reached the Tagg Run shelters at 12:00 and had a very difficult time finding the spring. No sign and no blue blazes to aid the hiker. Reached State Route 34 at 1:30 and hitchhiked into Mt. Holly Springs. Picked up mail, bought groceries, and ate a meal. Caught ride back to AT and resumed hiking at 4:30. Decided later that it was poor planning on my part to have gone into Mt. Holly Springs as the next day the Trail passed directly in front of a combination post office and grocery store in the little town of Allen, Pennsylvania.

I pushed on very hard after 4:30, as I knew there was not much more daylight. Figured I would reach Dark Hollow shelters by 8 p.m. at the latest; but when I reached Center Point Knob, a mile beyond the shelters, I knew that something had gone wrong. I learned later that the Dark Hollow shelters had been abandoned. Actually a supplement sheet to the guidebook had been issued and was in my possession; but I had not read it, so I had nobody to blame but myself. Hiked along the crest of White Rocks, a beautiful place; but I had neither the time nor inclination to enjoy it properly. Finally quit hiking at 9:00 and made my bed on the windward side of the mountain crest. Ate a cold supper and was in bed at 9:30. Hiked 22.7 miles. Saw deer on six occasions. About half the hiking today was on roads.

Let me comment at this point on those strange creatures, the 17-year locusts. On June 16 we crossed the "locust barrier" at US Highway 50. South of that point, I had neither seen nor heard the locusts. North of US 50 I was to hear their shrill singing for hours on end, whenever the temperature rose above a certain point. Along the Trail I had seen thousands of neat ⅜-inch round holes from which the locusts had emerged after a 17-year stay underground. Of late, I had been seeing dead locust bodies littering the Trail. A strange cycle of nature.

Thursday, June 25. Up at 5:20 and on the Trail at 5:40 without breakfast. Reached road in 20 minutes and hiked into the town of Allen, almost all the way on hard surfaced roads. Picked black raspberries (the first of year) and a half pint of cherries on the way in. Cooked breakfast over my Primus stove in the little cemetery across from combination store-post office. Also mixed up my first batch of "Citadel Spread." The postmaster gave me a letter from a Henry Finerfrock of New Cumberland, Pennsylvania, whom I had met at the ATC meeting in Shippensburg. He extended me a warm invitation to stay overnight at his home and asked that I telephone him. I tried to phone him from Allen; no answer. Left Allen at 10:00 and hiked on roads almost the entire day. Ate my fill of cherries and black raspberries. Crossed US Highway 11 in early afternoon. Lost Trail twice during the day; not too well blazed, very few signs. In mid-afternoon I was flagged down by two carloads of people, members of the Mountain Club of Maryland who had been tracking me for five hours. A number of them hiked with me all the way to the Darlington shelter. We reached there at 5:00. They came well equipped with big sandwiches, lemonade, cookies, etc. Very thoughtful of them to take off an entire day to provide a little companionship for one hiker, and I did enjoy meeting them.

To return again to my needless trip into Mt. Holly Springs. After noting the convenience of the combination store-post office at Allen, I made another one of many resolutions: that I will develop and publish a list of all convenient post office stops for the benefit of long distance AT hikers. This resolution I kept; and the list of grocery and post office stops appears in Appendix 3 to this book.

Hiked 16 miles today, warm and humid. Again having trouble with chafing.

Friday, June 26. Dark gloomy day; it rained hard during the night. Hiked the 12 miles into Duncannon; reached there 2 p.m. after a brief stop at Thelma Mark's shelter at 10:00. Picked up mail at post office and then moved over to quarters of the Volunteer Fire Department. Tried repeatedly to reach Finerfrock. No luck. Harry Baker of the Volunteer Fire Department offered me the use of the Recreation Room quarters overnight, and I gratefully accepted his offer. Fabulous setup; toilet facilities with water so steaming hot I could and did make coffee and tea with the tap water. A water cooler, tables to write on, a couch to sleep on, a TV if I wanted to use it. Had the whole building to myself. I stayed up until 1 a.m. catching up on my correspondence. Several of the firemen had apologized for the condition of the rest room. It was a bit litterstrewn, so as my contribution, I did clean the place spic and span clean. Went to bed at 1:30 a.m.

Saturday, June 27. Up at 6:00, left the firehouse at 6:30. Overcast day, rain threatened most of day. Crossed Clarks Ferry Bridge over the Susquehanna River, then crossed US 22 and the railroad tracks, then ascended the steep ravine. Reached Susquehanna shelter and met Bill Looney and group of 13 Boy Scouts from Canton, Pennsylvania. Looney is postmaster at Canton. Reached the Earl Shaffer shelter at 12 noon. Reached Clarks Valley shelter at 4:00, 14 miles for the day. This last shelter is the first concrete block shelter I have seen since Tennessee. Picked about one quart of black raspberries during the day. Yesterday, and again today, I saw the perforated four-inch metal ATC markers. I read that these were used in the early years of the Trail, but I don't recall ever having seen them on the Trail before.

Sunday, June 28. A clear, cool, delightful day. There are no shelters for a 27-mile stretch from Clarks Valley shelter until Applebee shelter. No shelters to inspect and none to sleep in, so I had made arrangements by telephone to sleep at the BSA Camp Bashore. Hiked through St. Anthony's Wilderness, one of the most beautiful areas on entire Trail. It is somewhat comparable to Laurel Fork Gorge in Tennessee. Met and visited with Mr. and Mrs. Marvin Kline, Class D members, of Mountain Top, Pennsylvania. St. Anthony's Wilderness is a fascinating place. The Trail is on the roadbed of the old stagecoach road. Within the quiet fastness of the Wilderness the hiker sees the remains of the once thriving town of Rausch Gap, the old town well, the little cemetery, the railroad beds, and the remains of the old trestles. I ate lunch at a pretty spot beside the rushing Rausch Creek.

At 1:30 I was hailed by Hank Finerfrock who had tracked me down by visiting the previous shelter and finding my green calling card with the date shown thereon. Thus he could fairly accurately predict where he would find me on the Trail. We hiked to Swatara Gap, the end of the section, 17 miles for the day. Reached Swatara Gap at 3 p.m. Had visited for a few minutes with a landowner, the elderly and very friendly Francis Ditzler, Jonestown, Pennsylvania. Hank and I then drove to Camp Bashore where I cancelled my sleeping reservation and visited with Jack Marcum, Earl Leiby, Warren Thompson and also Bennett Gordon of Falls Church. Thompson extracted a promise that I would drop him a line when I completed my hike at Mt. Katahdin. Camp Bashore is operated by the Lebanon, Pennsylvania, Council of the Boy Scouts.

Drove to the Finerfrock residence in New Cumberland, and I went to 5:30 Mass. I looked a little rough around the edges as I had not had time to change clothes or shave. That came later. I had a delicious steak dinner with the Finerfrocks; and after dinner I made a momentous decision! I needed a new Kelty pack! Some of the straps were wearing on my old Kelty and the fabric had taken quite a beating when my luggage rack tore loose from my car on our way down to Georgia in March. But more importantly I wanted more pack space. Even though it was a Sunday night I called Dan Couch, proprietor of Appalachian Outfitters in Oakton, Virginia, and he promised to send me the expedition size Kelty, a BB 5 model. Less than three days later, the pack arrived at Delaware Water Gap, Pennsylvania. It was there waiting for me when I hiked into the post office on July 6.

I heard no more 17-year locusts on that day, so I think I have passed through the locust country. I weighed 143 pounds stripped, 10 pounds under my normal weight.

Monday, June 29. Began hiking from Swatara Gap at 9:00 with Hank Finerfrock and 14-year-old Greg Grissinger, a friend of the Finerfrocks. We hiked very steadily as Hank had yet to put in a day's work beginning at 3 p.m. Covered the 10.6 miles to Applebee shelter in 4½ hours. Hank's daughter Jan, his wife Doris, and her mother had a hot lunch all laid out for us when we arrived. Such conveniences on the Appalachian Trail! And the day was just beginning. After the Finerfrocks left, Greg and I hiked to the nearby Lundgren cabin, a locked cabin belonging to the Blue Mountain Eagle Climbing Club of Reading, Pennsylvania. Bob Fisher, Trailmaster for the Blue Mountain Club, and his wife June were there. We visited, and enjoyed a delicious supper with them. Dick Kimmel, President of the Club, and his wife Hilda arrived from Lebanon in the early evening. More visting. Both couples left around 9:00; Greg and I then had the cabin to ourselves. Club members had spent hundreds of hours renovating the cabin, and it was a delightful spot in which to spend the night.

Tuesday, June 30. Up at 6:00, stoked up the fire, and had a huge breakfast of grilled cheese sandwiches, fresh milk, canned cherries, pie, and coffee. Not bad for a trail breakfast! Locked up the cabin at 7:20 and we were on our way. Pleasant day, mostly clear. Had a leisurely 14-mile hike to Neys shelter. Seemed odd that we were forced to walk for five miles on a gravel road in the hot sun. It would appear to have been more logical to have run the Trail through the nearby wooded area which was owned by the State of Pennsylvania. A group of 15 boys was already at Neys shelter when we arrived; but they shortly left and headed for an open campsite just south of Route 183. Cooked a freeze-dried beef steak supper given us by Hank Finerfrock. It was delicious. At 7:00 Maurice Forrester, a member of the Reading Club who had corresponded with me earlier, arrived and visited until 8:00. We saw deer walking inquiringly around the camp several times. Had a late snack of freshly popped corn.

Wednesday, July 1. A leisurely seven-mile hike to Port Clinton interrupted midway by my second encounter with a rattlesnake. Greg Grissinger was walking in front of me on the Trail when he suddenly jumped backward. Three feet in front of him was a four-foot rattle-snake with eight rattles. The snake was not coiled and had given no warning. He appeared indifferent to our presence, and we merely walked about three or four feet to one side of him and passed on.

A quarter-mile before reaching Port Clinton, we were met by the Finerfrock family and by Mrs. Grissinger. I picked up six letters at the post office and visited with a trailwise looking group of 16 Boy Scouts from Phoenixville, Pennsylvania who were on a 300-mile hike. The Finerfrocks and Greg Grissinger left at noon. I enjoyed my three-day hike with Greg, a good hiker and a very pleasant person.

I repaired to the Port Clinton hotel for a sandwich and signed the Appalachian Trail register maintained by Mr. and Mrs. Royle Car-baugh who operate the hotel. Within minutes, Bob and June Fisher picked me up and drove me to their home in Reading. Shortly there-after, Jan Jones, a reporter, and Bill Ader, a photographer from the *Reading Eagle* arrived for an interview and pictures. The story appeared in next day's paper.

Dinner at the Fishers. Afterward we were visited by three other members of the BMEC Club: Paul Lehman, Ann Hart, and Bruce Homan.

Thursday, July 2. Repacked groceries and weighed my pack, 43

pounds with my two canteens full of white wine, my heaviest weight
so far. A hot, humid, overcast day. Bob Fisher drove me back to Port
Clinton, and I began hiking at 8:45. Met Paul Lehman near Windsor
Furnace, and he hiked with me until 2:30. Much fog, no views from
the Pinnacles. Reached Hawk Mountain about 4:15. Met Bruce
Homan there, and we walked through the Hawk Mountain Sanctuary.
No view from lookout there either. Still foggy. Bruce got me back on
the AT at 5:30, and I found an envelope addressed to me. The letter
was from Norm Greist of North Haven, Connecticut. He had fastened
the letter to a cable across the Trail. Norm was hiking in the area and
was uncertain of my exact whereabouts. At 6:45 I reached the big
28-foot by 32-foot cabin owned by John Rarick, another member of
the BMECC. Cooked over a propane stove and had propane lighting
for the evening. Pretty luxurious for a trail hiker. Rarick and his wife
arrived about 9:45. He brought me a package of breakfast pastries.
He also brought up a half bushel of old bread and rolls for the many
raccoons in the area. They left at 11:30. To bed at 1 a.m.

Friday, July 3. Overcast and foggy all day. Missed all the views on
what is probably the most scenic part of the Trail in Pennsylvania.
Reached Allentown shelter at 10:00. The spring was dry, but fresh
water had been left there for me by John Himmelberger and Warren
Mengel. Very considerate people. Reached Route 309 at 1:00; and
just north of that point I began finding a series of envelopes addressed
to me, all from the same Norm Greist. The fourth letter contained
compass directions and distance to a little treat hidden near the Trail.
Treasure hunts on the Appalachian Trail? Yes, I found it!

Maurice Forrester joined me near Route 309. Reached New Tripoli
shelter at 3:00. It was occupied by 22 Scouts and their leaders from
the Wilmington, Delaware area. Reached Bake Oven Knob shelter at
5:00 and was joined by four more members of the BMECC. The
spring was dry at this shelter also, but the group had brought fresh
water with them. They left around 8:00. Before leaving, Forrester
gave me a copy of the July 2 issue of the *Reading Eagle.* We all
thought that the young lady reporter, Jan Jones, had done a very good
job. The picture taken by Bill Ader appeared in the *Reading Eagle.*

Saturday, July 4. Independence Day. Another hot humid day.
Reached Outerbridge shelter at 9:00, 8.1 miles. This shelter is unique
because of its stone work. The shelter is a large 21-foot by 18-foot
log structure with wooden bunks. There are no tables as such, but
there is about 30-square feet of flat stone work at table height built

on the rocky terrain immediately adjacent to the shelter. It is a very attractive shelter, but it was disfigured somewhat by 30 to 40 bushels of trash in an open pit 40 yards in front of the shelter. The next shelter is 30 miles farther north.

Met four boys at the shelter who were camping there, not hiking. Shortly after arriving, I was met by Hal Croxton, a Class D member of ATC from nearby Coupersburg. He hiked with me to Lehigh Gap. Shortly after crossing Lehigh River, I met a hiker at the top of a ridge who was taking his tent down. He proved to be a German engineer on a six weeks' hiking vacation to the US. I gave him one of the Pennsylvania hiking maps covering the area through which he would be hiking.

Found four more letters on the Trail today. These four were from LeRoy Smith of Nazareth, Pennsylvania. He asked that I contact him when I reached Wind Gap. Also walked through a concentration of sassafras trees today, the biggest such trees I had ever seen. The diameter of the largest was five inches at breast height.

Reached a paved road at Little Gap. Hitched ride into Danielsville and obtained a room ($4.00) at the Mountain View Hotel. Showered, shaved, and washed clothes. Have been hiking with wet feet for three days in hot humid weather and the stench from my socks is pretty awful. It felt wonderful to get into clean dry clothes. I hitched a ride into nearby Berlinsville to attend a 6:30 p.m. Mass. Caught ride back to the hotel with the Kean family who had also attended the Mass. Ate a chicken platter dinner at the hotel, wrote letters until 11:30. Things had begun to liven up in the hotel bar directly below me; the boom, boom, boom of the music kept me awake for a long time . . . all of five minutes!

Sunday, July 5. Left hotel 6:15. A 45-minute walk back to the Trail at Little Gap. Arrived at Smith Gap at 10:30 and met Tom Miller of Bethlehem, Pennsylvania, and his group of 20 horsemen. They had set up camp at a nice spot in the Gap; and with 20 people and a goodly number of horses, it was a busy place. They treated me to coffee, hamburgers, and a sip of wine.

Although I had seen evidence in a number of places that horses had used the Trail, the encounter at Smith Gap was the only time I actually saw them. The issue of horses using the Appalachian Trail is a thorny one. Horsemen, as well as bicyclists and motorcycle enthusiasts, have precious few places to pursue their hobbies except on highways where they must compete with roughly 100 million automobiles and trucks. To all of these groups the well-maintained Appalachian Trail looks very inviting. The hiking clubs maintain that since they (the hikers) have worked for 40 years to develop and maintain a 2,000-mile-long trail for hikers, that the other groups should go elsewhere. Moreover, the hiking clubs maintain that vehicles and horses do tremendous damage to the Trail, especially on steep slopes. A 1,200 pound horse with steel shoes climbing a steep slope will dislodge more ground cover and cause more erosion than hundreds of hikers will cause over a period of years. The National Trails System Act, Public Law 90-543, prohibits the use of the Trail by motorized vehicles and discourages but does not actually prohibit its use by horses. The matter is one that must be handled through regulation, as both the states and the federal government acquire rights to the lands over which the Trail passes.

Back to Smith Gap, named for the forebears of LeRoy Smith of Nazareth, Pennsylvania. As I left the Gap and began hiking the Trail, I experienced a strange feeling. It was as though suddenly I was back in Georgia and the time was early April. The Trail had a strange appearance. The sun shone brightly through the trees where I should have been in the shade! Here, for a five-mile stretch, the leaves had been stripped from all of the trees by gypsy moths. The forest was too, too bright; very few birds were in evidence. I experienced an eerie feeling. It made me think of Rachel Carson's *Silent Spring*.

I reached Wind Gap (State Route 115) at 3:45, 18 miles for the day. I promptly visited the nearby Gateway Motel where the Skinners had been treated so royally in 1968. The motel is operated by an Austrian family, the Domaters. While waiting for the LeRoy Smith family to pick me up, I purchased a huge ham sandwich for 50 cents and Mrs. Domater added a large slice of watermelon for good measure. The Smiths picked me up at 5:00. We drove to nearby Nazareth, Pennsylvania, and had dinner at the Smith home. Later, I was interviewed over the phone by Stan Schaffer of the *Allentown Morning Call*. A photographer came over later. Then, even though darkness was not far off, we drove back to the mountain; and LeRoy and I hiked up and inspected a site where the Delaware Chapter of the Appalachian Mountain Club planned to build a much needed trailside shelter. (The shelter was built in 1972—circa. The principal builder, Leroy Smith, died shortly thereafter; and the shelter was named the "Leroy Smith Shelter.")

Monday, July 6. Up at 5:00. A delicious sausage and egg breakfast. Left the Smith home at 6:30. As we were getting into the car, the newsboy bicycled into view and delivered the morning paper with the article and picture on my hike. Fast reporting! I reached the Kirkbridge shelter at noon and ate lunch there. As I was leaving, a man ran toward me and called me by name. He introduced himself as Joe Bell, another member of the Blue Mountain Eagle Climbing Club. While at work that morning, someone had shown him the morning paper with the article on my hike. During his lunch hour he had driven to the Kirkbridge shelter; he reasoned that I should reach that point at noon. Good calculation. I concluded that the BMECC had certainly cared for my welfare . . . even beyond that part of the Trail which they maintain.

I was now hiking the last few miles in Pennsylvania and approaching the Delaware River and the spectacular Delaware Water Gap. As I stood on the various view points looking down on the River, it reminded me very strongly of the view of the Potomac River and Harpers Ferry, which I had enjoyed on June 18. I arrived in the town of Delaware Water Gap at 3:45 and proceeded directly to the post office where I picked up a mountain of mail, some 15 letters and four packages. My new Kelty pack was there; and I promptly wrote a check and mailed it to Appalachian Outfitters. Even though I was pressed for time, I felt that such prompt service deserved prompt payment.

In addition to the Kelty pack, I had received three pounds of Claxton fruit cake from Claxton, Georgia, a heavier pair of hiking shoes sent from home, and the New York-New Jersey guidebook. I tied my various boxes together and began walking over the bridge to New Jersey and to the Park Service Visitor Center for the recently established Delaware Water Gap National Recreation Area. It is one thing to hike the AT with one pack and one pair of hiking shoes; it is another to do it with two of each. I reached the Visitor Center at 5:00; and shortly thereafter I was met by Harry Nees, a retired insurance executive, who lives in Garrison, New York. Nees, who is a long time member of the New York-New Jersey Trail Conference, personally maintains a section of the Trail in this area. He is also a fellow member of the ATC Board of Managers and I have known him for years. We drove to the Belleville Rod & Gun Club in Wallpack, New Jersey. We were the only occupants of the very spacious Clubhouse. After dinner, we assembled the new Kelty, feather light, seemingly very durable, and gobs of space. The Clubhouse is situated

Ed Garvey with Casey Kays at Sunfish Pond, July 7, 1970.

beside the Big Flat Brook; and in the twilight I walked along it, watched it, and listened to it. Many birds in this area.

On this date, July 6, I had completed my hike through seven States. Seven States still remained. I had hiked 1,156 miles and had 872 more to hike. On May 6, I had crossed from Tennessee into Virginia; and now, exactly two months later, I had crossed the Delaware River into New Jersey. Half the States and well over half the mileage was behind me. I had looked forward for days to reaching this point, and I was pleased that my hike had been so successful to date.

12. NEW JERSEY-NEW YORK, JULY 7 TO 18

Tuesday, July 7. This was to be a very eventful day. Harry and I drove back to the National Recreation Area Visitor Center, hiked the AT for a short distance, then hiked a side trail to the top of Mt. Tammany. The views of the Delaware Water Gap from various vantage points on Mt. Tammany are spectacular. It seems a shame that the Appalachian Trail is not routed over this very interesting spot. During the previous three months I had struggled to the tops of scores of steep mountain tops. When I reached the top, there was nothing to see; the mountain top was completely wooded. I wondered why trail planners had gone to such pains to put the Trail over the top of such mountains when there is no reward for the hiker when he reaches the top. But here in New Jersey the Trail comes within a mile of one of the most spectacular water gaps in the eastern United States, and for some unexplainable reason the Trail had been laid out to skirt the mountain top from which there were marvelous views.

Harry and I separated after lunch; and I began hiking on the AT towards Sunfish Pond, some four miles distant. Shortly thereafter, I met another lone hiker, also with pack. After a few exploratory remarks, he learned that I was the fellow he had hiked out to meet; he had read that morning in the paper about some character hiking the entire Appalachian Trail. For my part, I learned that he was Casey Kays of Hackettstown, New Jersey, a never-give-up conservationist whom I had been desirous of meeting for years. A factory worker, Casey was the first person to call public attention to the plans of utility companies to use Sunfish Pond, a glacial lake on Kittatinny Ridge, as the upper reservoir of a pumped storage electricity generating plant. For over five years he fought the good fight, writing and mailing thousands of letters, conducting hikes so that the public

could see the now famous pond, and testifying at hearings. Together
we hiked towards Sunfish Pond. I have included a picture taken on
the shore of this pond.

The pond itself is a rare jewel in a beautiful setting. As an outsider,
blissfully ignorant of all the ramifications, I can ask only two questions: (1) does this beautiful pond have to be sacrificed, and (2) if
the pond were not there, would all electricity generating activities
in New Jersey cease? (1978 note: Casey won the fight and Sunfish
Pond and the area surrounding it were deeded back to the State of
New Jersey!)

After leaving Casey and hiking on the AT around the pond, I was
distressed to note that the area seems to be suffering from wall-to-
wall camping and wall-to-wall littering. There seemed to be no
agency, state or federal, that was controlling the amount of camping
or was removing trash. I made no attempt to pick up litter near Sunfish Pond. Casey had given me detailed instructions on how to find
the spring at the north end of the pond, but it turned out that his
efforts were wasted. As I neared the spring area, I saw a large rock
directly beside the Trail. On it, in 2½-inch letters in blue paint had
been printed the following words:

E. Garvey
←

Spring

I was both amused and pleased with the sign; and I knew immediately what had inspired this sign and who had applied the
brush. Earlier in this chapter you have read of my difficulties finding
the water sources along the Trail—even to the point where I had
become lost in southwestern Virginia while looking for water. At the
ATC meeting in Shippensburg, Pennsylvania, I had appeared on the
program and had given a 20-minute discourse on the first 725 miles
of my hike. I had spoken with some heat about the poor identification of water sources. One of those in the audience was Herb Hiller
of Verona, New Jersey who resolved that he would identify the one
spring on his section of the Trail in a manner that would be unmistakable even to the nearsighted. On his next work trip he gleefully
did his sign work and waited for my reaction. I wrote to him
promptly, congratulating him on his originality. A day later at the
Stokes shelter, I heard some Boy Scouts talking about having stopped
at "The Garvey Spring." So, unless someone removes the large rock,

I have a spring named after me. A month or so after the completion of my hike, I received a letter from John W. Panko of Woodbridge, New Jersey, to which he attached an excellent 35 mm. color slide of the "E. Garvey Spring" sign. (*1978 note:* I have since received pictures and slides of this sign from many hikers.)

About two miles north of the spring there occurred one of the most unusual incidents of the trip. Approaching me from the north were two people walking single file. The first person was a young man, barefooted, wearing a pair of dungarees. I could not get a good look at the second person. However, when I drew abreast—and I choose that word carefully—I saw that the second person was a very curvaceous young lady; and she was not wearing dungarees, nor was she wearing anything else! She seemed a little new at the nudist game and somewhat ill at ease. As I came within speaking distance, she giggled and said, "Nice day, hunh?" I smiled and replied with an enthusiastic, "Indeed it is!" Shortly after passing these two, I heard a baby cry; and looking to my left I saw a 1½-year-old baby being comforted by a large naked young man. I spoke to him, and he returned my greeting. Beyond him were another eight or 10 young adults, all nude. I kept walking north, thinking over this unusual incident. Shortly thereafter I met Harry Nees who had hiked in from the north end of the section to meet me. I told him of my experience, and he shook his head sadly and said, "It just isn't right. I've maintained this section of the Trail for 15 years and have never seen anything more exciting than an occasional deer. Now you come up here from Virginia and the first day out you hit the jackpot!" Oddly enough, I think I was one of the few who encountered this band of nudists because others whom I met on the Trail who had come by that way shortly before me, or shortly after me had not encountered them. It does prove that hiking the AT can be a real adventure . . . also, that one should not hike with his eyes glued to the ground!

Harry and I reached Blairstown Road at 6:15. We stopped for a few minutes enroute to visit with a group of Puerto Rican Boy Scouts. We then drove back to the Belleville Rod and Gun Club and had a hearty dinner. There I learned a new method of cooking sweet corn, the Nees recipe: Put sweet corn in a kettle of cold water, add two-three tablespoons of sugar, bring the water to a boil, and, Presto, the sweet corn is ready to eat.

The day had been noteworthy in many other respects in addition to those I have already described. I met some 75 people on the Trail, a very high figure. I had picked up 15 cans and some 120 pieces of other litter, a very heavy day. I had learned to identify a new plant, Indian Pipe. I had seen deer on three occasions. And I had passed through another large area being defoliated by the two-inch-long caterpillar worms of the gypsy moth.

Wednesday, July 8. The following is quoted from my diary. "Up at 5:00, went to work on my notes, later Harry arose and cooked breakfast. I worked on my notes, wrote letters, repacked my new Kelty, and packed the old Kelty, my worn out shoes, and other material for mailing home. After lunch Harry drove me to the AT on Blairstown Road, and I began hiking at 1:30. Warm day. Made fairly good time, but blueberries slowed me down! Saw deer on three occasions, including one spotted fawn. Some beautiful views in this area, quite a few natural lakes. Reached Stokes shelter at 6:45. It was fully occupied by BSA Troop Two of Lakewood, New Jersey. They were kind enough to furnish me a tarp and helped me erect it. The boys also heated water for me, so I enjoyed the instant (five minute) beef stew (Mountain House, Freeze Dried Beef Stew) previously given to me by Bruce Homan. Must adjust to my new pack. Having that one huge compartment requires a different mode of packing. Enjoyed my visit with the three men of Troop Two: Carroll MacKenzie, Joe Maurer, and George Reese. Went to bed about 9:30. A few mosquitoes but no real problem."

Thursday, July 9. Hiked 15 miles from the Stokes shelter to High Point No. 2 shelter. Bought some delicious bakery products at Culver Gap and U.S. Highway 206 and washed them down with coffee, courtesy of Lakeside Sunoco. Had a long telephone conversation with John Broshkevitch, the Forester for the Stokes State Forest. Reached Gren Anderson shelter at 11:00; and five miles farther on, the High Point No. 3 shelter. At the latter shelter the roof was completely burned out; but the huge roof beams—and I do mean huge (9 inches by 12 inches by 21 feet)—were lying on the ground. Broshkevitch had informed me this shelter would have a new roof put on. Reached High Point No. 2 shelter at 5:30. Although the AT in New Jersey receives a tremendous amount of use, High Point No. 2 shelter, although in excellent condition, was obviously but little used. High grass almost obliterated the Trail to toilet and trash pit.

This was the heaviest litter pickup day to date: 15 cans, 160 pieces of other litter. Litter pickup in New Jersey is killing me!

Friday, July 10. It rained during the night and rained intermittently throughout the day, with torrential rains around 8 a.m. I was soaking wet by 8 a.m. and remained that way most of the day. Reached High Point No. 1 shelter at 10:00. North of this shelter the Trail extends into New York for a few miles before winding back into New Jersey. At 12:30 I reached Unionville, New York and searched for a restaurant. I was directed to a small place well back from the highway. It was fittingly named Side Road Pantry. What a find. I love homemade pies; and, as I approached the Pantry, I had an inkling of what I would find when I saw a lady come out of the entrance triumphantly carrying an armful of fresh baked pies. Inside was a large table completely covered with hot pies that had been set aside on the table to cool. All of the bread and rolls served to customers with their meals was homemade and of top quality. Another resolution made . . . and this one I'm sure I will keep . . . to return to the Side Road Pantry! At the Pantry my pack attracted the attention of Bill and Betty Knittel of Pompton Lake, New Jersey, who are Class D members of the Conference; and I had a brief visit with them. (1978 note: I did return to Unionville in October 1975 when researching my second book. To my dismay I found that the Side Road Pantry had closed a year or two earlier.)

After leaving Unionville, it began to rain again. Much of the Trail was along country roads. From the High Point No. 1 shelter, it is 45 miles to the next shelter in New York, so I knew I would have no shelter to sleep in on that day or the next. It was approaching 6:00 p.m., and I had hiked 20 miles. So as I near the community of Maple Grange, New Jersey, I asked and received permission from dairy farmer Lynn Presher to use his machine shed for the night. Not only that, but he permitted me to use the boiling hot water of the dairy room within the barn. Frankly, the machine shed was much more inviting than some of the shelters I had slept in. It was a pleasure to have steaming hot water for coffee, for shaving, and for washing dishes! I certainly completed my daily log and made my diary entries in some strange and varied places during the 158 days I was on the Trail; this night, July 10, I did my paper work while sitting on a feed sack in a machine shed of a New Jersey dairy farm.

Saturday, July 11. I was awakened at 5:10 a.m. by a cow that thrust her head through a hole in the machine shed wall and bawled impatiently at me. It was time for milking; and 10 minutes later Bill Presher, Lynn's brother, flicked on the barn lights. The cows ambled in, and the milking process began. I had begun making preparations for breakfast, but Bill invited me to his home. I accepted with alacrity. Much bacon, two eggs, and fresh banana nut bread. Water for coffee taken directly from the tap, the same boiling hot water used in the dairy room of the barn. Began hiking at 6:30, and at 8:15 I spotted a tent erected directly beside the Trail. I hailed the occupant, Gary Rutherford, a bearded, 27-year-old civil engineer from Pen Argyl, Pennsylvania. He hastily packed his gear, and we began hiking together. He expressed a desire to hike with me all the way to Katahdin. We ate lunch on the Warwick Turnpike, even finding a fruit stand 100 yards down the pike. The AT does offer some surprises now and then.

At 3:30 we reached Cascade Lake and went for a brief but delight- ful swim, my first of the year. Pushed on hiking steadily several miles high above the beautiful Greenwood Lake. At 5:30 we left the AT and hiked on the blue blazed Mountain Spring Trail to reach the resort village of Greenwood Lake, New York. We ate our evening meal and stayed overnight at Murphy's Hotel and Bar.

During the afternoon we had passed from New Jersey into New York. Eight States behind me; six more to go! Picked my first black- berries of the season. I am still seeing rhododendron in bloom and still seeing and smelling wild azalea.

Sunday, July 12. A clear, warm, and very humid day. Up at 6:00, went to eight o'clock Mass, and we both began hiking at 9:30. A hard climb to the top of a mountain; we reached the top at 10:00, dripping with sweat. Made poor mileage, many road crossings, met numerous groups of people with whom we stopped and visited. Hiked over miles of those big glacial conglomerate rock formations. The Trail is very steep in many places. Beautiful views of the New York lake area. While hiking we met three-fourths of the John Panko family, father, mother, and son Bob, of Woodbridge, New Jersey. They too are Class D members of ATC. I was later to meet the other son, Ron, in New Hampshire. As I wound my pleasant way north on the AT challenging everyone that I met, it seemed that the Class D-ers were literally coming out of the woodwork. To each I extended a warm invitation to meet me in June 1972, at the ATC meeting in Plymouth, New Hampshire. I hope that at the Plymouth meeting they provide large name plates for each person, for I will have many, many names and faces to recall.

At 6:30 we crossed State Route 17, near the New York thruway. By prearrangement we met Harry Nees at that point, and he whisked us over to his lovely home near Garrison, New York, with its magnificent view of the Hudson River Storm King area. I learned that Bill Hoeferlin, a long time stalwart of the New York-New Jersey Trail Conference and an enthusiastic hiker for 50 years, died today in a manner he would have wished, hiking with a group of friends.

Monday, July 13. Up at 5:30. Worked on notes and correspondence until the others arose. Had an out-of-this-world breakfast and lunch cooked by Harry's good Danish-born wife, Kirsten. After lunch, Harry drove us back to the AT at State Route 17. We hiked but eight miles for the day, our progress slowed by the need to inspect three shelters. Our hiking that day was entirely within the Harriman section of Palisades Interstate Park. The first six miles of our hike, from Route 17 to Lake Tiorati Circle, was on the very first section of the Appalachian Trail. That section had been opened on Sunday, October 7, 1923.

We reached the Letterrock shelter at 7:00 and found it occupied by a church group from New York City comprised of 20 boys. They cooked a hot dog and hamburger for both Gary and myself. With that and our own coffee and fruitcake we made out famously. As darkness enveloped the area, we were plagued with tiny little flies called "no-see-ums." Gary erected his two-man tent. The boys . . . in the 12- to 14-year-old class . . . played a little rough. The firecrackers, name calling, and an occasional rock banging on the tin roof of the shelter plus the hungry no-see-ums made sleep a little difficult.

Litter was again heavy: 10 cans and 80 pieces of other litter. We did not attempt to clean up the area around Island Pond as the area was saturated.

During the time I hiked with Gary, I lived a little higher on the hog insofar as coffee was concerned. He carried a small coffee pot with which he brewed real coffee over his gasoline stove. We both loved good fresh coffee; and he brewed it often, even at lunch time. His coffee pot was small; but we overcame that difficulty by brewing extremely strong coffee, then removing the percolator basket and adding water. The diluted mixture was still plenty strong enough for me, and by diluting the coffee there would be two full cups for each of us.

Tuesday, July 14. We began hiking at 8:00, but we lost a full hour because we hiked in the wrong direction! The second time I had done that. Met part of the group that had stayed at Letterrock shelter.

They had noticed us starting out in the wrong direction, but they were reluctant to challenge anyone who had hiked all the way from Georgia. I had the feeling that the group would not have given me a very high rating as a peerless woodsman!

Made slow time, encountered some very steep climbs. The views looking down on the New York lakes were superb. Somehow we missed the one shelter in this section, the West Mountain shelter. The shelter is 0.6 miles off the AT, and we observed no sign indicating the location of the shelter.

We reached the summit of Bear Mountain at 11:30 and then proceeded down the steep litter-strewn Trail towards the Bear Mountain Inn. During the day we picked up 10 cans and 150 pieces of other litter, most of it in the last mile. There seemed to be thousands of people milling about the playground area, concessions, and in the areas adjacent to the Inn and the museum. We had difficulty finding the Trail through this area. We reached the Bear Mountain bridge and paid the five-cent toll for crossing by foot—the only toll or admission I was forced to pay in 2,000 miles of hiking. I'm not complaining about the five cents. If you read of my attempt to cross the Kennebec River in Maine, on September 23, you will surmise (correctly!) that I would have paid many times that amount to cross the Kennebec. After crossing the Hudson, we were picked up by Harry Nees, driven to his home, and there made preparations for dinner at the Bear Mountain Inn where we were guests of the New York-New Jersey Trail Conference. We spent a most pleasant evening with George Zoebelein, Art Beach, Bob Bloom, Elizabeth Levers, and Harry Nees of the NY-NJ group plus Don Stewart, the Superintendent of the Palisades Interstate Park System.

Wednesday, July 15. We stayed at the Nees residence until noon. There we were joined by Art Beach and Mike Warren. At 2:00 p.m., the five of us (Beach, Warren, Nees, Rutherford, and I) began hiking from the Bear Mountain Bridge. We hiked only five miles for the day. It was a warm, overcast, humid day; and we walked through some areas where mosquitoes and deerfles were very troublesome. Gary was wearing shorts, and he did not have quite enough hands to keep the insects off.

We reached State Route 9 at 4:30, and walked up the steep hill to the Graymoor Monastery where Art Beach had made arrangements for us to stay. We ate a family style dinner at 5:40. A very interesting place, another one of those places to which I should like to return.

One of the buildings on the premises is used to provide temporary housing for derelicts from the streets of New York.

All through the southern Appalachians I had seen wild azaleas or flame azaleas as they are also called. They were of two colors, orange and pink. When I resumed hiking on June 6, I still would see a few of the fading azalea bushes at higher elevations; and each time I observed them, I recorded them as the "last azaleas" of the season. When I reached New Jersey, I was informed by Casey Kays that I would see a different type of azalea all through New Jersey and New York—smooth azaleas, he called them, and they would have white flowers. He was so right. We saw and smelled them on a number of days. However, on July 14 I saw the biggest azalea bushes of my trip—several of them standing 10 feet high.

Paint Blazing. Before leaving the state of New York it seems appropriate to make some observations on paint blazing. There are two areas on the entire Trail that are not paint blazed: the northernmost 40 miles of the Great Smoky Mountain National Park and most of the White Mountain National Forest in New Hampshire. There are sections of the Trail where the paint blazing is faded, where the blazes are too infrequent, where the blazes are missing at intersections thus leaving the hiker in a quandary as to which way he should proceed. The great proportion of the Trail mileage is, however, very well blazed, a tribute to the hard working trail clubs whose volunteer workers do the paint blazing. In a number of places on the Trail, I would smile appreciatively as I followed those clear sharp two-inch by six-inch white rectangles. I knew they had been placed there by an expert who had enough imagination to anticipate and to place a white paint blaze at every point where the hiker might experience uncertainty. In one seven-mile stretch of the Trail, north of Lake Tiorati Circle, I had observed paint blazing that was as close to perfection as any I was to see on the entire Trail. Upon inquiry, I learned that the careful workman was a Leonard Graydon whose address I promptly lost. On this date, July 14, I wrote him via the office of the New York-New Jersey Trail Conference a letter of congratulations on his expert blazing. Would that there were more such people! (*1978 note:* Leonard Graydon was mugged and killed in New York in 1975.)

Thursday, July 16. Began hiking at 8:15. A hot, humid, muggy, and buggy day. Hard rains from 11:00 to 1:00. At several places we hiked near swamps; the mosquitoes and deerflies were ferocious. Reached

Indian Lake shelter at 11:00. It began to rain at 12:00 and rained in
torrents for an hour. I was drenched from head to foot. Water squish-
ing out of my shoes at every step. We hiked through interesting
country, rock walls after rock walls. These places are not being farmed
any more. I reflected that it must have been extremely difficult trying to eke out a living from this rocky land in years past. Giant hemlock trees, plus mosquitoes much of the day. I used bug repellant
and wore a kerchief over my head and neck. We reached Fahnestock
State Park at 4:00. It brought back memories of the time when my
family and I had camped there in 1964 and when, on impulse, I had
written a note addressed to Chuck Ebersole who was hiking the
entire Trail that year with his son Johnny and beagle dog Snuffy. I
fastened the note to a tree beside the Trail. Three weeks later I
received a card from Ebersole. He wrote how he had seen the white
3 by 5-inch card from a distance on a foggy day . . . how, when he
came closer, he could make out writing on it . . . and how, when he
was within a few feet of it, he was amazed to see that it was
addressed to him. The Trail mail system can be most effective at
times.

On the highway near Fahnestock, I hailed Trooper Bill O'Connell
who drove me to the residence of Julian Cowan, Superintendent of
Fahnestock State Park. I visited with both men for a few minutes and
then pushed on towards Torrey Memorial shelter. I reached there
at 6:00.

Friday, July 17. Reached Farmers Mill shelter at 9:30 and State
Route 52 at 11:00. Visited with Harold (Dave) Schade, the proprietor
of a commercial nursery at that point. He brewed us a big pot of
coffee. We then pushed on to the village of Holmes. We reached
it at 3:00 and met veteran hiker Charlie Konopa on the way. Konopa
is also hiking the entire Trail, but he has been doing it in bits and
pieces. When we met him, he was using his camper as a base and
was hiking with a day pack only. We stopped at Holmes (grocery
store and post office) for groceries and refreshments, and I telephoned Norm Greist of North Haven, Connecticut, to let him know
of my whereabouts. At 6:00 we reached the outskirts of Pawling,
New York and were promptly flagged down by Norm Greist and
Newell Mitchell who had just driven up in their car. As we neared
Pawling, we noticed the new Edward Murrow Municipal Park; and we
received permission to camp there overnight. We also enjoyed the
luxury of a hot shower. Norm and Newell cooked supper for us and

left about 9:00. Meanwhile, I telephoned the city police office, notified them of our whereabouts; and they, in turn, located Charlie
Konopa's camper and informed him where we were. Charlie arrived
at 9:00 and visited with us until 10:00. We slept on the concrete
floor of the new pavillion, a happy choice both because it was free
of mosquitoes and because we were protected from the drenching
dew which settled that night. We had hiked 20 miles; and we had
seen two deer, several woodchucks and three more of those ugly
aerial survey panels littering the landscape.

Saturday, July 18. We began hiking at 6:00 through the quiet
streets of Pawling. At 6:45, we reached State Route 22; and by
prearrangement, we stopped for a ham and egg breakfast at Charlie
Konopa's camper which was parked at that point. In mid-morning
we plunged into the Pawling Nature Preserve Tract which was
extremely buggy and a veritable grass jungle near its northern end.
We emerged about 10:45 and moments later reached the Girl Scout
Camp, Sakajawea. Their leaders, Barbara and Chuck Chase, invited
us in. I spoke briefly about my hike to a group which was already in
a training session of some sort. Then we withdrew to the kitchen
where we were treated to a huge turkey sandwich, fruit, coffee, and
doughnuts. Around one o'clock we reached the side trail leading to
the Webatuck shelter and then spent a full 30 minutes making an
unsuccessful attempt to find it. Charlie Konopa had had no more
luck on his try to find it on the previous day. In mid-afternoon Norm
and Dorothy Greist plus Phil Houghton met us on the highway near
Webatuck. The two men hiked with us for over an hour; then they
departed for Connecticut to cook supper and await our coming.

Gary and I climbed steadily up the Schaghiticoke Mountain, signed
the register at the New York-Connecticut line (nine States and 1,315
miles behind me!), and then proceeded down the very steep Trail.
We reached Thayer Brook at 6:00 to find a fire burning and a spa-
ghetti and steak dinner awaiting. An excellent campsite in a shady
hemlock area beside the bubbling Thayer Brook. The Greist-Hough-
ton group left at 7:15, and I worked on my notes while Gary erected
his tent.

13. CONNECTICUT-MASSACHUSETTS, JULY 19 TO 29

Sunday, July 19. We left our impromptu campsite at 7:30 and
walked slowly and carefully down the very steep trail on Mt. Algo.
We reached the highway at 9:00 and left the Trail to walk into the

little village of Kent. I went to Mass after I first visited the church
basement where I changed clothes, shaved, and even trimmed some
of my shaggy hair. After church, I met Gary at the local restaurant
and we had a second breakfast. About noon we started walking
back to the AT, but we were given a ride by two churchgoers with
the very Irish names of Mamie O'Hagan and Claire Murphy. Such
names are music to the ears of one like me, three of whose grandparents came from Ireland!

We hiked but 13 miles today but encountered three shelters:
Chase Mountain, Macedonia Brook, and Mountain Brook. We
reached the last one at 7:15 p.m. and spent the night there. We had
difficulty finding the Macedonia Brook shelter; for it is 100 yards
off the Trail, with no sign or blue blazes to alert the hiker to its
presence. If there was a water supply there, we could not find it.
The Mountain Brook shelter had wire bunks for four, but wire mesh
on two was so badly damaged that it made them unuseable. Two
16-year-olds, Chuck Walsh and Howard Cramblitt, were occupying
the only two good bunks, so Gary and I slept outside. This was no
great inconvenience, and I mention the incident only to draw attention to the wire bunk situation. Once they become damaged, the
space they occupy becomes unuseable, as hikers do not wish to
subject their ground cloths, their air mattresses, their sleeping bags,
or their own carcasses to the jagged ends of a broken wire bunk.

Monday, July 20. We began hiking at 6:25. A moderately warm,
clear, day with low humidity, and a light breeze. Ideal for hiking.
We lost the Trail twice during the morning; and at one point, after
locating the Trail, we elected not to use it, as it was an uninviting
looking poison-ivy jungle. We took the longer way, via a dirt road.
We reached the town of Cornwall Bridge at 9:45, bought groceries
and one-half a gallon of ice cream. We opened up the ice cream
on the front porch of the grocery store, let the ice cream soften up a
bit, and then Gary and I each armed with a spoon began at opposite
ends. A very efficient and pleasant way of getting the job done.

We began hiking at 12:00. We hiked up Dark Entry Ravine, an
incredibly beautiful place that ranks with St. Anthony's Wilderness
in Pennsylvania and Laurel Fork Gorge in Tennessee for single-day
hiking beauty. We were very pleased to meet two young men, Todd
Foote of Greens Farm, Connecticut, and John Anderson of Westport,
Connecticut, who were working at cleaning up some of the litter in
the area on their day off from work. Many people talk about cleaning

up the environment; here were two men actually doing it. We pushed on very slowly, admiring the brook, the falls, and the cascades. Later in the day, we hiked through another beautiful area, Cathedral Pines. Near the end of the day, we encountered two shelters barely a mile apart, the Mohawk shelter and later a new shelter, Bunker Hill. We stayed overnight at the second. The shelter had a dirt floor covered with several inches of wood chips. It was quite satisfactory. A lone hiker, Dave Tilewick of Hamden, Connecticut, arrived and spent the night with us.

Tuesday, July 21. We began hiking at 6:45 and in 10 minutes reached the Red Mounain shelter—three shelters in a 1.4 mile stretch. Then, to quote from my diary, we "pushed hard for 3½ hours, reaching Pine Knoll shelter 10:45. Plain lucky to find shelter—obscure path—no sign—no blazes. Beautiful day for hiking—low humidity—strong breeze—beautiful mature forest—huge hemlocks, birch and other hardwoods. After hearty lunch with hot brewed coffee, I managed to locate spring. Guidebook instructions very ambiguous. Cool breeze—temperature at lunch 64 degrees.

"Pushed on over the very tough Barrack Mountain—reached Falls Village at 3:30. Pushed on to new Limestone Spring shelter—reached there at 5:00 p.m." *(1978 note:* Limestone Spring shelter burned down in 1975—circa.)

Wednesday, July 22. After breakfast, while I worked on my notes, Gary performed a major operation. First with scissors, then with razor, he removed his luxuriant big black beard! Quite an operation. We left the shelter 8:10. Stopped for some minutes to enjoy striking view of the Taconic Range. We reached US Route 44 at 9:30; and shortly thereafter, we were picked up, by prearrangement, by Robert Tabor, a Member of ATC Board of Managers from Charleston, West Virginia, and by Allerton Eddy of nearby Twin Lakes, Connecticut. We bought groceries in Salisbury and then spent two hours at the Eddy home on Twin Lakes. Began hiking on AT at 12:30 with Bob Tabor and the two Johnson brothers. Newell Mitchell of Southbury, Connecticut caught up with us at Lions Head. We picked blueberries until our tongues and lips were blue. Said goodbye to Tabor and the two boys at Bear Mountain. Newell, Gary, and I reached the locked AMC Riga cabin at 5:00. At 6:00, Norm Greist, Seymour Smith, and Howie Bassett, all members of the Connecticut chapter of the Appalachian Mountain Club (AMC) arrived. Norm then supervised the preparation of an outdoor banquet, the likes of which I had not previously experienced and perhaps never will again. First, the big outdoor table was covered with a gay tablecloth and decorated with ferns. We had a luscious chunk of steak, salad, baked potatoes, corn on the cob, and French bread. For dessert, we had a simple little thing—peach ice cream covered with sliced bananas, cherries, whipped cream, and candy topping!

Shortly after 9:00, we walked down to the parking lot—only 200 yards away, but in another state (Massachusetts) and said goodbye to Norm, Seymour, and Newell. Gary and I would stay another full day at Riga, and Howie Bassett would stay until the next morning.

Thursday, July 23. A gorgeous day, a high of 70 degrees, clear. A day for relaxing. This was one of only three days of the entire trip that I did not hike at least a few miles on the AT. I read all the mail that Greist had brought me from North Haven, wrote many letters, and brought my notes up to date. I washed clothes, shaved, and prevailed upon Gary to cut my hair. Howie Bassett left at 11:00. At 12:00, two family groups, the Browns and the Whites (honest!), stopped briefly enroute to the blueberry fields. In washing my clothes, I made one fatal mistake. All during the hike I had carefully used warm not hot water in the laundromats when I washed my permanent press slacks and shirts. At Riga we heated up a huge vat of boiling water, and I carelessly washed one pair of slacks and one green shirt. That particular shirt and slack outfit has never been the same since. Moral: warm water only!

The blueberry pickers returned about 4:00 and gave us a large quantity of berries, plus fresh milk and other goodies. After our evening meal, we were visited by Tim Nagler of Lakeville, Connecticut, who came up solely to cook an outdoor meal at this beautiful spot. Nagler, a former Eagle Scout, had done much AT trail clearing work as a youngster at the Pine Island Camp in Maine. He brought his double bitted axe with him and after his meal proceeded to split a big pile of wood. I love to watch an expert wield an axe, and this man handled that axe as a skilled surgeon would handle a scalpel.

For all practical purposes I had now hiked through Connecticut; Massachusetts was but a scant 200 yards away. Connecticut had surprised me. I really don't know what I expected, but I did not expect the Trail to be so rugged or so beautiful. We hiked through beautiful ravines, through pleasant wooded areas, up and down steep mountain trails, and we saw some spectacular views. We had good water, few insects! and the frosting on the cake was that wonderful day we had at the Riga cabin. The Connecticut Chapter, AMC, demonstrated that they would be outdone by none in the hospitality extended to a through-hiker of the AT!

I was surprised by another item in Connecticut—the paint blazing. I have commented previously on the standard 2-inch by 6-inch blaze prescribed in *ATC Publication No. 1*. I had seen variations of this here and there; and earlier in this Chapter I commented on some grossly oversized blazes on one short stretch in Virginia where I saw blazes 3 by 10 inches and a few as big as 3 by 14 inches. In Connecticut, it was the reverse. The blazes were woefully undersized. Generally they were 1 by 3 inches and frequently no bigger than 1 by 2 inches. I also learned of an interesting tradition in Connecticut, the annual spring marathon in which, on a given day, all 56 miles of the Trail are inspected by some seven or eight different teams. Being of a practical turn of mind, I could not help but reflect how much more productive these marathons would be if the inspection teams were furnished with paint cans, paint brushes, and 2-inch by 6-inch stencils!

I now had 10 States and 1,370 miles behind me. The next day I would be hiking in Massachusetts.

Friday, July 24. Massachusetts, six days and 84 miles. For reasons which the reader will soon perceive, this six days was one of the most pleasant, yet one of the most exhausting of the entire trip. Our last meal at Riga was a huge one, including among many other things, a large portion of fresh blueberries and fresh milk. We left the pleasant Riga cabin at 8:30, and within minutes we were walking along the beautiful Sages Ravine. Very shortly, we had crossed the ravine and entered into Massachusetts. We picked a quart of blueberries atop Race Mountain. At 1:00 p.m. we reached the summit of Mt. Everett, and I noticed a man with a camera standing on the first landing of the fire tower. He asked if I were the fellow hiking the entire Appalachian Trail; and when I assured him that I was, he began grinding away furiously with his movie camera. I had previously informed Art Koerber of Pittsfield, Massachusetts, a Vice Chairman of the Conference of the approximate time I would enter Massachusetts. I assumed that the photographer on the firetower was a newspaper photographer and that Koerber was responsible for his being there. However, he seemed so intense about his photography and took so many pictures from so many angles that I finally interrupted him and said, "Friend, would you mind telling me who you are and who you represent?" He introduced himself as Tex Griffin, a free lance photographer from Bronxville, New York. He had heard I was hiking the entire Trail, was captivated with the idea, and was determined to document parts of it both by color movies and by color slides. He was to meet me again in Vermont, New Hampshire, and at the end of my hike on Mt. Katahdin. In all, he made about 500 color slides of my hike. I have used a number of them in lectures I have given, and three of his pictures were used in the special Sunday article on backpacking in the *New York Times* of May 9, 1971. Other Griffin pictures appear in various parts of this book.

In addition to Griffin, there were three other people waiting for me farther down the mountain. One was Harvey Kreidemaker, the Superintendent of Mt. Everett Reservation. Another was George Gardner of the Massachusetts Department of Natural Resources. The third was Sam Steen of Kingston, New York, whom I had met in the Shenandoah Park in Virginia. Gardner delivered a message to me from Koerber and then drove me to a phone so I could call Koerber. Kreidemaker was most cordial and gave me much encouragement as to the possibilities of getting a trailside shelter built within the confines of the Reservation. I spent two hours at this point; and at 3:00, Gary, Sam, and I began hiking. We made slow time in climbing down the very steep and dangerous Jug End. We reached the highway at 6:00 and were met by Art Koerber who drove Gary and me to his home in Pittsfield, Massachusetts. Sam spent the night in his camper.

At the Koerber home I was provided with a combination office and bedroom with a typewriter and desk. I spent five hectic days at the Koerber establishment, hiking by day, writing scores of letters at night, plus writing one article for the September 1970, issue of *Appalachian Trailway News.* My article, appropriately enough, was on trailside shelters. My average time of going to bed was midnight, and of my average time for getting up was 5:45 or 6:00. It is difficult to say who was the more exhausted at the end of the five days, the Koerbers or myself.

During the first evening I learned that Art's wife, Sylvia, hailed from Minnesota, that I had worked with her brother Mauritz Seashore during my early days with the Soil Conservation Service at Winona, Minnesota, and that an older brother, Rosel, had been my high school science teacher in Farmington, Minnesota. Small world.

Saturday, July 25. Gary, Sam Steen, and I began hiking at 8:45.

The temperature was about 90 much of the day; there was a brief shower at 3:00. We did considerable road walking during first part of day through the pretty Massachusetts countryside. We crossed the Housatonic River for the umpteenth time, having crossed it several times in Connecticut. Water was scarce; the brooks and springs were running dry. We made it all the way to Benedict Pond, 15 miles, by 4:00 p.m. There Art Koerber met us and drove us back to Pittsfield. After supper, Rory O'Connor of the *Berkshire Eagle* arrived for a lengthy interview. Both Art and Max Sauter also participated in the interview. Sauter, an elder statesman among ATC members, is noted for two things: his undying love for the AT and a Swiss accent so thick you can cut it with a knife. (Max Sauter died in 1976. He had been made an honorary life member of the Appalachian Trail Conference in 1967.)

Sunday, July 26. I went to 7:00 a.m. Mass.; then in two cars we proceeded to our starting point at Benedict Pond. The Koerbers hiked with us part of the day. We reached Mt. Wilcox shelter at 10:30. This was another hard to find shelter, situated 100 yards off the Trail—no sign and no blue blazes to guide the hiker. At the shelter we met George Wright, a hiker from New York City, who asked if he might hike with us. George was on his first extended hike, carried a guitar, and sang professionally when the opportunity presented, sang for fun at other times. He was a traveling troubador, and his singing was to enliven our evenings until our paths separated at Sherburne Pass in Vermont.

We reached the Mt. Wilcox firetower at noon to find Max Sauter there with a noonday lunch ready. After lunch, our group, now reduced to four (Sam Steen, George Wright, Gary Rutherford, and I) pushed on rapidly to the beautiful little rural village of Tyringham. We reached there at 2:00. Although it was a clear, warm day with the temperature about 85, in the woods, it sounded as though there was a light rain falling continually. This was due to the hordes of gypsy moth caterpillars defoliating the trees around us. The insect droppings and the particles of leaves falling sounded just like rain. We were to be very conscious of this for the next two days. We reached US Route 20 at 5:00, a 15-mile day—which was fairly good time as we had not started until 9:45. Sam Steen was bushed. He felt light headed; and promptly after we reached Koerber's home, he took salt pills and rested a bit.

Monday, July 27. We hiked a scant eight miles on a clear, warm,

Ed Garvey with Mrs. Fred Hutchinson. (Photo: Joe Abrizzi, *Berkshire Eagle*)

humid day. We began at 8:45 at US Route 20 where we met George Wright. George had made out famously after we left him Sunday afternoon. He sang at a night club for meals and a stipend; after that one of the patrons took him to his home for the night and deposited him back on the AT at the point where he met us. We reached October Mountain shelter at 11:30, and I found a note there addressed to me from Helen Arnold, a hiker from Pennsylvania. At 12:00, we reached the home of Mrs. Fred Hutchinson at Washington Town Hall. Mrs. Hutchinson is, indeed, the grand old lady of the Appalachian Trail. Already waiting for us at the Hutchinson place was the photographer for the *Berkshire Eagle* who took pictures for the O'Connor article that appeared in next day's paper. Also on hand to greet us were Helen Arnold and a Mr. Poorman, hikers who had left a note for me at October Mountain shelter. The *Eagle* photographer took the picture of Mrs. Hutchinson and myself which is included here. Mrs. Hutchison had been expecting us and treated us to a delightful lunch with homemade bread and pie. After lunch, she read to us excerpts from a lengthy paper she had prepared concerning some of the many hikers she and her late husband had befriended over a 40-year period. At 2:30, we reluctantly said goodbye to this very wonderful person, hiked a mile to where Sam's car was parked, and drove back to Pittsfield. After supper, Art Koerber and I drove out to visit the Girl Scout Camp, Marian White; and I spoke briefly to some 85 senior Girl Scouts on my Appalachian Trail hike. In addition to their AT activities, the Koerbers have two other loves, the Girl Scouts and the Mt. Greylock Ski Club. Back at the Koerbers, I immediately resumed work on my *Trailway News* article which I finished well after midnight. (Genevieve Hutchinson died in 1972 at the age of 90.)

Tuesday, July 28. Max Sauter drove me out to Washington Town Hall. There I met George Wright who had stayed overnight at the Hutchinson residence. We stopped on Warner Mountain to pick blueberries and picked all we dared eat in 20 minutes from a single eight-foot high bush. We reached Dalton, Massachusetts, at 12:00; and as we walked through town, I was hailed by a police cruiser. Officer Richard Nicholas asked if I could delay my hike long enough for an interview and pictures for the local paper. I readily agreed, and minutes later reporter Marian Manning of the *Dalton News Record* appeared for the interview.

That afternoon we hiked through some interesting beech groves and later some white birch groves. We reached Cheshire, Massachu-

Ed Garvey on AT in New England with George Wright and Sam Steen. Photo by Joe Abrizzi, *Berkshire Eagle*.

setts at 5:30, having hiked 19 miles for the day. While walking on the street in Cheshire, we were approached by a man brandishing the July 28 issue of the *Berkshire Eagle* with the O'Connor AT article and a picture of George Wright, Sam Steen, and myself. He had just read the article, later had seen us hiking, and had correctly surmised that we were the hikers whose pictures appeared in the paper.

Back at Pittsfield in the Koerber home, I had a discussion with Gary Rutherford. He had not hiked the past two days since getting his shoes repaired among other things. His current plans were to resume hiking on July 29 back at US Highway 20 and to hike at a slower pace than mine. This was to be my last night at the Koerber home, and again I worked until well after midnight getting all the mileage I could out of the Koerber typewriter.

Wednesday, July 29. Had breakfast visit at Koerber home with Douglas Poland of the Massachusetts Department of Natural Resources (DNR). Under the Massachusetts law, Poland's department has responsibility for obtaining an Appalachian Trail right of way. Koerber and Poland and their agencies have been working quite closely, first, to move the Trail off the roads, and then to obtain easements and cooperative agreements from the landowners involved.

After breakfast, two cars left the Koerber home. Mrs. Koerber took Gary to US Highway 20 where he resumed his hike; and Max Sauter took me back to Cheshire where I resumed mine. My pack weighed 42 pounds, including my new supply of groceries. I reached the Kitchen Brook shelter at 10:30 and had an early lunch. During the morning I had encountered families of blueberry pickers on mountain tops. As I neared Mt. Greylock, I was met by Gordon Turnbull of Lee, Massachusetts. He too had read the account of my hike in the *Berkshire Eagle* and calculated correctly as to the time I would reach Greylock. I reached Bascom Lodge atop Mt. Greylock at noon and had a second snack there. I visited there briefly with a group of 10 to 12-year-old boys from a nearby camp.

According to my diary I "was somewhat horrified at Bascom to see about 40 or more waxed-paper wrapped sandwiches on the floor of the front porch. The sandwiches had been discarded by the boys from the nearby camp who were there when I arrived. The attendant picked them up and threw them in the trash. He said it happened every day!"

I learned that George Wright had conducted a songfest the previous night at Bascom Lodge and was somewhere ahead of me on the

Trail. Turnbull left me at 3:30. Shortly after, I arrived at Wilbur Clearing shelter. This is one of only four shelters in Massachusetts and the only really good one. It is a 15-foot by 20-foot shelter with a five-foot overhang in front. It has a very ingenious wood storage area underneath its rear overhang. I judged it would sleep 10 or 12 boys with ease. It was about to have its capacity tested when 35 boys and their leaders arrived at the same time I did.

I arrived at Blackinton, Massachusetts, shortly after 6:00 and at once went to the home of Mr. and Mrs. James A. Hardman, Jr. Hardman is owner and editor of the *North Adams Transcript* and is a good friend of the Appalachian Trail. Indeed the Trail goes through his property at this point and is within shouting distance of his home. After supper we were visited by Bill McArthur of Williamstown, Massachusetts, an indefatigable Trail worker, who had been largely responsible for a 12-mile relocation of the Trail in Vermont, the section which I was scheduled to hike the next day. The day was capped off by a refreshing swim in the Hardman's backyard swimming pool.

I had now hiked 1,451 miles and had all but completed my hike through Massachusetts, the eleventh State on my itinerary. Just as in Connecticut, I was surprised and pleased with the beauty of the country in the western part of the State through which the Trail passes. But, there is too much road walking; and the paint blazing, the shelter situation, and the wooden direction signs all need improvement. These deficiencies are recognized by both the Trail people and the Massachusetts Department of Natural Resources, and efforts are being made to correct them. Massachusetts was the first State to enact legislation for protection of the Appalachian Trail, its State legislation being designed specifically to supplement the National Trails System Act.

14. VERMONT, JULY 30 TO AUGUST 11

Thursday, July 30. My diary records: "Up at 5:30. Used the Hardman kitchen to quietly heat water for coffee. A long day ahead of me. The first 10-12 miles of the Trail were rerouted within past year away from roads. Big improvement. Visited Seth Warner shelter. Saw deer on two occasions, the first time in a week. Scared one woodchuck up a tree."

"It began raining hard at 3:00. Reached Congdon shelter about 3:45. Met George Wright and Craig Bumgarner. The new Trail relocation has excellent blazing and an excellent sign program. I pushed on from Congdon shelter and at 4:30 met Clifford Smith and his wife Margaret who left Mt. Katahdin June 14 headed for Georgia. Sorry I did not have more time to visit with them. They do not have a guidebook, only road maps. They buy their food for seven to eight days because they don't know where the next store is.

"I reached Route 9 about 7:00 and found a note for me on tree from Beth Oscanyan. Simultaneously I met Ben Rolston of Schenectady, New York, who had come to look for me. Drove into Bennington with Ben and his wife, to residence of Bob and Claire Santway. There Tyler Resch, editor of the *Bennington Banner* took pictures and interviewed Ben and me. I am in Green Mountain Club territory now. Met Marian Hardy, an old timer among GMCers and one of the first people to hike the Long Trail (Canada to Massachusetts)."

I had hiked over 20 miles that day and was tired. Some two miles south of Route 9 I had hiked through one spot where all the vegetation on both sides of the Trail for a considerable distance consisted only of ferns.

Friday, July 31. I spent the entire morning in Bennington hoping I would hear from the Oscanyans who were to meet me. They did not show, so at noon Bob Santway drove me out to the AT. I stopped briefly at the family farm of the Oscanyans; while there, a neighbor arrived. She said that the Oscanyans had suffered a misfortune. They were not coming back to the Bennington area. The message was for me to proceed. I stopped briefly at the Fay Fuller shelter, a rather dismal affair situated only 20 feet from a well-traveled road. Hiked only seven miles today; but much of it was up, up to the Glastenberry shelter at an elevation of 3,500 feet.

There were two young men at the shelter. At eight o'clock George Wright and Craig Bumgarner arrived. Foggy night. After nine o'clock, Bob Santway, Bill McArthur, and three others arrived and erected a tent. George played his guitar and sang, and 17-year-old Marty Gil chimed in with a harmonica.

Saturday, August 1. Beginning a new month. Hiked 14 miles that day from Glastenberry shelter to Vondell shelter. Breakfast was a congested affair with 10 men firing up stoves and packing gear in one shelter. Arrived at Caughnawaga shelter at 9:30 and at the Story Spring shelter at one o'clock. Intermittent rain all day. Reached Stratton Pond at 5:45. There are four shelters on this one pond, and all but one were filled to the saturation point on that Saturday night. Craig, George, and I moved into Vondell shelter and joined a couple who had arrived earlier. Met Art Steele, a Class D ATC member from Long Island, New York. Art and his group occupied the Bigelow shelter a scant 200 yards from our shelter. It began to rain again at 8:00 and became very dark.

Sunday, August 2. A turnabout in the weather. Today was sunny, low humidity, light breeze, ideal for hiking. Made a scant 14 miles for the day from Vondell shelter to Bromley Camp, my progress slowed by the need to inspect nine shelters in this 14-mile stretch. The heaviest concentration of shelters since I began my hike in Georgia. Met two Class D-ers at South Bourne shelter, Adolph Margus and Paul Rohrbacker. At North Bourne shelter we met Ed Carpenter, a 60-year-old woods-wise fisherman from Clarksburg, Massachusetts. He recognized me from the article in the *North Adams Transcript*. To prove he had read the article carefully, he informed (reminded would be a better word!) me of my age.

An amusing incident occurred at the shelter. Carpenter offered to heat up some coffee for us and we accepted. Even through all wood was saturated after the all day rain, Carpenter soon had a brisk fire going. I worked on my notes; and presently, without looking up, I inquired if the coffee was hot yet. "It must be," said Carpenter, "The coffee pot handle is on fire!" And so it was. He beat out the fire with his gloves and poured us each a potent cup of coffee.

We reached State Route 11 at 4:40 after having had extreme difficulty finding the Trail in the last mile because of the almost complete lack of paint blazes. At Route 11 we were hailed by Norm LaMoria, of Newfane, Vermont, a GMC member with whom we visited briefly. George and I reached the Bromley shelter at 5:30 to find Craig already there and talking with two other young men, Ken Lesenko and James Burdick, both of Saddle Brook, New Jersey. Craig cooked up a big batch of his Appalachian Trail Mix (see Chapter 3) fortified by a box of Rice-a-Roni which I supplied. It was a very congenial group. I had passed the 1,500-mile mark in my hike that day; and in honor of the occasion, George got up on the top bunk, played his guitar, and sang the folk song made famous by the Peter, Paul, and Mary trio—"500 Miles From Home."

Monday, August 3. Overslept. After breakfast I left the group and backtracked for one mile on the AT to again reach State Route 11. Almost immediately, I caught a ride with a French-Canadian, Don Dion. He drove me directly to the Forest Service office in Manchester Center since he had business there also. There I met and visited

with Alfred M. Johnson, the District Ranger. I learned to my surprise
that the Forest Service actually does some of the paint blazing for a
certain number of miles north of State Route 11. I had noticed those
blazes, deep axe marks filled in with paint. Johnson explained that
they no longer use the axe, only the paint brush. We discussed other
aspects of the Appalachian Trail maintenance; more particularly, the
absence of any signs in the Green Mountain National Forest indicating that the hiker was hiking the Appalachian Trail as well as the
Long Trail. The Long Trail predates the Appalachian Trail by approximately 20 years, but these two famous trails share the same route for
the first 100 miles from the Massachusetts line to Sherburne Pass.
Inasmuch as the Appalachian Trail is now a national scenic trail
recognized by federal statute, it would seem only proper that it
receive some recognition and identification along this 100-mile
stretch.

I did some shopping in Manchester Center and was given a ride
back to the Trail by Joe Gumberger, a college student and seasonal
employee of the Forest Service. He, like scores of people I met on my
hike, harbored a secret desire to hike the entire Appalachian Trail.
I gave him much encouragement.

I returned to Bromley shelter, changed clothes, and pushed on. I
reached Mad Tom shelter about 4:00 and found four young college
trainees already there. They were members of a roving trail maintenance crew which operated out of the Forest Supervisor's office in
Rutland, Vermont. They had several days supply of food and kept
urging me to stay overnight at the shelter. I was sorely tempted,
especially when they produced a quart of table wine; but I knew the
other group was expecting me at Peru Peak shelter. So I regretfully
pushed on and reached Peru Peak shelter at 7:00. Craig had cooked
a big batch of AT Mix fortified with a can of beef.

Trail blazing north of Route 11 left much to be desired. Some of
it was old, indistinct axe blazing. There was no blazing or signs
around the Bromley ski tower to assist the hiker in finding the Trail
north of the tower.

My litter pickup has dropped markedly in New England. Apparently, the big spring litter pickup drives have been effective.

My diary for that day reads: "Delightful evening—cool—64 degrees
at 7:00—got cooler. Nice big shelter—good fire going. George began
singing, and one minute later I was asleep—to be awakened later by
George clubbing a porcupine about two feet from my head!"

The porcupines do a great deal of damage, in Vermont especially. These animals actually chew to pieces the wooden toilets, tables, and shelter floors. I am sorry I did not obtain a picture of the one toilet with three walls completely eaten away. The newer toilets being installed are of metal. Most tables are covered with galvanized metal.

Tuesday, August 4. Ideal hiking day, cool all day. Visited five shelters during the day; four of which I rated Excellent, and one Very Good. Trail led through beautiful woods, ponds, and streams. Trail was in very good shape—easy to follow.

George and I reached the Lula Tye shelter at 3:00; there I learned that fellow Virginians were at Little Rock Pond shelter. We reached that shelter at 4:00 to find Bill and Beth Oscanyan. We decided to stay there overnight instead of going on to Greenwall shelter as originally planned. Took a brief swim—delightful. Hard to describe the beauty of this place—crystal clear pond, conifers and white birch trees along the shore. I had an enjoyable supper and visited with three Canadians who were also using the shelter. Took a walk around the pond to visit the other shelter. When we returned, George was singing at the lake shore. We sat and listened for almost an hour. I hated to see such a perfect day come to an end.

I am afraid I have heard and seen the last of the towhees for this trip. I enjoyed their company since that first day in Georgia. The Vermont border seems to mark the northernmost point of their territory. Their place has been taken by the white throated sparrow whose high pitched plaintive five-note song we now hear frequently.

Wednesday, August 5. Wakened at 3:30 by an owl hooting on far side of pond. Four notes, and then the same four notes immediately repeated. The sound traveled so clearly across the water. All of us were up at 5:30. Another nice day. George and I left the shelter at 7:20 after a most delightful visit with the Oscanyans. We made good time to Greenwall shelter but we were not in time to catch up with our three companions. There was a group of 12-14 boys at Greenwall still cooking breakfast when we arrived. We reached State Route 140 at 11:00 and found Craig Bumgarner waiting for us. He was discontinuing his hike at that point. At noon we reached the new Sunnyside lodge and enjoyed lunch with Charlie Geer and his sons. Clarendon Lodge shelter was reached at 3:30; and at 7:00, after hiking 19 miles, we reached the Governor Clement shelter. There were three separate groups at the shelter, 20 people in all, including Ken Lesenko and Jim Burdick. The latter two were as happy as two kids at their first Christmas. This was their first hike on the AT. They were uncertain of their ability; they had had rough going the first couple of days; but now, in the past two days, they had found that they could hike 15 or more miles per day, get into camp early, and not be too tired. After all were in bed, George got out his guitar and began singing, the last time I was to hear him—or so I thought at the time. He had a big audience that night, and the group was captivated.

Thursday, August 6. A leisurely hiking day by any standards. Up at 6:00 and only 10 miles of hiking by 5:00 p.m. when we reached Sherburne Pass (US Route 4). But then I had planned on a few of that type of day; and, as in the Smokies, I now wish that I had slowed down a bit more in the Green Mountains so as better to enjoy the ponds and lakes which dot the Trail there. It was 8:40 before the four of us left the Governor Clement shelter. After two hours of hiking we reached the new Tamerack shelter. I was very interested in the design of this shelter and of its older counterpart, the Glastenbury shelter, 70 miles to the south. They were unique among all of the 238 shelters I was to inspect on the entire Trail. Each had a wooden sleeping platform some four or five feet above ground level with room for perhaps six to eight people. This sleeping platform extended out into the shelter providing a spacious shelf underneath for either an immense amount of gear or four additional people. The Tamarack shelter was a big high structure which admitted light. It had a wide front overhang to provide protection from the elements.

We reached the Cooper lodge at noon. At this shelter, Churchill Scott, a member of the Green Mountain Club, was spending an entire week making a traffic count of hikers. When not counting people, he was making extensive improvements on this large shelter. From the lodge there is a trail leading 0.2 miles to the summit of Mt. Killington, the second highest mountain (4,241 feet) in Vermont. Since it was a clear day, we walked to the top to enjoy the spectacular views. Just below the summit is the upper station of a chair lift for a ski area. This brings large numbers of people within close proximity to the shelter. The shelter, consequently, suffers from vandalism; and its immediate environs suffer from litter and human refuse. We were warned not to drink the water from the spring which is located 40 yards south of the lodge. Unable to cope with the problem of constant glass breakage, the Green Mountain Club had replaced the conventional glass windows with clear plastic. Leaving Cooper, we hiked the three miles north to Pico Camp.

At that point our group split: Ken and Jim stayed there for the night; George and I hiked on to Sherburne Pass (US Route 4). We spent a few minutes at the Long Trail Lodge. Later, George spent a winter season at this place, singing professionally during the ski season under the name "Peregrine." I spent that night and the next two at a small guest building nearby which was owned by Mrs. Madeline Fleming. Mrs. Fleming and her next door neighbor, Mrs. Mersch, had, with their husbands, both now deceased, retired to this area some 10 years before. Both couples were long-time members of the Potomac Appalachian Trail Club and I had known them for years.

Friday, August 7. Breakfast at the Fleming home. No hiking for me today. At 9:30, Shirley Strong, President of the Green Mountain Club, arrived from Burlington; and we drove to the home of Wilbur Weston, President of the Killington Section of the same Club. We were shortly joined by Tony Bland, a reporter for the *Rutland Herald* who conducted an interview and took pictures. Later I drove to Rutland, visited the Forest Service Supervisor's Office and talked to Bill Baxondall and Frank Morrell. Much of the territory through which I had hiked since entering Vermont was in the Green Mountain National Forest. Since I was now sitting in the same room with representatives of both the Green Mountain Club and the Green Mountain National Forest, I could not let the opportunity pass without chiding them good naturedly about the total lack of recognition given to the Appalachian Trail along the 100-mile stretch between the Massachusetts-Vermont line and Sherburne Pass (US Route 4). I made the point that the Appalachian Trail was one of two national scenic trails recognized by the Congress in the National Trails System Act (Public Law 90-543); that the Forest Service was one of two agencies charged by the Congress with the administration of the Appalachian Trail, and that, accordingly, it seemed strange that the Appalachian Trail would not be accorded equal prominence with the Long Trail or other trails when the trail routes coincided.

I had supper with Mrs. Mersch and Mrs. Fleming. I later received visits from Tex Griffin and Mauri Wintturi, a GMC member from Massachusetts. Mauri, a man of undoubted Finnish extraction, told me at some length how he had been instrumental in getting a sauna bath built at the Zealand Falls AMC Hut in New Hampshire. He said that he had informed the hut boys at Zealand of my approximate arrival time; and when I reached there, I was to demand—not request, but to demand—that the sauna be heated up. I was uncertain as to how much influence Mauri had with the hut boys. Furthermore, I had never had a sauna bath; but with all the preparations that had been made, I concluded it would be best for me to have one when I reached Zealand!

Saturday, August 8. After breakfast, a party of seven was formed for a visit to the nearby Johnson shelter on the Long Trail. In addition to myself, there were Tex and Jean Griffin, Wes Weston and Dr. Howard, local GMC-ers, and Ray Secor and John Anlian, two of the four young Forest Service employees I had visited with at Mad Tom shelter. The GMC people were very proud of their new Johnson shelter. It is on the Long Trail about a mile north of the point where the Long Trail and the Appalachian Trail separate. The shelter sleeps eight people—on two upper and two lower wooden bunks. What makes it unique is the inside dining table and seating arrangement. The table is situated directly between the sleeping bunks. The table lacks the conventional and usually cumbersome movable benches. Instead, the lower bunk sleeping platforms extend far enough out into the room, and at just the right height, to provide a comfortable seat for the diners. I learned that Wes Weston, Dr. Howard, and Ray Secor had all had a hand in the building, along with Louis Stare, Jr. of Bass River, Massachusetts.

In the afternoon I made plans to attend 5 o'clock Mass at the little interdenominational church in Killington. The service was conducted by a priest who was also running for a seat in the Vermont legislature. Moreover, this was a folk Mass; and as I sat in the church before services began, I suddenly recognized one of the guitarists—George Wright! Whether it was a night club, a lonely shelter on the Appalachian Trail, or a church—there was George with his trusty guitar and his pleasant voice. During the two weeks I hiked with him, I had enjoyed immensely his companionship, his guitar, and his singing.

At this point I pass on to you a classic observation made by this same George Wright. It will strike a responsive chord with anyone who has hiked any distance on the Appalachian Trail. This was George's first hike on the Trail, and he confided to me that he had formed a mental picture of the people who painted the white blazes along the Trail. "I picture them" he said, "As two little men each with a paint brush and a can of paint walking together down the Trail. At one point, one of the painters announced, 'Let's put a blaze right here where they can't miss it.' And the other painter replies 'No! Let's put it over the top of the next hill. Make 'em guess a little bit!' " If you hike the AT and have trouble now and then finding those 2-inch by 6-inch white blazes, don't become angry. Think of it as a game. And think of the little man with the white paint and the gleeful smile on his face muttering to himself, "Make 'em guess a little bit!"

That evening Mrs. Fleming drove me over to the Long Trail Lodge where we had a final visit with George and with Ken Lesenko and Jim Burdick. George would resume hiking the next day . . . hiking on the Long Trail all the way to Canada. Within the past week he had joined the Green Mountain Club and looked forward to receiving one of the coveted "End to End" patches awarded by the GMC to those who hike the entire length of the Long Trail from Canada to Massachusetts. Ken and Jim were driving back to New Jersey the next day.

Sunday, August 9. Early breakfast; afterwards Mrs. Fleming and I joined Tex and Jean Griffin. The two ladies then drove on to Stony Brook shelter, while Tex and I hiked the distance, 4.1 miles. We reached the shelter at 10:00. Enroute we met two young boys, one of many groups I had met in Vermont, who were members of the Farm and Wilderness organization. One of the two boys was Peter Warburton of Chevy Chase, Maryland, whose parents are members of the Potomac Appalachian Trail Club. Mrs. Griffin and Mrs. Fleming were already at the shelter when we arrived. After shelter inspection and much picture taking, I said goodbye to all three and began the eight-mile hike to my shelter for the night, the Gulf shelter. I had had a rather busy, but very pleasant 2½ days in the Killington, Vermont, area and was deeply indebted to Mrs. Fleming for the use of her guest house, her typewriter, and for her intimate knowledge of the Appalachian Trail and its background in Vermont.

I reached the Gulf shelter at 4:30. I had not planned to spend the night there, but it looked too inviting to pass up. The overseer for the shelter had recently purchased and installed a variety of good skillets and cooking pots. Mauri Wintturi, who had been doing some paint blazing in the area, was at the shelter when I arrived. He left shortly thereafter, taking out my full litter bag with him. I had seen another six aerial survey panels still littering the landscape that day; I had seen 11 of them on August 5.

The weight of my pack when I left Killington was 35 pounds; my weight was 159. I was satisfied with both. I reflected that night that this was the first trailside shelter since Pennsylvania in which I had spent the night alone.

Monday, August 10. Up at 5:30, on Trail at 6:05—my quickest get-away in weeks. The reason: a cold cereal breakfast. I was now hiking in Dartmouth Outing Club (DOC) territory. Traditionally DOC has blazed the Trail with orange, black, and white blazes, but within recent months it had inaugurated a program of also providing the standard 2-inch by 6-inch ATC white blazes. For much of the day I followed both types of blazes. I was disturbed to find 17 aerial panels still on the ground some 20 months after they were put in place.

There were no shelters in the 18 miles I hiked for the day. At 9:00 o'clock I stopped for coffee and doughnuts with Rex Jillson and Steve Hough at the Jillson summer camp. Reached West Hartford at 3:15 and stopped for snack at Betty's Grocery, directly on Trail, before pushing on to the unlocked DOC Happy Hill cabin. Reached the cabin at 5:30 p.m. and made a revolting discovery. No water! Both the spring and the brook were dry. I had no water with me, but I did have a scant pint of wine. I ate an uncooked meal, washed down with the wine. No great punishment! It was the only time during my entire trip when I had to go without water overnight.

It had been a pleasant day of much up and down hiking over abandoned farms and over many delightful streams. The temperature was 90 degrees at 4 p.m. in West Hartford.

Tuesday, August 11. Left the cabin at 5:50 without breakfast. Ate my first breakfast at 6:20, when I found water running in a brook. Reached the Connecticut River at 8 a.m. Another milestone—12 States now behind me and almost 1,600 miles. I reached downtown Hanover, New Hampshire at 8:15 and picked up a mountain of mail. I judged that three-fourths of all the mail at the General Delivery window was mine. Visited Lou's Restaurant and had a more substantial breakfast of griddle cakes.

Observations on Vermont. The Green Mountain Club, which maintains all but perhaps 25 miles of the Trail in Vermont, is without a doubt one of the "buildingest" organizations within the Appalachian Trail Conference. In the 100-mile stretch of Trail between the Massachusetts line and US Route 4, there are 29 shelters for an average of one shelter every 3.4 miles. GMC is always building a shelter or two somewhere along the length of its long trail system. GMC is divided into a number of sections; and each section is a highly autonomous organization. Therefore one cannot generalize as to the condition of

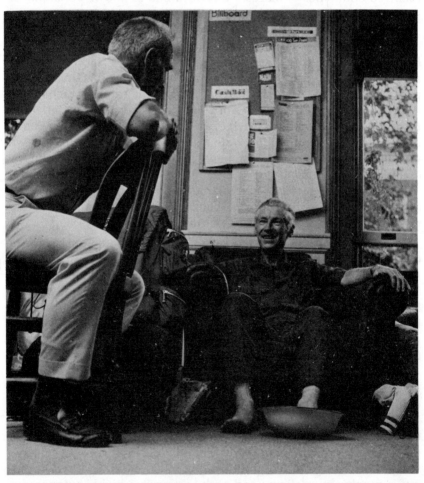

Ed Garvey soaks his feet and chat with Dartmouth outdoor activities director C. Allison Merrill. (Photo: Larry McDonald, *Valley News*)

the footway, the signs, or the paint blazes because these things can differ widely depending upon which "section" of the Club is doing the work. The Killington Section maintains the Trail in the vicinity of US Route 4 and two activities of that organization deserve comment.

On the litter front, the Killington group is taking one shelter at a time, removing all suggestion of any litter, removing any receptacle into which litter might be deposited, installing a trash receptacle at the nearest highway intersection, and then putting up signs at the shelter requesting the occupants to carry out all litter and informing them where the nearest trash receptacles may be found.

The sign program of the Killington Section is outstanding. It is largely the work of one man, Herbert Ogden of Windsor, Vermont. Not only is the workmanship top quality but the sign wording and the points where and the manner in which they are erected show great imagination.

15. NEW HAMPSHIRE, AUGUST 11 TO SEPTEMBER 12

Tuesday, August 11 (continued). After my second breakfast I proceeded to the office of the Dartmouth Outing Club in Robinson Hall. John Rand, who has directed the activities of DOC for years, was on vacation but Al Merrill, the ski coach, took care of me admirably. First, he showed me around the premises, carefully pointing out the new sauna bath and then the more conventional shower facilities and offering me the use of each. I thought this very kind of him but later reflected that perhaps he was not so much "offering" as he was "suggesting." After all I had hiked over 18 miles the previous day in temperature in the 90's! In any event I took advantage of his kind offer, took a much needed shower, and washed my socks. I was also provided with an office and the services of a secretary. After lunch I spent an hour participating in a taped inteview with Jeff Wulfson of the Dartmouth College radio station. I then spent another hour with Larry McDonald of the *Valley News*. McDonald, like many of the other reporters I had talked to during the course of my hike, was extremely knowledgeable, not only in the general field of outdoor recreation, but in such related subjects as overuse of trails and campgrounds, litter, water pollution, etc. We discussed the vexing question as to how much the use of the Appalachian Trail should be encouraged in the New England States without permanent damage to the ecology. This question had already been raised in my travels through Massachusetts, and even more strongly in Vermont. During the summer vacation months, it seems that big segments of the population from the hot cities gravitate to the cooler lake-studded New England mountain country. Both in the Green Mountains and even more so in the White Mountains, there are areas where the people-saturation-point has been reached—and some places where it has been exceeded.

I spent the entire day in "my office," bought additional groceries, and spent the night as a guest of Al Merrill.

Wednesday, August 12. Visited "my office" for about an hour to complete my paper work and began hiking at 9:00. Reached the unlocked DOC Harris cabin at noon and ate lunch there. The Harris cabin is a huge affair, a good 30-feet by 40-feet in size; and it must have been a dark and gloomy affair. But there have now been inserted in the roof two 4 foot by 12 foot traslucent plastic glass panels; and on a sunny day the inside of the cabin is as bright as a flourescent-lighted department store. I reached the Moose Mountain shelter at 3:00. My dairy then shows the following record: "Reached Goose Pond about 4:00—then my troubles began—lost the Trail twice in next two miles—then upon reaching Clark Pond I lost much time trying to find shelter. Blazes have been obliterated—Trail being re-located. Reached shelter at 6:00—had a delightful swim—then a light supper. Worked on notes—started a brisk wood fire at 8:30—and had another swim at 8:45. This was even more delightful. There was still some daylight. I could see the fire iluminating the interior of the shelter and could see an almost full moon coming up over the white birch trees. A truly wonderful sight. A joy to be alive and to be in the right spot at the right time. A little mosquito problem, but not bad. Crawled into sleeping bag—applied insect repellant to face and neck—and had no trouble. Not a ripple on the lake. I had earlier watched the sun go down as I sat on a rock working on my notes. End of a wonderful day."

Thursday, August 13. My diary for this day begins: "Up at 5:30—and went in pond for brisk and invigorating swim! Temperature 60 degrees, but no wind. Day dawning clear—pond is so beautiful—a little vapor hanging above the water and drifting slowly southward. I truly hate to leave and am dismayed that Dartmouth Outing Club and New Hampshire people are moving the Trail completely away from the pond."

I left Clark Pond at 7:00 and then reached firetower on Smart Mountain at 12:15. Ate lunch with the fire warden Gary Rosenthal.

Reached Cube Mountain shelter at 4:30 and met a group from the nearby Walt Whitman private camp. One of the leaders, Pat Orrell, invited me to visit their camp next day, as the AT goes directly by the camp. I found a note at the Cube Mountain shelter from Everett and Neil Skinner of Bristol, Vermont, informing me that they were returning. They did return after 5:00 with the makings for a huge steak dinner. They had hiked the entire Trail in 1968, and I had met them in the Shenandoah National Park in Virginia and cooked a meal for them. Little did we anticipate then that they would reciprocate a scant two years later. I had fun eating and visiting with them and comparing notes on some of our hiking experiences. To bed at 10:00 on the dirt floor of the shelter.

Friday August 14. Had one of my favorite breakfasts; sausage cakes, buckwheat pancakes, and Vermont maple syrup, all supplied by the Skinners. Left shelter at 8:45. Reached the Walt Whitman private camp at noon and ate lunch there. Learned that a front page story of my Appalachian Trail hike had appeared in the *Wall Street Journal* on August 12. One of the camp councilors produced a copy of the paper. Went for a swim in the camp swimming area. I left Walt Whitman camp at 4:00, crossed Highway 25-A, and immediately began finding survey stakes, lot subdivision stakes, and iron pipes marking the center line of a new road. These markings extended for half a mile and told an all too familiar story—another half mile of the Appalachian Trail was being blotted out.

I had planned to stay at the Wachipauka shelter, but I decided against it as the shelter was 0.8 miles off the Appalachian Trail and had no water. Instead, I camped at a delightful spot on the shore of Wachipauka Pond. I went for a swim immediately upon reaching camp. For supper I had two huge beef sandwiches, courtesy of Walt Whitman camp. A breezy night—had minimum trouble with the mosquitos.

Saturday, August 15. Began hiking 6:45. Reached Glencliff, New Hampshire, Post Office at 8:20. Picked up mail but not the three pound fruit cake from Claxton, Georgia, which I had ordered two weeks previously. However, five minutes after I arrived there, the mail truck arrived; and—Presto!—I had my fruit cake! Lucky. On the post office scales my pack now weighed 46 pounds with the fruit cake in it. That was a little disturbing because the elevation at Glencliff is only 1,540 feet and I was about to begin climbing to the top of Mt. Moosilauke which has an elevation of 4,810 feet.

My diary for the day shows: "At lunch I used some of my powdered tea that had taken so much weather as to be like taffy chunks.
Put the chunks in my shaker and shook vigorously. Oh well—the
shaking did impart some tea flavor to the water! Reached summit of
Mt. Moosilauke at 4 p.m.—tremendous viewing point, but day quite
hazy. Made slow progress towards Beaver Brook shelter. Trail very
steep and eroded, but along a beautiful cascade. I used the wooded
ladders and steel cables provided at the steepest points. Reached
shelter at 7 p.m."

There were six people at the shelter; and shortly after I arrived,
several of them approached me to ascertain if I were the individual
hiking on the Appalachian Trail from Georgia to Maine. It seems that
two of them had read the *Wall Street Journal* article, one had read
the *Valley News* article, and one had heard the taped Dartmouth
College radio program. I was well identified! One of the six was Ed
Brass, a Class D member of the Conference from Upper Montclair,
New Jersey, who with his son, was hiking through the White Mountains and using the AMC Huts. He was kind enough to loan me his
waterpoof tarp since he had no further use for it and I would be
going through areas where trailside shelters were scarce.

Sunday, August 16, Left Beaver Brook shelter at 8:00. At 8:15 I
crossed Kinsman Notch (State Route 112) and in so doing left that
part of the Trail maintained by the Dartmouth Outing Club and
moved into Appalachian Mountain Club territory. I would hike on
trails maintained by AMC for the next 100 miles, or until reaching
the Maine-New Hampshire line. Arrived Elisha Brook shelter at 12:45.
Met Russel F. Hansen of Hudson, Ohio, at shelter; and he furnished
me with a time tested method for making home-made beef jerky.
It was an extremely hot day. Paul Tutko, a Class D-er from Danvers,
Massachusetts, arrived suffering from the heat. I left the shelter at
3:00. Had a hot, hard climb up to the tops of the two Kinsman.
Reached Kinsman Pond shelter; an unimpressive 11 miles for the day.

There was only one occupant of the Kinsman Pond shelter besides
myself. The other person was Buck Canedy, a young apprentice op-
trician and a Class D member from Fall River, Massachusetts. The
White Mountains were suffering from a prolonged dry spell. The
spring at Kinsman shelter was dry; but I had been forewarned and
had brought two full canteens of water. Buck was boiling water from
the pond when I arrived. Buck also showed me a very clever device
he had made for transferring fuel from his aluminum fuel bottle to

the small one-half pint capacity gasoline stove he carried. This device is described and illustrated in Chapter 3. It was also described and illustrated in the May 1971 issue of *Appalachian Trailways News*.

One noteworthy item: I saw no aerial survey panels on the ground during the day's hike. It was noteworthy because in the previous four days I had seen 44.

Monday, August 17. Left shelter at 7:15 and arrived at the Lonesome Lake AMC Hut at 8:30. Coming from the south, Lonesome Lake is the first of the nine huts in the AMC system. Do not be mislead by that term "hut." Webster defines a hut as "an often small and temporary dwelling of simple construction; a shack." And again, as "a simple shelter from the elements." If you accept those definitions then the AMC structures are not "huts." I look upon them more as substantial mountain-type inns or hotels. The nine structures house from 30 to 100 guests. A crew of young men, called "hut boys," does the cooking and maintenance. Sleeping is dormitory style, women in one dorm, men in the other. Meals are excellent. Information and rates may be obtained from the Appalachian Mountain Club, Pinkham Notch Hut, Gorham, New Hampshire 03581.

I enjoyed hot coffee and hot muffins at Lonesome Lake; and I visited with Ross Morgan, the hutmaster. Reached Franconia Notch (U.S. Route 3) at 11 and walked on the highway to a pay phone at the Flume. Made a number of long distance calls arranging to meet people at the Crawford House Hotel on August 19. Walked back to the AT and began the long hard climb to the top of Mt. Lafayette. The elevation of the highway in the Notch is 1,420 feet; the elevation of Mt. Lafayette is 5,249 feet. The temperature on Lafayette was 58 degrees at 5 p.m. Decided I would push on all the way to Garfield Pond shelter; I reached there at 7:00. It was an overcast, windy, chilly night; and 33 members of a Boy Scout troop from Manchester, Massachusetts, were already in residence. Just before reaching the shelter, I crossed the outlet stream of Garfield Pond and took a copious drink. Moments later, I saw the sign on the shelter warning the water was not safe and should be boiled. Great! The shelter was pretty saturated with boys; but one of the Scout leaders provided me with a tent for my exclusive use, all set up and ready to sleep in. A very courteous thing to do. And I should state at this point that the two Boy Scout laws as to courtesy and kindness were certainly observed, insofar as I was concerned, by all of the Scout organizations that I met during my trip. I had met 65 people on the Trail and in shelters that day. I had hiked 15 tough miles, and I was tired. To quote from my diary: "Beautiful views from atop Lafayette—Lonesome Lake nestled down below me . . . the mountains to North and East—Mt. Washington and others. To Southeast there was Mt. Moosilauke . . . all etched so clearly against the sky. Wish now I had allowed an extra day for this traverse . . . a shame to hurry."

Tuesday, August 18. Up at 5:30. Temperature 46 and windy. Left shelter at 6:40. Shortly thereafter I met one of the AMC trail crews and also George T. Hamilton and his family. Hamilton, a fellow member of the Appalachian National Scenic Trail Advisory Council and an official of the New Hampshire Department of Resources and Economic Planning, was enjoying a few days of his vacation. We had much to talk about; but this wasn't the time to do it . . . one reason being that it was a very cool morning and the Hamiltons were attired in shorts. When I noticed them beginning to shiver, I hastily bade them farewell and was on my way. Reached the Galehead AMC Hut at 9:45 and met the hutmaster, Jeff Leich, the son of one of the Trail overseers for the Potomac Appalachian Trail Club. In the afternoon I visited the Guyot shelter which is ½ mile off the AT. Visited briefly on Trail with group of eight hikers from Camp Walt Whitman. I reached Zealand Falls Hut at 6:00—just barely in time to get washed up before the evening meal was served. After supper, Dough Teschner and Chris Hawkins, two of the hut boys, built a fire in the sauna; and at the appropriate time we stripped naked and walked gingerly into the smoky, unlighted sweat room. We absorbed much heat and steam and no little smoke from the fire below us. After we were sweating profusely we went outside and immersed ourselves in the ice-cold pool in the mountain stream. We repeated the operation once, then toweled off, put on clean clothes and returned to the hut. Quite an experience . . . and for some reason the immersing in the cold water is not quite the shock one would imagine. Worked on my notes in the well-lighted dining room and visited with the other guests—some 20 in all. Watched a full moon come up over the mountain in front of the shelter. It reminded me of my stay there in 1965 when I had visited all the AMC huts as a member of the annual AMC Range Walk.

Wednesday, August 19. Left the hut at 7:50. There was a full moon still showing in the morning sky. A beautiful day—excellent visability. Enjoyed the easy walk down the gentle grade of the old railroad bed. Reached Ethan Pond shelter at 10:00. Some 20 girls from a private camp were staying there. Very nice shelter. It has a stated capacity of 10, but I was assured that 17 girls had slept there the previous night. Back on the Trail. At 11:30 I met Art and Slyvia Koerber. They walked with me to Crawford Notch (US Route 302) and then drove me to the Crawford House hotel. There I met George McAvoy, the proprietor and manager, and also Mrs. Margaret Hill, the social hostess who hails from Dublin, Georgia. I changed my clothes, had lunch; and then the activity began.

First we were visited by Roy Kimball, a reporter for the *Manchester Union*; then by two representatives of the White Mountain National Forest, Robert Tyrrel and Russ Rogler, then by the photographer from Bronxville, New York, Tex Griffin; then by John Rand of the Dartmouth Outing Club; and lastly; by Joe May, Supervisor of Trails for the AMC, and three members of his trail crew. I thoroughly enjoyed exchanging ideas with these people. The AMC trail crew of 16 college-age young men is a very dedicated group; and the crew members I talked to that afternoon at Crawford House were very concerned with some of the problems facing them. During the evening meal and immediately afterwards, I had an opportunity to discuss the trail situation at some length with Tyrrel and Rogler of the Forest Service. Some of the urgent problems concerning both the Forest Service and the AMC are the following.

(1) How to cope with the frightfully increasing use, particularly by large organized groups, of shelters and shelter sites. This high useage causes problems with respect to water, sewage, litter, firewood, and breakdown of soil cover. (2) The feasibility of cluster camps with the AMC or the Forest Service providing custodians—somewhat like Liberty Spring, where the AMC has erected a number of tent platforms and where a resident AMC crew man supplies information and exercises some supervision of camping practices. (3) Total ban on use of firewood—with a requirement that any and all cooking be done with stoves using fuel other than wood. (4) The problems occasioned by increasing numbers of people camping out wherever they can find a spot.

After dinner, Tex Griffin showed movies and slides of pictures taken during my hike in Massachusetts and Vermont. And I gave a talk to a small audience of perhaps 25-30 people.

Thursday, August 20. Breakfast with the Koerbers and Tex Griffin. Sam Steen arrived from Kingston, New York, and will hike with me

for the next five days. There were no laundering facilities available
at the hotel, so I was most gateful to a Mrs. Dixon, a hotel employee,
who took my clothes home with her and laundered them.

Got all my gear packed, had lunch at the hotel with Mrs. Hill, said
my goodbyes, and shortly after one o'clock Tex drove Sam and me
back to the AT. It took us 4½ hours to hike appromimately 4½ miles.
The Trail was very steep, rocky, and eroded. Weather foggy — no
views. I saw some of the water bars (used to divert runoff water off
the Trail) which had been installed by AMC crews but concluded
they were fighting a losing battle. The answer is to completely re-
route many of the trails on more gentle grades.

We carried full canteens because we had heard that the spring at
the Nauman shelters was dry. We arrived at the shelters at 6:15.
There are two shelters 100 yards apart, each sleeping 14. The spring
was almost dry, its iron pipe discharging water one drop at a time.
Even so, two boys had spent several hours capturing 2½ gallons. We
had enough water for supper, but we borrowed breakfast water from
the two boys. Shortly after it became dark, a young man and his girl
friend arrived—no water—no stove. They used Sam's stove and all
our breakfast water to cook an evening meal. To bed at 9:00. It began to rain very hard at one o'clock and rained most of the night.

Friday, August 21. Delayed getting up until 6:30 because it was so
very dark and still raining slightly. Visited the spring and found that
water was now coming out in a steady stream. The long dry spell in
the White Mountains had been broken. Began hiking at 8:00.
Reached the big Mizpah Hut at 9:30 and stopped for hot coffee and
coffee cake. Reached Lake of the Clouds Hut at 12:30 and ate our
lunch there. At the hut we met James Dungan of Kinsport, Tennessee,
who is hiking from Mt. Katahdin all the way to Tennessee. We left
the Lakes Hut at 1:45 and the sky cleared—good views thereafter.
We hiked above the tree line most of the day, frequently above 5,000
feet, and went over Mt. Washington whose elevation exceeds 6,000
feet. My diary for the day shows: "Reached Thunderstorm Junction
about 6:00—decided to try for Crag Camp—reached there 6:45—
delightful arrangement—custodian, propane gas, running cold water,
utensils—all for $1. Cooked a good supper. Sam and I and the cus-
todian are the only occupants. Writing my notes with light from
Coleman lantern. I very much like this arrangement—immensely better than a lean-to; immensely cheaper than an AMC hut. Wish to explore the economics of this further. It is operated by Randolph

Mountain Club. Stars shinning brightly—town of Berlin, New Hampshire, glowing brightly down below."

I had passed the 1,700 mile mark—my hike was 85% completed!

Saturday, August 22. Up at 5:30 and used the 3-burner propane stove to make coffee and pancakes. Clear day, 44 degrees at 6 a.m. We reached the Madison Hut at 9:15 and stayed there for coffee. Met the MacDonald family of Alexandria, Virginia, fellow members of PATC, near the Hut. We climbed over the top of Mt. Madison, elevation 5,363 feet, and began the long slow hike towards the Pinkham Notch Hut and New Hamphire Highway 16. I had difficulty keeping my balance on top of Mt. Madison because of the strong wind. Both Sam and I were suffering from sore knees; the constant pounding from rock hopping, day after day, takes its toll. We met 12 groups of people in 8 miles—some 68 people in all—most of them heading for Mt. Madison Hut. We worried about some of these groups—family groups with small children—who, late in the day, were beginning the 8-mile uphill climb to the Madison Hut. One group whom we did not worry about was a group of 13 people, young adults, from Paul Petzold's Lander, Wyoming, National Outdoor Leadership School. We also met Ron Panko and his girl friend; they were also headed for Madison Hut. I had met Ron's parents and brother on the Trail in New York, some six weeks earlier. We lost the Trail shortly before reaching Pinkham Notch and came out on the highway. We reached the Hut at 5 and weighed my pack on one of the spring scales that is provided at each Hut for just that purpose. My pack weighed 40 pounds. I had a quick shower at the Hut, changed clothes, and drove in Sam's van to Gorham. We ate supper at a drive-in, and I went to 7:30 Mass. Then I telephoned my wife and wished her a happy birthday. The following are some random quotes from my diary and from my daily log form for that day: "Trail well marked with cairns and signs, but no AT white paint blazes. AMC Trail crews have installed perhaps 20-30 water bars and perhaps 10-12 wet-spot wooden walks. Much of Trail is steep and eroded." And then: "My 6-year-old L. L. Bean Pathfinder shoes have just about had it. Have worn them every day since I reached Delaware Water Gap on July 6—about 600 miles. Also, they are pretty smelly!"

We spent the night in Sam Steen's van which is equipped with a cot and had enough extra floor space (just enough—none extra) for one additional person . . . me!

Sunday, August 23. Woke up at 6 and lay in bed for an hour listening to the steady rain beating down on the metal roof of Sam's van. The weatherman predicted all day rain. The New Hampshire dry spell is definitely broken—two hard rains in less than three days. We had made reservations at the Carter Notch Hut; but in view of the weather, we cancelled the reservation and spent the day in the lobby at Pinkham Notch Hut.

Pinkham took on the atmosphere of an airport waiting room on a day when all planes are grounded. It had rained hard during the night; there was intermittent rain much of the day, low visability; and it was Sunday with many weekenders who had to get back home for the Monday-Friday workweek. All day, wet bedraggled hikers came down out of the mountains, took showers, made long-distance phone calls, waited for rides, and killed time. It was a quiet day during which I did much letter writing. I had an interesting one and a half hour discussion with Bruce Sloat, Manager of the AMC Hut system, who headquarters at Pinkham. I also met Ralph Etherington and his family, ardent ATC-ers from Lynchburg, Virginia, who were vacationing in the White Mountains.

Monday, August 24. Up at 5:30, breakfast, and over to Pinkham Notch Hut to obtain the weather report. It was posted at 8, it looked favorable, and we began hiking at 8:30. We reached the Gondola Lift at 11 and had our first lunch there. The temperature was 55. The climb to summit of Wildcat was vicious; the descent into Carter Notch even more so. Trails were wet and slippery from the long rain. Ate a second lunch at Carter Notch Hut. Made the tough climb to Carter Dome, then South Carter, Middle Carter, North Carter—all of these mountains have elevations in the 4,500-4,800 foot range. Then we made the steep and treacherous descent. Daylight was beginning to fade when we reached the Imp shelter at 7:45. Both Sam and I were beat. We hiked 13 miles over some of the roughest up-and-down climbing that I experienced. It was cool and windy at shelter, and we cooked a quick meal inside over Sam's Primus propane gas stove. I cooked a whole package of Lipton's green pea soup to which we added a can of sausages. Gad, but it tasted good!

It had been clear most of the day; and we obtained excellent views of Mt. Washington, Mt. Adams, Mt. Madison and the other mountains in the Presidential Range. We congratulated ourselves on *not* having hiked on Sunday. Not only would it have been sloppy and dangerous to have hiked in the rain and fog (it was dangerous enough as it was), but we would have missed so much. To quote from my diary: "I found today—as before—that the White Mountain trails are characterized by the three R's—Rocks, Roots, and Erosion. Even at Imp Shelter, the trail to the trash pit and toilet is almost straight up and down on a steep eroded trail."

An additional observation: I had not seen, nor would I see, any aerial survey panels on any part of the Trail maintained by the AMC.

Tuesday, August 25. Up quietly at 5:45, not wishing to wake Sam or the three teenagers still sleeping. Rinsed face and hands in swift flowing stream, made my shelter inspection, and brought my notes up to date—something I had not had time to do the previous day. Sam cooked a hot breakfast (his propane stove is a jewel) including a ham and scrambled egg mix that Norm Greist had given me way back at Riga cabin in Connecticut. (There is nothing like carrying food for hundreds of miles to be certain it is fully aged . . . I had carried this particular package for almost 400 miles!) We left Imp Shelter at 7:30 and made the very steep ascent of Mt. Moriah.

My diary relates: "Reached summit at 9 (4,092 feet). Six wooden signs at the junction of trails near the summit: three USFS signs and three AMC signs. Only one of the six signs gave indication that we were on the AT—the indication being the tiny one and one-eighth inch high AT symbol on one AMC sign. Saw four of the old type perforated 4-inch AT metal markers. Also saw some sporadic and old white AT paint blazing. Our knees are sore as boils, it hurts to walk. Reached Rattle River shelter 11:35. Ate a hearty lunch finishing up a lot of food I had carried for miles. Leaving shelter at 1:30. The temporary end of my hike is just an hour away. My knees need the rest! My shoes are a mess—worn down into the sub sole—right heel coming off."

We reached US Route 2 (near Gorham, New Hampshire) at 2 p.m. Caught a ride to Sam's car at Pinkham, showered, shaved, changed clothes, and began driving to Killington, Vermont. Stayed overnight at the home of Mrs. Fleming.

Wednesday, August 26. Spent the day traveling: by car to Sam Steen's home in Kingston, New York; and by bus from there to my home in Falls Church, Virginia.

Thursday August 27 to Wednesday, September 9. This two-week period was devoted to preparations for, participation in, and recuperation from my daughter Kathleen's wedding on September 5. A very lovely wedding in a downtown Washington church. The Anglos were seated on one side of the church—the Latins on the other. A bilingual priest with the very un-Spanish name of Father Sean O'Malley officiated. The marriage vows were exchanged in both Spanish and English. The marriage contract should not lack for formality! After the wedding, a reception at our home for 150 guests. Luckily the weather was beautiful, so guests could visit in our big yard. The cake cutting took place on our concrete basketball court.

The only untoward event occured as my wife, my two daughters (the bride and bridesmaid) and I were driving downtown to the church. My younger daughter Sharon suddenly became carsick. We made a hurried stop on the busy elevated Whitehurst Freeway in Georgetown. Sharon and I got out of the car so she could get some fresh air. Passing motorists were puzzled to see a young lady in full length dress and a gray-haired man in full morning dress standing at the rail of the busy elevated highway and seemingly enjoying the view of a concrete plant and a highly offensive rendering plant in Georgetown's industrial section!

Thursday, September 10. I took the bus from Washington, D.C. to New York. Tex Griffin picked me up at the bus station at 5:20 and drove me to his home in Bronxville. After supper we drove, in two cars, to the Griffin summer home in Millertown, New York.

Friday, September 11. After a big breakfast cooked by Jean Griffin, Tex and I took off in his VW for Gorham, New Hampshire. We reached there at 2:20 and went directly to post office where I mailed a package of Claxton fruit cake and a package of Appalachian Trail Mix to my self at the address, General Delivery, Monson, Maine. We quickly drove out to the AT and I began hiking at three o'clock. I wasted no time, as it was already mid-afternoon. The days were getting shorter, and I had almost 7 miles of hiking which involved some stiff climbs ahead of me.

For the last 300 miles of my hike I wore the rubber bottom L. L. Bean Maine Hunting Boots, 9 inches high. I wore heavier shirts and slacks. And my unlined 4 ounce windbreaker had now been replaced by a 25 ounce Holubar parka.

I reached the Gentian Pond shelter at 6:30 and found a Mike and Susan Humphrey already there. I ate a cold supper and worked on my notes until darkness intervened.

This is but one of the 13 highway crossing signs developed by the state highway departments of the states through which the Appalachian Trail passes. See page 36 for pictures of the others. The author at one time possessed all 13, having received them from the various state highway departments as they designed and completed their signs. The one pictured below (New Hampshire) is affixed in the Garvey garage; the others were delivered to the Appalachian Trail Conference in Harpers Ferry in 1972.

Appalachian Trail sign erected by New Hampshire Department of Public Works and Highways. (Photo: Joan Knight)

Saturday September 12. A clear beautiful day. Steam hovered over Gentian Pond. I left the shelter at 7:45 and reached Carlo Col shelter at 12:20. Both at the Gentian Pond shelter and later atop Mt. Success, I could smell the fumes of the paper factory at Berlin. I took a nasty spill at 11 a.m. while climbing on a rocky slab. My feet slipped out from under me, and I skidded downward. I had mittens on, but I suffered a small cut on my left wrist. I left the shelter 1:10 and in midafternoon I met Dave Allen and Doc Edwards, two AMC-ers from Boston. I reached Full Goose shelter at 5:20. I examined this structure with more than ordinary care because I had been told that it was one of the newer AMC shelters built with precut tongue and groove logs—each log being 7 inches high and 6 inches wide. It was an excellent shelter—30 feet by 12 feet in size with capacity for 14. Prices, shelter design, and construction hints may be obtained from Northern Products, Inc., Bomarc Road, in Bangor, Maine 04401.

I had been intrigued at several places by an AMC sign reading "Trident Shelter Removed—Lack of Proper Use." Think that one over a bit. A masterful bit of phrasing. It offends no one by saying that the shelter had been misused. It says merely that the shelter did not receive enough "Proper Use."

My diary reads: "Had beautiful views while hiking—could see Mt. Washington clearly—the carriage road—the smoke from the cog railway—and one time, the train itself etched clearly on the skyline. Could see and faintly smell fumes of the paper mill at Berlin even from atop the West Peak of Goose Eye."

I passed from New Hampshire into Maine at noon. Thirteen states and 1749 miles behind me.

Observations on New Hampshire. The White Mountains were one of two sections of the Trail that I faced with some apprehension . . . the other was the Smokies. I had a healthy respect for the Whites; for I had read of the sudden and violent changes in the weather, even in the summer months. The scenery in the White Mountains is some of the most spectacular on the entire Trail.

The trail passes through eight National Forests and the amount of trailwork done by each local trail club and that done by the Forest Service varies from Forest to Forest. In some cases, I suspected that the Forest Service was the "big brother" in the cooperative enterprise; while in the others the trail clubs themselves did a more substantial part of the total job. In the White Mountains the Appalachian Mountain Club is certainly full partner. For one thing, the AMC and the AMC trails were in existence long before the White Mountain National Forest. In 1970 the AMC had a 16-man trail crew working full time on trail and shelter maintenance during the summer months.

As in Vermont, I was dismayed at the scant recognition accorded the Appalachian Trail on that part that is maintained by AMC and by the White Mountain National Forest. The AMC signs do not mention the Appalachian Trail by name—the only concession being a tiny one and one-eighth inch high AT symbol on some—not all—of the signs that appear on the Appalachian Trail. The Forest Service is not much more generous in the recognition it accords the Appalachian Trail. On the other hand, where the Trail goes through State Park property, it receives very prominent recognition; and where it crosses State highways, there is a 24-inch by 72-inch sign erected by the New Hampshire Department of Public Works and Highways. Except for the failure to recognize the AT, I had nothing but praise for the AMC signs and cairns. They were excellent.

The great preponderance of AT mileage in the White Mountains does not have the conventional 2-inch by 6-inch white blazes. This puzzled me because the hiker needs all the assistance he can get in following the Trail; and the white paint blazes have proven to be one of the most reliable, vandal-proof methods of marking the Trail. Many of the AMC members I talked to were themselves somewhat puzzled at the lack of paint blazing. Perhaps the matter will be resolved as the National Park Service in collaboration with the Forest Service and the Appalachian Trail Conference issues guidelines on trail maintenance. The tentative *Guidelines for Planning Design and Management,* released in May 1971, for the Appalachian National Scenic Trail, does provide for the conventional white paint blazing and for a uniform system of signs along the 2,000 mile Trail. (Note: In 1972, the Appalachian Mountain Club applied white paint to all parts of the AT in the White Mountains!)

Foot trails, trailside shelters, and the Hut system are all big business in the White Mountain National Forest. In 1970 both AMC and the Forest Service were making painstaking appraisals of the hiker and camper use situation, the trail maintenance situation, and of many related activities. In April 1971, at the annual New England Trail Conference meeting in Northampton, Massachusetts, I listened to officials of both agencies announce changes that would occur in 1971: strict limitation on the number of campers permitted in one popular but overused area, a provision for cluster camps with a custodian, etc.

The most serious problem, as I saw it, was the severe erosion taking place on the Trail. The trails are very steep, having been laid out in a straight up and down route with no apparent effort having been made to observe a reasonable grade, to use switchbacks, or to use ballast to provide a stable trail. The only permanent solution is to build new trails at gentle grades which utilize all the techniques of modern trail design. This will take money—much money. A 1970 study in the Adirondacks disclosed that new foot trails would cost approximately $2,000 per mile.

Joe May, AMC's Supervisor of Trails, faced at present with the job of maintaining the existing steep trails, views the matter as a choice between two alternatives: to have a nice wide trail with much erosion or to have a much narrower trail with less erosion. With the narrower trail, the lacework of tree roots will assist in preventing erosion. But this means an annual program of trim, trim, trim, as tree branches must regularly be cut back to permit passage by the hiker. So much for the White Mountains—a fascinating piece of real estate.

16. MAINE, SEPTEMBER 12 TO OCTOBER 7

Sunday, September 13. I had been hiking in the Mahoosuc mountains for almost a day. My first few miles of hiking in Maine have already been described. On this date, September 13, I spent all day hiking but 8.1 miles; but this involved one of the toughest and most spectacular 8 miles on the entire Trail — from Full Goose Shelter through the famous boulder-filled steep walled Mahoosuc Notch, then a steep climb for 0.9 miles to the summit of Mahoosuc Arm, on past Old Speck Pond, and then the steep climb up Old Speck (elevation 4,180 feet). Finally, there was the slow steep descent into Grafton Notch and the Grafton Notch shelter.

I left Full Goose shelter at 7. Clear day, temperatures 44 at 7—only 60 at 1 p.m. Reached the Mahoosuc Notch at 8 and spent 1 hour and 25 minutes carefully threading my way over, under, and through the giant boulders in the Notch. Climbed and hiked steadily until 1:30 when I reached Old Speck Pond and shelter. Went for a very brief dip in the pond; the temperature of the water was 54 degrees. Met Dave Thurston and the advance guard of 20 members of the Freshman Class of Gould Academy, Bethel, Maine. Left the shelter at 2. Had beautiful views all day. Thurston and I walked to the observation tower atop Old Speck then down into Grafton Notch where Thurston's brother was waiting with a car. I proceeded to Grafton Notch shelter and reached there at 5:20 to find Andy Narva and his brother Bill already set up at the shelter. Andy had worked all summer as an AMC trail crew man, and we had much to talk about. Andy was enrolled at Harvard, but he was so gungho on the White Mountains and the AMC trails that I suspected it would take him a little time to unwind and get back into the routine of college work.

I found a note addressed to me at the shelter. It was from Dick Hudson, Croton-On-Hudson, New York, who had been completing the AT over a 5-year stretch. He had just missed me in a number of places. The note informed me that he had completed the entire AT at Grafton Notch in August 1970.

Monday, September 14. Had a leisurely breakfast with the Narva boys. Left the shelter at 10 but made only 8 miles for the entire day, including 1.3 miles of sightseeing on side trails. Clear, cool day, excellent visability. Temperature 50 degrees at noon. Enjoyed spectacular views from Table Rock, East and West Baldpate, and along the Frye Brook. My diary shows the following. "Hiked in T-shirt most of day despite low temperature. Poorest time I've made in months, but it was beautiful day and I promised myself a few of these. Reached Frye Brook around 4—not much water flowing but still spectacular with the Flume, the Cataract, etc. Reached shelter 4:30—made pudding, put prunes to soak, gathered firewood, and then to my diary. Hope I can get all paper work finished tonight and get an early start tomorrow. Frye Brook flowing 15 yards in front of shelter . . . will be lulled to sleep by it tonight. (later) Monday was one of real pleasant days of trip—in bed 7:30 . . . totally dark . . . went to sleep to sound of brook and light from camp fire. Glad I took it easy."

Tuesday, September 15. Made 18 miles today from Frye Brook shelter to Elephant Mountain shelter. Have been hiking since Grafton Notch, on trails with white paint blazers. Temperature reached a high of 48 at 12 noon. And from my diary: "Up at 6:10 awakened by alarm watch. Hot breakfast. On Trail at 7:10. Intermittent rain all day. Wore rain parka all day, and rain chaps most of day. Pleasant hiking —not strenuous—and I averaged 2.3 miles per hour to Squirrel Rock shelter. Went by three ponds—beautiful."

"From 11:15 to 11:30 a chipping sparrow preceded me on the Trail—alighting every few yards—sometimes flying into a tree and letting me pass—only to again fly ahead and resume the game. I counted 90 landings in the last 5 minutes. Estimated he made over 200 landings in about 1200 yards. Crazy business."

"Made slower time in P.M.—reached Elephant Mountain shelter at 4:30. Cold—42 degrees. Gathered water and firewood—cooked supper first—then got part of paper work done before darkness set in at 7. Watched fire—crawled into bed at 7:40. Began raining hard during the night and rained all night."

"Went through interesting forest area—some places all covered with moss—predominantly balsam—fairy-like appearance like some of the Disney movie scenes. Maine *is* pretty, but is a Wilderness."

That night for my evening meal, I cooked my old reliable, creamed tuna over rice. But this time I added an extra flourish; I put in basil leaves, krauterbutter, salt, pepper, the rest of my minced onion, and —when the meal was ready to eat—I garnished it with Lipton Garnish for Beef Stroganoff!

At the shelter I found a placard reading "Hikers—Join the Appalachian Trail Conference." Only the second such placard I have seen in 1780 miles!

Wednesday, September 16. Hiked only 11 miles from Elephant Mountain shelter to Sabbath Day Pond shelter. The all-night rain stopped at 6:45 a.m. Overcast and foggy most of day. Left shelter 8:20. Had tough hiking all day. Woods were dripping wet and slippery. Foggy, visibility 50 yards. I know I missed some beautiful views. Temperature never got above 50. It was somewhat eerie on top of the various Bemis mountains; the cairns and blazes were not too clear and fog made it doubly difficult to see. I was glad to get down into the timber. Sorry I could not have hiked this in August; I would have loved to have had a swim in these ponds and lakes. I walked to shore of Long Lake, a nice sandy beach, but I could not see more than 20 yards at the time.

Wore my rain chaps all day; they worked well. My shoes were wet, and my feet cold. I was wearing Beans' rubber bottom boots. The leather uppers got staturated, and water oozed down into my foot.

I reached Sabbath Day Pond shelter at 2:45 and had all my paperwork finished by 4. Laid in wood and built a fire with one of my fire starters. Was pleased that I was able to get a fire going immediately with the woods soaked as they were. I was joined at 5 p.m. by Chuck Miller, Vice President of Grand-Way, a division of Grand Union. He cooked up a huge freeze-dried four-man package of chili con carne. (Rich-Moor). Delicious. We dried more wood for breakfast. The

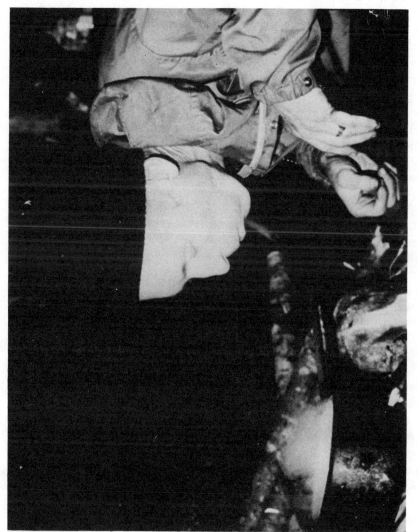

Garvey blowing on the fire for cooking his evening meal in Maine. (Photo: Tex Griffin)

weather cleared around 5, and a strong wind blew all night drying things quite well. To bed at 7:30; visited with Chuck until 9:15.

Signs and Markers. I was pleased with the excellent sign program in Maine and with the frequent use of metal markers. The signs were high quality: routed, attractive, light brown background, white lettering. They are placed at road crossings, trail intersections, and at shelters. Each shelter has a sign identifying the shelter and giving the name and distance of the next shelter north and the next one south.

Thursday, September 17. Hiked 12 miles to Piazza Rock shelter with four hours off for a trip to Rangeley, Maine. Left shelter at 6:50 and walked nonstop 6.1 miles to State Route 4. Reached there 8:40 and caught ride before I even got across the road! At 9:15 I was eating a second breakfast of hot cakes and coffee in Doc Grant's restaurant. Picked up mail, shopped for groceries, and bought a pair of after-ski boots. At 1 p.m. Postmaster Earl Fraiser picked me up and gave me a ride back to the Trail. He does this for any through-hiker of the Appalachian Trail.

Began hiking from Highway 4 at 1:15 and reached Piazza Rock shelter at 3:30. Immediately after arriving at the shelter I took off my rubber bottom boots and wet socks and donned my new wool socks and fleece lined after-ski boots. Gad, but they felt good. At the shelter I explored the Piazza Rock, a big table-like rock jutting out into space. Built a big fire, washed socks, wrote some letters by firelight, crawled into my sleeping bag early, and watched the fire die down.

During the day I had seen two robins, three grouse, and one striped warbler.

Seems late for the robins and warbler. Was amazed to see, this far north, a shagbark hickory tree which was 10 inches in diameter at breast height. Crossed the 1,800 mile mark today. Hike is 90% completed!

Friday, September 18. My diary for this day reads as follows: "Up at 5:50—reached Saddleback Mountain at 9:05—climbed over the Horn and, as I approached Saddleback, Jr., I met the three girls whom I had been expecting to meet somewhere in Maine—Nancy Peterkin, Evelyn Thielke, and Gale Dixon. Had a nice 45-minute visit. They began their hike at Mt. Katahdin. They told me there was a grocery store at Caratunk—also advised me to ford the Kennebec River because the water was so low. Good information to have. I reached Poplar Ridge shelter at 1, left at 1:20. Took four bad spills in an hour before reaching Orbeton Stream. My Bean hunting shoes have very little traction. Cut my left elbow—reopened cut on left wrist. Picked 12 apples at a one-time lumber camp—same place that Norm Greist and I picked three years ago. Reached Spaulding Mountain shelter 5:20. Cooked huge meal—creamed tuna over potatoes—combined with hot fresh apple sauce cooked in brown sugar and cinnamon. Overcast entire day, but visibility on Saddleback and the Horn was 5-8 miles. On Saddleback, Jr. visibility only 50 yards!"

I had hiked 16 miles that day and picked up only eight pieces of litter. The Trail was extremely clean all through Maine.

Saturday, September 19. Up at 5:30 and tried a new breakfast combination: Grapenuts mixed with the remains of the fresh apples I had cooked the night before. Washed down with hot coffee, it made a delicious breakfast. Left shelter at 7:40. The day was clear and became quite warm. I had difficulty following the Trail on the ski slopes of the Mt. Sugarloaf ski area. I built three cairns to help the cause. By prearrangement I met Joe May and his nine-year-old son Chris near Sugarloaf shelter. We ate lunch at the shelter. It was an absolutely gorgeous day; the trees were almost in full color at the lower elevtions. I reached Bigelow Village on State Routes 16 and 27 at 1 p.m. and then drove from there to—take a deep breath!—to Mooselookmeguntic Lake! The May family has a cabin on this beautiful lake; and we spent the rest of the day relaxing. I took a bath on the back stoop of the cabin with Joe pouring warm water over me . . . first bath of that type I had had in 45 years. We built a small driftwood fire on the lake shore at supper time and cooked hamburgers. The setting and weather for this outdoor meal were as delightful as one could ask for. I went to sleep that night listening to and watching the waves breaking on the rocky, pebbly shore.

Sunday, September 20. Went to 8:30 Mass in the little town of Oquossoc. Back to the May cabin, changed clothes, said goodbye to Joe's wife, and then drove with Joe, Chris, and Melissa back to Bigelow Village and the Appalachian Trail. Began hiking at 11 on a beautiful early autumn day. Before me lay one of the most beautiful mountain ranges in Maine, the Bigelow Range. I met ten people on the Trail in the first seven miles. Reached the two Horn shelters at 2:45, and reached the Avery shelter at 5:30. I missed the company of the very tame snowshoe rabbits who had visited us at the shelter when I had stayed overnight here in September 1967. I did have company of a Canada Jay who made countless trips to the fireplace six

feet in front of me to eat the shoestring potatoes which a previous
camper had discarded there.

I enjoyed beautiful views throughout the day, both from the highway looking up toward the impressive Bigelow Range and later, looking down on the valley from the top of that same range. I had seen
blueberries, clintonia, and bunch berry—all with fruit. I had also
taken another spill, and for the fourth time completely ripped open
the scab on my left wrist.

Monday, September 21. I left the shelter at 7:40 and made a leisurely
traverse of the Bigelows, hiking but 11 miles in the entire day. It
was a clear and sunny day; the temperature was 70 at noon and was
still 70 at 4 p.m. I saw seven spruce grouse in three groups and
marveled that this slow moving sluggish bird has not become extinct.
On top of Avery Peak I saw a sign reading "Mt. Katahdin, 184 miles."
I was getting closer!

In my diary I wrote: "Reached south end of Bigelow Crest at 12—
sunny, mild breeze. Ate snack in T-shirt—admired colors in trees all
along Bigelow Range—watched and listened to three ravens doing
aerial acrobatics below me. Saw moose tracks on Trail. Reached
Jerome Brook shelter at 3:30—quite warm—even had a few mosquitos! Worked on my notes first thing—then got supper. All finished
5:45—raining slightly—lucky me—got to shelter again before the
rain. Have a 16.5-mile jaunt ahead of me tomorrow and will have to
hustle to get to Monson by Friday. Before supper I opened an un-
marked (label removed) can of food I had picked up at Poplar Ridge
shelter—turned out to be chicken spread and that dictated the
menu for supper. Made a half batch of Liptons Chicken Stroganoff
and mixed in the whole can of spread. Completely filled one of my
3-cup sauce pans—delicious—and filling. Very very still except for
occasional car on the road 100 yards away. Will now (6 p.m.) wash
dishes and write a few cards to mail in Caratunk."

Tuesday, September 22. It rained all night. I left the shelter at 6:15;
I wore my rain chaps but only a T-shirt from the waist up. Reached
West Carry Pond Camp at 7:40 and had a big breakfast with Mr. and
Mrs. Elwyn Storey. I was one of the last paying guests as this well
known Maine Sporting Camp which was due to close permanently
on September 30 after 75 years of operation. Reached the East Carry
Pond Camp at 11:30 and had coffee and cookies with Mr. and Mrs.
Henry Spencer. Left there at 12 and reached the East Carry Pond
shelter at 12:30. The shelter in a beautiful spot, seven yards from the

lake shore. Left the shelter at one and made steady progress. Temperature reached 75 at 4 p.m. I was bothered by mosquitoes and no-see-ums. I reached a big lumbering operation one mile south of Pierce Pond Camp. There were perhaps 20-25 piles of wood, some hardwood, some softwood, each pile four to seven feet high, four feet wide, and 100-200 feet long. For one-third of a mile the Appalachian Trail is a mudhole where they have been skidding logs on it. Some trees were being cut directly beside the Trail. I reached the new Pierce Pond shelter at 4:10. It is an absolutely delightful place. I went for a swim. At 6:45 the pond was perfectly calm; the sun had set; the trees and mountains were mirrored in the pond.

Washed clothes, shaved, brushed teeth, had my swim, and felt wonderful. It was a warm evening. I went to bed at 7:30 on top of my sleeping bag.

Wednesday, September 23. Up at 5:30, left the shelter 6:30, and hiked the three miles to the Kennebec River in one hour. The three girls I had met the previous week had told me the river was quite low and could be forded. It was not low now. The current was swift, and there were occasional pieces of pulp wood flashing by. The guide book lists the width of the river as 0.2 miles which would be 350 yards. I judged it to be about 150 yards. I stripped down to my underwear, put my boots on to protect my feet, obtained an eight-foot pole, and began wading across. The water reached my crotch, then my waist, and one-third of the way across the water was chest high. I am a strong swimmer and could have swum across easily enough by myself although I would have ended up far downstream. With a 40-pound pack the situation was different. I had plenty of nylon cord with me with which to make a raft. But this would have taken considerable time, and there was always the chance of a mishap whereby I might have lost some of my gear or gotten it wet. I therefore returned to shore, dressed, poured the water out of my boots (one gets used to wet feet!); and backtracked on the Appalachian Trail for three miles. At that point, I left the Appalachian Trail and began walking south on a dirt road toward Bingham, Maine. I had hiked for six miles when I was given a ride by a French Canadian logger. He could speak little English but he looked at me and at my pack and said two words that sounded like "Oppolockian Trail?" I nodded "Yes." He gave me a ride all the way to Bingham which was perhaps 10-12 miles farther south. At 11:40 I walked into the Thompson Restaurant in Bingham, had a good lunch, and was given a ride back north to Caratunk by Emmons Casey and a companion whom I had met at the restaurant. At 1:15 I walked down to the east bank of the Kennebec where the Appalachian Trail resumes its course on dry land.

(*Note:* In 1978 hikers could be ferried across the Kennebec by Warren Ricker—phone 207-663-2241. Northbound hikers can make telephone arrangements at Williams Camp, also known as the Carrying Place—some 200 yards off the Appalachian Trail near Pierce Pond lean-to. Southbound hikers can call Mr. Ricker from Mitchell's store in center of Carratunk. Cost—$5 for one; lesser rate for two or more.)

I hiked into the little village of Caratunk and stopped for half an hour at the combination grocery store and post office. Picked up mail and had a pint of ice cream. Pushed on toward Pleasant Pond shelter, walking on hard surface road almost all the way. Within shouting distance of the shelter I met Robert Wing, a commercial logger from Bingham, who was working in the area with two French Canadian helpers. He invited me up to their shack for supper, and I accepted. The two Canadians, both equipment operators, were Norman Poulet and Victor Bourque; and their knowledge of English was quite limited. Bob Wing was bilingual so we got along famously as long as he was there. The two men worked five days a week in Maine and drove back to Canada each Friday night. They apparently liked me because after a bit they extended—via Bob Wing—an invitation for me to stay overnight in their cabin. I already had all my sleeping gear laid out on the shelter floor and declined the invitation, but I did accept their invitation to return for breakfast. I returned to the shelter at 9:20, and Bob Wing drove back to his home in Bingham.

It turned out to be a very pleasant day in spite of the initial disappointment of not getting across the Kennebec. I had hiked only nine miles on the Appalachian Trail but had hiked another eight miles on dirt roads.

Thursday, September 24. I got up at 5:20 and walked in the faint moonlight up to the logging shack. Everything very dark and quiet, and I had trouble finding the place. Woke up the two men and we had a very pleasant meal together. Returned to the shelter, packed my gear and began climbing Pleasant Mountain on the first leg of a 20-mile day. Reached Joes Hole Brook shelter at 10:35. Later I walked for one and one-half miles along Moxie Pond and saw a small animal swimming across the pond. I picked a spot where I thought it would emerge from water and waited. I was surprised to see that it was a mink. He had swum a good 200 yards across the south end of the pond; it seemed like a long swim for such a small animal. At two I reached the warden's cabin atop Moxie Bald Mountain and had coffee and cookies with two State of Maine employees, David Richards and Allan Scamman, who had come in by helicopter to do extensive repair work on the fire warden cabin. I was very impressed with the area atop Moxie Bald. The guide book describes it as an outstanding mountain with ledges and some of the Arctic features found at Katahdin.

I reached Moxie Bald shelter at 2:40 and left at 3:00. A beautiful spot, 40 yards from a nice pond. I hated to leave the place. It had plenty of table space, an assortment of pots and pans, a good spring, a nice pond. In my diary I made the notation "Would surely enjoy loafing up here for a couple of weeks. This Maine pond area is delightful."

The blazing, generally good in Maine, was poor north of Moxie Bald shelter. For the most part there was little attempt to paint a neat two-inch by six-inch blaze. The blazes were frequently old hatchet or axe wounds on the tree with white paint carefully painted inside the wounds.

Reached Breakneck Ridge shelter at 5:45. Had to work fast to make camp, cook my meal, and shave before darkness set in. All paper work deferred until next day. I had hiked 20 miles on another one of those beautiful fall days. And while I could not have foreseen it at the time, this was to be the last pleasant hiking day I was to have for some time.

Friday, September 25. Left shelter at 8:05. Intermittent rain all day. Passed through the little community of Blanchard and reached the town of Monson, Maine, at noon. Ate nooday dinner at Coffee Shop restaurant and visited with Bucky Owen and John Diamond, both of the University of Maine faculty. Owen was familiar with some of the Trail north of Monson since on several occasions he had assisted trail overseer, John Neff, in trail maintenance work in the vicinity of White Cap Mountain. I also made the acquaintance of Mrs. Manford Knowles, whose late husband had been very active in trail maintenance work.

I picked up a good deal of mail in Monson, including two packages of food that I had mailed myself from Gorham, New Hampshire.

I laundered all my clothes in the laundromat and bought ten dollars worth of groceries. I used the resetaurant as an office for reading my mail and writing letters. I ate my evening meal there and then received ride to home of Esmond Richardson who lives about two or three miles outside of town. I guess it would be proper to state that Richardson lives on the fringes of the wilderness. I base this on the fact that in his garden a week before he had shot a 100-pound bear cub and also on the fact that he had recently seen a moose in his yard. To me, that spells wilderness!

Repacked all my groceries in Richardson's kitchen—all the while having a pleasant conversation with him. He was a widower, a retired mechanic from the Great Northern Paper Co., and he enjoyed company. The three girls whom I had met the previous week had also stayed at his home, and he thought they were the greatest!

Saturday, September 26. Delicious bacon and egg breakfast cooked over a wood range stove. Worked out my schedule for the next ten days. I deliberately set a very slow schedule for two reasons: (1) my trip was nearing its end and I wanted to savor each day through the lake country of Maine, and (2) I would be sending the schedule to quite a few people and I wanted to be certain that I would disappoint no one by not showing up at a scheduled time.

Esmond drove me into town, and I typed up and mailed out my schedules. Steve Clark and his family arrived from Winslow, Maine. Steve and I walked on the Appalachian Trail out to the Richardson home, there I made a final check of my now heavily laden pack, and then Steve and I began walking toward the Old Stage Road shelter. His wife, Barbara, and children drove on to the Little Wilson campsite where they would camp out in the VW bus.

I was now on the last exciting leg of my journey. Monson, according to my mileage fact sheet, was the last grocery resupply point I would have. It was 118 miles from Monson to Mt. Katahdin, and I had deliberately set a slow schedule. I was carrying the heaviest supply of food for my entire trip and I judged my pack weighed between 52 and 54 pounds. A glance at a road map will show that from Monson, Maine, to Baxter State Park, the little dotted line representing the Appalachian Trail, goes through an almost roadless wilderness. I would see few people on the Trail the next ten days. I would travel through some beautiful lake country and would hike through an area that had the heaviest concentration of moose in the State.

It was an overcast day when we started out, with rain threatening any minute. We reached the shelter at 2:30 and found the area surrounding the shelter blanketed with red maple leaves. Steve performed the honors at supper, providing a shrimp cocktail, a haddock dinner, and a bottle of Chianti wine. Much visiting after supper. To bed at nine. It began to rain during the night and rained off and on all night.

Sunday, September 27. Up at six. Raining. We used our stoves to cook breakfast inside. I donned my rain chaps and rain parka and wore them all day. Slippery walking. Woods almost in full color. Took the 0.3 mile side trip to Little Wilson Falls. Reached the Little Wilson campsite at 12. It was here that Barbara Clark and their four children had spent the night. At that point, Steve took the children and the VW; and his wife Barbara hiked the next six miles with me to the Long Pond Stream shelter. We passed Bodfish Farm en route. Still raining. We reached the shelter at 3:30; and shortly thereafter the Clark family left for home. My company for the night was 22-year-old Sandy Thomson of W. Hartford, Connecticut. He had been on the Trail for 11 days and was almost out of food. Sandy writes poetry, and I was to see samples of some of it in the shelters farther north.

I had hiked six miles on roads; that is too much. The Trail should be rerouted to get it off the road.

Monday, September 28. Up at six. The temperature 38, the coldest since April. I made a hot breakfast and would continue to have hot breakfasts the rest of the trip. The day was clear, but the woods were saturated after three days of rain. I left the shelter at 7:35 and the first order of business was to ford the Long Pond stream which was a torrent after all that rain. At far side of stream I took off my shoes and socks and removed some of the water. Auspicious start!

In my diary I wrote: "Treacherous hiking—wore all my rain gear. Ate lunch at Cloud Pond shelter. Had made only four miles. Pushed on slowly using walking stick to keep from slipping. One of hardest days I've had—footway rough all the way—up and down all day. Beautiful views from various peaks. Color at, or almost at, peak. Particularly good views of Boarstone and Bodfish Intervale. Also many good views of Long Pond.

"Reached Chairback Gap shelter at 4:50. Used stove to cook supper and then cleaned up. By then it was 6:30 and too dark to write. In bed by seven—temperature in low 40's. Night clear—no moon now. Have 90 more miles to go."

The days were really getting short now. Imagine, going to bed at seven! But then there was really not much else to do.

Tuesday, September 29. It was 9 a.m. before I left shelter, for I spent a full hour on my notes and additional time sewing up the webbing on my pack frame. Clear weather in morning and Trail reasonably dry. A pleasure to hike without rain gear. Reached the East Chairback Camps at 10:30. They were closed, but the big mess hall had been left unlocked. Ate lunch there. Beautiful setting for a private camp. Reached the Pleasant River, took off shoes and socks and waded across the ice cold stream. A few minutes later, I left the Trail to visit the Hermitage area and to admire the virgin white pines towering 80 to 100 feet in height. This area now belongs to the Nature Conservancy. I pushed on steadily, frequently walking on roads. It rained slightly several times. Reached the White Brook shelter at 2:45. Found a bounteous supply of wood nearby so I decided to cook Appalachian Trail Mix (two parts whole rice, one part barley, one part lentils). I cooked it a full hour, adding one-half can of Spam. I was very pleased with the result. Before going to bed I had a final snack of popcorn from a supply I had found at Cloud Pond shelter.

It began raining steadily at six, and it was so dark I could barely see, even at that early hour. The fire was burning merrily; this helped to dispel the gloom. Had big pot of water boiling. Shaved for the first time since Saturday morning in Monson.

Wednesday, September 30. My diary for this date shows the following entries.

"A long day. It began at 1:05 a.m. when I looked at my watch. Moments later, I heard an animal in front of the shelter—sounded like a moose. Flashed my light, but could see only eyes—about seven feet high! Mr. Moose then came to within four feet of the shelter. There my light brought him clearly into view. Gad but they are big! He watched me four or five seconds, then meandered down toward the brook—twigs and branches snapping underfoot. So now I've seen my moose, but certainly not in a manner I had expected. Am writing these notes 6:15 p.m. at East Branch Tote Road shelter. Hiked 14.5 miserable miles today. It began raining even before I started. Arose at 5:30—lit a candle—got fire going immediately with birch bark. Heated water and heated up Appalachian Trail Mix left over from Tuesday night. With a dish of cereal this made a hearty breakfast. Left shelter 6:55.

"Elected not to put on rain chaps—a mistake. It rained hard, and I went through a lot of grown over trail. Soaked from hips down, including feet. Reached White Camp Mountain shelter at 10:45. Had hot chocolate—hot coffee—along with other stuff. Gasoline stove surely appreciated on cold wet raw days. Had reached top of White Cap Mountain (3,707 feet), but did not hike to tower because of rain and overcast. Slogged away until almost four, when I reached East Branch Tote Road shelter. Used stove again—put on dry clothes. How these warm pajamas and after-ski shoes are appreciated. Would be hell to sit around for hours in those cold wet rubber boots. Wrung water out of socks—drained water out of boots.

"Easy day tomorrow. By tomorrow night I will have hiked all of the Appalachian Trail, but not in one year. Another 64 miles to Mt. Katahdin. Surely hope weather clears. Finishing this at 6:30 p.m.—Raining—Dark!"

The reader will agree, I am sure, that judged by almost any standards, Wednesday, September 30 was not one of the most pleasant hiking days I had. But it takes a few like that to make one really appreciate the good days.

Thursday, October 1. Up at 6:30—another dark cloudy day with early morning rain. After breakfast and just before breaking camp, I had to face up to the dismal inevitability—taking off my warm dry clothes and ski boots and putting on trousers, two pair of socks, and rubber bottom boots that were all thoroughly wet and cold from yesterday's all-day rain.

Left shelter at eight and wore my rain chaps, but only after my trousers were thoroughly wet. My perspicacity at times amazes me. Made good time and at 9:15 reached the Kokadjo-B Pond road. At this point, I left the Appalachian Trail and hiked three miles on the road to the Yoke Pond Camps operated by Keith Skillin and his wife Cody. Had lunch there and got into a long discussion with Skillin on the use of the Appalachian Trail shelters by groups of undesirable people. Skillin feels very strongly that some way must be found of policing the shelters on the Trail. Bob Wing, the logger I had met at Pleasant Pond, had been just as emphatic on the same problem.

After lunch Game Warden Charles Howe of Greenville and a companion arrived. Their mission: to find and destroy a sick moose cow that had been seen staggering around for several days in a nearby area. I received permission to accompany them, and we paddled by canoe to the spot where the moose had last been seen. We found

Garvey awakened by moose. (Sketch by Sharon Garvey)

her tracks everywhere, found where she had lain down in the high grass for long periods of time; but we were unable to find her. Back to the camp kitchen for coffee and some more of Cody Skillin's home-made bread. I had lost track of time and hastily got my gear together and left Yoke Ponds Camp at three. Hiked the six miles to Cooper Brook Falls shelter, reached there at 5:30. I had stayed at this shelter in September 1969 when six of us hiked from Yoke Pond Camps to Katahdin. I could hear the continual roar of the falls about 20-30 yards from the shelter. Excellent deep swimming pool a mere 30 feet in front of shelter; but the day was chilly and overcast and I didn't have the usual zest for a swim. For supper I used the last of my Liptons potato soup, mixed in tuna, flour, rice, and milk, seasoned it well, and produced an excellent stew. Wrote my notes by candlelight.

Friday, October 2. Hiked a mere 11 enjoyable miles from Cooper Brook Falls to Potaywadjo Spring shelter. The record in my diary reads as follows:

"Left shelter at eight—looked longingly at the nice swimming hole at Cooper Brook Falls, but 38 is too cold! Made leisurely but steady progress—explored Cooper Pond some .22 miles to right of Trail. Reached remains of Old Antlers Camps on Little Joe Mary Lake and ate lunch there on the edge of the lake. Beautiful spot for a camp. Temperature 50 at 12—sunny. Proceeded to the sand beach, 1.62 miles north, where our group of six went swimming 13 months ago. It was about 75 then; today it was 50, with strong breeze. Heard a couple of loons crying out on lake. Reached Potaywadjo Spring shelter at 2:45. Found all the wood I needed from a single dead 3-4-inch diameter tree. Made a huge batch of Appalachian Trail Mix. Beautiful gushing spring at shelter, water temperature 42."

Saturday, October 3. Hiked a scant 12 miles from Potaywadjo Spring to the Wadleigh Pond shelter. In my diary I wrote the following.

"Up at six—rained during early hours and until about 10:30 a.m. Leisurely breakfast. On Trail at eight—dark in woods. Reached Mahar campground at 9:30. Saw a deer—first one in Maine. Steady drizzle—but rain parka too warm—wore chaps, but took off parka. Reached shelter at 11. Dismal little affair. Ate hearty lunch—topped off with hot popcorn. Delightful change in menu. Am enjoying Citadel Spread immensely. That and Claxton Fruit cake. Must husband them care-

fully for three more days! Two men from Millinockett drove up in
a jeep—first people I had seen on the Trail in six days.
"Left Nahmakanta Lake shelter at 12:45. At two I visited the sand
beach. Temperature 60, a strong wind, rolling clouds. Saw my second deer—then one of those great big owls which are frequently
heard but seldom seen. Began raining hard—then harder. Reached
Wadleigh Pond shelter at three. Found two medium sized potatoes,
boiled them, and cooked three freeze dried hamburgers given me
by Buck Canedy some 300 miles farther south. Heated up the rest of
my Appalachian Trail Mix from the previous day. Cleaned up all my
gear, and then the luxury of warm pajamas, dry socks, and fleece
lined ski boots. Crazy weather—lightning and thunder on October 3!
Am now only 35 miles from Mt. Katahdin. Have had seven days of
rain in the last nine—and have worn rain gear for nine straight days!
During the night it rained in torrents—shelter area a veritable lake
with a river running directly underneath the sleeping platform. I
was thankful for that good aluminum roof. Slept rather well despite
the cloudburst."

Sunday, October 4. My diary for this date shows the following.
"Up at 6:15. Had stopped raining about 1:30 a.m. Sun shining, hard
to believe! Left shelter at 8:15. Streams of water everywhere. Took
off boots and socks and forded the Pollywog Stream . . . water high—
well above knees. Reached Nahmakanta Lake Camp at 9:45. The
owners Paul and Frances Nevel not there, but the custodians John
and Audrey Richards were and they cooked me a second breakfast.
Informed me that yesterday's storm had raised the lake level three
feet and almost washed the boats and canoes away. Left there 10:30
and reached the outlet dam of Rainbow Lake at one. Got my first
glimpse of Katahdin with a few white clouds drifting around its summit. Magnificent sight. Reached Rainbow Lake shelter at 1:45—
extremely beautiful campsite with the Big Spring down by the lake
shore. Built fire—heated water. Aired all my clothing and sleeping
gear. Unbelievable—but as I write these notes—it has clouded up
again."

I spent much time down by the lake shore enjoying the beauty of
this spot and watching a family of six ducks out on the lake. I went
to bed at the very late hour of 7:15 with a good fire blazing merrily
in the makeshift stone fireplace directly in front of the shelter.

Monday, October 5. Up at 6:15 and had water boiling over the
open fire at 6:25. I visited the lake one more time before leaving—

Garvey climbing Baxter peak on Mt. Katahdin. (Photo: Tex Griffin)

beautiful spot. Hiked on to the Rainbow Lake Camps and had coffee and toast with Herb Hanson and his wife. These camps, owned by the Great Northern Paper Co., are used to house and entertain newsboys from various eastern cities. Hanson, too, was having troubles at the Rainbow Lake shelter which is on Great Northern property. His principal complaint was against fishing parties who left bushels of trash and even stole one of his boats. He is anxious to have the shelter torn down and a new one erected at a more remote spot where it would be restricted to those hiking the Appalachian Trail.

It was the end of the season for the Rainbow Lake Camps, and I helped Herb load some gear into a plane which had landed on the lake. We then moved some boats into drydock, and I left the Camps at 11. There is always something rather depressing about closing up a camp at the end of the season. I reflected somewhat sadly that my own "season" was about over also, as I was now only a few miles from Katahdin. From the Rainbow Lake Camps it is only 6.0 miles to the Hurd Brook shelter, and I reached the shelter at two. I had some beautiful views of Katahdin enroute from atop the Rainbow Ledges.

I had a quick lunch and laid in a supply of firewood. There was a 20-bushel open trash dump at the rear of shelter, similar to trash dumps I had seen throughout my hike. I now examined this trash dump more carefully to ascertain if it were hiker trash or trash left by others, i.e., picknickers, hunting parties, fishing parties. I concluded that no more than 5% of the trash was hiker trash. Hikers do not carry in their packs such articles as 32-ounce cans of fruit juice, one gallon cans of Coleman Fuel, 16-ounce cans of beer, one quart glass jars of Pream, just to name a few of the articles I saw in the trash dump. I am convinced that we are winning the battle of litter on the Trail. The matter of litter at the trailside shelters is a much more serious problem.

At 5 p.m. Tex and Jean Griffin arrived. What a pleasant surprise. Tex took many pictures and used his strobe light for interior shelter shots. We combined our food supplies and made out famously. We built a big fire and visited until a very late hour—like nine p.m.! Cool evening, temperature 42 at eight p.m.

Thursday, October 6. Up at six, temperature 37. Got wood fire going, cooked hot oatmeal (the last I had), cooked the last of my rice, used the last of my brown sugar, and finished the can of cinnamon that I had carried all the way from Georgia. All my food is about gone. Good planning! Left the shelter at eight. Clear beautiful day.

Reached the Millinocket-Greenville road at ten and put my pack in the Griffin car. Jean drove back to their base camp at Katahdin Stream Campground; while I shouldered a light day pack and with Tex began the nine-mile hike along the east bank of the Nesowadnehunk Stream. It would be hard to imagine a more perfect early autumn day. It had rained for a number of days. The Stream was high—scores and scores of cascades, small waterfalls, and two big ones. The fall color was at its absolute maximum. Even the air was clean. The woods had that fresh smell that fills the air after long rains. It was a hiker's and photographer's paradise. Tex went beserk on the picture taking—taking about 200 in all. We ate our lunch on a big rock slab extending far out into the water.

At 4 p.m. we reached the Katahdin Stream Campground which is located within boundaries of the Baxter State Park. I was met there by Jim and Lois Shores of Hyattsville, Maryland, both hard working members of the Trail Conference. They were vacationing in Maine and drove over to participate in the grand finale of my hike. Also met Helen Jensen of Downingtown, Pennsylvania, whose husband Dwayne was part way up Katahdin. He was camping out below tree line and was in touch with his wife by walkie-talkie.

I visited the ranger station and picked up a stack of mail including my Red Wing shoes. I also received in the mail a package of 300 form letters which I planned to mail to people from Georgia to Maine when and if I finished the hike up on Baxter Peak. Had a delicious steak supper with the Griffins. Reserved one of the open shelters for two nights and moved my gear into it. Later in the evening I went to the Shores-Jensen area of the camp, and we visited until almost ten. It was a clear night, the stars were shining, and it looked good for the next day's climb of Baxter Peak.

At this point, with all but 5.2 miles of my hike completed It seems appropriate to comment on the condition of the Trail in Maine. Some 276 miles of the Trail goes through Maine, most of it is not easily accessible by car; and the Maine Appalachian Trail Club has less than 100 members available for maintenance work. Substantial mileages of the Trail are assigned to other organizations for maintenance—organizations such as the Bates College Outing Club, and the Colby College Outing Club. With this assistance and the prodigious efforts of its own few members, the Maine Club (MATC) provides for the hiking public a most enjoyable hiking experience. There is a complete chain of excellent trailside shelters throughout the entire state,

The end of the hike. (Photo: Tex Griffin)

and in almost every instance the shelters are located very close to springs, streams, or ponds. The shelters are largely the work of former MATC president Louis Chorzempa with a big assist from Carl Newhall, Steve Clark, and others. The Trail in Maine is extremely well marked—excellent wooden directional signs, white and blue paint blazes, frequent use of metal markers and mileage markers. The Maine ponds and lakes are delightful and largely unspoiled, and one can only hope that they will remain that way for years to come. We Americans seem to have such tremendous capacity to destroy our wilderness areas that it seems almost inevitable that the wilderness experience the hiker enjoys in Maine will soon pass from the scene. Even though almost half of my hiking in Maine was done in the rain or in rain soaked woods, I found it to be a truly delightful place— another one of the many places to which I very much desire to return. (In Aug. '77 I rehiked the Trail from Katahdin to Monson. Tremendous area.)

Wednesday, October 7, 1970. Up at 5:20, still quite dark. Ate breakfast with the Griffins; and at 6:55 Tex and I began the 5.2-mile climb to Baxter Peak, the northern terminal of the Appalachian Trail. To climb Baxter Peak from the Campground involves a climb of 4,156 feet over a rough footway. It was a bright sunny day. Nature seemed to be rewarding me after all those rainy days of the previous two weeks. Tex took scores of pictures, especially after we climbed above tree line. Time slipped away from us until suddenly we saw dark clouds coming in on us rapidly from the West. We then began to hurry, since we had great respect for the sudden storms and low visibility that frequently beset Katahdin. We reached Thoreau Spring at 11 and had a light lunch there. We met Dwayne Jensen who had reached the summit of Baxter Peak and was on his way back to the Campground. We walked among the clouds. Visibility was low until we neared the summit of Baxter Peak. Then the clouds lifted nicely; and once more we were in sunshine with horizon to horizon visibility. We reached the summit at 12:15! The hike was finished. We took pictures of the huge cairn that marks Baxter Peak, of the bronze marker that tells the story of the gift of Baxter Park to the people of Maine by their former governor, and of the wooden sign that reads Baxter Peak, Mount Katahdin, and lists the distance to a number of places, including Springer Mountain, some 2,000 miles to the south in Georgia. I broke out the small bottle of champagne that the Griffins had given me for this very special occasion. Tex and I ate the

Celebrating the hike's completion on Katahdin. (Photo: Tex Griffin)

last morsels of Claxton Fruit cake and Citadel Spread that I had hoarded for this moment. It was indeed a time for rejoicing.

And then, at 12:40, we began the 5:2-mile trip back to the camp-ground. It had been exciting to climb that 5.2 miles to the summit. It was drudgery going down. We were both quiet, I particularly so. The trip I had planned for a whole year was finished, and the goal that I had hiked over 2,000 miles to reach was now behind me. I had not anticipated this emotional letdown, but it was certainly there.

As we neared the campground, we saw that we had a reception party waiting for us. There were Jean Griffin, Jim and Lois Shores, Dwayne and Helen Jensen, and John Peterson, a newspicture editor for United Press International in New York City. I was surprised and pleased to see Ken and Ingrid Parr who had motored over from East Burke, Vermont. Ken has been the assistant scoutmaster of the Boy Scout troop I had joined back in 1926 in Farmington, Minnesota. There were many pictures taken especially by Peterson who seemed to have a wide assortment of cameras and wide-angle lenses. We walked over to the shelter I was occupying—and in moments the table in front of the shelter was covered with champagne, wine, cheese, crackers, sardines, and kippered herring. Shortly afterwards, we moved to the Jensen camp where there were two big tables and a rousing fire. A delicious buffet supper was served, and our friendly group of ten sat and visited. It was a clear, mild evening; the food had been good; the fire burned brightly; the wine was heady; and the company unbeatable. I can say no more. At ten we decided to call it a day, and by 11 the campground was dark and quiet. A long long hike had been topped off by a big big day.

On October 8, the day after completion of my hike, I rode into Millinocket with the Shores and put up at the Millinocket Motel. Scores of people I had met during my hike had asked me to do them one favor when and if I finished—to mail them a card or letter from Maine informing them of the completion of my hike. I now went to work on the letter I had received the previous day, inserting on each the date I had finished my hike, writing a personal note to many of the people, signing, addressing, and stamping. Quite a job. The letter itself expresses in a few words my feelings about the 2,000-mile hike and some of my plans for the future. This is what I wrote:

Garvey at Katahdin Campground after completing his hike. (Photo: J. Peterson)

Millinocket, Maine
October 8, 1970

Dear Friend:

Thought you would be interested to know that I did finish my long hike on the Appalachian Trail . . . left Springer Mtn., Georgia, April 4 and arrived at Mt. Katahdin, Maine, the northern terminus of the Trail, on October 7. I took two breaks of two weeks each to return to my home at Falls Church, Va. The first break took place during the period May 25 to June 6 and for 3 days of that period I attended the 3-day meeting of the Appalachian Trail Conference at Shippensburg, Pa. The second break occurred from August 26 to September 10 when I came home to assist in the preparations for my daughter's wedding which took place on September 5. I then returned to Gorham, N.H., where I had temporarily discontinued my hike.

This was more than a 2,000-mile hike . . . it was also a people meeting expedition and a painstaking appraisal of the Trail, the trailside shelters, updating the guidebooks and a few other assorted chores. And I enjoyed them all . . . especially the people meeting bit! The hike afforded me an opportunity to meet scores and scores of new friends and a chance to have good visits with many old friends. My sincere thanks to those who extended courtesies to me during my trip . . . those who cooked meals for me on the trail, those who invited me into their homes, the patient newspaper reporters, the friendly employees of both the State and Federal parks and forests, Boy Scout and Girl Scout organizations and many, many others. I say with conviction that while hiking the Trail is in itself an adventure of a lifetime, it is the opportunity of meeting and visiting with people that makes the experience so much richer. Those who neglect this aspect of the hike miss so much.

Now to return to my home, sort through these voluminous notes I have and do what writing needs to be done. I plan to do a series of articles in forthcoming issues of Trailway News. I have plans for other writings. Time will tell whether or not I accomplish them. I am definitely planning to attend the June 1972 meeting of the Appalachian Trail Conference at Plymouth, N.H. and hope to see many of you there. Others I will see when I revisit sections of the Trail that I found particularly fascinating. And for all of you . . . Adios . . . and my sincere hope that sometime I will again have the opportunity of seeing you!

My very best wishes,

Edward B. Garvey

My wife arrived in Millinocket late in the afternoon, somewhat tired after a two-day 850-mile drive from Virginia. We enjoyed dinner and spent the early part of the evening at the home of Mr. and Mrs. Monroe Robinson in Millinocket. Then back to the motel to address a few dozen more letters. The next day we drove east to Maine's coastline and made our way slowly down the coast, spending part of one day at Acadia National Park. We reached home Tuesday night, October 13, to find a houseful of friends and neighbors who had gathered for a welcome home party. More champagne, a special cake, welcome home signs, and much good visiting.

The long trip was now officially over—and what a trip it was. I would be months and years getting all the pieces into place, writing up observations and recommendations for consideration by the Appalachian Trail Conference Board of Managers, conducting correspondence with a host of new friends, writing this book, and writing articles on various aspects of my hike. The recollection of places I had been, of experiences I had, and of the people I had met would influence the rest of my life.

THAT HORRIBLE WOODSY SMELL

Cathy Olsen, a 1978 Georgia to Maine hiker, left the Trail in North Carolina to visit the town of Franklin, one of her mail stops. Walking up to a tourist home she knocked on the door . . . and was promptly greeted by an elderly lady. The lady took one look at Cathy and her pack and announced "We don't take hikers here. We can't get rid of that "woodsy" smell after they leave!" Cathy tried to remonstrate but the lady was adamant. Eventually Cathy obtained lodging at another tourist home where they were not too concerned about that "woodsy" smell!

12
The Appalachian Trial — 1978

In Chapter 11 I described my day by day experiences along the Trail, as it was in 1970. In this chapter, written in early 1978, I will describe some of the changes that have occurred so that hikers will have a little better knowledge of what to expect. Probably one of the most important changes is an organizational one. The primary responsibility, as established by the National Trails System Act, for administration of the Appalachian Trail, rests with the National Park Service. Within the Park Service, the park superintendent is a key figure in terms of responsibility and authority for getting things done. It has been remarked on more than one occasion that the Appalachian Trail program would never really get off the ground until the Park Service put someone of park superintendent status at the helm. Action was belatedly taken in March 1976 when an Appalachian Trail Project Office was established in Boston, Mass. and David A. Richie was appointed as project manager. In rank, salary, and prestige Richie is equivalent to a park superintendent at one of the larger national parks. Since his appointment, Richie has worked tirelessly to acquire protection for the Trail. I feel guilty at times as I level my heavy artillery against the Department of Interior for its failure to acquire a single acre of land for protection of the Appalachian Trail, knowing that Richie is doing his level best to better the situation.

A second organizational change is the Appalachian National Scenic Trail Advisory Council provided for in the Trails Act. The first Council of which I was a member was largely ineffectual. Its chairman was a Park Service employee appointed by the Secretary of Interior. After three years of life, in which the Council had three different chairmen, the Department of Interior dealt the Council a death blow by removing its chairman, assigning him to another job, and not appointing another chairman to replace him.

311

Picture of Emblems relating to the AT. Bottom three were 2000 Miler suggested awards.

In June 1975, the Council was reactivated and the appointed chairman was *not* a Department of Interior employee. I have attended one general meeting and three regional meetings of the new Council, and have been impressed with the caliber of the Council members and the issues they consider and action they take.

One situation that has changed but little in the seven years since my hike is the ownership pattern of the land along the route of the Trail. Appearing in this chapter is an ownership chart prepared by the Appalachian Trail Project Office which shows by miles within each state the breakdown of land ownership along the 2029.3 miles of the AT as of May 1977. Two figures in that chart are worthy of special attention: (1) the total miles still in private ownership (661.7) and (2) the total miles on public roads (174.7). The total of those two figures—836.4 miles—represents over 41% of the entire Trail mileage.

Under the Nixon-Ford administrations little money was made available for protection of the environment or for acquisition of land for recreation purposes. The Department of Interior sought to have the 14 states acquire the land, feeling that this would be a better arrangement both from the standpoint of purchase and from the standpoint of management once the land was acquired. Even some of the states would prefer that the federal government stay out of the acquisition activity. But the states (Maryland excepted) have moved with painful slowness in their acquisition, and land costs continue to escalate at the rate of 18% per year. In May 1977, Assistant Secretary of Interior Robert L. Herbst, speaking to 1,000 members of the Appalachian Trail Conference at Shepherdstown, West Virginia, declared in ringing tones that the Department of Interior was ready to assume the land acquisition role assigned to it by the National Trails System Act of 1968. Furthermore, he committed the Department of Interior to acquiring 300 miles of the Trail by the time of the next general meeting of the Conference, August 1979! See Chapter 1 for details of legislative progress which occurred after the Herbst speech.

The Trail itself is much different than it was in 1970. For one thing there have been 254 changes in the Trail route, some of them major changes involving many miles such as the Mt. Rogers relocation in southwestern Virginia and the relocation over the Bigelow Mountain range in Maine. The paint blazing is better than in 1970. All of the Trail is now marked with the conventional white paint blazes but, in one area, the Great Smoky Mountain National Park, the blazes are very infrequent.

When I hiked the Trail in 1970, no permits were needed for any part of the route. That has changed. Permits are now required to hike through the two national parks, Great Smoky Mountain and Shenandoah, and through the Designated Wilderness Areas of the eight national forests. Fortunately all of these permits can be obtained by mail. If the hiker exercises just a little foresight, he can have all the permits in hand long before he reaches the restricted areas. There is no charge for any of the permits. The Appalachian Trail Project Office is seeking an arrangement whereby one permit would be recognized for all of the restricted areas, but as of early 1978, such efforts have not yet been successful. From south to north here are the places to write to for permits:

Great Smoky Mountains National Park, Gatlinburg, TN 37738. Advise the Park of your expected arrival date, number in party, and number of days expected to be in Park. Permit will be mailed to the pick-up point you specify. Should hikers fail to make the necessary arrangements in advance, they should contact the Twentymile Ranger Station (704/498-2327) near the South entrance, or the Big Creek Ranger Station (704/486-5616) near the East entrance upon arrival at the Park.

Shenandoah National Park, Luray, VA 22835. Provide the same information as for the Smokies above, but also specify the general location and date of each overnight camp. For those who have failed to do this, there is a register box some 30 feet north of the point where the AT leaves Skyline Drive at Rockfish Gap. The box provides instructions and directions for reaching the Rockfish Entrance Station to obtain a permit. If Entrance Station is closed, a permit may be obtained at Loft Mountain Campground 26 miles north or at Simmons Gap Ranger Station, 32 miles north, or from any Park Ranger. For southbound hikers, there is a register box at the north end of the Park where the AT leaves the Compton Gap fireroad. Contained therein are instructions for obtaining permit at Dickey Ridge Visitor Center, Piney River Ranger Station, Matthews Arm Campground or at Thornton Gap Entrance Station, 25 miles south on the AT. As of 1977 park rangers were instructed to discontinue the issuance of permits to the general public, but they were permitted to issue them to long distance through-hikers.

Lye Brook Wilderness area, Green Mountains, Vermont. Permits may be obtained in person or by writing:

Forest Supervisor	District Ranger
Green Mtn. Nat. Forest OR	Manchester Ranger District
Federal Building	Catamount Bank Building
151 West Street	Manchester Center, VT 05255
Rutland, VT 05701	

A permit may also be obtained at Stratton Pond or Bromley Lodge during the May-October hiking season.

Great Gulf Wilderness, White Mountains, New Hampshire. Permits may be obtained by writing:

Forest Supervisor	District Ranger
White Mtn. Nat. Forest	Androscoggin R.D.
P.O. Box 638 OR	80 Glen Road
Laconia, NH 03246	Gorham, N.H. 03581

A permit may also be obtained at Pinkham Notch Lodge, Lake of the Clouds Hut, or the Summit of Mount Washington during the May-October hiking season.

Those are the permit procedures as of 1978, but procedures do change and you would be well advised to write well in advance of your hike.

Before completing this chapter, I would be less than truthful if I did not mention some of the hazards that one must expect in 2,000 miles of Trail hiking. Injuries are sustained every year by some hikers, sprained or broken ankles and wrists, bad falls, cuts from sharp rocks, poison ivy infections, dog bites, stomach disorders, all the things that can happen at home plus a few more. And I regret to say there have been three deaths since my 1970 hike, one death by accident and two homicides. The accident was sustained by a young hiker attempting to cross a raging stream on a makeshift bridge in Vermont. He fell into the stream and his body was not recovered for several days.

Both of the homicides were bizarre affairs. The first occured on the AT near Cleveland, GA., in May 1974. An 18-year-old girl was hiking with her boy friend when a man they met on the Trail shot and killed the boy friend. The girl was forced to accompany the murderer for almost a day before she escaped and notified police. The killer was apprehended, tried, and sentenced to life imprisonment.

The other killing occurred at Vanderventer Shelter in Tennessee on April 21, 1975. A young woman hiking north spent the night at the shelter with an older man who was hiking south. The next morning while she was warming herself in front of the fire, the man, who had a history of mental instability and violence, drove a hatchet through her head. Gruesome. He turned himself in to the police and was later convicted of second degree murder and sentenced to 20 years in prison. He died within a year of his imprisonment.

There are many advantages to hiking alone and I was alone on about two-thirds of my 1970 hike. Yet, from the standpoint of safety, numbers of people lessen the danger from accidents or from being molested. Many hikers achieve the best of both worlds. In order not to get on one another's nerves, they hike alone during the day but cook the evening meal together and spend the night at the same camping spot.

Frequently I receive letters from hikers (or their parents) asking if it is wise or safe for them to begin hiking the Trail alone. Sometimes these letters are prompted by a situation in which the writer had planned to hike with a friend only to have the friend cancel out at the last minute. In all such cases I have urged the hiker to proceed on his own, knowing that he will meet many other hikers and he can quickly select another hiker or small group with which to hike. In 1976 and again in 1977, I enjoyed southbound April hikes in the Southern Appalachians, meeting and talking with northbound hikers who had assembled at Springer Mountain, Georgia for the annual pilgrimage to the distant Katahdin, some 2,000 miles north in Maine. The hikers travel singly, in pairs, or in small groups and the makeup of the groups sometimes changes from day to day as some forge ahead or drop behind to form other associations.

OWNERSHIP (in miles)

	GOVERNMENT							PRIVATE					
	NPS	Forest Service	Other Federal	State	Local	Roads *	TOTAL	Non-Profit	Corporate	Individual & Non-Corporate	Undefined	TOTAL	TOTAL
Maine	—	—	—	25.4	—	13.7	39.1	.2	223.2	14.0	.9	238.3	277.4
New Hampshire	—	86.3	—	8.8	.9	10.3	106.3	2.8	25.5	16.1	—	44.4	150.7
Vermont	—	64.2	—	2.7	—	9.0	75.9	1.1	18.8	35.3	2.6	57.8	133.7
Massachusetts	—	—	—	28.3	5.4	7.8	41.5	3.7	10.2	17.9	2.0	33.8	75.3
Connecticut	—	—	—	15.8	—	10.0	25.8	6.7	4.4	19.9	—	31.0	56.8
New York	—	—	—	24.8	—	27.3	52.1	5.0	7.0	22.0	—	34.0	86.1
New Jersey **	17.9	—	—	23.6	—	14.5	56.0	—	.7	6.4	—	7.1	63.1
Pennsylvania	4.2	—	—	104.8	—	23.0	132.0	10.5	14.0	61.0	—	85.5	217.5
Maryland	1.5	—	—	16.3	2.7	4.6	25.1	—	—	12.5	—	12.5	37.6
W.Va.-Va./No.***	.2	—	—	—	2.2	.5	2.9	—	—	14.5	—	14.5	17.4
W.Va.-Va./So.***	—	8.0	—	.8[v]	—	—	8.0	—	—	—	—	—	8.0
Virginia	112.2	227.6	4.9[s]	19.5	10.9	38.7	414.6	.3	5.7	57.3	—	63.3	477.9
Tennessee	—	52.8	2.1[t]	—	—	3.7	58.6	—	—	4.9	—	4.9	63.5
Tenn.-N.C.***	67.7	100.1	—	—	—	8.2	176.0	—	4.2	26.1	—	30.3	206.3
No. Carolina	—	74.2	.2[t]	—	—	3.4	77.8	—	—	3.6	—	3.6	81.4
Georgia	—	77.4	—	—	—	—	77.4	—	—	—	.7	.7	78.1
TOTAL:	203.7	690.6	7.2	270.8	22.1	174.7	1,369.1	30.3	313.7	311.5	6.2	661.7	2,030.8

* AT follows roads open to vehicular traffic.
** Includes 3.2 miles in N.Y. near Unionville.
*** Trail coincides with State boundaries.
(s) Smithsonian Institute.
(t) TVA.
(V) Virginia Polytechnic Institute.

836 MILES (41% OF THE ENTIRE TRAIL) STILL IN PRIVATE OWNERSHIP OR ON PUBLIC ROADS!

Prepared in May 1977 by the Appalachian Trail Project Office
*Boston, Mass. 02129

*NOTE: The Appalachian Trail Project Office of the National Park Service moved to Harpers Ferry, W.Va., in 1978.

Hostel in Damascus, Virginia, maintained by the Methodist church. (Photo: Ed Garvey)

13
Overnight Accommodations

As used in this chapter the term "overnight accommodations" refers to trailside shelters, AMC Huts, hostels, tents and tarps. The chain of overnight accommodations along the Appalachian Trail is one of its *most* distinguishing features and a feature that most intrigued me when I first became acquainted with the Trail a quarter century ago. As a boy living in southern Minnesota, fascinated with hiking and camping, I had read an article about the hostel system and I was captivated with the idea of these simple, inexpensive overnight shelters. Many years later our family moved to the Washington, D.C. area. Our oldest son Dennis had joined the Boy Scouts and I was finagled into leading 13 Boy Scouts on an overnight hike from Herbert Hoover Boy Scout Camp in the central section of the Shenandoah National Park. We stayed overnight at the Lewis Spring shelter (torn down by the Park Service in 1976), sharing it with its lone occupant, Dr. Francis A. Smith, mentioned elsewhere in this book. This was my first backpacking trip in 15 years and my first use of a trailside shelter. From that point on I used the shelters extensively, particularly in the Shenandoah National Park.

In 1959 I became Supervisor of Trails for the Potomac Appalachian Trail Club and that job necessitated inspecting trails and shelters in other parts of PATC territory—northern Virginia, Maryland, and southern Pennsylvania. The 18 PATC shelters were in rather sad shape at that time, and in 1962 I volunteered to renovate them. It was an exhausting but exciting job, and before the summer was over we had installed new roofs on 14 shelters, torn out wire bunks and replaced them with wooden bunks or sleeping platforms, installed a few tables and toilets and removed trash by the cubic acre. It can thus be seen that I had a deep interest in the shelters and was heavily involved in their construction and proper maintenance. This personal involvement will help explain the intensity with which I have defended the shelter system in the past.

In reading over the history of the Appalachian Trail, it seems that the shelter construction was completed in a series of spurts rather than as one planned effort. From ATC Publication 5, Chap. 8 appear the following excerpts:

> An event propitious for the completion of the Trail in Maine occurred in 1935 when * * * * the Appalachian Trail in Maine was made an item of the CCC program. Trail crews from four CCC Camps went over the existing Trail in 1935, widening, improving, and extending it. The work was continued through 1936 and 1937, and some 11 lean-tos were built along the route. The result was the creation of a wilderness trail of a high scenic order across Maine. [p. 72].

Continuing on this page is the description of the events of the eighth ATC meeting in June 1937 in which appears the first reference to a long-term plan for a complete shelter chain:

> A program was initiated in cooperation with the Federal and State Forest and Park Services for the completion of a chain of lean-tos along the entire route of the Trail [p. 73].

In the same publication on page 82 is the description of the progress reported at 1961 and 1964 meetings of the Conference; there are references to "Substantial progress" and "splendid progress" in completing the shelter chain. Many of the trail clubs had done a substantial amount of shelter building on their own, but there is no question that some of the federal programs—first CCC, later Mission 66, Operation Outdoors, Green Thumb, and others—played a major role in the construction. Among the trail maintaining clubs, the Green Mountain Club of Vermont gets my vote as being consistently the most active builder of trailside shelters.

When I made my 2,000 mile hike in 1970, there were approximately 240 shelters. Of this number perhaps 220 were the Adirondack type lean-tos with one side open or only partly closed in. Another nine were the AMC huts, some of which had been built around the turn of the century. The remainder were closed cabins, located mostly in Vermont and New Hampshire that were available to hikers on a first come-first served basis. Unfortunately many of the shelters built in the 1930's and 1940's were built on sites which in later years proved to be undesirable, primarily because they were directly beside or too close to automobile roads. In addition, shelters in the New England states, particularly in the White Mountains, were built on soils which were unable to withstand much use. As soon as foot traffic increased beyond a certain point, vegetation disappeared entirely and the area surrounding the shelter began to erode badly. The AMC had already removed a few such shelters, seeded the areas involved, and replaced them with wooden tent platforms with a summer time caretaker in residence to assist hikers. Even with the 240 shelters in 1970, there were stretches where there would be no shelters for two or three days of hiking. In such cases it was necessary for the hiker to use tent or tarp and camp where he could along the Trail or to seek shelter off the Trail at a motel or hotel.

The shelter program suffered a severe setback in September 1973 when the superintendent of the Shenandoah National Park issued tentative regulations in the *Federal Register* which, among other things, declared the 17 trailside shelters in the Park to be out of bounds for overnight use. The 94 miles of the Trail in the Park is within the jurisdictional area of the Potomac Appalachian Trail Club and I was president of the Club at the time. Unfortunately, for me, I had already committed myself to a 7-week contract tour in Eastern Siberia to participate in an outdoor recreation exhibit sponsored by the US Information Agency. Even so, from Siberia I wrote a strenuous letter of protest to the superintendent of the Shenandoah National Park and sent copies to the Potomac Appalachian Trail Club and to the Appalachian Trail Conference. In my letter I traced the history of the shelter program much as I have in this chapter. In addition, I pointed out that the National Trails System Act of 1968 provided for "campsites, shelters, and related-public-use facilities" on national scenic trails. I pointed out that the formal guidelines developed by the National Park Service and the Appalachian Trail Conference provided for trailside shelters in even more specific terms than did the law. I was confident that both PATC and ATC would object strenuously to the proposed regulations and that my letter would be published in *Appalachian Trailway News* and in PATC's *Potomac Appalachian*. When I returned to the Washington, D.C. area after almost 2 months absence, I was astonished to find that PATC had already sent a formal letter to the park superintendent acquiescing, without a word of protest, to the closing of the 17 trailside shelters in the Park. The Appalachian Trail Conference had acquiesced in another manner, by taking no action whatever. My letter had not been published in either the ATC or PATC publications. The constitutions of both organizations provide for a

Shelter at Jefferson National Forest, Pine Swamp. (Photo: U.S. Forest Service)

system of primitive camps along the Appalachian Trail. Benton MacKaye, in his 1921 article, in which he described his concept of an Appalachian Trail, provided for a chain of "shelter camps." He went on further to say that these shelter camps:

> "should be located at convenient distances so as to allow a comfortable day's walk between each. They should be equipped always for sleeping and certain of them for serving meals—after the fashion of the Swiss chalets."

And so, we have a situation in which the leadership of both organizations, without consulting the membership, acquiesced in an action that was contrary to the constitutions of both, was not in accord with either the National Trails System Act of 1968 or the National Park Service guidelines, and disregarded the precepts of the man who conceived of the Appalachian Trail and who helped organize the very Appalachian Trail Conference that disregarded his precepts. A very, very interesting chain of events!

Fortunately all was not lost. A number of us continued to press vigorously for the preservation of the shelter system. The editor of *Trailway News* reopened the issue and published letters both pro and con in several issues of the magazine. He then conducted a poll by mail, the results of which were overwhelmingly in favor of a shelter system. At the general meeting of the Appalachian Trail Conference at Boone, N.C. in June 1975, I introduced a resolution which was extremely critical of the National Park Service, both for closing the shelters in the Shenandoah National Park and for its failure, over a seven year period, to have acquired even a single acre of the Trail right-of-way. The resolution passed with only a few dissenting votes. Shortly thereafter, the resolution was inserted into the *Congressional Record* by Congressman Goodloe E. Byron of Maryland and I also received letters from several other concerned congressmen. In late 1976, Tom Floyd, PATC's new and extremely able Supervisor of Trails, wrote a very thoughtful letter on the shelter closing situation in the Park. Floyd's letter was published in the *Potomac Appalachian* and it produced a torrent of letters which were published in later issues. I introduced a resolution at the January, 1977 annual business meeting of PATC, favoring a complete shelter chain from Georgia to Maine and suggesting that the shelters in the Park be reopened for the hiker's use. The resolution passed by a substantial majority. Somewhat belatedly, the membership of both organizations had had their day in court, and the sentiments they expressed did not support the actions taken by the leadership.

Meanwhile on another front, David Richie, Appalachian Trail Project Manager, who had become alarmed at the deterioration of the shelter program, convened a meeting of thirteen people in October 1976. Those participating represented the Forest Service, National Park Service, and the Appalachian Trail Conference. I was one of those privileged to participate. There were two days of discussion by people of very diverse views. A visit was made to a number of nearby shelters. Following this meeting, Richie developed a statement of overnight-use principles for the AT. Over a period of months, and with input from many people, he kept refining it. By May of 1977, Richie felt that he had obtained a consensus and he presented the statement of overnight-use principles to the members of the Appalachian National Scenic Trail Advisory Council for consideration. The principles were adopted unanimously. Within the next three days, both the general membership of the Appalachian Trail Conference, meeting at Shepherdstown, West Virginia, and the Board of Managers of the Conference adopted the same set of principles without a dissenting vote. Several months later the Chairman of the Conference in separate letters to the Chief of the U.S. Forest Service and to the Director of the National Park Service sought assurances that the overnight-use principles were acceptable to and would be implemented by each of the two agencies. Those assurances were made.

The development of these principles and their unanimous adoption by three different groups and the heads of two government agencies represents a milestone in the overnight accommodation program of the Appalachian Trail. Further, the adoption of these principles is a tribute to David A. Richie's perseverance and ability to work out compromises among those holding strong and diverse views on a very controversial subject. The principles are reproduced at the end of this chapter.

Oh yes . . . about those shelters in the Shenandoah National Park. In November, 1977, the Superintendent of the Park met with representatives of the Potomac Appalachian Trail Club to work out general arrangements for the reestablishment of overnight accommodations within the Park. No effective date was set but hopefully, some accommodations will be available for the 1978 hiking season. It seems fairly certain that some shelters will be torn down, others

Shelter in Shenandoah National Park (one of 17 closed for overnight use in 1974). (Photo: Ed Garvey)

relocated, and some new shelters or campgrounds for backpackers built. One plan tentatively advanced by the superintendent is the construction of a sizeable camp at each end of the Park, a sort of Welcome Station as it were for backpackers, comparable in concept to those erected by state highway departments for motorists who cross over a state border on primary highways. These two entrance camps would each have overnight sleeping accommodations and other facilities to permit the hiker to dry clothes, bathe, and to generally regroup for his 100-mile hike through the Park. A caretaker would be in residence during the busy hiking months to explain the backpacking regulations within the Park and to otherwise render assistance to the hiker. I personally believe this entrance station campground idea has tremendous potential and I hope it materializes.

Now to leave the trailside shelters for the moment and to describe a fairly recent and pleasant phenomena, the off-the-Trail, near-the-Trail church related hostels that have sprung up since 1970. It may have been because of the tremendous increase in long-distance hikers beginning in 1972; it may have been because of the lack of enough suitable trailside shelters; but it was more likely because of a deep-seated desire among even the most avid of back-country hikers to return to civilization now and then, to obtain a shower, to wash clothes, to resupply with food, to receive and dispatch mail, and to visit with the townspeople. Whatever the reason, the hostels have come into being, the hikers look forward to reaching them, much as they look forward to receiving a letter from home. To the best of my knowledge there is only one American Youth Hostel along the entire Trail: this being the hostel on the Maryland side of the Potomac River across the bridge from Harpers Ferry, West Virginia. This hostel charged $2.50 per night for lodging in November 1977. The other hostels of which I spoke are those operated by church groups and no fixed fee is set for the lodging and other amenities they provide. They depend upon donations from the hikers. They hope to be self-supporting but they seldom are. This is because some of the hikers are in straitened circumstances and can pay but little. All of the hostels report a few hikers who contribute most generously. Unfortunately many who could afford to pay their share choose not to, preferring to believe that since no fixed fee is collected, the lodging, showers, and other amenities provided are "free" and hence no donation or only a token donation is in order.

The hostels, the "Good Samaritans" as one of my friends dubbed them, perform a tremendous service to the hikers, providing not just for his or her physical needs but adding a personal touch and bit of warmth as well. Many of the through-hikers are young people; the AT hike is their first long period away from home and constant rains in the Appalachians can become demoralizing to even the hardiest souls. Small wonder that the written and spoken comments of the hikers who have used the hostels reveal their heartfelt gratitude for the shelter and friendship they have received.

I have made arrangements with the editor of *Appalachian Trailway News* to write a series of articles on the hostels, the firehouses, and other facilities being made available to hikers of the AT. The first such article on the Holy Family Hospice at Pearisburg, Virginia, appeared in the November 1976 *TN*; the second on the Jesuit hostel at Hot Springs, North Carolina, appeared in the January 1978 *TN*; following that will be the Methodist Church hostel in Damascus, Virginia, and so on.

Despite the existence of trailside shelters and hostels, there will always be some situations in which the hiker must use his tent or tarp to protect himself from rain. Of the 47 2,000 Milers of 1976 who completed questionnaires for me, approximately 30 carried tents. The remaining 27 either carried no protection or carried tarps. One, Rex A. Riffle, used two different types of tube tents without much success. Then he switched to a 9-by-10-foot Eureka tarp with sewn-in grommets. He stated that he used the tarp from Harpers Ferry, WV to Katahdin. It kept him dry, was light in weight (39 oz.), and could be erected in various shapes and sizes. Although it did not provide bug protection, he stated he would use the tarp for the entire trip if he were to hike the AT again.

In my 1970 hike, I carried no tent or tarp. I was forced to sleep out about six times and lucked out every time. In recent years I have carried either an inexpensive tube tent or a tarp. Both the tube tents and the tarps can be used as ground cloths when sleeping in shelters or for sleeping out in the open when rain is not expected. I was rather surprised to find that eight or ten of the 1976 hikers carried no tent or tarp. Even though I did it myself, I would not do it again and I recommend that some type of shelter be carried.

The last type of shelters to be described in this chapter are the AMC huts in the White Mountains of New Hampshire. There are but nine of them, each a moderate day's hike apart. They are unique to the White Mountains and their operation poses some unique problem for the AMC. Many of the huts are above tree line. They are in or near exposed areas that are subject to some of the worst weather in North America. The route of the Trail that runs from one hut to the next is largely through an area that has been designated by the US Forest Service as a "Restricted Use Area" (RUA). Restricted use means that all camping and fires must be below timberline; must be at least 200 feet off the trail; and must be one-fourth mile away from any road, hut or shelter. Many of the 1976 through hikers were especially resentful of the restrictions placed upon them in their traverse of the White Mountains. They seemed to feel that they (the hikers) were captives in a vicious system that forced them either to stay at the AMC huts and pay the tab ($13 a night for lodging and two huge meals), or to walk far down off the mountain to one of the open shelters or tent platforms. Granted that for the hiker, who is both short of money and dead tired after an all day hike, neither of the alternatives may be satisfactory, but that's the way it has to be. Hikers should be aware of the fact that most of the huts were located where they are long before there was an Appalachian Trail and the Trail route was selected so as to use existing AMC trails and to permit the hiker to take advantage of this unique hut system. The AMC is keenly aware of the problems of the long-distance hiker and it has prepared a 6-page leaflet entitled *Facilities and Regulations Along the Appalachian Trail in the White Mountain Area*. Those planning to traverse the Whites should by all means obtain this document by writing to: Pinkham Notch Hut, AMC, Gorham, NH 03581. It contains a wealth of information as to the opening and closing schedules of the huts, location of trailside shelters, tentsites, and campgrounds, fees for use of overnight accommodations, etc.

HARD TIMES

Said the Rev. Richard Stephens, vicar of a church in Cheshire, England: "Our forefathers did without sugar until the 13th century, without coal fires until the 14th, without buttered bread until the 16th, tea or soap until the 17th, without gas, matches or electricity until the 19th, without cars, canned or frozen foods until the 20th. Now, what was it you were complaining about?"
—Quoted in Pasadena, Calif., *Star-News*
Readers Digest Jan. '73

Introduced by the Use-Problem Work Committee. Considered and approved by Appalachian National Scenic Trail Advisory Council on 5-27-77.

Appalachian Trail Overnight-Use Management Principles

Purpose

Principles guiding overnight-use along the Appalachian Trail have been developed in response to changes in the character of back-country recreation and its management, and to perceived trends adverse to the traditional Trail shelter. The belief exists that negative attitudes toward shelters and inadequate maintenance and management efforts have led to shelters being removed or closed without full consideration to the impact of such actions on the overall Trail experience.

The following principles encourage consideration of shelters and other overnight-use sites as a fundamental part of the Appalachian Trail. Neither the footpath nor its overnight camping opportunities should be considered independently of each other.

Shelters are an important part of the history of the Trail: they should not be discarded without compelling reasons for doing so.

Overnight-Use Management Principles

1. It is necessary to assure appropriate opportunities for backpackers along the Appalachian Trail to make overnight stops. Hostels, cabins, mountain huts and lodges, Adirondack lean-tos and other primitive shelters, primitive campsites, and dispersed camping can, under suitable conditions, serve this function.

2. New structures serving overnight-users should be located so as to be reasonably accessible from the Trail, but far enough away not to affect adversely the quality of the Trail environment. They should also be far enough removed from vehicular access so as to discourage use by non-hiking groups. Existing shelters, located immediately adjacent to the Trail, need not be removed or relocated based solely on conflict with this principle. Prior to removal of problem shelters,

consideration should be given to rerouting the Trail—making their location less accessible.

3. Shelters are amenities which contribute to many hikers' experience, but they are not necessary and may be removed or relocated when there are compelling environmental or management reasons for doing so.

4. Decisions about changing, removing or relocating overnight-use sites should be approached on a case-by-case basis. In arriving at these decisions, primary consideration should be given to protection of the resource and the essential needs of the backpacker. Tradition, continuity of similar overnight-use sites, and the provision of a variety of opportunities for backpackers should also be considered.

5. Research, including studies of the ecology of the site as well as the attitudes of hikers, should be encouraged to support management decisions related to overnight-use.

6. Provision for adequate management, which may include on-the-Trail education for caretakers should be included in the planning for any facilities. Principles of good Trail camping etiquette and sanitation should be widely disseminated to Trail users by the most effective and least obtrusive means possible. These techniques have the potential to diminish some of the negative consequences associated with different types of overnight-use.

7. Restrictions on overnight-use by backpackers should be avoided when possible so as to retain the unregimented character of the Appalachian Trail experience.

8. Trail-maintaining clubs, and, where practicable, other user representatives should be consulted and given an opportunity to participate in decisions affecting shelters and other types of camping along the Trail.

NICE PEOPLE!

I have traveled all over the world . . . Germany, Japan . . . many other points . . . and I've never met a nicer group of people than the Appalachian Trail hikers!

Keith Shaw
Monson, Maine
Aug. 27, 1977

14
Flowers Along the Trail

In Chapters 14 through 18, I will discuss the more common flowers, edible wild plants, birds, trees, and animals that the hiker will encounter during his 2,000-mile hike of the Trail. The comments and observations are strictly those of a layman. I have no special competency in any of these fields.

Of the five classes, I felt most keenly my lack of knowledge of flowers and trailside plants. There are those who maintain it is unimportant to know the names of plants, flowers, trees, etc. If you recognize them by sight, the name is immaterial. In my home neighborhood and at the place where I work, I like to be able to recognize by sight and speak to by name those people with whom I come in contact most frequently. So it is with the birds, flowers, and trees. I like to identify by name, as well as by sight, those things which I can expect to see most frequently. For maximum enjoyment, I would urge—and I wish I had done it myself—that some time be spent in advance of such a hike in studying and learning to identify the more common flowers and plants. I would suggest that you carry with you the smaller, lightweight versions of books that identify the more common flowers, birds, trees, and animals that you will see.

Among the flowers, plants, and flowering woody plants, such as mountain laurel, those which I saw with greatest frequency were:

Mountain Laurel, Rhododendron, Wild Azalea. These three flowering woody plants, all high on my list of all time favorites, were seen from Georgia to New England.

Spring Beauty (Claytonia Virginica). I saw this beautiful spring flower from Georgia to Virginia. I did not learn its name until I visited the nature center building at Peaks of Otter in Virginia.

Trillium, Purple, yellow, pink, and white. I designated May 12 as

"Trillium Day." I walked through six miles of them north of Turkey Gap shelter in southwestern Virginia.

Poison Ivy.

Bluets, May Apples, Iris, Violets.

Tiger Lily

Jack-in-The Pulpit

Lady Slippers

Jewel Weed

Honeysuckle

Columbine

Indian Pipe

Bunchberries

Mountain Cranberries

Wood Astor

Clintonia

A lightweight, easy-to-carry booklet that identifies the more common flowers in the Appalachians is: *Flower Finder*, by May Theilgaard Watts, Nature Study Guild, Publishers. For the flowers in New England I know of only one book, *The Mountain Flowers of New England* published by the Appalachian Mountain Club, 5 Joy St., Boston, Mass. 02108.

A more comprehensive book, *Wildflowers in Color* by Arthur Stupka, Harper and Row, 1965 is available.

Letters to the Author—Always Welcome. Send to Appalachian Books, Box 249, Oakton, Virginia 22124. If reply is desired, enclose stamped, self-addressed envelope.

15
Edible Wild Plants

This is a new chapter. I did not cover this subject at all in my original book. In Chapter 14 on Flowers, I conceded my ignorance on the subject, ignorance which I corrected to some extent by learning to identify by name many of the more common flowers to be found along the AT. Not so with the edible wild plants. I started out ignorant and, 2,000 miles later I knew little more than when I began the hike. The identification and proper preparation of edible wild plants is a skill or body of knowledge that seems to have been almost totally lost within a few generations after the white man came to the New World. It is only through the efforts and writings of people like Euell Gibbons and Bradford Angier that our interest in this subject has been reawakened in recent years.

One of my first assignments at Appalachian Outfitters was to get in touch with Euell Gibbons and ascertain if he would be willing to come to the northern Virginia area and teach a course in identification and preparation of wild foods. In March 1972, I visited the Gibbons home near Middleburg, PA, and had a most enjoyable and educational visit with Euell and his very knowledgeable wife Frieda. Euell felt that he already had too many commitments to permit him to participate in another wild food course but he put us in touch with one of his most ardent disciples—a Miss Edelene Wood of Parkersburg, WV. Miss Wood readily agreed, and in August 1972, she and her mother set up shop near the Appalachian Outfitters store in Oakton, VA and for a solid week educated a group of some 100 enthusiastic adults in the art of identifying and preparing wild foods. Those who desired to take the course were required only to agree to teach their newly acquired skills to others after the course was completed. We secured permission from land owners and walked across fields, along narrow country roads, along power lines, and elsewhere. Everywhere we became acquainted with weeds . . . er . . . uh . . . "edible plants" that were there for the effort of taking. At the end of the course, we had a wild food dinner consisting of plants that had been gathered during the week. The course was repeated the following spring at another Appalachian Outfitters location in Winston-Salem, NC. At the wild food dinner at Winston-Salem, several people had donated from their freezers, wild animals previously killed and cleaned. Unfortunately, the donors had other commitments that prevented their cooking the animals they had donated. I was thrown into the breach—a do or die situation! With frequent references to a wild game cook book, plus helpful suggestions from some of the other cooks working in the kitchen with me, I roasted, barbecued, or otherwise prepared one beaver, one raccoon, four rabbits, and a venison roast. I learned that in cooking wild game the almost universal custom is first to parboil. This simply means to boil thoroughly and to throw away the water. This process serves both to tenderize the game and to remove some of the gamey taste which some find objectionable. So much for game. Now back to plants.

My bible in the identification and cooking of wild plants is the book *Stalking the Wild Asparagus* by Euell Gibbons. It's a paper back, 300 pages, selling for $4.50 in 1978. I refer to it frequently, carry it in my camper most of the time. It's well illustrated, but in black and white sketches only. Gibbons' intense love of his subject is evident throughout and his practice of providing a little history of the plants and of relating some of his personal experiences in foraging for them make for interesting as well as educational reading. Edelene Wood, in her own discourses on wild plants, segregates them into three groups: (1) survival, (2) supplemental or make do, and (3) gourmet. In this chapter I've omitted the gourmet types and concentrated on the first two. I have listed plants which I have actually observed along the AT, those which are reasonably easy to identify, from which the edible part of the plant can be easily harvested, and those which are easy to prepare and cook. It must be remembered that the AT is a mountain ridge top trail, a type of terrain in which edible wild foods are not too abundant. It is only when the Trail drops down into valleys, goes along fence lines, across abandoned farms and gardens, across power lines and through areas of relatively recent fires, that the wild food is found in abundance; and it is in these places that the hiker should take pains to look for and collect them. Also I have divided my list of some 20 foods into two groups: (1) the "pick and eat raw" fruits and (2) all other foods that generally require some preparation and cooking before being eaten.

THE FRUITS

For the most part I provide only brief descriptions of these. There is no preparation required, one need only pick and eat. Perhaps, because I have picked and eaten most of these since childhood, I assume that others know them also. Most of them have been domesticated and are on sale in fruit markets so that even city dwellers should be able to identify them: an exploratory taste should either confirm or negate the identification. Another method of learning to identify these fruits would be to acquire one of the catalogues that comes out in February or early March of each year in which oversize fruits are pictured in mouth watering color photographs.

Strawberries: A low growing plant, 3 to 6 inches off the ground, white flowers in May, red fruit ripe in Southern Appalachians in early June. The wild variety is less than half the size of the domesticated one but infinitely sweeter. Gibbons describes the wild strawberry as one of the most delicious of all wild fruits. Very plentiful in Virginia.

Blackberries, red raspberries, black raspberries: All three of these are members of the *rubus* species, all grow on canes from 3 to 8 feet tall (most of which have thorns that scratch skin and clothes) and all three can be found in various places in the AT from Georgia to Maine. While the backpacker will eat most of them right from the cane, all three can be used for delicious pies and cobblers. A word of warning: delicious as these berries are, do not eat too many of them on an empty stomach. They are tart and acidulous and (voice of experience speaking) eaten in the course of strenuous hiking, they can make you very sick.

Wineberries: Another member of the *rubus* species but an immigrant from Asia. Like its three cousins above, it too grows on prickly canes. I have found it on roadsides. It has a husk that opens only when the berry is ripe. In color, the ripe fruit is similar to the red raspberry.

May apple or American mandrake: This is a really fascinating plant and the Georgia to Maine hiker will see the plant coming out of last years dead leaves, emerging like a tiny umbrella that is only partially opened up. Each day the umbrella opens a bit more as the plant grows taller. It eventually reaches a height of 12 to 18 inches, bears a single white flower, and produces a single fruit, egg shaped and egg in size. The fruit is greenish yellow in spring and becomes entirely yellow, softer, sweet, and tasty in late summer. All parts of the plant except the ripe fruit are considered somewhat poisonous. The root has medicinal qualities but Gibbons advises amateurs to refrain from experimenting with this powerful drug. The ripe apple is pleasant to eat raw; also makes excellent jam.

Mulberry: The mulberry grows on trees that reach heights of from 15 to 30 feet, possibly higher. We have two kinds in the US; the native mulberry that bears a deep purple colored fruit when ripe and the imported mulberry that bears a white fruit. The white mulberry was imported as part of the unsuccessful attempt to establish a silk industry. The fruit is similar in shape to the boysenberry. The trees that I have seen are prolific bearers. We are fortunate to have, purely by chance, trees of both types on the Appalachian Outfitter property in Oakton, VA. Employees have a June strawberry shortcake festival and an August peach shortcake festival; no reason why, with 4 or 5 heavily bearing mulberry trees, we should not have a mulberry festival. Gibbons suggests that plastic sheets be spread out underneath the trees and the trees shaken to collect the fruit. The fruit can be eaten as is or made into jellies and pies. It contains no pectin so if it is to be cooked, artificial pectin must be added.

Pears and apples: In the course of his 2,000-mile hike the Appalachian Trail hiker will occasionally pass through or near abandoned orchards of both pears and apples. At other times he will frequently find wild apple and pear trees which have grown from seed. The fruit of the wild tree bears little resemblance in either shape or taste to the fruit from which the seed was produced. The wild fruit is generally smaller, firmer, and more tart than the domestic fruit. But the very qualities which make the wild fruit less pleasant to eat raw make it more satisfactory for cooking. Cut the apples up in quarters, remove any wormy areas, add sugar and water and cook. I generally carry a bit of cinnamon in my sack of condiments. A batch of apple sauce cooked over a fire on a cool autumn evening is an excellent dish; and a bit of cinnamon does wonders for both the olfactory nerves and the palate.

Persimmon: This fruit, also known as the sugar-plum, in the latitude of northern Virginia, becomes ripe during the first part of October, frequently later. Its late date for maturing makes it more enjoyable because by October and early November when the persimmon is at its best, the other fruits have long since disappeared. They are at their best when they fall from the tree onto soft surface and when the fruit itself is soft and mushy. They are a pale orange when ripe and have a high sugar content and delicious flavor. Gibbons tells of finding some of this delicious fruit in January. My own most memorable experience with the persimmon occurred on a New Year's day with the snow heavily crusted. The persimmons, partially dried and frozen had dropped on the firm surface and rolled into depressions from which they were easily gathered. They were sweet and tasty as dates. The ripe fruit, when found in the wild, is seldom more than an inch in diameter. Gibbons comments that in Pennsylvania they seldom have seeds. The ones I have eaten in Virginia *always* have seeds. The persimmon should be eaten only when fully ripe. The unripe fruit has a strong puckery quality that is very unpleasant.

OTHER EDIBLE WILD FOODS

Acorns: My first recollection of people eating acorns was in the 1950's when the Washington, D.C. newspaper carried an article about a middle age couple hiking through the Shenandoah National Park. The couple ran out of food and resorted to eating acorns. Both became very ill from the experience. The illness was undoubtedly caused by the tannin content of the acorns. The same tannin is highly sought in oak tree bark for curing leather but apparently the human stomach finds the tannin unacceptable. How then to treat the acorn so that it can be eaten? The answer is to leach out the tannin by boiling it in water, using successive changes of water until the water remains clear. Gibbons recommends a two-hour boiling process.

I have on several occasions at our wild food parties eaten muffins and breads made from flour that was composed of equal parts of acorn meal and wheat flour. Preparatory to writing this chapter I gathered up about 18 freshly fallen acorns, removed their shells with a pocket knife, and ate part of one nut raw. It was quite bitter and I suspected it was high in tannin. I shelled all the rest and boiled them about 40 minutes changing the water once. I then ate one of the nuts as it was. Not too exciting to the palate but the bitterness was gone. I then roasted them in a pan on top of the stove in melted butter. Even this did not make them highly palatable.

Later I made a bowl of cream of mushroom soup and added the acorns a la Chinese cuisine. Very satisfactory. Gibbons gives other methods of roasting, glazing and making meal. It was Gibbons observation that throughout man's history, the acorn has probably provided nourishment for more millions of people than have the more recent cereal grains. It seems particularly important that AT hikers be aware of the food value of the acorn because it is so plentiful even at high elevations where other foods are relatively scarce.

Ramps: Although referred to as a "ramp," this plant, a member of the lily family, is listed in the dictionary as "rampion." It grows throughout the southern Appalachians seeming to thrive at elevations of around 4,000 feet. Both the stalk above ground and the bulb underground have a strong onion-garlic flavor. It grows to a height of 3 to 5 inches and frequently grows out of soft humus in the forest making it quite easy to remove from the ground. It is at its succulent best during the early weeks of April. I have made good use of the ramp by cutting up the bulb and the lower part of the stalk into small pieces, sauteeing same in butter, and then mixing them in various freeze dry foods and in Tuna Helper (see Chap. 3). Each April some southern mountain towns have ramp festivals, such festivals being preceded by a tremendous amount of foraging throughout the mountains.

One word of caution on ramps. During early April another member of the lily family is sometimes mistaken for the ramp. The other plant is the hellebore which is poisonous. The hellebore, as it gets larger, has very pronounced ridged leaves, whereas the ramp leaves are smooth. Also, the hellebore frequently grows up in spiral fashion, whereas the ramp does not. If in doubt, just nibble on the bulb. The onion-garlic taste is so unmistakeable in the ramp that one nibble will identify it immediately as the ramp or something else. A picture of the ramp showing both the plant and one of the extracted bulbs appear on page 339.

Poke salad (poke weed): Although referred to by either name I prefer "poke salad." Sounds nicer! Also known as garget, inkberry, and pigeonberry. This is one of four "weeds" that I learned to identify in our wild food classes, weeds that I had been removing from my garden for decades. The other three were lambs quarter, Jerusalem artichoke, and purslane. I now have a feeling of friendship

Rampions. (Photo: Ed Hanlon)

for these former enemies and I can't quite bring myself to eradicating them entirely even if I could. I rather enjoy seeing the rascals come up each spring.

Once you learn to identify poke, you will be surprised to find it almost anywhere along the AT, for it ranges from Florida to Maine. The plant is most easily identified in the late summer and early fall when it is *not* edible. It develops stalks almost an inch thick and from 5 to 8 feet tall. Also, as the plant matures the green stalk gradually takes on a reddish hue and the berries turn a dark purple, almost black; hence the common name, "inkberry." Everything about the plant is poisonous: root, berries, and mature stalk. What you look for in the spring are the tender young shoots and leaves, identifying them as much by last year's dead stalks as by their own distinctive lance shaped heavily veined leaves.

There are many recipes for cooking poke; some are so simple that they are particularly attractive to the backpacker. One is the "asparagus approach" which I have used many times. Take a number of young stalks leaving on the unfolded leaves, cut into 1-2 inch lengths, boil in plenty of water for perhaps 10 minutes, then throw the water away. Add a small amount of fresh water, also add butter, bacon grease or other shortening, season, and boil or simmer slowly so that the seasoning permeates the "asparagus." Then serve and eat as is. Or, if you are skilled in making cream sauce, use that method.

Another method is to skin the young stalks, roll them in corn meal, and then fry them. The practice of skinning the stalks seems to obviate the need for that first boiling. Most people prefer to parboil to remove any trace of the medicinal element. The poke has a huge root (like a Paul Bunyan-size potato) which has medicinal qualities.

The last recipe to be included here was given to me by Anne Panagatos of North Lebanon, PA. We will call this one the "spinach approach." Parboil the tender young leaves (not the stalks) twice, using a pinch of baking soda in the water. Drain the second water, and return the leaves to a skillet. Add shortening and seasoning and fry slowly, adding either fresh eggs or freeze-dry eggs. Stir the eggs while cooking. When the eggs are cooked the entire contents of the skillet are ready for eating, a one pot backpacker's meal.

Milkweed: This is an excellent food for backpackers. Its very name is so descriptive that identification is easy and certain. I have known this plant since early childhood but, until my participation in the wild food classes, did not know of the plants edible qualities. Gibbons gives this plant a very high rating, explaining that it has not just one, but four uses as a food at its different stages of growth. I urge you to consult the Gibbons book for description of the four phases and the sketch of the plant. Then, if on your hike or food foraging trip, you spot a plant that even half way resembles the sketch, give it the test: break off a piece of the leaf or the stalk and if a thick, sticky, white fluid emerges, you've got it! It's that simple.

I have eaten the milkweed plant in two of its phases: (1) the unopened flower bud stage when they are eaten like broccoli or fresh peas and (2) the young pod stage when they can be cooked like okra. I've cooked them only in the unopened flower bud stage both on canoeing and backpacking trips. Gibbons makes quite a point of mentioning that the entire milkweed plant posses a bitter quality that is removed only by immersing the stalks, buds, leaves, or pods in boiling water, boiling hard for one minute, throwing away the water, then repeating for two more cycles the one minute boiling process with fresh boiling water. On the occasions when I've cooked the tender flower buds I have not had Gibbons' book handy and have cooked the buds just as I would fresh peas (which the buds resemble in both shape and size). On some occasions I have not thrown the water away at all, on other occasions I've drained the buds just once. I've not been aware of any bitter taste, but perhaps the final product would have been tastier had I proceeded as suggested by Gibbons.

From July 3 to 5, 1977, I accompanied (mostly via my camper van) and performed the cooking chores for a number of Georgia to Maine hikers through the central section of the Shenandoah National Park in Virginia. I also did some maintenance work on a blue-blazed trail that intersects the Appalachian Trail at Milan Gap. Near that intersection are some 30 to 40 milkweed plants and in the space of but a few minutes, I was able to gather some 1½ quarts of flower bud clusters. That night for the evening meal I cooked hamburger, potatoes, onions, and a big pot of milkweed buds. For the other hikers it was a first experience with the milkweed and this fresh green vegetable was thoroughly enjoyed. Milkweed grows throughout the entire length of the Trail and I especially urge backpackers to become familiar with and to use this plant in its various stages.

Lamb's quarters or pigweed: This plant, a close relative of the garden beet and spinach plants, grows throughout much of the United States. It is one of the most common and persistent garden weeds I've ever encountered. It seems to grow especially well in gardens or along the edge of cultivated fields. Pick the young plants under a foot high. New plants keep sprouting up from spring to frost so you can enjoy these fresh greens for many months of the year. Once you have picked enough for a meal you can cook them in the same manner as spinach except that no parboiling is necessary.

Jerusalem artichoke: This is a native American plant, a member of the sunflower family. It is *not* an artichoke and it does not come from Jerusalem. I have these on the edge of my garden, the stalks grow from 6 to 10 feet high and have yellow flowers. On this plant it is the undergrond tuber that you eat. Friends of mine from Missouri, who are enthusiastic organic gardeners, stoutly maintain that in a given area of their garden they can obtain more food from the Jerusalem artichoke than they can from domestic potatoes. It is best eaten after the first frost, any time you can find it in winter, and well into spring. Locate the stalks, do a bit of digging, and locate the tubers. The tubers are best eaten raw just as you dig them, or sliced up in a salad. They can be cooked as potatoes but the cooked product is not nearly as tasty as the uncooked. The long distance backpacker develops a hankering for crisp raw vegetables and if he can locate just a few of these hardy plants, his appetite will quickly be satisfied.

Day lily: This member of the lily family grows to a height of about two feet, has orange colored flowers, is easily identified, and seems to grow everywhere. It is an ideal plant for the backpacker because all parts of the plant can be eaten. The flower buds can be cooked and eaten like green beans, the flowers themselves (both today's freshly opened flowers and yesterday's withered ones) can be added to soups or stews; the small tubers can be eaten raw, boiled, or roasted. The early spring stalks can be cut up and cooked like asparagus. I've eaten the flower buds and flowers, also the tubers. So far I have not cut and eaten the stalks but that will come later. Not only do I have these plants growing wild along my property line but I have transplanted a number of them into a flower bed. A most desirable food and decorative flower.

The above described plants are some of the most commonly found ones along the Appalachian Trail. Learn to identify them and learn how to cook or otherwise prepare them for eating. Even though he reads reams of descriptive literature on a plant, the novice is somewhat hesitant about eating a plant that someone else has not positively identified for him. Participate in wild flower hikes and pester other participants to identify for you the plants I have described here. Ask other hikers. Read other books in which these plants are shown in color. Check with the food editor of your local paper to ascertain if there are wild food enthusiasts or clubs in your area and if there are, participate in their foraging hikes. If you are persistent you can learn to identify and enjoy these edible wild plants and your hiking experience will be much the richer for having done so.

A few words about Euell Gibbons. For years he participated as the featured guest at the annual Nature Wonder Weekends held in late September at the North Bend State Park in West Virginia. I was invited to attend in 1972, '73, and '74 but was out of the country on each occasion participating in outdoor recreation exhibits. In September 1975, I did participate in the affair and in the course of doing so I had several good visits with Gibbons. He was then in his 60's, he had spent a lifetime in the study of wild plants, in experimenting with the cooking of them, and in writing and lecturing on the subject. It was only in his later years that public recognition and success had crowned his efforts. He died but a few months after the September, 1975 weekend at North Bend.

(Note: Illustrations in the Gibbons book are in black and white. For purposes of identification readers may desire to consult *Field Guide to Edible Wild Plants* by Bradford Angier, Stackpole Books, 1974. It contains over 100 *color* reproductions of edible plants.)

16
Birds Along the Trail

I felt much more at home in the identifying of birds than I did identifying flowers. I had acquired an interest in bird identification when I earned my bird study merit badge as a Boy Scout. I still have those journals, with the dates 1930 and 1931 on them, which list 50 and more birds I needed to identify for that merit badge. Many of the birds along the Appalachian Trail will be heard rather than seen. Therefore, one who desires to do some advance study will do well to obtain Bird Song and Bird Call phonograph records from a public library. Look in the library card index under "bird songs" and "bird calls."

Here are some of the birds I saw or heard. My list begins with the bird which I saw the first day of my hike, on April 4, in Georgia, and which I was to see and hear every day thereafter, until I reached Vermont.

Towhee: By all means, learn to identify this bird by sight and by his *two* songs. He will be your one most constant bird companion for most of your hike.

Black cap chicadee.

Tufted titmouse: Be certain to learn the song of this little fellow. you will hear him daily but seldom see him.

Crow.

Blue jay and Canada jay: The blue jay will be seen in most of the states along the Trail. His cousin, the Canada Jay, is also known as Camp Robber and Whiskey Jack. He will be seen in Maine.

King bird.

Turkey vultures and black vultures: I had two unusual experiences with these birds. One is recorded in Chapter 11 under date of May 19. The other occurred on the fourth day of my hike, on April 7, north of Tesnatee Gap, in Georgia. I surprised two vultures feeding on two long-since-dead dogs directly beside the

344

Trail in a remote area. I have often wondered how two dogs would die in one place at one time.

Whippoorwill: You must learn to recognize this bird by his call. You will see him often, but you will never get a good look at him because he appears when twilight is giving way to darkness. He has a piercing call; and you will hear him often, frequently at close range.

Woodpeckers: red headed, hairy, downy: You will see all three.

Flicker.

Wood thrush, hermit thrush, brown thrasher: The hermit thrush is a famous songster and you should learn to identify him through his song.

Pileated woodpecker: Not common. You may see only a few, but I list him because he is such a striking bird that you will be thrilled to see and identify him.

Black and white warbler: Again, a not common but a small bird with striking colors who frequents tree trunks where you can get a good look at him.

Great horned owl: Frequently heard at night, seldom seen. I think I saw only two, but I heard their deep, penetrating hoot on scores of nights.

Ruffed grouse: Seen almost daily from Georgia to Maine. They take off from the ground like fighter planes, waiting until you are only within a few feet from them before zooming into the air. In early May, investigate the point from which the hen takes off. You will, if you are lucky, find the nest. In late May and early June, the hen will frequently charge towards you, seeking to divert your attention from the young chicks. On a still day, you will hear a far away drumming or pounding sound; it is made by the male as part of the courting process.

Spruce grouse: You will see these birds only in New Hampshire and Maine. They are entirely different from the ruffed grouse in their habits. Whereas the ruffed grouse takes off suddenly in flight and flies quickly out of sight, the spruce grouse prefers to run slowly, keeping about five to ten yards away. If he feels he must fly, he flies only to a nearby, low-hanging limb.

Robin.

Cardinal.

Scarlet tanager: Not seen too often, but a thrill to see and recognize.

Sparrows: Song sparrows, chipping sparrows, white throated sparrows: The ones most frequently seen were the song and chipping sparrows, but the one that intrigued me the most was the white throated sparrow. Somewhere around the Massachusetts-Vermont line I realized that I was no longer seeing or hearing the towhee. At that same time, I became aware of a new bird call, five slow, distinct, high pitched, plaintive notes. It was five days before I found someone who could identify this distinct call as belonging to the white throated sparrow. And it was another three days before one of these handsome little fellows came down close to our group and let us examine him at some length.

Slate colored junco: One of the most frequently seen birds. They nest on, or near the ground; and they will frequently betray the location of their nests by leaving them suddenly as you approach. I found many of these nests directly beside the Trail.

Wild turkey: I saw these on a number of occasions, particularly in Virginia.

Loon: I saw and heard these birds only on the lakes of Maine. These are very large water birds and are excellent divers. They have a loud, yodel-like call that carries long distances across water.

EXPERIENCE IS A GOOD TEACHER

In 1972 Jeffrey Lawton, then a 17-year-old from Philadelphia, Pennsylvania, took his first hike on the Appalachian Trail—July 1972 letter:

"I really enjoyed your book and I appreciate the warning about not hiking in new boots. Unfortunately I did and that is why I'm back home reading your book and writing you this letter while allowing a pair of badly blistered and cut-up feet to heal. When people, like myself, a month ago, read warnings such as yours, I don't think they take them seriously enough. I guess experience is the best teacher."

17
Trees Along the Trail

The hiker, if he wishes, may largely ignore the flowers, plants, birds, and animals along the Trail—although some plants (like poison ivy), some birds (like the whippoorwill) and some animals (like bears, skunks, and porcupines) may insist on being recognized. Trees, however, are so much a part of the Trail that they must be recognized day in and day out. The trailside shelters are made from tree products. The wood for cooking fires comes from trees. Trees provide food in the form of cherries, mulberries, and nuts. Fallen trees sometimes block the hiker's path.

The hiker will wish to become acquainted with the most frequently seen trees on the Trail. He cannot be expected to know all the species of each tree (54 species of oak, 34 of pine, etc.). I have therefore listed only those trees which I saw most frequently on my own hike. These are:

Pine: White pine and balsam are those which I saw most frequently—the balsam primarily in the Smokies and in Maine.

Hemlock.

Flowering dogwood. In late April and all through May the white dogwoods and the contrasting redbuds provide a welcome splash of color in the woods.

Sugar maple and red maple.

Black walnut, butternut.

Hickory: Many varieties, but pignut and shagbark are the most common. The shagbark will be recognized immediately from its very shaggy, scaly bark. I was surprised to see one as far north as Maine.

Black locust, honey locust.

Sassafras.

Mulberry.

Sweet gum.

Birch, yellow, white, brown, black.

Black cherry.

Beech.

American chestnut: This tree has been largely exterminated by the chestnut blight; but I found live chestnut trees from Georgia through Virginia. The quickest way to identify them is to note last year's large thorny seed-pods on the ground. This tree was once so numerous that along parts of the Appalachian Trail one can even now walk for hundreds of yards by walking only on dead and fallen chestnut trees. Many of the early trailside shelters and many of the old cabins seen along the Trail were built of chestnut.

Oak: Particularly, white oak and chestnut oak. The latter is so named because its leaf closely resembles that of the American chestnut.

Yellow poplar or tulip poplar: This tree can be easily distinguished in May and June by its large tulip-like greenish-yellow flowers. The largest known specimen of the yellow poplar is in North Carolina, about one mile south of the Wallace Gap (US Highway 64) and one-half mile off the Appalachian Trail on a well-signed trail. This tree was identified and measured by Duke Barr, the district ranger of the US Forest Service in Franklin, North Carolina.

A booklet *Master Tree Finder* by May Theilgaard Watts, Nature Study Guild, contains 144 species of Eastern Trees. The same author also has written *The Winter Tree Finder*. It is published by the same firm.

18
Animals Along the Trail

Ordinarily, one who is hiking the entire Appalachian Trail in one year cannot expect to see too many animals. For one thing, the Trail follows the ridge top throughout much of its length; and I do not think the animal population is as heavy there as it is further down the mountain, where water and food are more plentiful. Furthermore, the hiker is walking briskly along the Trail; and his movements, his noise, and scent alert animals to his presence. George Miller, who hiked the entire Trail in 1952, kept a very accurate log of his journey. He reported seeing no bears, a deer only now and then, and very few other animals.

Judging by the frequency of animal tracks and animal droppings on or near the Trail, it would seem that more animals use the Trail than do humans. The tracks and droppings of deer, bear, and moose are easily recognizable. I suspected that on many occasions I saw droppings from fox, wildcat, raccoon, and oppossum; but I was not certain of this. Likewise, the widespread rooting by wild pigs in the southernmost 30 miles or so of the Smokies was unmistakable; but I saw none of the pigs. (Saw the Mollies Ridge Shelter pig on my 1977 hike of the Smokies. The pig had rooted up so much of the shelter area that it looked as if it were ready for spring garden planting!)

In contrast to George Miller, who saw deer only "now and then," I saw them frequently . . . almost daily, from Georgia through Vermont. On one day in Pennsylvania, I encountered deer on six occasions; this was in the 22-mile stretch immediately south of Allen, Pennsylvania. I saw no deer in New Hampshire, and I saw them on only two occasions in Maine. Other animals seen frequently were squirrels—red squirrels, gray squirrels, and other varieties, plus chipmunks—these were seen almost daily—sometimes I saw many on a single day. Other animals seen were:

349

Woodchucks: Saw perhaps 30 to 40 of these.

Shrews: Saw four of them . . . all dead . . . on different parts of the Trail, at widely separated points.

Raccoon: Saw only one . . . and he was almost a household pest . . . at Doyle River cabin in the Shenandoah National Park.

Bear: Saw just one, in Georgia.

Beaver: Saw beaver cuttings, beaver trails, beaver dams, and beaver houses. However, I saw no beaver.

Mink: Saw one in Maine swimming across Moxie Pond.

Porcupine: Numerous in Vermont; but I saw only one.

Moose: They are numerous in New Hampshire and Maine. Their huge tracks and droppings are seen frequently on the Trail. I saw only one moose, at a shelter in Maine, at 1:05 a.m. (Saw moose on two occasions in my 1977 hike.)

Mice: Your most frequent companion in the trailside shelters. You see them occasionally, hear them frequently, and now and then you will feel them as they run across your sleeping bag or your head.

19
Reflections on the Adventure of a Lifetime

I began my hike on April 4, 1970, and finished on October 7, 1970. With time out for the two trips home, I spent 158 days on the Trail. I examined the footway, the paint blazing, the wooden directional signs, and, with a few exceptions, I made a careful inspection of all of the 238 trailside shelters that were being used in 1970. I visited with scores of people—with employees of the US Forest Service, the National Park Service, with members of many trail clubs—all of whom have a direct interest in the protection and maintenance of the Appalachian Trail. After having done all this, what are my conclusions with respect to the Appalachian Trail?

1. Hiking the entire Appalachian Trail, whether done in one year, or over a space of many years, is a thoroughly delightful experience.

2. The footway throughout the length of the Trail is excellent. This was the single most outstanding feature of the Trail as I observed it.

3. The marking of the Appalachian Trail is very good. Marking includes paint blazing, wooden directional signs, metal markers, and in Maine, the mileage markers. In most places, the marking was excellent or very good. In a few places, it was fair or poor. Overall—very —very good.

4. The identification of water sources near the Trail is poor. For some unexplainable reason this aspect of trail marking has been sadly neglected.

5. The chain of trailside shelters is in good condition—excellent on some fairly long stretches of the Trail, poor in some areas, almost nonexistent in a few places.

6. The use of the Appalachian Trail, both by short-distance hikers and those hiking the entire distance, is increasing at a very rapid rate.

The words written so far in this chapter are exactly as they appeared in my original book written almost 7 years ago. The observations I made then are still applicable today except that we generally have made progress on signs and on identification of water sources. My prediction as to the increased use of the Trail was right on target. Example: In one year, 1973, there were 92 people who completed the entire 2,000-mile Trail, which is 1½ times as many as had completed it in the first 30 years of the Trail's existence. Today we estimate that approximately 4 million people each year hike on some part of the Trail.

In the last paragraph of Chapter 11, written in 1971, I predicted that my 2,000 mile hike of the Appalachian Trail "would influence the rest of my life." *How prophetic that statement turned out to be!* In the next few paragraphs I will relate some of the aspects of my life from 1971 through 1977 . . . events that were related directly to my long hike of the AT.

May 31, 1971—finished Appalachian Hiker manuscript, mailed last chapter to publisher, boarded plane for Europe.

June 1-Oct. 3—touring many countries of Europe by car with wife and son.

Dec. 1—Began working at Appalachian Outfitters.

Dec. 4—*Appalachian Hiker* book published.

Feb. 1972—I was elected president of the 2,000-member Potomac Appalachian Trail Club.

Sept. 1-Oct. 10, 1972—Participating in Outdoor Recreation Exhibit, Zagreb, Yugoslavia, then trips to Greece, Tunisia, North Africa, Italy, and Vienna, Austria. In Vienna, Austria Airport picked up copy of October 1972 *Readers Digest* describing my hike of the Appalachian Trail.

Jan. 9-Feb. 22, 1973—Participating in Outdoor Recreation Exhibit, Skopje, Yugo (near Greece) then trips to Rome, Majorca, Spain Portugal.

May 15-July 18, 1973—Outdoor Recreation Exhibit, Moscow, USSR, then trips to Leningrad, Helsinki, Stockholm, Edinburgh. In Stockholm I spent one afternoon visiting factory that makes Optimus, Primus, Svea stoves.

Sept. 12-Oct. 28, 1973—Outdoor Recreation Exhibit, Irkutsk, Eastern Siberia, USSR. Took plane to Moscow, then 4 days and nights on Trans-Siberian railroad to Irkutsk. Article describing an unusual 2-

day hike in Siberia appeared in 1974 *Potomac Appalachian* magazine and in July 1974 issue of *American Forestry*.

June 28-Sept. 25, 1974—A 3-month trip which ended with participation in late September at the last of the Outdoor Recreation Exhibits. This one was in Budapest, Hungary. The 2-week exhibit was preceded by six weeks of hiking and backpacking in the Alps of northwestern Yugoslavia and nearby Italy and Austria with two PATC companions: Ed Hanlon and Bill Husic. A fabulous hiking trip in which I visited 30 of the huts in those countries and slept in 17. Then a month of sightseeing with my wife in Italy, Austria, and Hungary, then the exhibit. The exhibit itself, the last of 11 of them, held in Yugoslavia, USSR, and Hungary, was terrific—250,000 visitors in nine days in Budapest.

May-Nov., 1975—Researching and writing a second hiking book— *Hiking Trails in the Mid-Atlantic States.* Drove 9,000 miles and hiked many miles in the mid-Atlantic states of Virginia, West Virginia, Pennsylvania, Maryland, Delaware, and New Jersey.

Apr. 1976—Backpacking trip with Ed Hanlon and Bill Husic—140 miles on Appalachian Trail from Wesser, N.C. to Springer Mt., GA and on to Amicalola Falls.

May, 1976—Book, *Hiking Trails in Mid-Atlantic States*, published.

Apr. 1977—Backpacked through the Smokies and south to Wesser, N.C., 95 miles.

May, 1977—Attended general meeting of Appalachian Trail Conference in Shepherdstown, WV. Re-elected to Board of Managers (I had terminated my eight year membership on the Board in June 1972 at the time my proposed amendment to the ATC constitution had been adopted, an amendment which limited length of tenure for board members).

Aug. 1977—Backpacked with Ed Hanlon and Bill Husic on Appalachian Trail from Katahdin to Monson, Maine, 118 miles.

Throughout these past six years, I have continued to work on a part-time basis at Appalachian Outfitters and I expect to continue the affiliation for many more years. The affiliation permits me to keep abreast of new equipment coming into the market, to receive feedback from hiker-customers, and to personally check out new hiking boots, new tents, new sleeping bags and backpacks. I've continued my active participation in both the Potomac Appalachian

Trail Club and the Appalachian Trail Conference. During the first years after the completion of the long hike in 1970 I really did little serious hiking. (Big talk, much write, no hike!) but in 1976 and 1977 I began rehiking sizeable distances on the AT. I plan to continue this so that after a period of time I will have hiked the Trail a second time. And on May 7, 1977 I participated in one of the zaniest hikes of my life, a one-day 100 kilometer hike on the Chesapeake and Ohio Canal towpath. If you are not up on your metric conversions, the distance of 100 km's is equal to 62.2 miles. Some 45 other somewhat demented people assembled with me at 3 a.m. on a Saturday in Georgetown, the older part of the Nation's Capital. I finished my hike some 21 hours later at midnight at the American Youth Hostel near Harpers Ferry, WV. If my health permits, I plan to participate in this long distance hike each year, if for no other reason than that it will afford an incentive for me to get in tip top shape at least once each year. (For those who might wish to participate in one of these hikes, write to Hiking Coordinator, Sierra Club, 330 Pennsylvania Ave., S.E., Washington, D.C. 20003.)

THE REWARDS OF WRITING THE BOOK

Writing is hard work. The financial returns only rarely net the author much more than day labor wages. But there are other rewards and I have had much more than my share on *Appalachian Hiker*. First there is the satisfaction, after having labored for months on your manuscript, of finding a publisher who considers your product good enough for him to risk his time and a considerable outlay of his cash to get your book edited and printed. There is another thrill when the book is actually printed and you hold the printed product in your hand, and you see your book on the shelves of book stores and outdoor stores. And finally, the greatest satisfaction, for me at least, was and is the tremendous reaction from readers. Never could I have foreseen the impact the book would have. Letters from people of all walks of life, from teenagers to retirees and grandparents. Letters thanking me for the enjoyment the book provided, letters thanking me for a recipe or for a backpacking tip, letters asking questions, letters in which the writers related that as they read the diary part of the book they felt that they were hiking right along with me. I've received cards from Springer Mountain in Georgia and from Katahdin in Maine. In my book I designated May 12 as Trillium Day. In 1975, I received a postcard written from a shelter in North

Carolina. It was signed by six Georgia to Maine hikers who just wanted me to know that they too were celebrating Trillium Day!

If I was pleased to receive letters, the personal encounters were even more satisfying. So many people have made it a point to introduce themselves and then thank me for a helpful piece of information furnished in it or to thank me for just having given them the confidence or desire to give backpacking a try. These encounters have occurred on the Trail, at the outdoor store where I work, and in other walks of life. But the most surprising of these encounters occurred at the Plitvice National Park in Yugoslavia in 1974. Accompanied by a fellow member of the Potomac Appalachian Trail Club, Ed Hanlon, we approached an information booth to seek information regarding a third member of our party with whom we had planned to rendezvous at that point. The young English speaking attendant readily helped us and then, after a long look at the AT patch on my sleeve, he asked almost apologetically, "Did you by any chance write a book about the Appalachian Trail?!" Hard to say who was the most surprised, Hanlon, the young man, or I. When I pursued the matter a bit, he explained that he had read the book from cover to cover within the past month at the reading room of the American Consul office in Zagreb, Yugoslavia.

If one is fighting for a cause, then a book, whether it be an adventure book, a "how-to" book, or a guide to hiking trails, provides an excellent platform from which one can bring the facts out into the open. Few people with whom I've come in contact within recent years have any doubt as to the two causes that I am vigorously espousing: (1) the preservation of the Appalachian Trail (i.e., getting it into public ownership) and (2) the preservation and enhancement of the overnight accommodations for the backpacker. Not only does the book win converts for the cause but the very fact that you have written a book that has gained public acceptance gives one greater credibility when he later testifies or writes other articles on behalf of this cause. And so, while sitting hunched over a typewriter for hours at a time does not come within my definition of fun, I have found that the rewards more than compensated for the sacrifice.

OBITUARIES

Throughout Chapter 11, I made a number of parenthetical notes to record the deaths of a number of people who were still very much alive when I made my long hike in 1970. In this chapter I provide more details regarding three people who have passed on in the intervening years: Benton MacKaye, Emma Gatewood and Genevieve Hutchinson. Each lived to an advanced age; each gained fame and affection for widely different reasons.

Benton MacKaye: Born March 6, 1879, died December 11, 1975 at the age of 96.

I have already devoted some space in Chapter 1 to Benton MacKaye and one of his letters is reproduced on the inside covers of the book. He was a fabulous gentleman. I began corresponding with him in 1967 and my wife and I drove to Shirley Center, Mass. in May 1969 to pay him a visit. He had a wide circle of friends from many walks of life and kept in constant touch with them by mail and phone. Almost totally blind in his last years, he gratefully accepted the services of a battery of neighbors to perform his secretarial chores.

In 1925 he, and a handful of other trail enthusiasts, met in Washington, D.C. and organized the Appalachian Trail Conference. Ten years later, with seven other men, he again met in Washington, D.C. to organize the Wilderness Society. The Appalachian Trail was especially dear to his heart, and yet it seemed that the Appalachian Trail Conference was less appreciative of his contribution and held him in less esteem than did the Wilderness Society. At the time of his death, the Wilderness Society devoted almost an entire issue of its quarterly magazine (*The Living Wilderness*, January/March, 1976) to MacKaye's life and his accomplishments. The ATC was much more modest in its *Trailway News*.

Early in 1966, the Department of Interior announced its highest Departmental awards to nine individuals and two organizations for efforts in the conservation of natural resources. Benton MacKaye was one of those named. It was shortly after this that I realized that the Appalachian Trail Conference had never bestowed an honorary lifetime membership upon the very man who was so responsible for creating the Trail and the organization itself. I proposed his name to the Conference Board of Managers and its Executive Committee promptly approved. The announcement of Honorary Life Time Membership was made in *Trailway News*, September 1966. At the 1967 general meeting of the Conference, I was asked to prepare and then to read to the membership a citation for Benton MacKaye.

I thought the citation had long been lost but have since found it—handwritten on the back of the hotel stationery where the Conference was held. It has not heretofore been published and it is quoted below:

Benton MacKaye   Shirley Center, Mass.

In recognition of his foresight in conceiving, writing, and planning for an extensive foot trail which would follow generally the crest of our eastern mountain range from Maine to Georgia; for his continuous letter writing campaigns over a 40-year-period to legislators and conservationists on behalf of the Appalachian Trail; for his contributions in other fields such as participation in formation of the Wilderness Society; for his conception and writing on "townless highways," the forerunner of our interstate highway system. For these and many other accomplishments, the Appalachian Trail Conference confers honorary membership upon Benton MacKaye of Shirley Center, Mass.

Under the date of June 4, 1976 Mr. MacKaye wrote me acknowledging and extending his thanks to the Conference for the honor bestowed. He also furnished "A MEMORANDUM to the Appalachian Trail Conference" in which he furnished many priceless details of the March 1-3, 1925 meeting and many more details of the "prenatal" years preceding that meeting. I should have furnished that "MEMORANDUM" to the Conference years ago but neglected to do so. Having now rediscovered it in my files, I will make copies and furnish same to the Conference for publication in *Trailway News* and/or the Conference archives.

No description of MacKaye's last years would be complete without mentioning his next door neighbors, the Johnson family, who took ever increasing care of him. In the very last years, it was Mrs. Lucy Johnson who acted not only as housekeeper, cook and guardian, but also as his eyes, reading mail and publications for him and frequently, along with other neighbors, writing letters for him. It came to be that visitors to Shirley Center looked forward to visiting not just one person but two: Benton MacKaye and Lucy Johnson, two wonderful people.

Mrs. Emma Gatewood: In August 1973, I wrote the following article shortly after Mrs. Gatewood's death. It was published in somewhat abbreviated form in the October 1974 issue of the Potomac Appalachian.

THE MEANING OF "DESIRE"

GRANDMA GATEWOOD DIES IN OHIO

Mrs. Emma "Grandma" Gatewood, probably the best known of all those who have hiked the entire Appalachian Trail, died on June 4, 1973 at Gallipolis, Ohio. She first hiked the entire Trail from south to north in 1955 when she was 67 years old. Two years later she repeated the trip. Then in the course of extensive hiking on the Trail in 1960, 1963, and 1964 she covered the Trail a third time, with a hike of the Long Trail in Vermont thrown in for good measure. (See the *Appalachian Trailway News*, Jan. 1956, Jan. 1958, and Jan. 1965 for details.) In 1959 at age 72 she walked the Oregon Trail as a part of the 100th anniversary of the Oregon Trail.

In 1970 when I hiked the Trail myself from south to north I found that among landowners along the Trail Grandma had become a living legend. Her name and her exploits were mentioned more times than those of all previous hikers combined. There was something about that little old lady doggedly pursuing her goal in good weather and bad that seemed to make an everlasting imprint on the minds of those she met.

In 1972, at the age of 84, she attended her first Appalachian Trail Conference meeting at Plymouth, New Hampshire. Her picture appears on the cover of the September 1972 *Appalachian Trailway News* along with fifteen others who had hiked the entire Trail. I had the opportunity for a couple of brief visits with her during the Plymouth meeting. Among other things, I did verify one piece of information that had been repeated to me a number of times, concerning her footwear. "Is it true Mrs. Gatewood," I asked, "that you wore sneakers during the course of your three hikes on the Appalachian Trail?" "Indeed it's not true," she replied indignantly, "I wore Keds!" A fine point of distinction perhaps, but she went on to explain that on her AT hikes she wore the high-top Ked basketball-type shoe and on the road walking out to Oregon she wore the low-cut variety.

While most of the hiking public is aware that Grandma made three successful hikes of the entire Trail, very few know that her first attempt, made in May, 1954, ended in dismal and almost tragic failure. She started at the north end on that first hike, climbed Katahdin, and then set out south on what was hopefully the Appalachian Trail. At that time she was unaware that the Trail was marked by white paint blazes. "I carried no guide books, no maps, no nothin' that I didn't need!" But apparently she did have *some* unneeded items for the first two or three days because she stopped at the first Maine sporting camp (presumably Twin Pines) and had her suitcase with extra clothes mailed home. A day or so farther south she stopped overnight at Rainbow Lake Camp and the next day became lost. She came to a lake and stayed near or around the area for several days trying to find her way back. She built a fire and sent up smoke signals. She waved at a low flying plane. All to no avail. Her food supply was exhausted. Finally she located a promising looking trail that took her back to Rainbow Lake Camp. She was flown to Millinocket, where, because of her appearance, she had difficulty getting into the very hotel she had occupied a week earlier. Her clothes were torn and dirty, one eye was blackened, she had broken her glasses and patched them together with white tape, her face and arms were scratched. When she got into her hotel room and looked into a mirror she was horrified. "I looked like I'd been dug out of the gutter!" she remarked. She promptly bought herself a new wardrobe in Millinocket and left for home. Interviewed by a reporter she explained that she had gone to Maine and had climbed Mt. Katahdin "and I never told anybody anything else."

Her hiking gear and techniques will be of interest to present day hikers. Her "pack" consisted of one yard of denim cloth fashioned into a sack with a drawstring at one end. In it she placed plastic sacks containing food, clothing, and a few other possessions. She carried no cooking utensils. Occasionally she would find food at shelters and would eat it as is or cook it with whatever cooking utensils she found at the shelter. She carried no sleeping bag, but did carry a blanket and sweater. She fashioned a long rain cape from some plastic material she found at a shelter. The cape served as both a garment and as a shelter at night providing warmth and protection from the rain. Her pack rarely if ever exceeded 17 lbs. She boasted that she was the only one of the through hikers of the Trail that really roughed it, and she was probably right. She lacked most of the pieces of equipment that hikers consider absolutely essential, but she possessed that one ingredient "Desire" in such full measure that she never really needed the other things.

Edward B. Garvey

Mrs. Genevieve Hutchinson: Mrs. Hutchinson, whose picture appears in Chapter 11 under the date of July 27, died on Feb. 6, 1974, at the age of 90. Mrs. Hutchinson did not participate in the formation of prominent organizations as did Mr. MacKaye; nor did she hike the AT three times as did Mrs. Gatewood, rather she achieved fame for being the No. 1 hostess for Appalachian Trail hikers over a 35-year period. The tradition for hospitality which she established at the big frame house (which at one time was a stage coach stop on the old Boston-Albany post road) is still being carried on, both by her daughter Mrs. Elmer Allen (who lives across the road from the former Hutchinson home) and by Midge Tufts, who lives in a log cabin near the October Mountain lean-to.

STUPIDIOS

During the years 1948-1951 I undertook the designing and building of a block and brick home which eventually, with breezeway and double garage, extended to a length of exactly 100 feet. I received tremendous help from my then 18-year-old brother Jerry and later from my wife Mary on the lighter jobs. Since it was a first time effort, we made more than our share of mistakes—some of them errors of judgment, some errors of clumsiness. However, we never owned up to any of these errors, attributing all of them to a fictional character we invented whose name was J. Herman Stupidio. In time any simple act of clumsiness came to be called a "stupidio." So it was that on my 2,000-mile hike I was guilty of some of these same stupidios. These are recounted in Chap. 11 such as finding and carrying for 500 miles some freeze dry foods; or leaving a shelter, hiking for two hours, and finding myself back at the same shelter from which I had begun hiking. Even the act of getting lost on May 14 in southwest Virginia, separated from the shelter and my pack overnight, was not an act that was an example of mental brillance. I recounted these acts with some apprehension fearing that their disclosure would make my readers write me off as an incompetent. My fears were groundless. The readers loved it. They seemed to say, "Hey . . . here's a guy that's able to walk the entire Appalachian Trail and he admits to making the same stupid mistakes that we do!" They felt that I was not talking down to them but sharing my experiences with them. Emboldened by my success in describing the aforementioned stupidios, I will now describe two more and give the reader just a hint of the third one.

View toward White Mountains of New Hampshire July 1974. (Photo: Don Fortunato)

The genes that I inherited from my forebears included very few of the mechanical aptitude type. When I resumed hiking on June 6 after my first break, I was carrying a cook kit sold by Gerry of Denver, Colorado. It had a metal gripper that could be used on any pot. The gripper had a round ring on the end of the handle that proved to be nothing but an annoyance as I tried to get a good grip on one of my cooking pots. I assumed the ring was intended for locking the two handles together when the cook kit was being carried in the pack. When I reached central Pennsylvania, I was met one evening by a group from the Blue Mountain Eagle Hiking Club. While I was in the shelter, I overheard the group discussing my cooking equipment. One of them said, "This is a nice cook kit that Garvey's got. Look at this metal gripper. It has a metal ring on the handle that you can lock in place so that it becomes almost like a permanent handle on any cooking pot you're working with." Aha I thought. So that's what that ring is for. But I said nothing to my visitors. But from that point on the metal ring was used in the manner that it was intended to be used.

At Delaware Water Gap, PA, I received my new Kelty pack and I noticed that it had two cord loops near the top of the pack. I had to assume that the two loops were there for a purpose but what purpose? A few days later I began hiking with Gary Rutherford who had a pack similar to mine. I noticed that when he finished stowing all his gear into his pack he would tighten the draw strings and then bring the dangling strings up to the top of the pack and slip the knotted end of each through those cord loops. I followed suit in a business like manner that I hoped would convince Gary that I knew exactly what I was doing.

The third incident occurred on the Bigelow Range in Maine. It was really an experiment . . . conceived in haste . . . regretted for a full day. In the course of writing this revision I related the incident to my daughter Sharon and asked her advice. She considered it for a long moment and then said "Dad, I've known you for 23 years and I've had time to adjust. But I'm afraid your readers are not quite ready for that one yet. I'd leave it out." And so, I think I will leave that incident for the next revision of this book. By that time I will be about 70 years of age and it will make little difference if people question my sanity.

THE 2,000 MILERS—CLASS OF 1976
COST OF HIKING THE ENTIRE TRAIL

There were 40 items in the questionnaire and some items had several parts. Questions were asked as to type of equipment used, adequacy of overnight accommodations, adequacy of guide books and other informational literature, total cost of trip, etc. A few of the hikers completed the questionnaire in the briefest manner possible but the majority elaborated upon their answers on the back of the forms or in separate letters. It was this extra information that really provided an insight as to the type of experience enjoyed by each hiker. The completed questionnaires are really fascinating. I, and a few others to whom I have loaned them, have spent hours poring over them. Some day, when time and ambition are simultaneously available in proper quantities, I will make an orderly tabulation of the answers. Now, however, I have used the questionnaires to obtain just one vital piece of information.

Cost of Hiking the Entire Trail

On my own hike, I maintained detailed daily records of expenses incurred and recorded them on my daily log form (see page 152). Like other through hikers, I had the expense of getting to the starting point in Georgia and the expense of getting home from Katahdin in Maine. Further, I had two breaks during my hike which entailed additional transportation expense. I also used my Volkswagen Camper for eight days of shuttle service from June 6-13. Despite these additional expenses, the total cost of my 158 days on the Trail came to only $768. But that was in 1970 and costs of food, lodging, and transportation have all risen sharply since then. In reviewing the 47 questionnaires I pulled off three pieces of information: (1) total days on trail (2) daily cost of food including restaurant meals and (3) total cost of trip including transportation, food, lodging, restaurant meals. Remember that these are 1976 cost figures. If you are planning your hike for the 1980 hiking season, you will need to make adjustment for the cost of living increases which may have (WILL HAVE) occurred since 1976.

There were six of the 47 hikers who finished the hike in 120 days or less, There were four (the lucky ones!) who enjoyed leisurely trips of over 180 days (6 months or more). The great majority spent from 121 to 179 days on the Trail—over 4 months, less than 6 months. Avoiding the extremes, the questionnaires show that average daily food costs (including restaurant meals) to be in the $2.50 to $4.00 range and the total trip costs to be in the $600 to $900 range. Ten people had total costs exceeding $1200 and just four hikers whose total expenses did not exceed $400.

One of those whose food cost figures I was especially interested in was Mike LaRouche of Fitchburg, Mass. I met Mike at one of the shelters in North Carolina in April 1976 and he informed me of the extensive food preparations he had made for the hike. He had purchased 50 lbs. of peanuts, 20 lbs. of flour, 10 lbs. oatmeal, 12 lbs. of honey, etc. He spent much time preparing and packaging these foods and had boxes of them sent to him at various post office stops along the Trail. The average cost of his prepared foods come to 39¢ per meal. When he added in cost of postage, cooking fuel, restaurant meals, fresh fruits purchased it brought the cost up to 57¢ per meal or about $1.70 per day. Interesting LaRouche statistic—he used an Optimus alcohol stove—and for the 157 days he spent on the Trail, he used a total of 5 gallons of alcohol, (cooking fuel alcohol that is!) at a total cost of $12. Even an economy minded housewife could make no complaints on those costs.

What do all these cost figures show? That those who are really pinched for money can make the long hike if they can discipline themselves to simple foods and do not use motels or hotels for overnight lodging. The questionnaires also show that most hikers succumb to the desire to live it up now and then—to buy a good restaurant meal and to occasionally sleep between clean sheets. So, while you *can* live the Spartan life for the 150 or so days you will be on the Trail, and you *can* get by for a total expenditure of $400, the chances are you will do like most of the 2,000 Milers of 1976 and you will wind up spending something more like $700 to $800.

Observations and Impressions

The comments from just a few of the 1976 "2000 Milers" plus those from a few hikers of earlier years are included in this section. For those who really wish to become familiar with the experience of others, there is the two volume "Hiking the Appalachian Trail," 2,000 pages, over 100 color photos. It is published by Rodale Press, edited by James R. Hare (with much assistance from a 2,000 Miler by the name of Charles Konopa) and available in many libraries. It contains the experiences of 46 people who have hiked the entire Trail.

June Parsons Gallagher, Texarkana, Texas on food, "I had prepared about 150 lbs. of pemmican and baked 58 2½ lb. fruit cakes and made about 25 lbs. of beef jerky before starting the Trail. Had this food mailed to us in 15 food pickups at post offices."

Author's comment—"WOW! How the Lewis and Clark expedition could have used Mrs. Gallagher's talents!"

Ron Keal, Vine Grove, Ky. on dogs, "I had many problems with dogs. Other hikers agree that dogs are a major problem. A dog bit me in New York, and I had to stop hiking for about 8 days. I suggest that ALL hikers carry a canaster of HALT, the same thing that postmen carry to defend themselves against dogs. A severe dog bite could ruin a trip. It almost caused me to quit my hike."

Dr. Edward B. Selby, Jr. on cost of the long hike, "the major 'cost' to fully employed persons in their productive years is the normal income that they would have to forego while hiking for close to five months. Also, persons in that category would have many expenses that would continue even while on the Trail—car payments, house payments, insurance, food and clothing for the family left at home, etc. Some measure would also need to be made of the loss of seniority, advancement opportunities, or even the loss of job itself. These reasons I believe go far in explaining why most all of the through hikers doing the Trail in one year are the young and the retired. The opportunity costs and continuing expenses for these groups are the lowest of all."

Author's comment, I wrote to Dr. Selby commenting that "I have many times found myself making the same kind of evaluations as you set forth only to become irritated at myself for doing so. One can set a dollar value on the minus features (loss of income, expenses incurred) but not on the plus features (better health, happier outlook, friendships made, etc.)."

Roger Leavitt, New Vernon, NJ on hiking boots, "but hikers must make sure their boots are big enough, because their feet are going to get swollen throughout the trip."

Tom Ridley, Murfreesboro, Tenn. commenting in the questionnaire as to an 18-year-old female hiking the Trail alone, "Anyone,

Sign marking a bridge on Long Trail, Vermont July 1974. (Photo: Don Fortunato)

short of a wheel chair victim, can walk the AT provided one has enough time. The Trail is a lot safer than walking the streets."

Gary Spanovich, Miami, FL on the New England insect problem in early summer, "We started in Maine (May 8) mainly because we had never been to the state. After canoeing the swamps of Florida, I couldn't imagine insects being that bad in Maine. I, however, was dead wrong. The swarms of black flies we experienced in Maine and N.H. and to a lesser extent down through the rest of New England were the worst exposure to insects I have ever experienced."

Miss Carole Flint, age 23, Kent, England hiked a big chunk of the Trail in 1974 and came back to the USA to finish her hike in 1976. She too completed one of the questionnaires and with it she sent this beautiful letter, "The Trail system in the USA is excellent for backpackers. In England we have nothing to compare with such "organized" hiking. We have only 8 Long Distance footpaths, most of which are not well marked and we have no shelters at all. For the inexperienced backpacker, the Trail is easy to follow and use, and enables most people, regardless of age or physical ability, to gain enjoyment from mountain walking.

I was very impressed with the system of trail shelters and also how well the trails were marked considering their use and access-ability. I would very much like to see a similar system in Britain.

I was amazed by the length and the challenge of the Appalachian Trail when I first heard of it and it kindled an interest which grew until I was able to hike it. The experience I gained can never be forgotten and can only be remembered with the greatest pleasure and I sincerely thank all those Americans who have made the Trail as enjoyable and as challenging as it is.

When I think about the Trail, I remember the other hikers and the people I met on the way. My impression of American people grew when I lived in the mountains with such kind, understanding, yet fun-loving people. I felt that US Hikers must be race apart, until I found the same friendliness, interest, and generosity in the people in the towns by the Trail. It was a pleasure to be with them.

My only complaint is that the AT is not long enough! I never wanted to finish it, even though the joy of reaching Katahdin was unsurpassed, I wanted the Trail to go on and on, so I would never have to leave such an idyllic life. Reality hits us all though so

Katahdin was reached and the AT was ended, leaving me with a wonderful experience accomplished, an address book full of much loved friends and an understanding of the mountains and the people of America.

In 1972, 25-year-old Jill Davenport, a New York City girl who had never backpacked before, began hiking the AT at Springer Mounter, GA. Some seven weeks and 600 miles later, discouraged by loneliness and continuous rains, she left the Trail just north of Roanoke, VA. A month later, back in New York City, she wrote a long letter regarding her experiences. One part of that letter is quoted, "When I began my hike, I was a total raw novice, never having hefted a pack or built a campfire in my life. Now I'm an experienced woodswoman and have certainly seen just about everything, bear, rattlers, wild pigs, skunks, spiders, and other frightening beasts which are only frightening if you've never faced 'em. I grew healthy, brown, and thin, experienced the best of all possible feelings, confidence in my self-sufficiency. Really I mean this. The hike was the best thing I ever did in my life. I kept a thorough, vivid journal of my travels and have been working on it since I got back, trying to feel out some shape and form. It seems to be developing into a book and I just hope that I might be as successful as you were in finding an interested publisher."

Jill returned to the Trail in 1974, finished hiking it, and in the course of so doing, met another 2,000 Miler, Bert Gilbert, married him, and in 1977 they became proud parents of a baby girl.

The last item to be quoted is a paragraph from a letter written by 61-year-old Jim Maddox of Black Mountain, NC, who hiked the Trail in 1973. Writing from the Travel Town Motel in Roanoke, VA., Jim observed that,

"Most of the people hiking the Trail this year are young men from 20 to 30 years of age although occasionally there are two women hiking together or very occasionally there is a man and wife hiking together. Some are merely logging so many miles per day but most seem to be drinking in the beauty that keeps unfolding before their eyes. Many seem to be seeking something that they have failed to find in their routine of life. However as a whole I find this group to be as fine a group of people as I have ever met anywhere. There seems to be a spirit of camaraderie among trail hikers that bridges the generation gap."

Chris Wile on a hike in the Green Mountains. (Photo: Don Fortunato)

The feeling of satisfaction, exuberance, even sheer joy as expressed by the Carole Flints, the Jill Davenports, the Jim Maddox's are, I am convinced, a permanent part of the makeup of any person who has hiked the entire Trail. The experience also evoked in me a feeling of tremendous wealth, especially in the spring, as I hiked through some of the national forests and national parks, a new season in the making, birds returning, trees and plants leafing out, the knowledge that I was walking on public land, my land, as a citizen, these tremendous acreages of the finest forest land in the eastern United States. This feeling of wealth was expressed so nicely by Henry David Thoreau over a century ago. Living in a simple cabin near Walden Pond, he wrote in his journal of occasional mornings on Walden Pond—days when he would paddle out to the middle of the Pond and then let the wind and waves take him to whatever part of the shore they wished. Thoreau described these times as

"days when idleness was the most attractive and productive industry. Many a forenoon have I stolen away preferring to spend thus the most valued part of the day; *for I was rich, if not in money, in sunny hours and summer days, and spent them lavishly;* nor do I regret that I did not waste more of them in the workshop or the teacher's desk." (italics added)

(From the book *Walden,* published 1946 by Vail-Ballou Press Inc.)

The long hike affected me in other ways. Inasmuch as I took two breaks of almost two weeks each, it meant that I had to hustle, hustle, hustle if I was going to reach Katahdin before bad weather set in. As a result, my stride is much quicker than before the hike began. Even now it is difficult for me to slow down to keep pace with people who walk more slowly. I've always been somewhat of an early riser, but again that feeling that I must get up at the crack of dawn, break camp, and get going, still persists. I no longer observe the daily ritual of a detailed reading of the newspaper. After all I went without it for over five months in 1970 and I realized that much of what I had been reading was not that essential. I became more tolerant of a lot of things, of the food that I ate, of the shelter I slept in, yes, even more tolerant of dirt! I think all the 2,000 Milers become a little more philosophical about life—like the Graymoor Friar's philosophy—"I'd Pick More Daisies" quoted on page 135.

CONCLUSION

Despite the exasperatingly slow pace at which the Department of the Interior is moving to protect the Appalachian Trail, despite the fact that the Trail is not marked as well as it should be, and despite the fact that much work needs to be done to improve the trailside shelter situation—despite all these things, and possibly a few more, the Appalachian Trail offers a superlative outdoor adventure to millions of Americans and Canadians who live within a single day's automobile drive of the 2,000 mile long Trail. To those who will hike the Trail for a few days or a few weeks, I wish you happy hiking. May the skies be sunny, the springs full and the shelters clean and dry. For the comparatively few who have the time and the stamina to hike the entire Trail, I say "Welcome to the Club!" I know that for them, as well as for myself, it will be "The Adventure of a Lifetime!"

AT 2,000-Miler Plaque awarded to Garvey.

AT in southwestern Maine.

Appendix 1

Sources of Information on Hiking and Backpacking and Publications for Hiking the Appalachian Trail

General

Backpacking One Step at a Time, Harvey Manning, 1975, Vintage Books.

Movin' Out, Harry N. Roberts, 1975, Stonewall Press.
Roberts is experienced in the eastern outdoors; expert coverage on equipment.

The New Complete Walker, Colin Fletcher, 1978, Alfred A. Knopf.

Backpacking, R. D. Rethmel, Burgess Publishing Co., rev. 1974.

Hikers Guide to the Smokies, Sierra Club Totebook, 1973.

Backpacking for Fun, Thomas Winnett, Wilderness Press, 1972.

Hiking Trails in the Mid Atlantic States, by Ed Garvey, Contempory Press, Chicago, Il.

Specific Books and Publications on the Appalachian Trail

Hiking the Appalachian Trail, edited by James R. Hare, Rodale Press, 1975; 2007 pages, 2 volumes, 131 color pictures. Describes the experiences of 46 people who have hiked the entire 2,000 mile Appalachian Trail. Contains a bibliography of 140 books and also contains 22 pages showing elevations of all important points along the AT.

The Appalachian Trail, Ronald M. Fisher, National Geographic Society, 1972.

Reproduced below is the 1978 price list of books, maps, trail guides, and other items available from the Appalachian Trail Conference, Harpers Ferry, WV 25425. If ordering after 1978, write or telephone for current price list (Telephone (304) 535-6331).

ATC PRICE LIST—1978

Item No.	How Many	Name of item	Retail Price	Member Price	Total Price
		GUIDES TO THE APPALACHIAN TRAIL (including maps)			
101		Maine, 1975 8th Edition	8.00	6.80	
102		New Hampshire and Vermont, 1968 2nd Edition	5.83	5.00	
103		Massachusetts and Connecticut, 1977 4th Edition	5.50	4.67	
104		New York and New Jersey, 1977 8th Edition	4.95	4.21	
105		Pennsylvania, 1977 4th Edition	9.25	7.85	
106		Susquehanna River to Shenandoah National Park, 1974 9th Edition	8.15	6.93	
107		Shenandoah National Park, 1977 8th Edition	8.70	7.40	
108		Central and Southwestern Virginia, 1974 7th Edition	6.10	5.20	
109		Tennessee and North Carolina: Cherokee, Pisgah and Great Smokies, 1976 5th Edition	6.70	5.70	
110		The Great Smokies, the Nantahalas and Georgia, 1973 5th Edition	6.70	5.70	
		PATCHES			
201		AT Shoulder Patch, circular, 3" diameter. 'Maine to Georgia'	1.00	.85	
202		Rockers 'Member ATC' (for members only)		.50	
203		2,000 miler rocker (for those who have completed the Trail)	.60	.50	
		MAGAZINE			
301		Appalachian Trailway News (bi-monthly, except July) Includes Newsletters and Relocations	5.00		
302		Current Issue, single copy	1.25		

303	Back Issues	5.00	4.00

MAPS

401	New York-New Jersey color map (included with NY-NJ Guide)	1.25	1.00

Following four maps are included with the Pennsylvania Guide No. 105
KTA 1, 2, 3 and 4: (Sold only as a set of four)

402-A	Pennsylvania: Delaware Water Gap	4.00	3.40

Following three maps are included with the Pennsylvania Guide No. 105
PATC 1, 2-3 and 4: and Susquehanna No. 106

406	Pennsylvania: Susquehanna to Cumberland Valley	1.25	1.00
407	Pennsylvania: Cumberland Valley to Caledonia Park	1.25	1.00
408	Pennsylvania: Caledonia Park to Pen-mar	1.25	1.00

Following three maps are included with the Susquehanna Guide No. 106
PATC 5-6, 7 and 8:

409	Maryland: northern and southern half	1.25	1.00
410	Northern Virginia: Harpers Ferry to Snickers Gap, Rt. 7 (northern half)	1.25	1.00
411	Virginia: Snickers Gap to Chester Gap, Rt. 522 (southern half)	1.25	1.00

Following three maps are included with the Shenandoah National Park Guide, No. 107
PATC 9, 10 and 11:

412	Virginia: Shenandoah National Park (northern section)	1.50	1.25
413	Shenandoah National Park (central section)	1.50	1.25
414	Shenandoah National Park (southern section)	1.50	1.25

BOOKLETS

502	The Appalachian Trail Conference History and Anthology (formerly ATC No. 5), 1976	1.50	1.25
503	A Manual of Trail Construction and Maintenance Techniques (formerly ATC No. 1)	1.50	1.25

No.			
504	Appalachian Trail Data Book (formerly Mileage Fact Sheet), 1977	3.00	2.55
505	Pennsylvania Hiking Trails	2.50	2.00
506	Circuit Hikes in the Shenandoah National Park	2.00	1.60
507	100 Favorite Trails of the Great Smokies and the Carolina Blue Ridge	1.50	1.25
508	The Appalachian Trail Conference (formerly ATC No. 17) a brochure	.50	.42
BOOKS			
601	Backpacking Equipment: William Kemsley and the Editors of Backpacker Magazine	8.95	
602	Be Expert with Map and Compass: Bjorn Kjellstrom	6.95	
603	Medicine for Mountaineering: James A. Wilkerson	7.95	
604	Mountaineering First Aid: Dick Mitchell	2.50	
605	Backpacking with Small Children: James & Ann Stout	6.95	
606	Winter Hiking and Camping: John Danielson	4.50	
607	Backpacking 'One Step at a Time': Harvey Manning	2.95	
609	Appalachian Trail—Wilderness on the Doorstep: Ann and Myron Sutton (Paperback)	3.95	
610	Hiking Trails in the Mid-Atlantic States: Ed Garvey	5.95	
611	Hiking Trails in the Northeast: Thomas A. Henley & Nessa Sweet	5.95	
612	Hiking Trails in the Mid-West: Jerry Sullivan & Glenda Daniel	5.95	
613	Hiking Trails in the Southern Mountains: Jerry Sullivan & Glenda Daniel	5.95	
614	The Appalachian Hiker: Ed Garvey	6.50	

* Member prices apply to current and new member applicants.

TOTAL

Postage & Handling (excluding contribution)

Special Handling

TOTAL AMOUNT ENCLOSED

Please allow 10 work days for ATC processing.
U.S. Dollars only, please. NO STAMPS, CASH or C.O.D.'s.
Prices subject to change without notice.

Appendix 2

Some Speciality Backpacking and Wilderness Camping Stores in the Eastern United States

These stores usually have a good to wide selection of packs and frames, tents, hiking boots, sleeping bags, trail foods, lightweight stoves and cooking equipment.

* Stores identified by an asterisk are 90 minutes or less by auto from the Appalachian Trail.

Maine

L. L. Bean
Main St.
Freeport, ME 04033
(207) 865-3111

*Hanson's
395 Main St.
Brewer, ME 04412
(207) 989-7250
55 miles from AT

New Hampshire

*Dartmouth Coop
Hanover, NH 03755
on AT
(603) 643-3100

*Stod Nichols, Inc.
Theatre Building
43-45 Main Street
Littleton, NH 03561
9 miles off the AT, Franconia
    Notch
(603) 444-5597

*Skimeister
Main Street
North Woodstock, NH 03262
(603) 745-2767

*EMS
Main Street
North Conway, NH 03860
(603) 356-5433

*IME
Box 494
Main Street
North Conway, NH 03860
(603) 356-5287

*Peter Limmer and Sons
Cobblers
Intervale, NH 03845

EMS
Vore Farm Road
Peterborough, NH 03458
(603) 924-7231

Vermont

Dakin Mountain Shop
227 Main Street
Burlington, VT 05401
(802) 864-4122

EMS
Dorsett Street
South Burlington, VT 05401
(802) 864-0473

*Ski Haus
Mountain Sports
Middlebury, VT 05753
(802) 388-2823

Massachusetts

Eastern Mountain Sports
1041 Commonweath Ave.
Boston, MA 02215
(617) 254-4250

Moor and Mountain
63 Park Street
Andover, MA 01810
(617) 475-3665

*Don Gleason's Camper Supply
9 Pearl Street
Northhampton, MA 01060
(about 1 hour from AT)
(413) 584-4895

EMS
1 Winthrop Square
Boston, MA 02108
(617) 482-4414

EMS
189 Linden Street
Wellesley, MA 02181
(617) 237-2645

*EMS
Rt. 9 Box 12
Amherst, MA 01002
(near AT, ½ hr.)
(413) 253-9504

Paddlers & Packers
1615 Riverdale Street
West Springfield, MA 01089
(413) 737-0267

Rhode Island

Summit Shop
185 Wayland Ave.
Providence, RI 02906
(401) 751-6166

Connecticut

Outdoor Traders
Main Street
Essex, CT 06426
(203) 869-7950

Outdoor Traders
79 East Putnam Ave.
Greenwich, CT 06830
(203) 869-7950

Outdoor Traders on-the-Green
Litchfield, CT 06759
(203) 567-8010

The Ski Hut, Inc.
15 Whitney Ave.
New Haven, CT 06510
(203) 236-0878

The Ski Hut, Inc.
Kieeler Building
Wilton, CT 06897
(203) 762-8324

Great World, Inc.
250 Farms Village Road
Box 250
South Simsberry, CT 06092

EMS
1 Civic Center Plaza
Hartford, CT 06103
(203) 278-7105

New York

EMS
725 Saw Mill River Road
Ardsley, NY 10502
(914) 693-6160

EMS
174 Glen Cove Road
Corle Place,
Long Island, NY 11514
(516) 747-7360

EMS
Lake Placid
Main St., Box 910
Lake Placid, NY 12946
(518) 523-2505

Camping Specialties
15 E. Main Street
Conton, NY 13617
(315) 386-8360

Liverpool Sports Center
125 1st Street
Liverpool, NY 13088
(315) 457-2290

*Rock and Snow
44 Main Street
New Paltz, NY 12561
(914) 255-1311

American Youth Hostels
132 Spring Street
New York, NY 10012
(212) 431-7100

Kreeger and Son
30 W. 46th Street
New York, 10036
(212) 575-7825

Eureka Camping Center
625 Conklin Rd.
Binghamton, NY 13902
(607) 723-4179

Paragon Sporting Goods
867 Broadway
New York, NY 10010
(212) 255-8036

Outdoor Outfitters
Box 56
New Hartford, NY 13413

Nippenose
3006 Erie Blvd.
Syracuse, NY 13224
(315) 446-3838

Nippenose
Dewitt Mall
215 N. Cayuga Street
Ithaca, NY 14850
(607) 272-6868

Nippenose
Stevens Square
81 State Street
Binghamton, NY 13901
(607) 724-4363

Nippenose
Parinton Hills Mall
Rt. 250 E31
Fairport, NY 14450

*Campus Center
635 White Plains Road
Tarrytown, NY 10591
(914) 631-0409

*EMS
1270 Niagara Falls Blvd.
Tonawanda, NY 14150
(716) 838-4200

Hansons Trail North
960 A Troy-Schenectady Rd.
Latham, NY 12110
(518) 785-0340

A.B.C. Sport Shop
185 Norris Drive
Rochester, NY 14610
(716) 271-4550

Inside Edge
624 Glen St.
Glens Falls, NY 12801
(518) 793-5677

New Jersey

The Nickel
354 Nassau Street
Princeton, NJ 08540
(609) 924-3001

The Nickel
150 Main Street
Flemington, NJ 08822
(201) 782-1600

J. D. Sachs
114 King's Highway East
Haddonfield, NJ 08033

Overall Outfitter
62 Rt. 22
Greenbrook, NJ 08812
(201) 968-4230

Hills and Trails
93 Brant Ave.
Clark, NJ 07066
(201) 574-1240

Wilderness Shop
9 West Mill Road (Rt. 513)
Long Valley, NJ 07853
(201) 876-4648

Delaware

Chestnut Hill Plaza
Newark, DE 19711
(302) 737-2521

Wicks
1201 Philadelphia Pike
Wilmington, DE 19809
(302) 798-1818

Pennsylvania

Base Camp
121 N. Mole St.
Philadelphia, PA 19102
(215) 567-1876

J. D. Sachs
880 W. Lancaster Ave.
Bryn Mawr, PA 19010
(215) 527-3616

J. S. Sachs
10 Penn Valley Dr.
Yardley, PA 19067
(215) 493-4536

James Cox
931 Lancaster Ave.
Bryn Mawr, PA 19010
(215) 525-3163

James Cox
23 State Road
Paoli, PA 19301
(215) 644-9325

*Pathfinder
Cedar Cliff Mall
1104 Carlisle Rd.
Camp Hill, PA 17011
(717) 761-3906
(15 Min. from AT)

Pathfinder
137 E. Beaver Ave.
State College, PA 16801
(814) 237-8086

Pathfinder
Station Mall
1109 9th Ave.
Altoona, PA 16601
(814) 943-4016

Wicks
403 Pottstown Pike
Exton, PA 19341
(215) 363-1893

Wicks
321 W. Woodland Ave.
Springfield, PA 19064
(215) KL 3-5445

Maryland

*Appalachian Outfitters-Baltimore
11400 York Road
Cockeysville, MD 21030
(301) 666-2721

*Appalachian Outfitters-Baltimore
8563 Baltimore National Pike
Ellicott City, MD 21043
(301) 465-7227

Appalachian Outfitters-D.C.
1910 Seminary Place
Silver Spring, MD 20910
(301) 587-5100

Hudson Bay Outfitters
10560 Metropolitan Ave.
Kensington, MD 20795
(301) 949-2515

Hudson Bay Outfitters
315 East Diamond Ave.
Gaithersburg, MD 20760
(301) 948-2474

The Ridge Runner
10431 Stevenson Road
Pikesville, MD
(301) 486-6088

H and H Surplus
424 N. Eutaw St.
Baltimore, MD 21201
(301) 752-2580

West Virginia

Pathfinder of W. Va.
2910 Grand Central Ave.
Vienna, WV
(304) 295-6062

Pathfinder of W.VA.
182 Willey Street
Morgantown, WV 26505
(304) 296-0076

Ohio

Appalachian Outfitters
951 Batavia Pike
Cincinnati, OH 45245
(513) 752-3032

Pathfinder of W.VA.
13 W. State Street
Athens, OH 45701
(614) 593-7129

Wilderness Outfitters
3962 Linden Ave.
Dayton, OH
(513) 257-5006

District of Columbia

Appalachian Outfitters
Box 249
2938 Chain Bridge Road
Oakton, VA 22124
(703) 281-4324

Appalachian Outfitters
1910 Seminary Place
Silver Spring, MD 20910
(301) 587-5100

Georgetown Mountain Sports
Canal Square
3110 M St., N.W.
Washington, D.C. 20007
(202) 965-4510

Eddie Bauer
1800 M St., N.W.
Washington, D.C. 20036
(202) 331-8009

Virginia

*Appalachian Outfitters
Box 249
2938 Chain Bridge Road
Oakton, VA 22124
(703) 281-4324
(90 min. from AT)

*Appalachian Outfitters
Rt 3 Box 7A
Logan's Barn
Salem, VA 24152
(703) 389-1056
(15 driving min. from AT)

Alpine Outfitters
818 W. Grace St.
Richmond, VA 23220
(804) 358-2101

Alpine Outfitters
11010 Midlothian Turnpike
Richmond, VA 23235

*Blue Ridge Mountain Sports
1417 Emmet Street
Charlottesville, VA 22901
(804) 977-4400
(30 driving min. from AT)

Blue Ridge Mountain Sports
881 N. Military Highway
Norfolk, VA 23502
(804) 461-2767

*Blue Ridge Mountain Sports
Forest Hills Shopping Center
2844 Linkhorn Dr.
Lynchburg. VA 24503
(804) 384-9113
(40 min. from AT)

Hudson Bay Outfitters
9683 Lee Highway
Fairfax, VA 22030
(703) 591-2950

Wilderness Center
Mount Vernon Plaza
Richmond Highway
Alexandria, VA
(703) 765-3615

North Carolina

Appalachian Outfitters
Box 4856
4240 Kernersville Rd.
Winston-Salem, NC 27107
(919) 784-7402

Appalachian Outfitters
2805 Hope Valley Road
Durham, NC 27707
(919) 489-1207

*Mountaineering South
344 Tunnel Rd.
Asheville, NC 28805
(704) 298-4532
(60 min. from AT)

*Footslogger
835 Faculty Street
Boone, NC
(704) 264-6565
(20 min. driving from AT)

Jesse Brown's
2843 Eastway Drive
Charlotte, NC 28205
(704) 568-2152

*Jesse Brown's
4369 S. Tryon St.
Charlotte, NC 28210
(704) 523-9094

East Coast Outdoor Sports
4403 Wrightsville Ave.
Wilmington, NC 28403
(919) 799-1114

Blue Ridge Mountain Sports
2805 Battleground Ave.
Greensboro, NC 27408
(919) 288-7477

Carolina Outdoor Sports
Lake Boone Shopping Center
2446 Wycliff Road
Raleigh, NC 27607
(919) 782-8288

*Nantahala Outdoor Center
Star Route Box 68
Bryson City, NC 27514
(704) 488-6404

Trail Shop
3114 Hillsboro Street
Raleigh, NC 27607

Carolina Outdoor Sports
844 W. Lee Street
Greensboro, NC 27403
(919) 274-1862

Tennessee

*Blue Ridge Mountain Sports
5201 Kingston Pike
Knoxville, TN 37919
(615) 584-9432
(40 min. from AT)

*Outdoor America
9110-C Executive Park Dr.
Cedar Bluff Shopping Center
Knoxville, TN 37919
(615) 693-5262
(60 min. from AT)

*Trek Mountain Sports
1010 Commonwealth Ave.
Bristol, VA 24201
(30 min. from AT)
(703) 669-1213

Camp and Hike
4674 Knight Arnold Road
Memphis, TN 38118
(901) 365-4511

Campers Corner
2050 Elvis Presley Blvd.
Memphis, TN 38106
(901) 946-2566

The Packrat
4004 Hillsboro Road
Nashville, TN 37215
(615) 297-0569

Kentucky

The Great Outdoors
3824 Wilmington Ave.
Louisville, KY 40207
(502) 895-7353

Sage, Inc.
209 E. High Street
Lexington, KY 40507
(606) 255-1547

South Carolina

*Wilderness Outfitters
Wade Hampton Mall
Greenville, SC
(803) 233-4035

Georgia

*High Country, Inc.
1544 Piedmont Ave.
Atlanta, GA 30324
(404) 874-5821

*High Country, Inc.
6300 Powers Ferry Road, N.W.
Atlanta, GA 30339
(404) 955-1866

*High Country, Inc.
2138 Henderson Mill Road, N.E.
Atlanta, GA 30345
(404) 491-8217

*American Adventures
6300 Powers Ferry Rd., N.W.
Atlanta, GA 993-9644

Georgia Outdoors
1945 S. Candler Road
Decatur, GA 30032
(404) 289-9717

*Blue Ridge Mountain Sports
Lenox Square Shopping Center
3393 Peach Tree Road, N.E.
Atlanta, GA 30326
(404) 266-8372

Wilderness Southeast
133 Montgomery Crossroads
Savannah, GA 31406
(912) 927-2071

Charbon Outfitters
257 W. Broad Street
Athens, GA
(404) 548-7225

Florida

Trail Shop
1421 University Blvd. North
Jacksonville, FL 32211
(904) 744-2292

Trail Shop
206 West College Ave.
Tallahassee, FL 32303
(904) 222-5608

Trail Shop
1518 NW 13th Street
Gainesville, FL 32601
(904) 372-0521

Wilderness Shop
1426 Lake Drive, Box 3325
Cocoa Beach, FL 32922
(305) 632-3070

Bill Jacksons
1120 4th St. South
St. Petersburg, FL
(813) 896-8636

Campers Gear
1935 1st Ave. South
St. Petersburg, FL 33712
(813) 822-7592

Campers Paradise
9735 N.W. 27th Ave.
Miami, FL 33147
(305) 696-1693

Allon's
3448 W. University Ave.
Gainesville, FL 32607
(904) 373-9233

South Face Wilderness
609 South Federal Highway
Ft. Lauderdale, FL 33301
(305) 463-6489

The Challenge Shop
115 Candace Drive
Maitland, FL 33301
(305) 831-7449

Major Manufacturers from Whom Cataloges May be Obtained

North Face
1234 5th Street
Berkeley, CA 94710

Sierra Designs
4th and Addison
Berkeley, CA 94710

Kelty Pack
Box 639
Sun Valley, CA 94710

Lowe Alpine Systems, Inc.
Box 189
Lafayette, CO 80026

Camp Trails
Dept. OB, Box 23155
Phoenix, AZ 85063

Woolrich
Woolrich, PA 17779

Alpenlite
Box 851
Claremont, CA 91711

Cannondale
35 Pulaski Street
Stamford, CT 06902

Pivetta Boots Corp.
2110 5th St.
Donner Mountain
Berkeley, CA 94710

Frostline
452 Burbank
Bloomfield, CO 80020

Vasque
113 Main Street
Red Wing. MN 55066

Coleman Peak
250 N. Francis
Wichita, KA 62201

Eureka Tent
625 Conklin Road, Box 966
Binghamton, NY 13902

Danner Boots
110 SE 82nd St.
Portland, OR 97216

Jansport
Paine Field Industrial Park
Everett, WA 98204

Stephenson Warmlite
RFD 4 Box 398
Gilford, NH 03246

Fabiano
Dept. A-3
850 Summer Street
S. Boston, MA 02127

Bishops
Box 4
Oakton, VA 22124
(703) 281-4576

Camp 7—Calico Kits
802 S. Sherman
Longmont, CO 80501

Optimus Stoves
Box 4147
Fullerton, CA 92634

Mountain Safety Research
631 S. 96th Street
Seattle, WA 98108

Pacific Ascenté
Box 2028
Fresno, CA 93718

Silva Compasses
2466 N. State Road 39
Lazate, AZ 46350

Trailwise
1615 University Ave.
Berkeley, CA 94703

Food Suppliers

Mountain House/Tea Kettle
Oregon Freeze Dry Foods
Box 1048
Albany, OR 97321
(503) 926-6001

Natural Food Backpack Dinners
Box 532
Corvalis, OR 97330

Richmoor Foods
Box 2728
Van Nuys, CA 91401

Stowaway Foods
166 King St. (Cushing Hwy.)
Cohasset, MA 02025
(617) 383-9116

Perma-Pak Camplite Foods
40 E. 2430th, South
Salt Lake City, UT 84115

Appendix 3
MILEAGE FACT SHEETS
Preface

The fact sheets are provided as an adjunct to the guide books and not as a substitute. The fact sheets will be useful in planning a trip of a few days, a few weeks, or a 2,000-mile trip of the entire Trail. For details as to locations of water source, for nearby points of interest off the Trail, for the exact location for overnight shelters, for capacity of shelters, and for many other things the hiker will need to use the guidebooks.

All distances shown on these fact sheets are the distances from south to north, starting at Springer Mountain, the southern terminus of the Trail.

Hikers finding errors or omissions in these fact sheets are urged to contact the Applachian Trail Conference promptly, giving as much detail as necessary so that the pertinent fact sheet may be immediately corrected.

To conserve space symbols are used on the fact sheets to designate such things as shelters, cabins, camp grounds, etc. The symbols used and the meaning of each follows:

C —Locked Cabin. For Virginia, Maryland, and Pennsylvania cabins, contact Potomac Appalachian Trail Club, 1718 N St. NW, Washington, D.C. 20036. For Vermont and New Hampshire cabins, contact Dartmouth Outing Club, 22 Robinson Hall, Hanover, N.H. 03755.

CG —Camp Ground. A developed site generally with tables, water, toilet facilities.

CS —Undeveloped Campsite . . . has water, usually nothing else.

G —Groceries.

L —Lodging as in a motel, hotel or private home.

LT —Lean-to, an open faced shelter. Some have wooden floors and bunks, some only wire bunks, and others no bunks or floors.

M —Meals, as in restaurants.

m —Miles.

n, s, e, w, r, and l—Directions.

NW—No water supply. Non-existent, unreliable or unsafe. Refer to guide book for details.

S —Shelter. A four-sided but unlocked shelter for housing hikers overnight.

PO —Post Office. Always shown with the 5 digit zip code.

Where such things as grocery stores and post offices are located away from the Trail, the direction and distance will be shown, e.g., "G 2.3 m. l." meaning a grocery store will be found 2.3 miles to the left of the Trail.

Separate copies of these fact sheets or later revisions thereof may be purchased from Appalachian Books, Box 249, Oakton, VA 22124.

Copies of the Appalachian Trail Data Book may be purchased from the Appalachian Trail Conference, Box 236, Harpers Ferry, West Virginia 25425.

HISTORY OF THE MILEAGE FACT SHEETS

Early in 1970, Mr. Maurice A. Crews (now living in Southwest Harbor, Maine) reviewed the ten Appalachian Trail guide books and typed up copies of a list of significant points along the Trail (trailside shelters, grocery resupply points, and highway crossings). The mileage points were listed in cumulative fashion, beginning with a zero point at Springer Mountain in Georgia, and reaching a mileage of slightly over 2,000 at Baxter Peak on Katahdin in Maine. These sheets were made in preparation for the scheduled 1970 Crews-Garvey hike of the Trail. Mr. Crews was unable to make the hike but I used his fact sheets extensively throughout my hike, making many corrections and additions to them based on my on-the-Trail observations. After the completion of my hike in October 1970, Mr. Crews and I further revised the fact sheets and early in 1971 we made them available to Col. Lester L. Holmes, then Executive Director of the Appalachian Trail Conference. The mileage fact sheets were made available to the public in 1971, both as a separate publication of the Conference and by Appalachian Books as an appendix to the book Appalachian Hiker.

From 1971 through June 1975, the demanding and laborious task of correcting and reissuing the fact sheets became a personal project of Col. Holmes. Had it not been for his perseverance and championing of the fact sheets concept, they would probably have ceased to exist. After 1975 the Publication Committee of the Conference assumed the responsibility and in 1977 issued a completely new book entitled *The Appalachian Trail Data Book.* The new book was prepared on a north to south basis, had many more points of interest, and contained eight columns of figures, both in mileages and in kilometers.

For this revision of Appalachian Hiker, I have reverted to the south to north concept as that is the direction in which most long distance hikers travel. To make the fact sheets more simple, I have eliminated many of the points of interest shown in the AT Data Book and I have shown but a single column of mileages (no kilometers . . . yet!). Those who desire the additional information are urged to purchase the more complete AT Data Book.

These fact sheets were prepared in March 1978, using the mileage distances as shown in the 1977 AT Data Book. Copies of the fact sheets were then sent for review and correction to knowledgeable Trail people and to maintaining clubs and government agencies. The fact sheets as contained in this appendix are as accurate as we could make them as of April 1978. It must be realized by users of these sheets that they will never be completely accurate. Even if 100 percent accurate at time of going to press (a very unlikely assumption!), they will have some inaccuracies by the time they reach the user. The Trail is a constantly changing thing—relocations are made, shelters removed, new shelters erected. The prudent hiker will obtain the most up-to-date Data Book or Mileage Fact Sheets that he can, and will update the information thus obtained by reviewing current issues of *Appalachian Trailway News* and by querying other hikers as to changes which may have occurred.

I am indebted to many long distance hikers who have furnished me information as to Trail changes and as to off-the-Trail facilities such as restaurants and inexpensive places of lodging. I am particularly indebted to Warren E. Doyle of the Eastern State Connecticut College, University of Connecticut, who has hiked the Trail on a south to north basis on three occasions and who made available to me his extensive notes. And all of us are indebted to that army of volunteers who maintain the Trail, who carefully measure the distances, and who provide detailed descriptions of it, thereby making possible the issuance of guide books and mileage fact sheets such as these.

Edward B. Garvey, 1978

APPROACHES TO THE APPALACHIAN TRAIL IN
GEORGIA AND MAINE

Most of the 2,000 Milers begin their hike down in Georgia. The Georgia Appalachian Trail Club, P.O. Box 654, Atlanta, GA 30301 receives so many inquires that it has prepared a handout which is quoted below. The information shown was accurate as of 1978. Those desiring more current information in later years may write directly to the Club. Sending a stamped self-addressed envelope is most helpful. In addition to the quoted information below, I have talked to a number of through hikers who, upon arriving at the Atlanta airport, have bargained with a cab driver at the airport for a firm price for a trip direct to the Amicalola Falls State Park. Allow yourself a full day of strenuous hiking to get from the Visitor Center at the Park to the top of Springer Mountain.

TRANSPORTATION INFORMATION TO GEORGIA
APPALACHIAN TRAIL

While the southern terminus of the Trail is at Springer Mountain, it is necessary to hike to that terminus from either Big Stamp Gap (which is located on a forest service road north of Springer Mountain) or from Nimblewall Gap via the blue blazed approach trail which leads from Amicalola Falls State Park (which is to the south of Springer Mountain). The most popular approach for through hikers is to start at Amicalola Falls State Park. Public transportation via Greyhound Bus Line is available from Atlanta, Georgia, as shown below:

Depart Atlanta	Arrive Gainesville
7:30 a.m.	9:15 a.m. daily
1:15 p.m.	2:42 p.m. daily
5:00 p.m.	7:05 p.m. daily except Saturdays, Sundays and holidays
5:30 p.m.	7:35 p.m. daily except Saturdays, Sundays and holidays
6:30 p.m.	8:15 p.m. Saturdays only
10:00 p.m.	11:15 p.m. daily

One-way fare is $3.70, including tax.

From Gainesville, Veteran's Cab will take you to Amicalola Falls for $20.00 (no extra charge for one additional passenger). Call 534-5355 for 24-hour service. A phone is available at the Greyhound

Terminal in Gainesville or, with some advance notice, Lance Holland will take you to or from the Falls for $15. Lance will also shuttle cars and deliver hikers to other points on the Trail. Write or call Lance Holland, Star Route, Dawsonville, Georgia 30534, phone 404/265-3714 for further details.

If you have a ride to Dahlonega, transportation to Amicalola Falls is available at the L. C. Poore Union 76 Service Station on the town square (phone 404/864-3304 days or 404/864-3363 nights, 12 to 24 hours in advance). Transportation from the Poore Station is also available to and from other points on the AT in Georgia.

Please note that hikers arriving at the Atlanta Airport may catch a city bus (MARTA #72) into Atlanta itself and by transfer (to MARTA #10) get to within a block or so of the Greyhound Station. The fare is $0.15, one way, including transfer. The buses do not run on a regular basis from the airport, but a call to the MARTA information office (404/522-4711) can give you the times closest to your arrival.

The above is subject to change and you should always double-check in advance.

Maine

Bangor, Maine is the city closest to Katahdin that is reachable by either air or bus. From Bangor, the hiker must negotiate his own transportation to Millinocket. There is taxi service from Bangor to Millinocket and from Millinocket to the Katahdin Stream Campground. Both in 1970 and in 1977, I stayed at the Millinocket Motel and in '77, we arranged with the motel owner to drive us out to the Katahdin Stream Campground which is the usual jumping off place to climb Baxter Peak, the exact northern terminal of the Trail.

MILEAGE FACT SHEET SUMMARY

This booklet is comprised of ten mileage fact sheets, each sheet corresponding to one of the ten guidebooks available from the Appalachian Trail Conference. A summary of the ten sheets on a south to north basis follows:

Sheet No.	Mileage	Area Covered	Cumulative Mileage
1	162.2	Georgia and North Carolina	162.2
2	274.9	North Carolina and Tennessee	437.1
3	352.6	Southern Virginia	789.7

4	106.6	Shenandoah National Park	896.3
5	172.2	Northern Virginia to	
		Southern Pennsylvania	1068.5
6	141.8	Pennsylvania	1210.3
7	155.9	New Jersey and New York	1366.2
8	139.3	Connecticut and Massachusetts	1505.5
9	292.9	Vermont and New Hampshire	1798.4
10	276.1	Maine	2074.5

MILEAGE FACT SHEET NO. 1

Extending from Springer Mountain, Georgia (0.0 miles) to Fontana Dam (Little Tennessee River) in North Carolina (162.2 miles).

Approach to Springer Mountain

Amicalola Falls St. Park Visitor Center	0.0 miles
Nimblewill Gap	6.5
Springer Mt.	8.8

MILE-
POINT

ITEM

0.0	Springer Mountain
0.1	Springer Mt. LT
3.2	Big Stamp Gap LT
9.6	Hawk Mt. LT
18.8	Gooch Gap LT
22.4	Woody Gap, Ga. Hwy. 60. PO: Suches, GA 30572 1.6 m. l.; G
31.1	Blood Mt. S (no water)
33.2	Neels Gap, US Rts 19 & 129; Snacks, freeze dry foods; water, fuel
38.9	Tesnatee Gap, Ga. Hwy. 349 (water 0.5 m. r.)
39.7	Whitley Gap LT (1.0 m. r. off trail)
44.2	Low Gap LT
51.0	Rocky Knob LT
53.8	Unicoi Gap, Ga. Hwy. 75 CG
58.4	Tray Gap, Tray Mt. Rd.
59.7	Montray LT 0.1 m. l.
65.0	Addis Gap LT 0.4 m. r.
70.4	Dicks Creek Gap, US Rt. 76 G 4.5 m. l.; Also stove fuel
74.7	Plumorchard Gap LT
79.1	Bly Gap, N.C.-Ga. Line

81.7   Muskrat LT
85.5   Deep Gap CG
86.0   Standing Indian LT
94.0   Carter Gap LT
100.4   Big Spring LT
105.6   Rock Gap LT
105.9   Rock Gap CG 1.5 m. l. (no water)
106.3   Wallace Gap, US Rt. 64; PO: Franklin, NC 28734; L; M; G;
        15 m. r.
113.2   Siler Bald LT 0.7 m. r. of Trail
115.1   Wayah Gap
122.5   Burningtown Gap   G; M; 3.5 m. l.; PO: Aquone, NC 28703
123.6   Cold Springs LT
127.2   Tellico Cap
131.6   Wesser Creek LT
134.6   US Rt. 19, Nantahala Outdoor Center   G: M: L: Laundry;
        Fr. Dry foods, fuel
140.5   Sassafras Gap LT
146.5   Stekoah Gap
155.0   Cable Gap LT
160.4   N.C. Hwy. 28, G; L; M; 2.0 m. l.; PO: Fontana Dam, NC 28733
162.2   Fontana Dam (Little Tennessee River)

Cumulative mileage from Springer Mountain, Georgia (southern terminal of the Trail) to Fontana Dam (Little Tennessee River)....162.2

MILEAGE FACT SHEET NO. 2

Extending from Fontana Dam (Little Tennessee River) in North Carolina to Damascus, Virginia. Total Distance 274.9 miles.

0.0   Fontana Dam (Little Tennessee River)
5.2   Birch Spring LT
9.7   Mollies Ridge LT
11.8   Russell Field LT
14.2   Spence Field LT (G in Cades Cove 1.5 m. l.)
20.2   Derrick Knob LT
25.6   Silers Bald LT
27.3   Double Springs Gap LT
30.1   Clingmans Dome
33.2   Mt. Collins LT
37.6   Newfound Gap, US Rt. 441

40.3	Boulevard Trail
40.6	Ice Water Spring LT
44.0	False Gap LT (scheduled for destruction in 1978)
47.9	Pecks Corner LT (LT is 0.4 m. to r.)
52.8	Tri-Corner Knob LT
60.5	Cosby Knob LT
67.5	Davenport Gap LT
68.4	Davenport Gap, Tenn. 32, NC 284 (G at Mt. Sterling Village, 1.5 m. r.)
70.3	Big Pigeon River (limited G, 2.25 m. r.)
71.0	Interstate 40
73.3	CS
78.2	Groundhog Creek LT
87.4	Lemon Gap, NC 1182, Tenn. 107 (Max Patch Road)
88.3	Walnut Mt. LT
92.5	CS
98.0	Deer Park Mt. LT
100.9	Hot Springs Hikers Hostel
101.2	Hot Springs, NC PO 28743; US Rts. 25 & 70, NC 209; M: G: L:
105.9	CS (Mill Ridge—Pond, 2 springs)
112.0	Spring Mt. LT
115.6	Allen Gap, Tenn. Rt. 70, NC Rt. 208 (G: 0.1 m. r.)
120.4	Little Laurel LT
127.0	Jerry Cabin LT
133.5	Locust Ridge LT
134.9	Devils Fork Gap, NC 212
137.3	CS
142.7	Sams Gap, NC Rt. 23 (Limited G: 2 m.r.)
151.0	Little Bald, CS 0.35 m. l.
154.3	Spivey Gap US 19W (CG 0.2 m. s.)
158.9	No Business Knob LT
164.5	Nolichucky River (M: L: G 1.5 m. r.) PO: Erwin, TN 37650
168.8	Curley Maple Gap LT
181.0	Cherry Gap LT
183.7	Iron Mt. Gap; Tenn. Rt. 107; NC Rt. 226; G 1.5 m. r.
188.6	Homestead LT; 0.2 m. n. of Trail
191.8	Hughes Gap
196.5	Carvers Gap (Roan Mtn.) Tenn. Rt. 143, NC Rt. 261
198.0	Grassy Ridge LT
199.3	Low Gap LT

204.6   Hump Mt.
207.1   US 19E; M; L; also at 1.5 m. r. is Elk Park, NC PO 28622;
         G: M: L
208.3   Sunset Orchard CS
216.7   Moreland Gap LT
224.1   Laurel Fork LT
231.9   Tenn. Hwy. 67 (G, M, L) Rat Branch
235.7   Watauga Dam Rd.
241.7   Vanderventer LT (water limited)
248.6   Iron Mt. LT
249.8   Nick Grindstaff Monument
253.2   Tenn. Hwy. 91
256.6   Double Spring LT
259.9   Low Gap, US 421
264.7   Abingdon Gap LT
271.2   Tenn.-Va. State Line
274.9   Damascus, VA, US Hwy. 58; M: G: L: PO 24236

Cumulative mileage from Springer Mt., GA (southern terminal of the
Trail) to Damascus, VA 437.1

MILEAGE FACT SHEET NO. 3

Extending from Damascus, Va. to the Shenandoah National Park
(352.6 miles)

  0.0   Damascus, VA, PO 24236 (M, G, L) US Hwy. 58 (Hiker check-
         point at Post Office)
  8.3   Taylors Valley (L)
 19.4   US Rt. 58, Summit Cut
 24.1   Whitetop Mountain
 27.0   Elk Garden (Va. Hwy. 600)
 29.0   Deep Gap LT
 30.5   Mt. Rogers (elev. 5,729—highest pt. in Va.)
 36.2   Old Orchard LT
 44.2   Hurricane and Grindstone Campground Trail
 46.5   Dickeys Gap (Va. Hwy. 16), G; M; 0.5 m. r.
 48.8   Raccoon Branch LT
 53.6   Teas, Va. (village)
 63.0   Glade Mt. LT
 67.2   US Route 11 (M; L)
 75.3   Big Walker LT (LT is 0.1 m. r.)

82.5	Monster Rock LT
83.5	US Rts. 21 & 52; Big Walker Lookout (M) fuel
93.0	Turkey Gap LT (r. 100 feet)
101.2	High Rock LT
104.7	Va. Hwy. 42; Crandon, VA (G) fuel
115.0	Wapiti LT (0.4 m. l. on blue bl. trail)
125.5	Doc's Knob LT
133.2	Pearisburg, VA, PO 24134; G; L; M
149.5	Pine Swamp LT
152.2	Interior (village), G 2.0 m. r.
153.8	Bailey Gap LT
161.8	War Branch LT
166.2	Big Pond LT
173.6	Va. Hwy. 42; G at Newport 0.2 m. r.
197.5	Trout Creek LT (0.5 m. r.)
208.5	St. Rt. 311, Catawba Mt.; (M) (Note: Emergency relocation on this area April '78—Details not available at time of publication)
209.6	Boy Scout LT; 0.1 m. r.
218.3	Lamberts Meadow LT
229.1	US Rt. 11, Cloverdale, VA, PO 24077 (G; M; L)
232.5	Fullhardt Knob LT
238.1	Wilson Creek LT
240.9	Black Horse Gap, F.S. Road 186
245.8	Bobblets Gap LT
248.3	Bearwallow Gap, Va. Hwy. 43
254.8	Middle Creek CG
263.1	Cornelius Creek LT, 0.1 m. r.
265.3	Parkers Gap Road, F.S. Rd. 812
267.3	Thunder Hill LT
271.7	Petites Gap For. Serv. Road 35
273.9	Marble Spring LT
279.3	Matts Creek LT
281.9	James River (US Rt. 501) (G 0.8 m. l.) PO Snowden, VA 24591
284.3	Johns Hollow LT
292.7	Punchbowl Spring LT
293.1	Blue Ridge Parkway; Punchbowl Mt. Crossing
301.1	Brown Mt. Creek LT
302.9	US Rt. 60; G 1.0 m. l.
308.8	Wiggins Spring LT (LT is 0.5 m. l.)

310.7   Salt Log Gap; Va. Sec. Rd. 634
317.0   Fish Hatchery Road
321.1   Crabtree Farm Road
322.1   Priest LT
327.4   Tye River, St. Hwy. 56; G 1.2 m. r.; PO Tyro, Va. 22976
329.5   Harpers Creek LT
335.5   Maupin Field LT
336.9   Reeds Gap; Va. Sec. Rd. 664
346.4   Humpback Gap; Va. Rd. 609
352.6   Rockfish Gap, US Rt. 250 and Int. 64; M, G, L 3.0 m. l.; PO
      Waynesboro, VA 22980

Cumulative mileage from Springer Mountain, Georgia (southern
terminus of the Trail) to the Shenandoah National Park 789.7

MILEAGE FACT SHEET NO. 4

Extending from Rockfish Gap (US Rt. 250 and I-64) to US Route 522
in Virginia (106.6 miles).
(NOTE: All lean-tos in Shenandoah National Park closed for overnight use in 1974; a few expected to be available in 1978; more later.
Obtain information and permits at Park entrance. There are 25 points
in this 106.6-mile stretch where the AT and the Skyline Drive intersect. See PATC Maps 9, 10, and 11.

  0.0   Rockfish Gap (US Rt. 250, I-64) (G, M, L 3.0 m. l.) PO Waynes-
      boro, VA 22980
  7.6   Jarmans Gap
  9.9   Sawmill Run LT (LT 0.3 m. l.)
 19.8   Black Rock Gap LT
 25.1   Doyle River C
 26.8   Loft Mt. CG (G in season)
 29.1   Ivy Creek LT
 32.9   Pinefield LT
 41.0   Hightop LT
 44.2   Swift Run Gap, US Rt. 33
 47.1   South River LT (LT 0.3 m. r.)
 50.8   Pocosin C
 52.5   Lewis Mt. CG (G in season)
 53.5   Bear Fence Mt. LT (LT 0.2 m. r.)
 60.4   Lewis Spring LT (removed by Park Service—1976)
 61.4   Big Meadows CG (G, L, M, 0.5 m. r.)

64.9   Rock Spring C
65.1   Byrd Nest No. 2, Hawksbill Mt. LT
66.3   Hawksbill LT (LT 0.3 m. r.)
69.1   Skyland (M & L in season)
72.6   Shavers Hollow LT (LT 0.3 m. l.)
73.2   Pinnacles Picnic Gr.
75.5   Byrd Nest No. 3 LT
78.5   Thornton Gap, US Rt. 211 (M in season)
79.9   Pass Mt. LT
82.5   Byrd Nest No. 4 LT
86.7   Elk Wallow LT (M in season at Elk Wallow Wayside on Sky-
        line Drive)
88.2   Range View C
93.1   Gravelly Springs LT (LT 0.2 m. r.)
101.0   Indian Run LT (LT 0.5 m. r.)
103.0   Floyd LT
106.6   US Rt. 522 (M, L, G 6.0 m. l.; PO Front Royal, VA 22630)

Cumulative mileage from Springer Mountain, Georgia (southern terminus of the Trail) to US Rt. 522 is 896.3
This fact sheet supplements the *Guide to Trails in the Shenandoah National Park* available from the Potomac Appalachian Trail Club, 1718 N St., N.W., Wash., DC 20036.

MILEAGE FACT SHEET NO. 5

Extending from US Route 522 in Northern Virginia to the Susquehanna River. Total distance is 172.2 miles.

0.0   US Rt. 522 (M, L, G 6.0 m. l.; PO Front Royal, Va. 22630)
3.6   Mosby LT
6.6   Linden (St. Rt. 55), G; PO Linden, Va. 22642
10.5   Manassas Gap LT
19.8   Ashby Gap, US Rt. 50; M; PO Paris, Va. 22130
27.9   Three Springs LT
30.8   Snickers Gap, Va. St. Rt. 7
36.9   Wilson Gap LT
44.3   Keys Gap LT (Va. St. Rt. 9)
50.4   PO Harpers Ferry, WV 25425; G, M, L 1.5 m. l. off Trail;
       headquarters Appalachian Trail Conference
50.7   Sandy Hook Bridge on US Hwy. 340 (over Potomac River)

51.3   Chesapeake & Ohio Canal Towpath
51.8   Weverton CS
59.3   Crampton Gap, Gathland State Park CG; Md. St. Rt. 572
59.9   Crampton Gap LT (LT 0.3 m. r.)
64.1   Rocky Run LT
66.0   Turners Gap, US Alt. Rt. 40 (M)
68.0   Washington Monument St. Park CG
71.4   US Route 40, I-70
71.8   Pine Knob LT
79.5   Hemlock Hill LT
79.6   Smithburg Rd., Md. St. Rt. 153
84.2   Devils Racecourse LT 0.5 m. r.
89.4   Pen-Mar Park
89.6   Pa.-Md. State Line; Mason Dixon Milestone No. 91
91.3   Pa. St. Hwy. 16; G, L, M; 5.0 m. l.; PO Waynesboro, Pa. 17268
91.4   Mackie Run LT
95.5   Antietam LT
96.6   Tumbling Run LT
101.1 Mont Alto-Sanatorium Rd.; G 1.0 m. r.; PO South Mountain, Pa. 17261
103.8 Raccoon Run LT's
105.7 Caledonia State Park CG (G, M, 1.0 m. l.) US Rt. 30
108.1 Quarry Gap LT's
112.8 Milesburn Cabin
115.2 Birch Run LT's
118.2 Michener Cabin (C 0.3 m. r.)
121.2 Toms Run LT's
123.3 Pine Grove Furnace Cabin
125.5 Pine Grove Furnace St. Park; CG: G: Pa. St. Rt. 233
132.9 Tagg Run LT's 0. m. r.
134.1 Pa. St. Rt. 34, Hunters Run Rd.
136.4 Pa. St. Rt. 94
137.1 Moyer CG; G
147.6 Allen, PA St. Rt. 174; PO Allen, PA 17001
153.5 US Rt. 11
158.4 Donnellytown (Pa. St. Rt. 944)
160.8 Darlington LT
167.3 Thelma Marks LT (limited water)
171.6 Duncannon, PA; PO 17020; M, G, L
172.2 Susquehanna River

Cumulative mileage from Springer Mountain, Georgia (southern terminus of the Trail) to the Susquehanna River ....1068.5 This fact sheet supplements the *Guide to the Appalachian Trail from the Shenandoah National Park to the Susquehanna River*.

MILEAGE FACT SHEET NO. 6
PENNSYLVANIA

Extending from the Susquehanna River to the Delaware Water Gap. Total distance is 141.8 miles.

0.0	Susquehanna River
0.9	Susquehanna LT
5.0	Pa. St. Rt. 225
6.5	Zeager LT (no water)
8.6	Shaffer LT
14.4	Pa. St. Rt. 325 (Clarks Valley)
25.4	Rausch Gap LT
29.1	Greenpoint General Store
31.6	Swatara Gap, Legislative Rt. 140
41.4	Pa. St. Rt. 645
43.0	Pa. St. Rt. 501
46.5	Hertlein CS
50.0	Pa. St. Rt. 183, Rentschler Marker CS
56.5	Neys LT
63.6	Port Clinton, Pa. St. Rt. 61; (M, L, G) Church pavillion available for lodging; PO Port Clinton, PA. 19549
65.8	Pocohontas Spring and CS
68.9	Windsor Furnace LT
85.2	Allentown LT (no water)
89.4	US Rt. 309
91.6	New Tripoli LT (0.3 m. l.)
96.3	Bake Oven Knob LT (limited water)
104.0	Outerbridge LT
104.7	Lehigh Gap; G, M, L at 2.0 m. l. and at 3.0 m. r.
110.0	Little Gap; M, L 2.0 m. r.
112.6	Bucha Farm Campsite (1.2 m. r.)
121.2	Leroy A. Smith LT
125.9	Wind Gap Pa.; L at Gap; (M, L, G 1.5 m. r.) PO Wind Gap, Pa. 18091
134.5	Fox Gap, Pa. St. Rt. 191
135.2	Kirkridge LT (no water in Winter)

141.8 Delaware Water Gap (M, L, G); PO Delaware Water Gap, PA 18327

Cumulative mileage from Springer Mountain, Georgia (southern terminal of the Trail) to the Delaware Water Gap is ....1210.3 This fact sheet supplements *Guide to the Appalachian Trail in Pennsylvania* and is available from ATC, Box 236, Harpers Ferry, WV 25425.

MILEAGE FACT SHEET NO. 7
NEW JERSEY AND NEW YORK

Extending from Delaware Water Gap, PA to the New York-Connecticut State Line. Total distance is 155.9 miles.

0.0	Delaware Water Gap (M, L, G; PO Delaware Water Gap, PA 18327)
4.9	Sunfish Pond
13.0	Blairstown—Millbrook Road
24.1	Brink LT (LT 0.2 m. l.)
27.9	US Rt. 206, Culvers Gap (G, L, M)
30.9	Gren Anderson LT (LT 0.2 m. l.)
34.1	Crigger Road
36.7	Mashipacong LT
39.3	Rutherford LT (LT 0.2 m. r.)
41.9	NJ Rt. 23
43.3	High Point Monument LT
49.2	NY Rt. 284, Unionville, NY, PO 10988; G and light meals
57.8	NY Rt. 94, Maple Grange (L 0.6 m. r.) (G and PO Vernon, NJ 07462—1.5 m. r.)
66.2	Warwick Turnpike
76.0	NY Rt. 17A
87.0	NY Rt. 17
91.5	Fingerboard LT
93.0	Lake Tiorati Circle
94.1	William Brien Memorial LT
97.5	West Mt. LT (LT 0.5 m. r. on TT trail-blue)
102.9	Bear Mt. Bridge (M, L)—10¢ toll!
105.2	Hemlock Spring CG
107.7	US Rt. 9, Graymoor Monastery (M, L)
112.2	Indian Lake LT (LT 0.1 m. l.), water 0.2 m. w.
113.7	Canopus Valley Crossroads
116.2	CS 0.1 m. l. on Dennytown Road (water from pump) north from Trail

119.6	Fahnestock St. Park CG, NY Rt. 301
125.1	Taconic State Parkway
129.2	Farmers Mill LT (LT 0.1 m. r.)
130.9	NY Rt. 52
137.9	NY Rt. 292 (G 0.1 m. r.), PO Holmes, NY 12531
139.6	NY Rt. 55
140.9	NY Rt. old 55
141.8	CG Edward Murrow Memorial Park (hot showers in season)
142.2	Pawling, NY, PO 12564; NY Rt. 22
150.7	Webatuck LT (LT 0.4 m. r.; water—0.2 m. past LT)
151.7	NY Rt. 55, Ten Mile River Crossing
155.9	Ct.-NY Line

Cumulative mileage from Springer Mountain, Georgia (southern terminal of the Trail) to the New York-Connecticut state line is 1366.2 This fact sheet supplements *Guide to the AT in New York and New Jersey*.

MILEAGE FACT SHEET NO. 8
CONNECTICUT AND MASSACHUSETTS

Extending from New York-Connecticut State Line to the Massachusets-Vermont State Line. Total distance is 139.3.

0.0	New York-Conn. St. Line
3.8	Conn. Hwy. 341 (M, L, G), PO Kent, Conn. 06757; 0.3 m. r.
7.3	Chase Mt. LT
13.8	Housatonic River Rd.
14.5	Mt. Brook LT
20.8	US Rt. 7 (G; fuel), PO Gornwall Br., CN 06754
28.2	Mohawk No. 2 LT
29.4	Mohawk No. 3 LT
29.6	Conn. Hwy. 4, Bunker Hill
29.8	Red Mountain LT
31.6	Conn. Hwy. 43
38.7	Pine Knoll LT (LT 0.1 m. l.)
42.6	US Rt. 7 (M)
44.2	Falls Village Bridge across Housatonic River
49.2	Salisbury, CN PO 06068 (G, M, L) Conn. Rt. 41; 0.3 m. l.
56.1	Sages Ravine, Massachusetts-Connecticut Line
64.6	Jug End
67.2	MA Hwy. 41
70.5	US Rt. 7 (M)

77.9   MA Hwy. 23, Lake Buel Rd.
80.7   Benedict Pond CG
82.3   Mt. Wilcox LT
88.8   Tyringham, MA; PO 01264
95.0   US Rt. 20 (M, L), Jacobs Ladder Hwy.
101.8 October Mt. LT (no water)
112.3 MA Hwys. 8 & 9; Dalton, MA PO 01226 (G, M, L)
121.3 MA Hwy. 8; Cheshire, MA 01225; (G, L, M)
125.1 Kitchen Brook LT
129.0 Mt. Greylock, Rockwell Rd., Bascom Lodge (M, L)
132.3 Wilbur Clearing LT (LT 0.2 m. l.)
135.3 MA Hwy. 2, Williamstown, MA PO 01267 (G, M, L, 1.5 m. l.
       at shopping center)
139.3 Massachusetts-Vermont State Line

Cumulative mileage from Springer Mountain, Georgia (southern terminal of the Trail) to the Massachusetts-Vermont State Line is 1505.5
This fact sheet supplements *Guide to the Appalachian Trail in Massachusetts and Connecticut* . . . ATC Publication 21.

MILEAGE FACT SHEET NO. 9
VERMONT AND NEW HAMPSHIRE

Extending from Massachusetts-Vermont State Line to the Maine State Line. Total distance is 292.9 miles.

0.0   Vermont-Massachusetts Line
2.8   Seth Warner LT (0.3 m. l.)
10.0 Congdon S
14.2 Vt. Hwy. 9 Molly Stark Hwy.
15.6 Melville Navheim LT
23.9 Glastenbury Mt. LT
28.1 Caughnawaga and Kid Gore LT's
31.6 Story Spring LT
33.3 Stratton Road
37.3 Bigelow LT
37.4 Vondell LT
37.9 Stratton View LT
39.6 South Bourn Pond LT
40.0 North Bourn Pond LT
43.2 William B. Douglas LT
49.7 Vt. Hwy. 11 (G, M, L 4.0 m. l.) PO Manchester Center, VT
      05255

50.5   Bromley Camp S
55.0   Mad Tom LT
59.4   Peru Peak LT
59.9   Griffith Lake CS
64.0   Lost Pond LT
65.7   Big Branch LT
66.9   Danby-Landgrove Road
68.8   Lula Tye LT
69.5   Little Rock Pond LT
74.2   Greenwall LT
76.1   Vt. Hwy. 140 (G 3.0 m. r.) PO Wallingford, VT 05773
78.7   Sunnyside Camp S
81.4   Vt. Hwy. 103
82.2   Clarendon S
87.8   Gov. Clement S
90.8   Tamarack LT
91.9   Cooper Lodge, Killington Peak, S
94.8   Pico Camp S (Pico Ski Shop 1.0 m. l.; back-packing equip-
       ment and trail food)
97.3   Sherburne Pass (M, L) US Rt. 4
97.8   Junction Point; Appalachian Trail—right (east); Long Trail—
       straight ahead (north)
98.8   Gifford Woods State Park (LT's)
99.0   Vt. Hwy. 100 (G, M, L 1.0 m. r.) PO Killington, VT 05751
105.2 Stony Brook LT
106.9 Chatauguay Road
113.5 Gulf LT
115.5 Vt. Hwy. 12
119.8 Pomfret Road
121.5 Cloudland LT
127.2 Vt. Hwy. 14 (G); West Hartford, VT PO 05084
128.0 Interstate Hwy. 89
131.2 Happy Hill Cabin S (Unlocked)
136.2 Connecticut River
136.7 Hanover, NH (G, M, L) PO Hanover 03755
136.8 Dartmouth College, Thayer Hall—Meals
137.6 Velvet Rocks LT (0.6 m.r.; NW)
143.7 Harris C (0.1 m. r.)
149.5 Trapper John LT
156.4 Smarts Mt. LT

163.5	Mt. Cube LT
165.0	NH Hwy. 25-A
171.2	Armington C (C 0.3 m. l.)
171.7	NH Hwy. 25-C
175.0	Wachipauka Pond
177.5	NH Hwy. 25, Glencliff, NH, PO 03238
179.5	Great Bear C (0.1 m. l.)
183.0	Mt. Moosilauke S
186.1	Beaver Brook LT (LT is 0.1 m. r.)
186.5	Kinsman Notch, NH Hwy. 112 (M, G, L 4.0 m. r.) PO N. Wood-stock, NH 03293
193.7	Eliza Brook LT
197.5	Kinsman Pond LT
199.4	Lonesome Lake Hut
202.4	US Rt. 3, Franconia Notch
204.7	Liberty Spring CS (Resident Caretaker)
208.5	Greenleaf Hut, Mt. Lafayette (Hut 1.1 m. l.)
212.3	Garfield Ridge CS
215.0	Galehead Hut
218.3	Mt. Guyot LT (LT is 0.5 m. r.)
222.8	Zealand Falls Hut
226.7	Ethan Pond LT
230.2	Crawford Notch US Rt. 302
236.0	Mizpah Spring Hut
240.6	Lake of the Clouds Hut
242.1	Mt. Washington (M)
245.7	Edmands Col (*Emergency* Shelter Only)
248.2	Madison Huts
255.4	Pinkham Notch Hut
261.5	Carter Notch Hut (Hut is 0.1 m. r.)
268.5	Imp S
274.3	Rattle River LT
275.9	US Rt. 2 (M, L, G 3.6 m. l.) Gorham, NH 03581
286.0	Dream Lake CS
288.3	Gentian Pond LT
292.9	Maine-New Hampshire Line

Cumulative mileage from Springer Mountain, Georgia (southern terminal of the Trail) to the New Hampshire-Maine State Line is ....1798.4 This fact sheet supplements ATC Publication No. 22, *Guide to the Appalachian Trail in New Hampshire and Vermont.*

Explanatory Notes:

1. The word *Hut* appearing on the fact sheet for New Hampshire refers to a chain of eight structures providing dormitory facilities and meal service. These huts extend some 60 miles beginning with Lonesome Lake Hut and terminating with Carter Notch Hut, farther north. The Pinkham Notch Hut is open all year. The others are open only during the hiking season. Cost for breakfast and lodging in 1978 was $11.00 per night. Write to Appalachian Mountain Club, Pinkham Notch Camp, Gorham, New Hampshire 03581 for information. It is best to make reservations in advance.

2. The symbol C used on the New Hampshire Fact Sheet refers to cabins operated by the Dartmouth Outing Club. With two exceptions these are locked cabins. Arrangements for their use should be made with the Dartmouth Outing Club, Robinson Hall, Hanover, New Hampshire 03755. The Harris Hollow Cabin is left unlocked and is open for use by the hiking public. There is also one room of the Moosilauke Winter Cabin that is left unlocked.

MILEAGE FACT SHEET NO. 10
MAINE

Extending from the New Hampshire-Maine State Line to the northern terminal of the Appalachian Trail atop Baxter Peak on Katahdin. Total distance is 276.1 miles.

0.0	Maine-New Hampshire Line
0.5	Carlo Col Shelter (LT is 0.3 m. l.)
4.9	Full Goose Shelter
7.2	Mahoosuc Notch, E. end
9.6	Speck Pond Shelter
10.9	Old Speck
14.4	ME Hwy. 26
14.9	Grafton Notch LT
21.6	Frye Brook LT
21.9	Andover B-Hill Rd.
28.5	Hall Mt. LT
31.9	ME Hwy. 5
37.8	Elephant Mt. LT
45.7	ME Hwy. 17
49.5	Sabbath Day Pond LT
54.0	Little Swift River Ponds Campsite
58.7	ME Hwy. 4 (M, L, G 9 m. l.) PO Rangely, ME 04970

60.1   Piazza Rock LT
68.7   Poplar Ridge LT
71.0   Ford, Orbeton Stream
75.7   Spaulding Mt. LT
81.5   Crocker Cirque Campsite
88.6   ME Hwy. 27 (M, L, G 5.0 m. l.) PO Stratton, ME 04982
93.9   Horn Ponds LT's
96.9   Myron Avery Memorial LT
107.4   Long Falls Dam Road
107.5   Jerome Brook LT
117.6   East Carry Pond LT (LT is 0.1 m. r.)
123.6   Pierce Pond LT (Make arrangements at the "Carrying Place,"
        0.1 m. n. of LT for crossing Kennebec River)
127.3   Kennebec River and US Rt. 201
127.8   Caratunk, ME PO 04925 (Limited groceries)
132.8   Pleasant Pond Mt. LT
140.8   Joes Hole Brook LT
145.9   Moxie Bald Mt. LT
152.8   Breakneck Ridge LT
156.3   Blanchard Village, ME Hwy. 15
161.8   ME Hwy. 15; PO Monson, ME 04464 (M, G, L); last supply
        point for 100 miles north
166.8   Old Stage Road LT
173.0   Little Wilson Stream CG
176.6   Bodfish Farm
179.6   Long Pond Stream LT
183.5   Cloud Pond LT (LT is 0.2 m. r.)
190.2   Chairback Gap LT
193.6   Ford of West Branch, Pleasant River
199.4   Gulf Hagas Mt.
200.2   Sidney Tappen Campsite
204.0   White Cap Mt. LT
205.6   West Branch Ponds Road
212.2   East Branch Tote Road LT
215.6   Kokadjo B-Pond Road (North End)
218.9   Cooper Brook Falls LT
226.7   Lower Joe Mary Pond (Old Antlers Camps; one cabin left
        unlocked for use by hikers)
230.6   Potawadjo Spring LT
237.2   Nahmakanta Lake LT

241.8   Wadleigh Pond LT
244.6   Pollywog Stream Ford
246.7   Rainbow Stream LT
258.1   Hurd Brook LT
261.6   Abol Bridge CS (G) fees charged at this site
268.9   Daicey Pond Campground and LT's; fees charged
270.8   Katahdin Stream Campground; reservations needed—Baxter
        Park Authority, Millinocket, ME 04462
275.1   Thoreau Spring
276.1   BAXTER PEAK, KATAHDIN!!

Cumulative mileage from Springer Mountain, Georgia (southern terminal of the Trail) to Baxter Peak on Katahdin is ....2074.5 This fact sheet supplements the *Guide to the Appalachian Trail in Maine.*

Northbound hikers should purchase enough groceries at Monson, Maine to last them until reaching the all season grocery store at Abol Bridge.

NOTE: In 1978 hikers could be ferried across the Kennebec River by Warren Ricker, phone: (207) 663-2241. Northbound hikers can make radio telephone arrangements at Williams Camp (also known as the Carrying Place) some 200 yards off the AT near Pierce Pond lean-to. Southbound hikers can call Mr. Ricker from Mitchell's store in center of Caratunk. Cost: $5 for one person; lesser rate for two or more.

OFF TRAIL FACILITIES

Over the years the long distance hikers have ascertained the locations of many low cost places of lodging, eating places, laundromats, etc., that are located close to the Trail. The information is exchanged between northbound and southbound hikers; is left via notes at hostels and shelters; and much of it is furnished to Mrs. Jean Cashin, the attractive gray haired lady who works at the front desk at the ATC headquarters in Harpers Ferry. The 2,000 Milers, class of '76, in their completed questionnaires, furnished me the names and locations of many of these "super places" they had discovered in their travels. These off trail facilities are listed in the following pages in the same order as the Mileage Fact Sheets are arranged. Space is left between each of the ten lists so that hikers may write in new places as they learn of them from other hikers.

Mrs. Cashin of ATC keeps an up-to-date list of all these places, reproduces copies of her list and furnishes them free of charge to hikers who visit ATC headquarters. Would be hikers who desire an updated list may obtain same from ATC by furnishing a stamped self addressed envelope.

Some of these facilities are well known, are located immediately adjacent to the Trail, and are already included in the Mileage Fact Sheets. Examples of these are the Hikers Hostel at Hot Springs, North Carolina and the Nantahala Outdoor Center at Wesser, North Carolina. Others are listed below. Hikers learning of new places should furnish the information to ATC Headquarters in Harpers Ferry.

MILEAGE FACT SHEET NO. 1—Georgia and North Carolina

Neals Gap, GA (Walaysi Center) Hikers Supplies, freeze dried foods, snacks.

Fontana Dam Village—everything: groceries, cafeteria, rooms, post office

Fontana Dam (Little Tenn. River)—showers (free at the dam)

MILEAGE FACT SHEET NO. 2—North Carolina and Tennessee

Erwin, Tennessee—Lodging at YMCA for $1 . . . Bath and pool 50c extra

MILEAGE FACT SHEET NO. 3—Southern Virginia

Damascus, VA—Hostel at Methodist Church (Donations)
US Route 11—Motel, restaurant, groceries and post office 2 miles left at Atkins
Pearisburg—Hospice at Holy Family Church (Donations)
Crandon—groceries and stove fuel
Newport—lodging at pavillion or covered bridge, store 0.5 miles right
Waynesboro—free lodging at Fire Station, shoe repair shop

MILEAGE FACT SHEET NO. 4—Shenandoah National Park

No camping in lean-tos or within sight of lean-tos; permits required.
All campgrounds have groceries, laundry, stove fuel, showers.
Skyland, Big Meadows, Panorama—restaurants

MILEAGE FACT SHEET NO. 5—
Northern Virginia to Southern Pennsylvania

Snickers Gap (St. Hwy. 7. Va)—Snackbar
Keys Gap (St. Hwy. 9) Va-WV. 100 yards left—groceries and water pump at Shell Station
Harpers Ferry, WV—ATC Headquarters, post office, grocery stores, "all you can eat" buffet suppers at Hilltop House, KOA Campground, free camping under Sandy Hook Bridge
Sandy Hook, MD (Across bridge from H. Ferry) American Youth Hostel
Crampton Gap, MD (Gathland State Park) soda, telephone, water, picnic area
Washington Monument State Park, MD.—Campground, water
Greenbrier State Park, MD.—Just before crossing Int. 70, go left on US 40 for 1.0 miles; lake, showers, campground; snack bar restaurant across from entrance to Park
Duncannon, PA—Free lodging at Fire Station
Allen, PA—Approx. 2 miles north of Allen, PA is Musser Farm and vegetable stand. For A.T. hikers Mr. Musser will provide water, tentspace and toilet access free of charge—modest charge for food, shower, shelter, store items. Store *closed on Sundays;* the Mussers NOT to be disturbed on that day!

MILEAGE FACT SHEET NO. 6—Pennsylvania

Swatara Gap—Groceries, motel
Port Clinton, PA—free lodging at church pavillion, Port Clinton Hotel
Delaware Water Gap, PA—Hostel at Presbyterian Church, backpack
store, donations

MILEAGE FACT SHEET NO. 7—New Jersey and New York

US Route 206—Excellent bakery to left in Worthington, NJ.
Unionville, NY—Lodging in American Legion Hall or camp in adja-
cent field; also lodging at Fire Hall.
Greenwood Lake, NY—Free Lodging at Appalachian Cottage 3 miles
south of Rt. 17A. See "Crazy Roger" sign with directions on it.
Rt. 9 Hwy. Crossing—Graymoor Monastery, NY—Lodging and Meals
—Donations.

MILEAGE FACT SHEET NO. 8—Connecticut and Massachusetts

Kent, Ct.—Lodging at Volunteer Fire Department
Salisbury, Ct.—Lodging at Episcopal Church
Jug End, MA—Hostel
Tyringham, MA—Lodging for $5 at Carolyn Cannons, showers, light
meals
Bascom Lodge (atop Greylock)—lodging and food
Dalton, MA; Shower at Fire House—no lodging
Cheshire, MA—Lodging at Catholic Church
Williamstown, MA—Free lodging at Williams College
N. Adams, MA—Free lodging at N. Adams State College

MILEAGE FACT SHEET NO. 9—Vermont and New Hampshire

Rutland, VT—Montgomery Ward—huge breakfasts, very reasonable
prices
Killington, VT—Mountain Meadows Lodge—Bed and Breakfast $4.50;
1 mile north of point where App. and Long Trails separate.
Hanover, NH—Dartmouth College, Free Rooms; "all-you-can-eat"
meals at Thayer Hall.

N. Woodstock, NH—SkiMeister backpacking store; guest house across from SkiMeister; Cascade Tourist Home; Swiss Chalet restaurant— "all-you-can-eat" breakfasts for $3.

Gorham, NH—Mrs. Stinson's Tourist Home (room $3); Alpine Guest House $6.50.

MILEAGE FACT SHEET NO. 10—Maine

Stratton—Dorms in basement of Hotel; The Hilltop Inn—$3.00 lodging, shower, kitchen privileges; fill fuel bottles at Stratton Power Saw.

Rangely—Viola's Tourist Home $5.50; Judkins $4.50.

Pierce Pond LT—The "Carrying Place" 200 yards n. of LT—excellent all-you-can eat meals, reasonable prices, showers, friendly people.

Monson—Shaw's Boarding House—Lodging and 2 meals $7.50.

Millinocket—Brookside Restaurant 1.0 mile west of town—excellent meals, reasonable prices . . . a place to celebrate the completion of the 2,000 mile hike!

AVERAGE CLIMATIC CONDITIONS ALONG THE
APPALACHIAN TRAIL FOR APRIL-OCTOBER

		Elev. Feet	Av. Daily Max & Min Temps. (F)							Average Precip. (inches)	
			Apr	May	Jun	Jul	Aug	Sep	Oct	Wettest	Driest
1.	Greenville, ME	1060	48	62	72	77	74	67	55	Jul	Apr
			26	37	47	52	50	42	34	4.02	3.20
2.	Mt. Washington, NH	6252	31	36	51	53	54	44	30	Aug	Apr
			17	23	39	42	43	34	16	7.19	5.46
3.	Barre-Montpelier, VT	1122	51	64	74	78	76	68	58	Aug	Sep
			31	41	51	55	52	44	36	3.22	2.66
4.	Somerset, VT	2080	48	61	70	75	73	66	56	Sep	Oct
			27	38	47	51	49	42	33	4.92	4.00
5.	Pittsfield, MA	1170	53	66	75	79	78	69	59	Jul	Oct
			33	43	52	56	55	47	37	4.89	3.25
6.	Bear Mountain, NY	1300	55	66	75	79	77	70	61	Jul	Oct
			38	48	57	63	61	54	44	5.66	3.41
7.	Pocono Mts., PA	1915	58	67	76	80	77	70	60	Aug	Oct
			33	43	51	56	54	47	38	5.25	4.32
8.	Harrisburg, PA	338	64	75	83	87	85	78	67	May	Oct
			42	52	61	65	63	56	45	3.76	2.57
9.	Hagerstown, MD	560	63	74	82	86	84	78	67	May	Oct
			40	50	59	63	61	54	43	3.62	2.49
10.	Shenandoah Nat. Pk. Big Meadows, VA	3535	59	67	74	76	75	69	60	Aug	Apr
			37	46	54	57	56	50	41	5.47	3.63
11.	Peaks of Otter, VA	2605	64	72	77	81	79	73	63	Aug	Oct
			43	52	58	63	62	56	46	5.50	3.51
12.	Burkes Garden, VA	3300	62	70	76	79	78	73	64	July	Oct
			38	45	52	56	55	48	38	4.78	2.39
13.	Banner Elk, NC	3710	61	69	75	77	77	73	64	July	Oct
			36	44	52	55	54	48	38	5.47	3.34
14.	Gatlinburg, TN	1454	71	79	86	88	87	83	73	July	Oct
			42	50	58	59	60	55	43	6.37	3.03
15.	Blairsville, GA	1917	70	77	83	85	85	80	71	July	Oct
			41	49	57	61	60	54	42	5.11	3.09

Due to differences in elevation, the above listed temperatures may not always be representative. In order to approximate the average temperature for the actual elevation of the trail, 3½ °F per 1000 feet may be subtracted where the trail is higher than the nearest recording station. Precipitation tends to be greater at higher elevations.

Data extracted from various Environmental Data Service publications with varying periods of record.

Prepared by the National Climatic Center
Ashville, North Carolina 28801
(204) 258-2850

WIND CHILL TABLE

Temperature in Celsius; wind speed in kilometers per hour

DRY BULB TEMPERATURE (°C)

Dry Bulb	WIND SPEED (km/h)										
	6	10	20	30	40	50	60	70	80	90	100
20	20	18	16	14	13	13	12	12	12	12	2
16	16	14	11	9	7	7	6	6	5	5	5
12	12	9	5	3	1	0	0	— 1	— 1	— 1	— 1
8	8	5	0	— 3	— 5	— 6	— 7	— 7	— 8	— 8	— 8
4	4	0	— 5	— 8	— 11	— 12	— 13	— 14	— 14	— 14	— 14
0	0	— 4	—10	—14	— 17	— 18	— 19	— 20	— 21	— 21	— 21
— 4	4	— 8	—15	—20	— 23	— 25	— 26	— 27..—	27	— 27	— 27
— 8	— 8	—13	—21	—25	— 29	— 31	— 32	— 33	— 34	— 34	— 34
—12	—12	—17	—26	—31	— 35	— 37	— 39	— 40	— 40	— 40	— 40
—16	—16	—22	—31	—37	— 41	— 43	— 45	— 46	— 47	— 47	— 47
—20	—20	—26	—36	—43	— 47	— 49	— 51	— 52	— 53	— 53	— 53
—24	—24	—31	—42	—48	— 53	— 56	— 58	— 59	— 60	— 60	— 60
—28	—28	—35	—47	—54	— 59	— 62	— 64	— 65	— 66	— 66	— 66
—32	—32	—40	—52	—60	— 65	— 68	— 70	— 72	— 73	— 73	— 73
—36	—36	—44	—57	—65	— 71	— 74	— 77	— 78	— 79	— 79	— 79
—40	—40	—49	—63	—71	— 77	— 80	— 83	— 85	— 86	— 86	— 86
—44	—44	—53	—68	—77	— 83	— 87	— 89	— 91	— 92	— 92	— 92
—48	—48	—58	—73	—82	— 89	— 93	— 96	— 98	— 99	— 99	— 99
—52	—52	—62	—78	—88	— 95	— 99	—102	—104	—105	—105	—105
—56	—56	—67	—84	—94	—101	—105	—109	—111	—112	—112	—112
—60	—60	—71	—89	—99	—107	—112	—115	—117	—118	—118	—118

Example: A Celsius temperature of minus 20 combined with wind speed of 40 kilometers per hour produces wind chill factor minus 47 (−47) Celsius

Appendix 4

The Metric System

The Board of Managers of the Conference has approved a resolution providing for conversion to the metric system on guide books and other publications effective as of 1980. Presumably distances will continue to be shown in miles for some time after that, but at the very least we will begin seeing hiking trail distances in meters and kilometers in 1980.

The metric system of weights and measures was officially adopted by France (where the system originated) in 1799. It was officially adopted by the United States in 1890 and the metric system is now in use in most parts of the world except in the English speaking countries who have stubbornly refused to recognize the new system. But even in England and the US there seems to be a growing feeling that the metric system is THE system that should be used.

Within the Conference, Pennsylvania seems to be most eager to go all the way with metric and the particular club that leads the way is the Penn State Outing Club which built and maintains the Mid-States Trail. The Club points out that by pure serendipity the initials MST also stands for Metric System Trail. Its guide book is published in the metric system and we are indebted to one of its members, Dr. David L. Raphael for computing and providing the "miles to kilometers conversion table" reproduced in this appendix.

Also reproduced in this appendix is a wind chill table which is expressed in Celsius temperature readings and in wind speeds of so many kilometers per hour. This table appeared in the *Newsletter* of the Keystone Trails Association, and is reproduced by permission.

Miles to Kilometers Conversion Table

	0.0	1.0	2.0	3.0	4.0
0.0	0.000	1.609	3.219	4.828	6.437
0.1	0.161	1.770	3.380	4.989	6.759
0.2	0.322	1.931	3.541	5.150	6.598
0.3	0.483	2.092	3.702	5.311	6.920
0.4	0.644	2.253	3.862	5.472	7.081
0.5	0.805	2.414	4.023	5.633	7.242
0.6	0.966	2.575	4.184	5.794	7.403
0.7	1.127	2.736	4.345	5.955	7.564
0.8	1.288	2.897	4.506	6.116	7.725
0.9	1.448	3.058	4.667	6.277	7.886

	5.0	6.0	7.0	8.0	9.0
0.0	8.047	9.656	11.266	12.875	14.484
0.1	8.208	9.817	11.426	13.036	14.645
0.2	8.369	9.978	11.587	13.197	14,806
0.3	8.530	10.139	11.748	13.358	14.967
0.4	8.691	10.300	11.909	13.519	15.128
0.5	8.851	10.461	12.070	13.680	15.289
0.6	9.012	10.622	12.231	13.840	15.450
0.7	9.173	10.783	12.392	14.001	15.611
0.8	9.334	10.944	12.553	14.162	15.772
0.9	9.495	11.105	12.714	14.323	15.933

	10.0
0.0	16.094
0.1	16.254
0.2	16.415
0.3	16.576
0.4	16.737
0.5	16.898
0.6	17.059
0.7	17.220
0.8	17.381
0.9	17.542

Example: 7.4 miles
Equals 11.909 Kilometers.
0.01 miles = .0161 km.

Appendix 5

Names and Addresses of Clubs Maintaining the Appalachian Trail

The Appalachian Trail Conference has a number of categories of membership, ranging from a category for clubs actually maintaining a portion of the 2,074-mile footway to individual memberships, youth memberships, and life-time memberships. The honored category is the "A" category—rightfully accorded to the clubs that maintain the Trail. In this appendix is listed the names and addresses of the 60 clubs in the Class A category. The list is reproduced just as it was furnished by the Conference. If you live anywhere near the Appalachian Trail you will be able to find in this list the name and address of an organization near you that is involved in trail maintaining activities. If you are interested in trail maintenance work or if you wish to join one of the organizations listed, write to them at the address shown. Newcomers and volunteers are always welcome.

These are in order from Maine to Georgia.

Mr. Don Witherill, President
Maine Outing Club
Memorial Union Building
University of Maine at Orono
Orono, ME 04473

Mr. Dave Field, President
Maine Appalachian Trail Club
Box 183-A, RFD # 2
Bangor, ME 04401

Troop # 69, B.S.A.
c/o John Seiler
Box 21
Springfield, ME 04487

Mr. Gerald R. Ireland, Pres.
Sierra Club Group
River Road, RFD # 2
Orrington, ME 04474

Mr. Henry Banks, President
Colby Outing Club
Roberts Union, Colby College
Waterville, ME 04901

Mr. Donald Hanson, President
Fairfield Troop # 470
RFD # 1, Box 284 A
Fairfield, ME 04937

Carl A. Newhall, Trail Boss
Maine Trail Trotters
RFD # 3
Winthrop, ME 04364

Mr. Stuart Rosenthal, Pres.
Bowdoin Outing Club
Moulton Union Box
Brunswick, ME 04011

Dewlyn Downes
A.M.C., Maine Chapter
126 Concord Street
Portland, ME 04103

Mr. John V. Cleary, President
Bates College Outing Club
Bates College, Box 389
Lewiston, ME 04240

Mr. Donald E. Feeney, Director
Gould Academy Outing Club
Gould Academy
Bethel, ME 04217

E. Louise Young, President
A.M.C., Narrangansett Chapter
25 Cobble Hill Road
Lincoln, RI 02865

Mr. Robert D. Proudman
Appalachian Mountain Club—
Boston
Gorham, NH 03581

Mr. Mark M. Winkler, President
Dartmouth Outing Club
P.O. Box 9
Hanover, NH 03755

Mr. Joseph E. Frank, President
The Green Mountain Club, Inc.
P.O. Box 889, 43 State Street
Montpelier, VT 05602

Mr. Donald I. Craft, President
Mt. Greylock Ski Club, Inc.
P.O. Box 478
Pittsfield, MA 01201

Marion B. Rhodes, President
Metawampe-Univ. MA Faculty
Outing Club, Russell Road
Sunderland, MA 01375

Mr. Walter L. Haynes, President
A.M.C., Berkshire Chapter
5 Weymouth Street
Springfield, MA 01108

David P. Sinish, Chairman
A.M.C., Connecticut Chapter
20 Dyer Avenue
Collinsville, CT 06022

Mr. Walter Houck, President
New York-New Jersey Trail Con-
ference, 305 W. 86th St., # 3A
New York City, NY 10024

Lawrence J. Gross, President
A.M.C., New York Chapter
113 W. 95th Street
New York, NY 10025

Westchester Trails Association
c/o Miss Linda Hellmann
632 Warburton Ave., Apt. 6K
Yonkers, NY 10701

Mr. Robert G. Lommel, Pres.
Woodland Trail Walkers
34 Hillcrest Drive
Wayne, NJ 07471

Mr. Tom Yoannou, President
Conservation & The Outdoors
Box 284
New York, NY 10031

Mr. Marland Whiteman, Pres.
Green Mtn. Club, NY Sect. Inc.
360 E. 72nd St., Apt. # C2005
New York, NY 10021

Miss Suzanne Gillespie, Pres.
Adirondack Mtn. Club, Inc.
New York Chapter,
110 DeHaven Drive
Yonkers, NY 10703

Ms. Nancy Cooper, President
Short Hills Outing Club
P.O. Box 1127
Union, NJ 07083

Mr. Nathan Levin, President
Union Co. Hiking Club
1358 Franklin Street
Rahway, NJ 07065

Mr. Fred Caiocca, President
New York Ramblers
508 East 78th Street
New York, NY 10021

Iven Rinard, Chairman
Sierra Club, Atlantic Chapter
800 2nd Avenue
New York, NY 10017

Montague G. Ball, Jr., Pres.
Pine Island Camp
P.O. Box 10128
Greenville, SC 29603

Mr. Richard Austin, President
West Jersey Hiking Club
34 Laurie Road
Landing, NJ 07850

Prof. J. J. Copeland, President
The Torrey Botanical Club
351 Bedford Avenue
Mt. Vernon, NY 10553

Maurice J. Forrester, Jr., Pres.
Keystone Trails Association
Road 3, Box 261, Factory Road
Cogan Station, PA 17728

Ms. Jane Galloway, President
Springfield Trail Club
c/o Ms. Wilma Flaig
P.O. Box 441
Media, PA 19063

Ms. Peggy Flanagan, President
Batona Hiking Club
301 Broadway
Westville, NJ 08093

Mr. Robert L. Prichett
A.M.C., Delaware Valley Gap
Rd. 3, Box 303
Bath, PA 18014

Mr. George Eddy, President
Philadelphia Trail Club
1522 Huntington Road
Abington, PA 19001

Mr. Leonard L. Reed, Sr., Pres.
Blue Mtn. Eagle Climbing Club &
Wilderness Park Association
122 W. High Street
Womelsdorf, PA 19567

Mr. Bill Bevan, President
Allentown Hiking Club
124 S. 16th Street
Allentown, PA 18102

President
Brandywine Valley Outing Club
Box 7033
Wilmington, DE 19803

Mary W. Ludes, President
Susquehanna A.T. Club
87 Greenwood Circle
Wormlesbury, PA 17043

Mr. Bernard Frick, President
York Hiking Club
347 S. George Street
York, PA 17403

Mr. John Eckard, Jr., Pres.
Mountain Club of Maryland
4415 LaPlata Avenue, Apt. E
Baltimore, MD 21211

Mr. Scott Johnson, President
Potomac Appalachian Trail Club
1718 N Street, NW
Washington, D.C. 20036

William B. Bundick, President
Maryland Appalachian Trail Club
3 Fernwood Lane
Hagerstown, MD 21740

T. I. Diamond, Jr., President
Shenandoah-Rockfish A.T.C.
1520 Mulberry Street
Waynesboro, VA 22980

President, Old Dominion
Appalachian Trail Club
P.O. Box 25283
Richmond, VA 23260

Mr. Mike Ashe, President
Tidewater Appalachian Trail Cl.
P.O. Box 62044
Virginia Beach, VA 23462

Mr. Henry L. Lanum, Jr., Pres.
Natural Bridge A.T. Club
P.O. Box 32
Madison Heights, VA 24572

Mr. John W. Bowles, President
Roanoke Appalachian Trail Club
2416 Stanley Avenue, SE
Roanoke, VA 24014

Mr. Warren Woomer, President
Kanawha Trail Club
1411 Sweetbriar Road
Charleston, WV 25314

Mr. Steve Hiser, President
Virginia Tech Outing Club
P.O. Box 459
Blacksburg, VA 24061

Mr. Tom Harmon, President
Piedmont A.T. Hikers
307 S. Chapman
Greensboro, NC 27403

Mr. Dan Schunke, President
Mt. Rogers A.T. Club
29 Shadow Grove Circle
Bristol, VA 24201

Mr. Robert W. Miller, Pres.
Tennessee Eastman Hiking Club
P.O. Box 511
Kingsport, TN 37662

Mr. John Tompkins, President
Carolina Mountain Club
1 Baird Mt. Road
Asheville, NC 28804

Mr. Sam Tillett, President
Smoky Mountains Hiking Club
P.O. Box 1454
Knoxville, TN 37919

Mr. Donald W. McLean, Pres.
Nantahala Hiking Club
Rt. 1, Box 162
Franklin, NC 28734

Ms. Nancy Shofner, President
Georgia Appalachian Trail Club
1351 Springdale Road, NE
Atlanta, GA 30306

Appendix 6

Honorary Members of the Appalachian Trail Conference

Article I, Sec. 3 of the ATC Constitution as revised provides for a special category of Honorary Members. The Constitutional language is "Upon recommendation of the Executive Committee, Honorary membership may be conferred by the Board of Managers at a regular meeting of the Conference on an individual who has made a distinguished contribution to the Appalachian Trail project." In the 53 year history of the Conference only 19 memberships have been so awarded. The 19 members so honored can truly be considered as comprising the Appalachian Trail Conference "Hall of Fame." There has never been published a listing of these 19 Hall of Famers; indeed, until Lester L. Holmes, ATC Archivist, completed several months of searching of old records, did we even know how many there were or who they were. Both Col. Holmes and I felt that the list should be compiled and published; after this it will be easy to maintain the list of future people selected for the honor.

The selecting and awarding of the Honorary Memberships has proven to be a delicate operation. If the Conference waits too long to confer the honorary membership, the intended recipient may either be dead or so advanced in years or in such poor health that he does not really appreciate the honor being bestowed. On the other hand, if the honor is conferred too early in life, the intended recipient may reason that the Conference is attempting to shove him or her out of the main stream of Conference activity. On two occasions the intended recipient has angrily refused to accept the honor for that very reason! My own feeling is that the Conference should award the honor whenever a member has met the criteria of having "made a distinguished contribution to the Appalachian Trail Project" and that the conferring should take place regardless of whether the recipient is 50 years of age or 80.

Col. Holmes has prepared two lists; one a chronological listing showing names of recipients and the date of award; the other showing names and addresses of the 11 recipients who are still living. I have met the 16 recipients who received their awards in 1964 or later and I have worked closely with many of them. The awards have been richly deserved. I would hope that the Conference would be able to locate or reconstruct the citations for each of the 19 recipients. Their "distinguished contributions to the Appalachian Trail Project" have in many cases spanned periods of from 20 to 40 years. It would be a worthy addition to the Conference building at Harpers Ferry to have a Hall of Fame section where names, dates of award, pictures and citations of each of the Hall of Famers would be on display.

Also included in Appendix 6 is a picture of Benton MacKaye and a narration by Col. Holmes of his last visit with Mr. MacKaye in October 1976.

HONORARY MEMBERSHIP

*Myron H. Avery	1952
(Designated as Honorary Chairman)	
*Frank Place	1955
*Harlean James	1955
*Marion Park	1955
Paul M. Fink	1955
Rev. A. Rufus Morgan	1964
*Frederick F. Schuetz	1964
*Max Sauter	1967
*Benton MacKaye	1967
Murray Stevens	1967
*Thekla Stephan	1972
Dr. Jean Stephenson	1972
Seymour Smith	1972
Sadye Giller	1972
Walter Boardman	1972
G. F. Blackburn	1972
Florence Nichol	1975
Stanley A. Murray	1975
Thomas Campbell	1977

*Deceased

ADDRESSES OF THE LIVING HONORARY MEMBERS
OF THE CONFERENCE

Mr. G. F. Blackburn
5028 Allan Road
Washington, DC 20016
(202) 229-8084

Mr. Walter Boardman
5663 Rogers Ave.
Port Orange, FL 32019
(904) 767-8121

Thomas Campbell
3521 Richards Blvd. S.W.
Roanoke, VA 24018
(703) 774-2879

Paul M. Fink
Jonesboro, TN 37659
(615) 753-3314

Miss Sayde Giller
1421 Massachusetts Ave. N.W.
Washington, DC 20005
(202) 462-0193

Dr. A. Rufus Morgan
Rt. 1, Box 164
Franklin, TN 28734
(404) 939-3172

Stanley A. Murray
P.O. Box 3356
Kingsport, TN 37664
(615) 323-4993

Seymour R. Smith
P.O. Box 413
Watertown, CT 06795
(203) 274-2157

Miss Florence Nichol
5416 Fourth Street S.
Arlington, VA 22204
(703) 671-0431

Dr. Jean Stephenson
Washington, DC 20005

Murray H. Stevens
Meriden, NH 03770
(603) 469-3306

BENTON MacKAYE 1879-1976

In October 1976, little did I know that it would be my last visit with Benton. We sat talking about the Trail and especially about a project close to both of us; NATURE and its appreciation and protection.

Benton had written in 1932 about his wish for people in the cities to come to the mountains and enjoy nature. He had hoped that they would appreciate the natural beauty of the woodlands and streams and would protect them. He had voiced concern that apparently no one in the Conference had pushed for a definite program to become "acquainted with scenery; to absorb the landscape and it influence as revealed in the earth and primeval life. How to read the story of the earth—a particular part of the earth—the Appalachian earth and the life thereof. The earth story is told in the structure of the Appalachian Range; the earth's life is disclosed in the forest on its slopes."

Some years earlier I had put together a series of color slides taken on and adjacent to the Trail showing scenery, the wild flowers. the critters and the rock formations. Each visit with Benton would include the topic of "our show," and a report of where it had been shown and the reaction of the audiences. His suggestions were invaluable.

On this visit while we were talking I took some shots of Benton sitting in his chair by the window. While his sight had failed, his mind was as keen as it had ever been. He recalled incidents of years past and quoted from his many writings as if it were composed yesterday.

He seemed to be quite happy and contented on this visit in October 1976.

Lester L. Holmes, 1978

Benton MacKaye, October, 1976. (Photo: Col. Lester L. Holmes)

Appendix 7

On Joining Hiking Organizations

In this last appendix to the book there are included names, brief descriptions, and membership application forms for two organizations: the Appalachian Trail Conference, a regional organization; and the American Hiking Society, a newly formed national organization.

The 53-year-old ATC is truly remarkable for what it has accomplished during the past half century, operating as it has, almost entirely with volunteer employees. Its first paid employee was a part time office assistant hired in 1966. Even today it has but eight paid employees at Harpers Ferry, WV, who service the 10,000 individual members and who work with federal and state agencies and with some 63 hiking clubs in the continuing effort to maintain a continuous hiking trail which is rapidly approaching 2,100 miles in length. The Conference relies primarily upon membership dues to finance its activities.

The American Hiking Society was organized in late 1976 by a number of people prominent in the hiking and backpacking field. One of the founders was the late Congressman Goodloe E. Byron of Maryland, some of whose activities on behalf of the Appalachian Trail are described in Chapter 1. Another of the founders was Bill Kemsley, the publisher and executive editor of *Backpacker* Magazine. The names of the others read like a "Who's Who" of those activities in hiking and backpacking. A public research report released late in 1977 shows that 10% of the American public hike on remote trails and that 19% hike on more accessible trails. The American Hiking Society was founded to provide a voice for this large segment of our population whose needs and desires seem to have been largely overlooked. A personal appeal from the President of the Society appears in this appendix. If you are interested in hiking and backpacking trails on a national basis you would do well to join this organization.

THE AMERICAN HIKING SOCIETY . . . for those who enjoy the natural world on foot.

If you enjoy walking on soft earth and fallen leaves, if you come alive with a face full of wind while treading a ridgeline, if you are at home with a pack on your back and no one else in sight, there are some things you should know. You are among the people most neglected by our representative system of government. More importantly, there has been no organization of national influence seeking to educate the public in the pleasures of hiking and the use of foot trails. There has been no national organization effectively promoting research in what things hikers enjoy, who they are, or where they go. And there has been no national organization effectively promoting educational programs to reach the millions of people who have only recently discovered the pleasures of walking, hiking, backpacking, snowshoeing and ski-touring. The American Hiking Society is for those who want too see these things changed.

Studies by the Heritage Conservation and Recreation Service indicate that hiking will grow tremendously in the years ahead. Will sufficient land be set aside for trails? Will goverment be responsive to the needs of hikers? Will hikers themselves be properly educated in the use of foot trails? An effective national organization can help see that these questions are answered properly.

Here are the goals of the American Hiking Society:

1. To educate the public in the appreciation of walking and the use of foot trails.

2. To provide for and protect the interests of hikers.

3. To encourage hikers to build and maintain footpaths.

4. To encourage others to enjoy the esthetic and spiritual experience of hiking in the natural world.

5. To foster research related to these goals.

Benefits of membership.

The American Hiking Society will not be a one-way street. You will receive many benefits of membership as well as knowing that you are furthering the interests of hiking and backpacking in America. Benefits include:

The *AHS NEWS,* a quarterly publication with much information of interest to hikers.

"Alert" Newsletters eight times a year, giving members up-to-date reports on legislative matters and items of immediate concern to hikers.

A deadheading service, search and rescue insurance, a membership card and decal are additional benefits.

Privilege of doing something.

By joining the American Hiking Society you can have the privilege of knowing that you have done something important to help preserve hiking opportunities in America. This is the most important benefit of all. For it will benefit not just you and the other hikers of today—but all future generations of hikers, as well.

The American Hiking Society
18600 SW 157 Avenue
Miami, Fl. 33187

YES count on me. I want to be a member of **The American Hiking Society.** My $15.00 dues for the current year will be paid as follows:

☐ Bill me.
☐ I'd rather pay now & save AHS the expense of billing me.

Name _____

ADDRESS _____

CITY _____ STATE _____ ZIP _____

PHONE _____

I would like to volunteer the following services: _____

Appalachian Trail Conference

For over 50 years, private citizen-volunteers have built and continue to maintain the Appalachian Trail—one of the few wilderness resources in the East. Now, the demand for land for industry, second homes, and utilities has placed the Appalachian Trail in constant jeopardy. Your membership preserves this unique natural resource for now, forever.

ATC headquarters.

Join the appalachian trail conference now!

Name _____

Address _____

_____

_____

Date _____

Optional
Information _____

Hiking Club Affiliation

Age

Occupation

You will receive a subscription to the
Appalachian Trailway News.

Individual

$12.50 plus $2.50 entrance fee for
first time applicants only

Life
$200.00 (Time Payment Available)

An assortment of experimental AT metal markers—copper, enamel, perforated, galvanized iron. (Photo: Chuck Young)

BE CONSIDERATE

1. Respect Property

Treat the property of others—public as well as private—even better than you would like others to treat yours. Honor no trespassing signs. Close gates. Respect privacy.

2. Avoid Littering

Bring appropriate containers. Carry out leftover food and trash. (If trash barrels are available and not overloaded, you may use them, of course.) Go an extra step, carry out trash that less thoughtful people may have left. Leave the area better or no worse than you found it.

3. Protect Plants and Animals

Respect the natural balance. Don't feed "nice" animals, but also don't harm or tease any wild animal, including poisonous snakes. Don't remove or deface trees or other plants.

4. Be Careful of Fires

Use a portable stove. Light wood fires only in an emergency. Tend your fire at all times. Extinguish fires thoroughly. Except in designated areas, obliterate all evidence of your fire. Respect local fire rules.

5. Be Hygienic Discreetly

When facilities are provided, use them. Brush your teeth, wash self and dishes away from stream or lake. For elimination of body waste, get well away from trail or water, dig small but adequate hole, bury toilet paper, replace dirt and sod.

6. Restrict Size of Group

Suggested maximums: 10 for backpacking, 20 for day hikes. For hiking, consider the trail situation—popularity, wetness, fragility. For camping, keep within any established limit for facilities.

7. Respect Trails

When following a trail, stay on it—don't take shortcuts at switchbacks. This can cause erosion. Try not to widen the trail.

8. Choose Backcountry Campsite Carefully

Stay out of "sight and sound" of trail and other campers. Move if vegetation becomes worn. Honor no camping signs.

9. Keep Vehicles Where They Belong

Park only in areas provided or acceptable. Always leave room for cars to pass or get out. Recognize that barriers may need to be opened for emergency vehicles. Do not drive where vehicles are not permitted.

10. Be Prepared

Carry and know how to use map, compass and first aid kit. Have adequate food and water. Have essential clothing but don't overload yourself. Keep track of time and weather. Know alternate routes off the mountain.

11. Minimize Problems of Being Lost

Tell others what you plan. If lost, stay in one place. Stay calm. Respond to calls from rescuers. If in a group, stay together.

12. Consider Those You Meet

Be friendly but respect the privacy of others. Encourage courtesy within your own group and from your group to others. If you bring a dog or firearm (restricted in many places), exercise particular care for the safety and enjoyment of others. If you have a radio, keep the volume low. End your party early.

Reprinted by permission of the Potomac Appalachian Trail Club. Additional copies of this document may be obtained by sending stamped self addressed envelope to PATC, 1718 N St. NW, Wash DC 20036

Other Appalachian Books

Blue Ridge Voyages, Vol. I, III, IV
  By Corbett and Matacia

Potomac Trail Book
  By Robert Shosteck

Canoeing Whitewater
  By Randy Carter

Potomac Whitewater
  By John Seabury Thomson

Appalachian Waters, by Walter F. Burmeister
  Vol. I—*The Delaware & Its Tributaries*
  Vol. II—*The Hudson River & Its Tributaries*
  Vol. III—*The Susquehanna River & Its Tributaries*
  Vol. IV—*Southeastern U.S. Rivers*
  Vol. V—*The Upper Ohio & Its Tributaries*

NOTES

NOTES

NOTES

NOTES

NOTES

NOTES

NOTES

NOTES